Lecture Notes in Computer Science   9748

Commenced Publication in 1973
Founding and Former Series Editors:
Gerhard Goos, Juris Hartmanis, and Jan van Leeuwen

More information about this series at http://www.springer.com/series/7409

Aaron Marcus (Ed.)

Design, User Experience, and Usability

Technological Contexts

5th International Conference, DUXU 2016
Held as Part of HCI International 2016
Toronto, Canada, July 17–22, 2016
Proceedings, Part III

 Springer

Editor
Aaron Marcus
Aaron Marcus and Associates
Berkeley, CA
USA

ISSN 0302-9743   ISSN 1611-3349   (electronic)
Lecture Notes in Computer Science
ISBN 978-3-319-40405-9   ISBN 978-3-319-40406-6   (eBook)
DOI 10.1007/978-3-319-40406-6

Library of Congress Control Number: 2016940901

LNCS Sublibrary: SL3 – Information Systems and Applications, incl. Internet/Web, and HCI

Printed on acid-free paper

This Springer imprint is published by Springer Nature
The registered company is Springer International Publishing AG Switzerland

Foreword

The 18th International Conference on Human-Computer Interaction, HCI International 2016, was held in Toronto, Canada, during July 17–22, 2016. The event incorporated the 15 conferences/thematic areas listed on the following page.

A total of 4,354 individuals from academia, research institutes, industry, and governmental agencies from 74 countries submitted contributions, and 1,287 papers and 186 posters have been included in the proceedings. These papers address the latest research and development efforts and highlight the human aspects of the design and use of computing systems. The papers thoroughly cover the entire field of human-computer interaction, addressing major advances in knowledge and effective use of computers in a variety of application areas. The volumes constituting the full 27-volume set of the conference proceedings are listed on pages IX and X.

I would like to thank the program board chairs and the members of the program boards of all thematic areas and affiliated conferences for their contribution to the highest scientific quality and the overall success of the HCI International 2016 conference.

This conference would not have been possible without the continuous and unwavering support and advice of the founder, Conference General Chair Emeritus and Conference Scientific Advisor Prof. Gavriel Salvendy. For his outstanding efforts, I would like to express my appreciation to the communications chair and editor of *HCI International News*, Dr. Abbas Moallem.

April 2016   Constantine Stephanidis

HCI International 2016 Thematic Areas
and Affiliated Conferences

Thematic areas:

- Human-Computer Interaction (HCI 2016)
- Human Interface and the Management of Information (HIMI 2016)

Affiliated conferences:

- 13th International Conference on Engineering Psychology and Cognitive Ergonomics (EPCE 2016)
- 10th International Conference on Universal Access in Human-Computer Interaction (UAHCI 2016)
- 8th International Conference on Virtual, Augmented and Mixed Reality (VAMR 2016)
- 8th International Conference on Cross-Cultural Design (CCD 2016)
- 8th International Conference on Social Computing and Social Media (SCSM 2016)
- 10th International Conference on Augmented Cognition (AC 2016)
- 7th International Conference on Digital Human Modeling and Applications in Health, Safety, Ergonomics and Risk Management (DHM 2016)
- 5th International Conference on Design, User Experience and Usability (DUXU 2016)
- 4th International Conference on Distributed, Ambient and Pervasive Interactions (DAPI 2016)
- 4th International Conference on Human Aspects of Information Security, Privacy and Trust (HAS 2016)
- Third International Conference on HCI in Business, Government, and Organizations (HCIBGO 2016)
- Third International Conference on Learning and Collaboration Technologies (LCT 2016)
- Second International Conference on Human Aspects of IT for the Aged Population (ITAP 2016)

Conference Proceedings Volumes Full List

Design, User Experience and Usability

Program Board Chair: **Aaron Marcus, USA**

- Sisira Adikari, Australia
- Claire Ancient, UK
- Arne Berger, Germany
- Jan Brejcha, Czech Republic
- Hashim Chunpir, Germany
- Silvia de los Rios Perez, Spain
- Marc Fabri, UK
- Tineke (Christina) Fitch, UK
- Patricia Flanagan, Australia
- Steffen Hess, Germany
- Long Jiao, P.R. China
- Nouf Khashman, Canada
- Khalil R. Laghari, Canada
- Tom MacTavish, USA
- Judith A. Moldenhauer, USA
- Francisco Rebelo, Portugal
- Kerem Rızvanoğlu, Turkey
- Christine Riedmann-Streitz, Germany
- Patricia Search, USA
- Marcelo Soares, Brazil
- Carla Spinillo, Brazil
- Virginia Tiradentes Souto, Brazil
- Manfred Tscheligi, Austria
- Ryan Wynia, USA

The full list with the program board chairs and the members of the program boards of all thematic areas and affiliated conferences is available online at:

http://www.hci.international/2016/

HCI International 2017

The 19th International Conference on Human-Computer Interaction, HCI International 2017, will be held jointly with the affiliated conferences in Vancouver, Canada, at the Vancouver Convention Centre, July 9–14, 2017. It will cover a broad spectrum of themes related to human-computer interaction, including theoretical issues, methods, tools, processes, and case studies in HCI design, as well as novel interaction techniques, interfaces, and applications. The proceedings will be published by Springer. More information will be available on the conference website: http://2017.hci.international/.

General Chair
Prof. Constantine Stephanidis
University of Crete and ICS-FORTH
Heraklion, Crete, Greece
E-mail: general_chair@hcii2017.org

http://2017.hci.international/

Contents – Part III

DUXU in Virtual and Augmented Reality

DUXU for Smart Objects and Environments

Mobile DUXU

Comparison of Mobile Input Methods

Gencay Deniz[1,2(✉)] and Pinar Onay Durdu[2]

[1] Department of Computer Engineering, Graduate School of Natural
and Applied Sciences, Kocaeli University, Izmit, Kocaeli, Turkey
zinedyacneg@gmail.com
[2] Human Computer Interaction Research Laboratory, Kocaeli University,
Izmit, Kocaeli, Turkey
pinar.onaydurdu@kocaeli.edu.tr

Abstract. This paper presents the results of an experimental study that compared the usability of four different input methods in the context of smart phones with touch screen property. Twenty users were asked to fill in a questionnaire with four different input methods which were radio button, text field, spinner and button. Time required to fill in the questionnaire and the errors occurred were recorded. Overall, radio button was found to be the fastest by causing no error while text field was found to be the slowest input method and more error prone. In addition, participants were asked about their perceived performance before and after filling in the questionnaire. These results were compared with their actual performance. Most of the users could not predict their performance before use and many of the participants still could not make correct predictions about their own performance after use.

Keywords: Mobile input methods · Performance of mobile input methods · Perceived performance

1 Introduction

Interacting with mobile technologies has been widespread since the use of smartphones has increased. Nowadays, these devices are used to perform many of the daily routines conducted with computers such as social networking, gaming or entertainment [1]. People connect web through their smartphones as well. Therefore, they come across form elements on their mobile devices to input information. Users have to fill in forms to buy goods in an e-commerce website, to join a social network or to get their things done with productivity based applications such as online banking. Form elements stand between the goals of users and applications and unusable web forms lead to loss of users [2]. Thus, the research subject of usability and effectiveness of form elements has been carried to mobile context.

Developers of mobile applications should consider usability issues related with form elements to get information timely and accurately from their users with satisfaction. Although there has been substantial research conducted related to usable web form elements [3–5], to the extent of our knowledge, there are not any studies conducted with form elements accessible through mobile devices. In traditional web environment, the mostly studied form elements for performance and satisfaction were

© Springer International Publishing Switzerland 2016
A. Marcus (Ed.): DUXU 2016, Part III, LNCS 9748, pp. 3–13, 2016.
DOI: 10.1007/978-3-319-40406-6_1

button, radio button, text field and drop down buttons [4, 6–8]. While text field is advantageous in that it enables inputting free form of data, it is a slower input method. On the other hand, button, radio button and drop-down box are used to gather input from pre-determined options [9]. In the mobile context, since the display area is much smaller than traditional web environment, screen real estate becomes another major concern. In this study, an experiment was conducted to investigate the performance of different mobile input methods which were button, text field, radio button and spinner with a touch-based smart phone since these form elements affect the performance of form usage. The chosen input types and their descriptions are given in Table 1. Specifically, we examined which mobile input method provides faster and more accurate data input and which one is more preferred by the users by conducting a user test in our laboratory. Our work is expected to make the following contributions to HCI research field:

- Determine which input method produces faster data entry with less error and more user satisfaction.
- Present the first detailed investigation of performance of mobile input methods in the context of smart phones with touch screen property.

Table 1. Mobile input methods [10]

Control Type	Description
Radio button	Similar to checkboxes, except that only one option can be selected in the group
Text field	An editable text field
Spinner	A drop-down list that allows users to select one value from a set
Button	A push-button that can be pressed, or clicked, by the user to perform an action

2 Related Work

Many of the web based applications use online forms for registration or communication purposes. Users generally do not want to fill in the forms or they leave the forms without filling all questions because the forms designed are unusable requiring long time or causing difficulties to its users. As it was stated above there were some usability evaluation studies conducted in traditional web environment, in this study we are mainly focusing on input types of form elements such as text field, button, radio button and, spinner (which is used instead of drop down box in mobile context) which weren't studied in mobile context. In this section, we will summarize the most important results of the studies about usability of online forms. Although many of these studies were conducted in traditional desktop environment, their results will shed light to our findings.

One of the early work of investigation of usability of form controls was conducted by Gould et al. [11]. They evaluated seven different methods for calendar input by both experienced and inexperienced computer user groups in traditional web environment.

They reported that text entry method was faster and more accurate than selection methods in both groups.

Tullis and Kodimer [6] conducted a study that investigated the usability of seven input methods in a database application in a Windows® environment. They tried to determine which input techniques were easier to learn and use as well as the most preferred. According to their results, radio button and one entry text field input methods were found to be better based on all three dimensions of practice, time and subjective satisfaction. Miller and Jarret [5] emphasized the use of drop-down to save the screen real estate and the use of radio button since it provided visibility of all options together. Heerwegh and Loosveldt [8] discussed the effect of two response formats which were radio buttons or drop-down boxes that were used in web surveys regarding data quality. They reported drop-down boxes were more difficult to use and required more time than radio buttons but they also concluded that the choice among two different response format was not self-evident. Healey [4] conducted an empirical study to investigate the effect of radio button or drop down to the responses of participants of web surveys and could not find out any significant effect on survey completions, number of non-substantial answers or time to completion but found evidence that at individual question level drop downs took longer response times. Actually, this was not a surprising result based on the Keystroke-Level Model [12] because drop downs require more clicks, first to open the drop down and then select the option, than radio buttons.

Bargas-Avila et al. [3] proposed 20 guidelines for usable web forms and they included items related with input types. Seckler et al. [13] conducted an empirical evaluation of these guidelines. In that study, users mostly mentioned about the requirement of easy and fast filling in of the forms during interviews which were conducted to determine their negative experiences with the forms. In another study [14], input methods of button, combo box, radio button and text field were compared according to their performance on web form filling and it was found out that button input type was the fastest and text field was the slowest contrary to Tullis and Kodimer's [6] study. In addition, Bargas-Avila et al. [3], compared six input methods of date entry used in an interactive form on the web and found out that using a drop-down is the best when format errors were to be avoided but text field input was faster and had higher user satisfaction.

Apart from these studies, Welch and Kim [15] conducted an empirical study to investigate the effect of menu element size on mobile applications regarding the effectiveness and efficiency issues. Although the main objective of this study was actually different from our study's scope it is worth to mention about it. Their study didn't not focus on different input elements but they used different sizes for menu elements. They reported the element size had a direct correlation to increased user preference and usability.

3   Method

In this study we performed a user test to examine which input method provides faster and more accurate input in a touch based smartphone environment. Four different input methods which were button, text field, spinner and radio button were evaluated.

3.1 Participants

Twenty participants (8 female, 12 male) took part in the study. Their age ranged from 20 to 59. Average age of participants was 34. Participants were grouped as adults and elderly, according to their age. The first group was between the ages of 20 to 30 and the other group was between the ages of 50 to 60. They were grouped in two age groups based on the median age. First group who were between 20 and 26 years old was determined as young participants and the second group who were between 27 to 59 years old was determined as elderly participants. We grouped participants who had been using smartphone for equal or less than two years as novice and participants who had been using smartphone for equal or more than three years as expert. Participants' smartphone's operating system information was also gathered but two of the participants did not reported (NR) about this information. Only one of the participants had owned the smartphone that was used in this experiment. The details can be seen in Table 2 below.

Table 2. Demographic and smartphone related information of the participants

Gender		Age		Smartphone usage experience		Mobile phone operating system		
Male	Female	Young (20–30)	Elderly (50–60)	Novice (<=2 years)	Expert (>=3 years)	Android	iOS	Others
12	8	15	5	10	10	10	7	3

3.2 Data Gathering Tools

We applied two questionnaires to our participants. One of the questionnaires was to gather their demographic information including gender, age as well as participants' previous experience with any smartphone or the smartphone that we have used in our study. We also included a question regarding their perceived performance of input methods before and after use in this questionnaire. The second questionnaire was used as a "test questionnaire" on the smartphone and included questions related to the personal preferences of participants on general subjects.

A mobile application was developed in Java programming language. Samsung Galaxy S4 smartphone which had an Android OS was used in the experiment. In this mobile application, four versions of the test questionnaire, with different input methods, were used as can be seen in Figs. 1, 2, 3 and 4. The questions and their answers were shuffled for each user and for each trial in order to minimize the learning effect. Application has its own chronometer. It started to track the time at the background of the application when the participant started to fill in any version of the test questionnaire until s/he pressed the complete button. Error correction was disabled in the mobile application to determine which of the input method provided more accurate data input. In the "Text Field" method, the backspace button was disabled and in the other three methods after any of the choices was selected, the others became invisible.

Fig. 1. Button input method

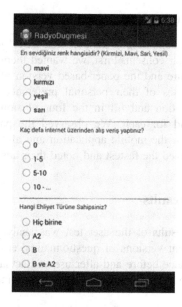

Fig. 2. Radio button input method

Fig. 3. Text field input method

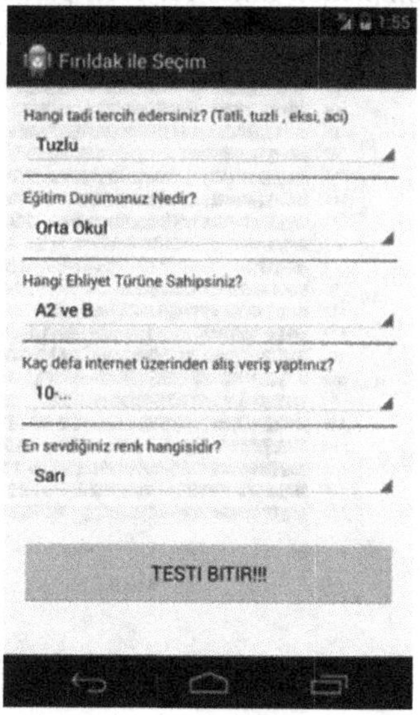

Fig. 4. Spinner input method

3.3   Procedure

At the beginning of the user test, we informed the participants about the procedure and got their consent. First, we wanted them to fill in the demographic information questionnaire and the paper-based version of the test questionnaire to gather their correct responses of their personal preferences. Then we asked them to use the mobile application and fill in the four versions of the questionnaire using different input method for each. We observed the participants while filling in the questionnaire through the mobile application and afterwards asked them which input method they perceived the fastest and noted their answers.

4   Results

The results of the user test was analyzed regarding the required time to fill in the different versions of questionnaires, errors occurred and participants' perceived performance before and after use and actual performance among the four different input methods in a mobile context. We summarized these in the following sub-sections.

4.1   Task Completion Times

Task completion time of four different input methods were recorded during the test. Task completion times for each participants' each method can be seen in Fig. 5.

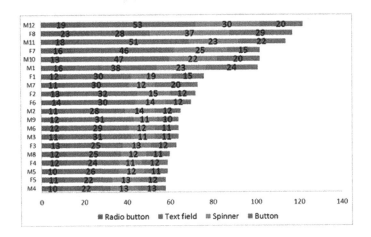

Fig. 5. Task completion times for all participants with four input methods (Color figure online)

There was a statistically significant difference in task completion times depending on the four different input methods, $\chi^2(3) = 39.963$, p = 0.000. Post hoc analysis with Wilcoxon signed-rank tests was conducted with a Bonferroni correction applied, resulting in a significance level set at p < 0.008. Mean values of task completion times for radio button, button, spinner and text box running trial were can be seen in Fig. 6. Radio button was significantly faster than text box (Z = −3.924, p = 0.000) and

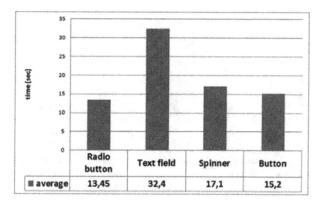

Fig. 6. Average task completion times of four input methods

spinner (Z = −3.188, p = 0.001) whereas there was no significant differences in task completion times between radio button and button running trials (Z = −1.746, p = 0.081). Text-box is significantly faster than spinner (Z = −3.848, p = 0.000) and button (Z = −3.848, p = 0.000). There was no significant differences in task completion time between spinner and button (Z = −2.653, p = 0.008). This result was mainly related with the number of keystroke required to fill in the questionnaire with the used input method. Text field and spinner data entries required more time since they required more keystrokes as can be predicted with the Keystroke-Level Model (Card et al. [12]). Spinner method required two steps to input data while radio button and button methods required one step.

Figure 7 shows comparison of average task completion times by age. The fastest input method is radio button among all age groups and text field is the slowest. Young participants performed significantly better than elderly. Performance differences were statistically significant at p < .05 among age groups with all input methods.

We also analyzed the task completion times according to participants' gender as can be seen in Fig. 8. Males performed better than females with three of the input

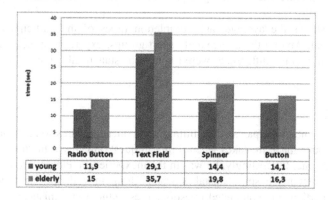

Fig. 7. Average task completion times by age groups

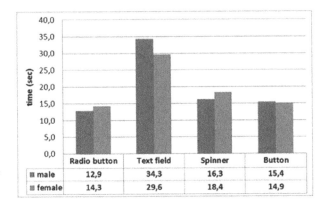

Fig. 8. Average task completion times by gender

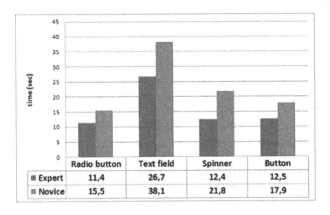

Fig. 9. Average task completion times by experience levels

methods; however, females performed better than males with text field input. However, the difference among the gender groups was not found statistically significant at $p < .05$.

Figure 9 shows the average task completion times of the participants by their experience level. Among the novice and expert groups, expert group performed better than novices and all the differences were found to be statistically significant at $p < .05$.

4.2 Errors

Errors made by the participants while filling in the questionnaires were recorded. Most of the participants made mistakes when filling in questionnaires with "text field" input method except one. Interestingly, he was in the inexperienced elderly group. All of the experienced users made some mistakes when filling in with the "text field" input method. All participants completed questionnaires without any mistakes in the other three input methods.

4.3   Perceived and Actual Performance

We asked participants about their perceived performances before and after the experiment. Participants' perceived performances differed after the experiment; however, their actual performance was also different. Before the experiment only 30 % of the participants stated they would perform better with radio button. After the experiment this percentage increased to 35, however 65 % of the participants performed better with radio button. 25 % of the participants perceived they performed better with spinner after the experiment; however, none of them performed better with this input method. The details can be seen in Fig. 10.

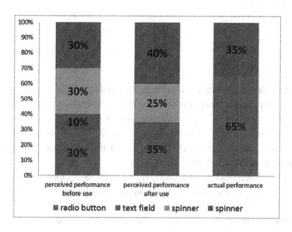

Fig. 10. Participants perceived and actual performances (Color figure online)

5   Discussion

The analyses we have performed on the task completion times of participants with four different input methods indicate that "radio button" is the best of the four approaches studied for this form filling task in the context of smart phones with touch screen property. This result is similar to the previous study's findings [6] although it was in a different context. Form filling with a text field required more time since it required more typing as it was defined in Keystroke level model [12]. Moreover, participants performed more errors with text field. Even we required from the participants to type very short answers by the use of a virtual keyboard of the smartphone, they made errors. There are findings of studies that show people often make errors with virtual keyboards [16].

Another finding of this experiment was related with the people's perceived and actual performances. Our participants weren't able to predict their performance before experiment which is a consistent finding of Dillon's [17] studies. Moreover, they could not predict their performance after the experiment.

The results of this study shows that use of radio button will provide faster form filling in mobile context. Since there is not any statistically significant difference among radio button and spinner input methods, mobile interface designer can prefer spinner while considering screen real estate. In addition, they should avoid text field input as much as possible since it takes longer and causes more errors.

There are some limitations regarding with this study. First of all, this study was conducted in a laboratory setting which could be considered as an artificial environment for mobile context. Because mobile users use these input methods while they are moving and that requires more cognitive overload. Another limitation is that the sampling of the study included few number of participants. They also cannot be considered as well-representative or the population since convenience sampling was used. Therefore, similar studies should be conducted in a more natural setting with more representative users.

References

1. Flurry Analytics: Personal and Professional Productivity: The Next Frontier for Mobile Apps (2014). http://www.flurry.com/bid/109655/Personal-and-Professional-Productivity-The-Next-Frontier-for-Mobile-Apps#.VQqB8tKsW-Y
2. Wroblewski, L., Spool, J.: Web Form Design, pp. 1–374. Rosenfeld Media, New York (2008). http://www.amazon.com/Web-Form-Design-Filling-Blanks/dp/1933820241/ref=sr_1_1?s=books&ie=UTF8&qid=1309070243&sr=1-1
3. Bargas-Avila, J.A., Brenzikofer, O., Tuch, A.N., Roth, S.P., Opwis, K.: Working towards usable forms on the world wide web: optimizing date entry input fields. Adv. Hum.-Comput. Interact. **2011**, Article No. 202701, 8 (2011)
4. Healey, B.: Drop downs and scroll mice: the effect of response option format and input mechanism employed on data quality in web surveys. Soc. Sci. Comput. Rev. **25**, 111–128 (2007)
5. Miller, S., Jarret, C.: Should I use a drop-down? Four steps for choosing form elements on the web (2001). http://formsthatwork.editme.com/files/Articles/dropdown.pdf
6. Tullis, T.S., Kodimer, M.L.: A comparison of direct-manipulation, selection, and data-entry techniques for reordering fields in a table. Proc. Hum. Factors Ergon. Soc. Annu. Meet. **36**(4), 298–302 (1992). SAGE Publications
7. Hogg, A., Masztal, J.J.: Drop-down, radio buttons, or fill-in-the-blank? Effects of attribute rating scale type on web survey responses. In: Proceedings of ESOMAR Congress, Rome (2001)
8. Heerwegh, D., Loosveldt, G.: An evaluation of the effect of response formats on data quality in web surveys. Soc. Sci. Comput. Rev. **20**(4), 471–484 (2002)
9. Shneiderman, B.: Designing the User Interface: Strategies for Effective Human-Computer Interaction (vol. 2). Addison-Wesley, Reading (1992)
10. Android Developers: Input Controls (2014). http://developer.android.com/guide/topics/ui/controls.html
11. Gould, J.D., Boies, S.J., Meluson, A., Rasamny, M., Vosburgh, A.M.: Entry and selection methods for specifying dates. Hum. Factors: J. Hum. Factors Ergon. Soc. **31**(2), 199–214 (1989)
12. Card, S.K., Moran, T.P., Newell, A.: The keystroke-level model for user performance time with interactive systems. Commun. ACM **23**, 396–410 (1980)

13. Seckler, M., Heinz, S., Bargas-Avila, J.A., Opwis, K., Tuch, A.N.: Designing usable web forms. In: Proceedings of the 32nd Annual ACM Conference on Human Factors in Computing Systems - CHI 2014, 1275–1284 (2014)
14. Adak, M.F., Durdu, P.O.: Form elemanlarının form doldurmadaki performansa etkisi. Int. J. Inf. Technol. **4**, 11–18 (2011)
15. Welch, S., Kim, S.-J.: Determining the effect of menu element size on usability of mobile applications. In: Marcus, A. (ed.) DUXU 2013, Part IV. LNCS, vol. 8015, pp. 740–749. Springer, Heidelberg (2013)
16. Chen, T., Yesilada, Y., Harper, S.: What input errors do you experience? Typing and pointing errors of mobile web users. Int. J. Hum. Comput. Stud. **68**(3), 138–157 (2010)
17. Dillon, A.: Beyond usability: process, outcome and affect in human-computer interactions. Can. J. Libr. Inf. Sci. **26**(March), 57–69 (2002). http://arizona.openrepository.com/arizona/handle/10150/106391

Where-How-What Am I Feeling: User Context Logging in Automated Usability Tests for Mobile Software

Jackson Feijó Filho[(⊠)], Wilson Prata, and Juan Oliveira

Nokia Technology Institute, Av. Torquato Tapajós, 7200 - Col. Terra Nova,
Manaus, AM 69093-415, Brazil
{jackson.feijo,wilson.prata,
juan.oliveira}@indt.org.br

Abstract. This work proposes the use of a system to implement user context and emotional feedback and logging in automated usability tests for mobile devices. Our proposal augments the traditional methods of software usability evaluation by monitoring users' location, weather conditions, moving/stationary status, data connection availability and spontaneous facial expressions automatically. This aims to identify the moment of negative and positive events. Identifying those situations and systematically associating them to the context of interaction, assisted software creators to overcome design flaws and enhancing interfaces' strengths.

The validation of our approach include post-test questionnaires with test subjects. The results indicate that the automated user-context logging can be a substantial supplement to mobile software usability tests.

Keywords: Usability · Automation · UXDX · Mobile phones · User research

1 Introduction

In mobile software application stores, consumers frequently find themselves unable to decide which ones to acquire, considering that many of them have the very same functional features. It is very likely they will prefer the application that presents their functionalities in the most usable manner [1].

In [2] Harty debates how several organizations do not execute any usability evaluation. It is considered too expensive, too specialized, or something to address after testing all the "functionality". This is habitually prioritized because of time and other resource constraints. For these groups, usability test automation can be beneficial.

The assessment of usability in mobile applications delivers valuable measures about the quality of these applications, which assists designers and developers in identifying opportunities for improvement. But examining the usability of mobile user interfaces can be an exasperating mission. It might be extensive and require expert evaluation techniques such as cognitive walkthroughs or heuristic evaluations, not to mention expensive usability lab equipment.

© Springer International Publishing Switzerland 2016
A. Marcus (Ed.): DUXU 2016, Part III, LNCS 9748, pp. 14–23, 2016.
DOI: 10.1007/978-3-319-40406-6_2

In addition to the resources constraints, there is the desktop versus mobile software matter. Most of the usability methods (e.g. usability inspection, heuristics, etc.) are both valid to desktop as well as to mobile phones software, although it is more difficult for a mobile usability testing context to accomplish relevant results with conventional assessment methods. The reason is that the emulation of real-world use during a laboratory based evaluation is only feasible for a precisely defined user context. Therefore, due to physical restrictions, it is difficult to extract solid results from such varying user context [7].

Recent work has been published regarding tools for low-cost, automated usability tests for mobile devices. In [8], these tools have been reported to help small software development teams to perform fairly accurate recommendations on user interface enhancements. However, these tools do not consider neither emotional feedback nor contextual awareness of users towards mobile software.

1.1 Emotions and Usability

Emotional feedback is a significant aspect in user experience that chronically goes un-measured in several user-centered design projects [9], especially with small development groups. The examination of affective aspects through empirical user-centered design methods supports software creators in engaging and motivating users while using their systems [10]. Collecting emotional cues will provide another layer of analysis of user data, augmenting common evaluation methods. This results in a more accurate understanding of the user's experience.

1.2 Automated Tests and Unsupervised Field Evaluations

It is important to reference the importance of automated tests, while being performed for mobile devices. In contrast to desktop applications or web sites, mobile applications have to compete with stimuli from the environment, as users might not be sitting in front of a screen for substantial amounts of time [11]. Due to the natural mobility in this scenario, in a real-world context, users might as well be walking on the street or sitting on a bus when interacting with mobile software. Hence, it is important not to ignore the differences of such circumstances and desktop systems in isolated usability laboratories without distractions [7].

2 Related Work

Previous work has been published about automated software usability tests, specifically for mobile devices. Here we divide related work in two groups: "UI Interactions, Automated and Unsupervised Logging and Analytics" and "Emotions Logging Systems".

2.1   UI Interactions, Automated and Unsupervised Logging and Analytics

Several commercial frameworks for logging user statistics on mobile devices, such as Flurry[1], Google Analytics[2], Localytics[3] or User-Metrix[4]. However, these frameworks focus on user statistics such as user growth, demographics and commercial metrics like in-app purchases. These solutions approach automation of usability tests, but ignore emotional feedback, user context and even UI interaction information.

Flurry Analytics. Commercial solutions such as Flurry, which is taken as an archetype for commercially available analytic frameworks (i.e. Localytics[5], Mobilytics[6], Appuware[7] and UserMetrix[8]), try to get an audience perception. They deliver usage statistics based on metrics like average users per day or new users per week. To use these frameworks, the development teams offer support and code snippets to integrate the framework with existing applications. However, developers are responsible for adding framework functionality at the right place in their applications. Besides the option of collecting demographic information (i.e. gender, age or location), the framework also offers a possibility to track custom events. However, metrics that provide assumptions about the quality of user interfaces are generally missing. In contrast to these frameworks, our approach directly focuses on associating UI interaction, emotions and user context logging.

EvaHelper Framework. In 2009, Balagtas-Fernandez et al. [16] presented an Android-based methodology and framework to simplify usability analysis on mobile devices. The EvaHelper Framework is a 4-ary logging system that records usability metrics based on a model presented by Zhang et al. [18]. Although Balagtas-Fernandez et al. focus on the part of automatically logging user interaction, they do not focus on the evaluation of the collected data. For the visualization of their results, they use third-party graph frameworks that are based on GraphML[9] to visualize a user's navigational graph. Compared to our approach, they solely provide navigational data for single application usages. They do not augment the graph with some kind of low-level metrics to enable the identification of emotional feedback or contextual adversities.

Automatic Testing with Usability Metrics. This work presents a methodology and toolkit for automatic and unsupervised evaluation of mobile applications. It traces user interactions during the entire lifecycle of an application [8]. The toolkit can be added to mobile applications with minor changes to source code, which makes it flexible many

---

[1] http://www.flurry.com.

[2] http://www.google.com/intl/de/analytics.

[3] http://ww.localytics.com/.

[4] http://usermetrix.com.

[5] http://www.localytics.com/.

[6] http://www.mobilytics.com/.

[7] http://www.appuware.com/.

[8] http://usermetrix.com/.

[9] http://graphml.graphdrawing.org.

types of applications. It is also able to identify and visualize design flaws such as navigational errors or efficiency for mobile applications.

2.2 Emotions Logging Systems

Some techniques and methodologies have been reported about gathering affective data without asking the users what and how they feel. Physiological and behavioral signals such as body worn accelerometers, rubber and fabric electrodes can be measured in a controlled environment [19]. It is also feasible to evaluate users' eye gaze and collect electrophysiological signals, galvanic skin response, electrocardiography, electroencephalography and electromyography data, blood volume pulse, heart rate, respiration and even, facial expressions detection software [9]. Most of these methods face the limitations of being intrusive, expensive, require specific expertise and additional evaluation time.

UX Mate. UX Mate [17] is a non-invasive system for the automatic assessment of User eXperience (UX). In addition, they contribute a database of annotated and synchronized videos of interactive behavior and facial expressions. UX Mate is a modular system which tracks facial expressions of users, interprets them based on pre-set rules, and generates predictions about the occurrence of a target emotional state, which can be linked to interaction events.

Although UX Mate provides an automatic non-invasive emotional assessment of interface usability evaluations, it does not consider mobile software contexts, which has been widely differentiated from desktop scenarios [7, 11, 12]. Furthermore, it does not take into account the contextual awareness of the user.

Emotions Logging System. It [15] proposes the use of a system to perform emotions logging in automated usability tests for mobile devices. It assess the users' affective state by evaluating their expressive reactions during a mobile software usability evaluation process. These reactions are collected using the front camera on mobile devices. No aspects of user context are considered in this work.

3 Contribution

Our proposal supplements the traditional methods of mobile software usability evaluation by:

1. Monitoring users' spontaneous facial expressions automatically as a method to identify the moment of occurrence of adverse and positive emotional events.
2. Detecting relevant user context information (moving/stationary status; location, weather conditions; data connections availability;
3. Systematically linking them to the context of interaction, that is, UI Interaction (tap/drag) and current app view.

4. The automated test generates a graphical log report, timing
   (a) current application page;
   (b) user events e.g. tap;
   (c) emotions levels e.g. level of happiness;
   (d) emotional events e.g. smiling or looking away from screen;
   (e) moving/stationary status;
   (f) location;
   (g) weather conditions;
   (h) data connection availability (WLAN/3G/4G);

3.1 Example Scenarios

According to [9], the gazing away from the screen may be perceived as a sign of deception. For example, looking down tends to convey a defeated attitude but can also reflect guilt, shame or submissiveness. Looking to the sides may denote that the user was easily distracted from the task.

The work in [15] clearly addresses this matter, by logging the event of "gazing away" from the screen. Although there are certain scenarios where this is perfectly acceptable even if the user is fully committed to the UI interaction:

- While waiting at a bus stop: user has to constantly gaze away from screen, to check for coming buses;
- In a conversation: user has to constantly gaze away from screen, to demonstrate e.g. any media on an application, to the conversation partner.

These are examples of the evident need of user context awareness during automated and unsupervised mobile software usability tests.

3.2 System Structure

The basic system structure is displayed in Fig. 1.

The running application uses the front camera to take photos of the user every second. This image is converted to base64 format and is sent via HTTP to the server. The server decodes the base64 information into image and runs the emotion recognition software, which returns the numerical levels of happiness, anger, surprise, smile (true/false) and gaze away (true/false). This information is sent back to the phone via HTTP and written to a text file, with a set of other interaction information. When the user exits the application, the log file is sent to the server, which stores and classifies the test results in a database, which can be browsed via a web front-end.

For the user context gathering, an additional layer of software periodically logs user's location, appointments schedule (time to next appointment), moving status (walking running, etc.), data connection availability, weather information, UI interaction and current application page. When the user exits the application, the log file is sent to the server, which stores and classifies the test results in a database, which can be browsed via a web front-end.

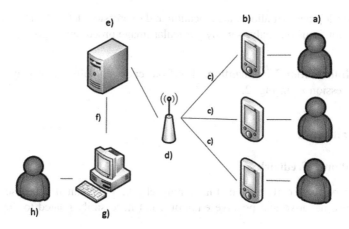

Fig. 1. (a) User; (b) mobile phone; (c) sends face images, GPS location, appointments schedule, moving status (walking, running, etc.), data connection availability, weather information, UI interaction (tap, drag, flick, etc.) and current application page; (d) WLAN, GPRS or HSDPA; (e) emotions recognition software, user context framework, UI interaction integration; (f) emotions and user context log; (g) log data visualization; (h) developer.

Interaction Information Logging. The applications to be tested are written using the library (.dll) we implemented. When the application is started by the user, a log file is created, registering the time, current page, emotional feedback and user context. For simplicity analysis, we are logging only tap interaction - tap/click (true or false). When tap is true, logs position of tap and name of the control object tapped e.g. button, item on a list, radio button, checkbox, etc.

The generated log file is comma separated value format, enabling visualization in tables, as displayed in Tables 1 and 2.

Emotion Recognition Software. The emotion recognition software was developed using the well documented Intel RealSense SDK [13]. Among many features, this

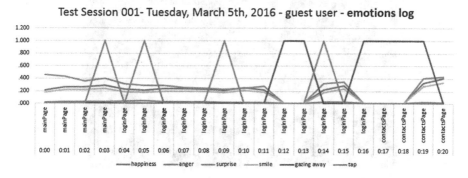

Fig. 2. Emotions log from a 20 s test session (Color figure online)

software development kit allows face location and expression detection in images. This paper does not focus on analyzing any particular image processing algorithms to detect emotions.

Usability Information Visualization. The front-end web software display one quick (20 s) test session as in Fig. 2.

4   Experiments

4.1   Emotional Feedback

In order to perform early system functioning check, we planned a test session that would induce negative and positive emotions, not necessarily related to the interface design.

To test negative feedback, we asked one male adult (32 years old) to login to one of his social networks accounts and post one line of text to his timeline. During this task, we turned the WLAN connection on and off, in intervals of 30 s. After 5 min of not being able to execute a considerably simple task, the test subject was noticeably disappointed. The emotional feedback logged by our system was in successful accordance to the test session.

Fig. 3. Path of user during test. Circle size shows amount of stationary time. Clicking on each circle will show user context and emotional feedback (Fig. 4).

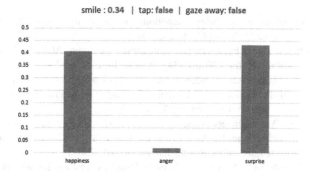

Fig. 4. Emotions and context information at given time

To test positive feedback, we asked one male adult (27 years old) to answer a quiz of charades and funny answers. The emotional feedback logged by our system was successful, as the user smiled and even laugh about the funny text and imagery.

The test session displayed in Fig. 2 show another example of one test session we have run. The user was asked to login to one instant messaging application in development stage in a research institute.

4.2 User Context

In order to perform early system functioning check, we planned a test session that would log an example user context information.

The user was asked to lo login to one instant messaging application in development stage in a research institute, while leaving an office premise, crossing the street and walking towards a bus stop. See Fig. 3.

5 Future Work and Discussions

This work presents an early approach to user context and emotional feedback logging for mobile software usability evaluation. The problem space was narrated through referencing other usability automation research. Some relevant related work was described and distinguished from the present proposal. A system was developed as a proof-of-concept tool to our hypothesis and experiments where performed to raise argumentation topics to provoke advances on the current matter.

Our system logs user context information and emotional feedback from users of mobile phone software. It stands as a solution for automated usability evaluation.

Future work will investigate a more in-depth applicability of the logged interaction information. More importantly, it will research the integration of the different possible variables to be added to this framework.

Additionally, this technique will be compared to other usability methodologies to validate the benefit of our approach.

References

1. Brajnik, G.: Automatic web usability evaluation: what needs to be done. In: Proceedings of Human Factors and the Web, 6th Conference, June
2. Harty, J.: Finding usability bugs with automated tests. Commun. ACM **54**(2), 44–49 (2011)
3. Witold, A.: Consolidating the ISO usability models. In: Presented at the 11th International Software Quality Management Conference and 8th Annual INSPIRE Conference (2003)
4. Rubin, J., Chisnell, D.: Handbook of Usability Testing: How to Plan, Design, and Conduct Effective Tests, 2nd edn. Wiley, New York, NY (2008)
5. Vukelja, L. et al., Are engineers condemned to design? A survey on software engineering and UI design in Switzerland. In: Presented at the 11th IFIP TC 13 International Conference on Human-Computer Interaction, Rio de Janeiro, Brazil (2007)
6. Dumas, J.S., Redish, J.C.: A Practical Guide to Usability Testing: Intellect Books (1999)
7. Oztoprak, A., Erbug, C.: Field versus laboratory usability testing: a first comparison. Technical report, Department of Industrial Design - Middle East Technical University, Faculty of Architecture (2008)
8. Lettner, F., Holzmann, C.: Automated and unsupervised user interaction logging as basis for usability evaluation of mobile applications. In: Proceedings of the 10th International Conference on Advances in Mobile Computing & Multimedia, pp. 118–127. ACM (2012)
9. de Lera, E., Garreta-Domingo, M.: Ten emotion heuristics: guidelines for assessing the user's affective dimension easily and cost-effectively. In: Proceedings of the 21st British HCI Group Annual Conference on People and Computers: HCI... but not as we know it, vol. 2, pp. 163–166. British Computer Society (2007)
10. Spillers, F.: Emotion as a Cognitive Artifact and the Design Implications for Products that are Perceived as Pleasurable (2007). http://www.experiencedy-namics.com/pdfs/published_works/Spillers-EmotionDesign-Proceedingspdf. Accessed 18 Feb 2007
11. Madrigal, D., McClain, B.: Usability for mobile devices, September (2010). http://www.ux-matters.com/mt/archives/2010/09/
12. Kaikkonen, A., Kallio, T., Kekäläinen, A., Kankainen, A., Cankar, M.: Usability testing of mobile applications: a comparison between laboratory and field testing. J. Usability Stud. **1**, 4–16 (2005)
13. Hertzum, M.: User testing in industry: a case study of laboratory, workshop, and field tests. In: Proceedings of the 5th ERCIM Workshop on "User Interfaces for All" (1999)
14. Kjeldskov, J., Skov, M.B.: Was it worth the hassle? Ten years of mobile HCI research discussions on lab and field evaluations. In: Proceedings of the 16th International Conference on Human-Computer Interaction with Mobile Devices and Services. ACM (2014)
15. Feijó Filho, J., Prata, W., Valle, T.: Mobile software emotions logging: towards an automatic usability evaluation. In: Proceedings of the 13th Annual International Conference on Mobile Systems, Applications, and Services. ACM (2015)
16. Balagtas-Fernandez, F., Hussmann, H.: A methodology and framework to simplify usability analysis of mobile applications. In: Proceedings of the 2009 IEEE/ACM International Conference on Automated Software Engineering (2009)
17. Staiano, J., Menendez, M., Battocchi, A., De Angeli, A., Sebe, N.: UX mate: from facial expressions to UX evaluation. In: Proceedings of the Designing Interactive Systems Conference, pp. 741–750. ACM DIS (2012)

18. Zhang, D., Adipat, B.: Challenges, methodologies, and issues in the usability testing of mobile applications. Int. J. Hum. Comput. Interact. **18**(3), 293–308 (2005)
19. Picard, R.W., Daily, S.B.: Evaluating affective interactions: alternatives to asking what users feel. In: Presented at CHI 2005 Workshop Evaluating Affective Interfaces (Portland, OR, 2–7 April 2005). Anderson, R.E.: Social impacts of computing: codes of professional ethics. Soc. Sci. Comput. Rev. 10(2), pp. 453–469 (1992)

QAZ Keyboard: QWERTY Based Portrait Soft Keyboard

Hiroyuki Hakoda[✉], Buntarou Shizuki, and Jiro Tanaka

University of Tsukuba, Tsukuba, Japan
{hakoda,shizuki,jiro}@iplab.cs.tsukuba.ac.jp

Abstract. In this paper, we present a QAZ keyboard, which is a QWERTY keyboard that facilitates one-handed thumb input for a mobile device with a large touchscreen. To design the keyboard, we first conducted experiments to investigate pointing performance on a large mobile touchscreen using one-handed thumb. The results showed that vertically long areas around the center of the touchscreen would be suitable to place a keyboard in terms of accuracy and time of pointing. Based on this finding, we designed and implemented the QAZ keyboard for Android-based devices. A longitudinal study with 4 participants showed that the mean text entry speed was 18.2 wpm, and the mean error rate was 9.1 %. Moreover, a comparative study of the QAZ keyboard compared to a QWERTY keyboard showed that the QAZ keyboard's error rate was significantly lower than the QWERTY keyboard.

Keywords: Text entry · Software keyboard · Virtual keyboard · Smartphone · Mobile devices · Touch screen · One-handed interaction · One-handed thumb · Pointing

1 Introduction

While it has been reported that users of mobile devices expect to use it with one-handed thumb [6], the size of mobile touchscreens is enlarging owing to the demand for increasingly larger screens. This trend inevitably enlarges the touchscreen area that users can no longer reach by using only a thumb. As a result, users are forced to use the device with two hand or change the manner in which they hold the device.

To address this problem, we designed the QAZ keyboard (Fig. 1), which is a portrait QWERTY-based keyboard. We rotated a QWERTY keyboard 90 degrees to make the keyboard cover more area where thumb can easily press keys, thus making text entry on a QWERTY keyboard with one-handed thumb input easier on a large mobile touchscreen.

Before designing the keyboard, we conducted two experiments to investigate the pointing performance with one-handed thumb input on large mobile touchscreens. Based on the results, we designed and implemented the QAZ keyboard on Android-based devices. We also conducted a long-term user study to measure the basic performance of the keyboard. This paper reports the results of those experiments and presents the QAZ keyboard.

© Springer International Publishing Switzerland 2016
A. Marcus (Ed.): DUXU 2016, Part III, LNCS 9748, pp. 24–35, 2016.
DOI: 10.1007/978-3-319-40406-6_3

Fig. 1. QAZ keyboard.   **Fig. 2.** Normal QWERTY keyboard.

2   Related Work

The characteristics of one-handed thumb input have been extensively researched (e.g., [5,15–17,21]). As a result, it has been shown that each location on a touchscreen has different accuracy and time of pointing; therefore, by using a compensation function that shifts the user's touches, the touch performance can be improved [5,21]. As a result, design of the user interface of a touchscreen should avoid key locations that require excessive thumb flexion or extension such as the bottom right and top left on the touchscreen.

Based on characteristics of touch behavior, text entry methods utilizing characteristics of one-handed touch input were designed. Takahama and Go [20] proposed a one-handed text entry method which provides a stable holding position, where users can input text by rubbing the screen with a thumb on a small touchscreen area. Kimioka et al. [7] proposed a text entry method by adopting two arc shaped keyboards for two-handed multi-touch gestures by using both thumbs on a tablet. While these research papers proposed novel text entry methods which were designed ergonomically, the layouts were totally different to those of existing keyboards. On the other hand, novices can use a QAZ keyboard with ease.

Some researchers have proposed keyboards that dynamically adapt the shape and position of a key to users' hands. Sax et al. [18] and Kuno et al. [8] proposed a keyboard where a user can perform touch-typing using a soft keyboard. iGrasp [2] is a system which provides a soft keyboard to users based on how and where users grasp the devices. In contrast, we found the proper area to place a keyboard on a touchscreen based on the results of our preliminary experiments which investigated characteristics of one-handed thumb input, thereby allowing users to use the keyboard without dynamic adaptation.

To improve text entry performance, *static* keyboard layouts were explored. Some researchers have proposed high-performance keyboard layouts by optimizing the motion of a finger [12,23]. Layouts that a user can easily learn have also been investigated [1]. Sipos et al. [19] presented a layout suited for thumb navigation on one-handed devices. Half-QWERTY [14] is a keyboard which only has the left-hand keys of the QWERTY layout for one-handed typing. Users can type the right-hand keys by holding the space bar to mirror the right-hand keys onto the left ones. The 1Line Keyboard [9] condenses the three rows of keys in a normal QWERTY layout into a single line with eight keys by using a language model. While these layouts show high performance, it was also reported that users rarely preferred spending their time learning a new keyboard layout [1,13]. This result motivated us to adopt the QWERTY layout to design our soft keyboard.

3   Experiment: Pointing Performance

We conducted experiments to investigate pointing performances with one-handed thumb input using a large mobile touchscreen in order to find an optimum region to place a keyboard. 12 participants (9 males and 3 females) ranging in age from 21 to 24 years (mean = 22.8; SD = 1.14) took part in the experiments as volunteers. We used a smartphone (LG Electronics Optimus G L-01E, size: 137 mm × 69 mm × 9.6 mm) with a 4.7 in. touchscreen.

3.1   Procedure

We asked the participants to hold the device with their right hands. They were then asked to tap a target on the touchscreen as a trial with their right thumb (Figs. 3, 4).

Our study consisted of two experiments, Experiment A and B. In Experiment A, we motivated the participants to change the way they hold the smartphone depending on the position of a target (free hand posture) for better performance. In Experiment B, we instructed them to keep their hand posture as fixed as possible. In total, each participant performed 1440 (5 sessions × (16 × 9) targets × 2 experiments) trials.

3.2   Results and Analysis

Figures 5 and 6 show the accuracy and time of the pointing tasks, respectively. The results show that the center of the touchscreen shows high performance, and the center of the right side shows high accuracy while the time was slow in both experiments.

Therefore, to find an optimum region to place a keyboard, it is necessary to compare pointing performance among various regions where we can place a keyboard by taking both accuracy and time into account. To realize this, we first calculated the average accuracy and time within the regions shown in Fig. 7 and Tables 1, 2. Then, to evaluate each region, taking both accuracy and

Fig. 3. All participants were instructed to put their elbow on a desk.

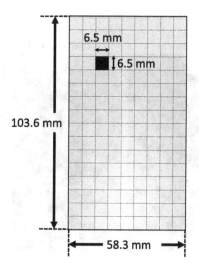

Fig. 4. A target presented on the smartphone's touchscreen.

time into account, we used the following *Cost* function that roughly models the performance of text entry when a keyboard is placed on a certain region:

$$Cost(P, T) = NT(1 + M(1 - P)/P)$$

Here, *Cost* is the estimated time to type a specific text using the keyboard placed on a certain region. Specifically, the parameter P is the success rate of the keyboard (i.e., pointing accuracy of the region). The parameter T is the average time of pointing for the region. N is a constant which is the ideal number of taps necessary to type the text (e.g., if the number of characters in a given text

Experiment A   Experiment B

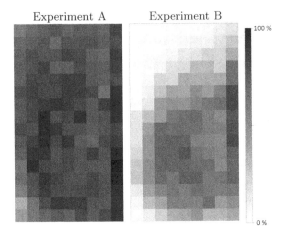

100 %

0 %

Fig. 5. Accuracy in Experiment 1. The darker the area is, the higher the accuracy of the area.

Experiment A   Experiment B

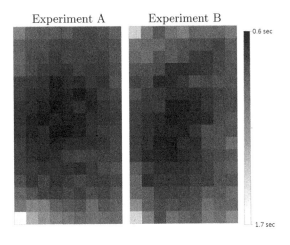

0.6 sec

1.7 sec

Fig. 6. Time in Experiment 1. The darker the area is, the shorter the time of the area.

is 100, it is necessary for the user to tap keys n times to type one character, $N = 100n$). Therefore, NT is the ideal total time required to type the text. Moreover, because typing usually contains errors, we model this by adopting M, which is the number of taps required to recover from an error input (usually $M = 2$ because recovering from one error input requires two taps: tapping Back Space key to delete the error input and then tapping the correct key). Because $(1 - P)/P$ is the error rate, $NTM(1 - P)/P$ is the additional time required for recover. In summary, if a region has low $Cost$, based on the pointing performance, the region is considered suitable for text entry.

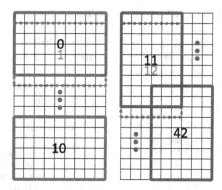

Fig. 7. Analyzed regions: 11 landscape regions (red; ID $= 0, \cdots, 10$) and 32 portrait regions (blue; ID $= 11, \cdots, 42$), which have almost the same footprint as the built-in QWERTY keyboard. (Color figure online)

Based on Tables 1, 2, we adopted Region 23, which is portrait and the region showing the lowest *Cost*.

4   QAZ Keyboard

Based on the results of our experiment, we designed a portrait soft keyboard, which we designated a QAZ keyboard, and then implemented the keyboard as an Android application shown in Fig. 1. We show the design principles below.

QWERTY layout
   Our keyboard adopts the QWERTY layout because many people are familiar with this layout.

Portrait region
   Regions showing high performance might also be suitable to placing a keyboard in terms of accuracy and fast typing. Hence, our keyboard arranges the keys of a QWERTY keyboard on a portrait region that showed the highest performance in the experiment.

5   Evaluation

We conducted a long-term user study to measure basic performance of the QAZ keyboard. Four participants (P1-P4; 4 males) ranging in age from 22 to 24 years (mean $= 23.25$; SD $= 0.83$) took part in this user study. They were all right-handed. They were all Japanese. Regularly, one participant used a soft QWERTY keyboard; two participants used Grid Flick (a method for inputting Japanese text); and one participant used both methods. They were all familiar with the QWERTY keyboard because they were currently using a QWERTY keyboard to control their PCs. They were compensated with 820 JPY (approximately 8 USD) / hour for their participation. We used the same apparatus as used in Experiment A and B.

Table 1. Experimental data in Experiment A. ID is region ID. *Cost* 1 indicates calculated *Cost* as $M = 1$, $N = 100$. *Cost* 2 indicates calculated *Cost* as $M = 2$, $N = 100$. These data are sorted from the highest to the lowest performance.

ID	accuracy	ID	time (sec)	ID	Cost 1 (sec)	ID	Cost 2 (sec)
41	83.8%	22	0.672	23	80.5	23	93.8
23	83.6%	23	0.673	22	80.9	22	94.7
24	83.5%	30	0.675	5	81.5	5	95.0
5	83.4%	4	0.677	4	81.6	24	95.3
40	83.4%	21	0.678	24	81.8	4	95.5
42	83.3%	31	0.679	15	82.0	15	96.0
25	83.3%	5	0.680	21	82.1	6	96.3
6	83.3%	29	0.680	31	82.2	21	96.4
39	83.1%	15	0.680	14	82.4	31	96.6
33	83.1%	14	0.681	6	82.5	14	96.8
7	83.0%	24	0.684	30	82.5	39	97.4
22	83.0%	28	0.686	33	83.2	30	97.5
4	82.9%	20	0.686	39	83.3	32	97.6
15	82.9%	3	0.687	29	83.3	40	98.1
32	82.7%	6	0.687	3	83.6	13	98.4
21	82.6%	32	0.688	13	83.7	3	98.5
14	82.6%	38	0.690	38	83.8	16	98.6
31	82.5%	13	0.690	16	83.9	38	98.6
16	82.5%	39	0.692	20	84.0	29	98.7
8	82.5%	16	0.692	40	84.1	7	98.9
13	82.5%	37	0.693	37	84.5	20	99.4
34	82.4%	36	0.697	7	84.5	37	99.7
38	82.3%	12	0.701	28	84.7	25	100.3
26	82.3%	40	0.701	36	85.7	41	100.5
3	82.2%	7	0.701	12	85.8	33	100.8
37	82.0%	27	0.701	25	86.0	28	100.9
30	81.8%	19	0.705	33	86.2	12	101.5
9	81.8%	2	0.705	2	86.4	36	101.6
20	81.7%	35	0.711	41	86.4	2	102.4
12	81.7%	33	0.716	19	87.2	8	103.1
29	81.6%	25	0.717	27	87.6	19	103.9
17	81.6%	11	0.723	8	87.7	35	104.7
2	81.5%	8	0.723	35	87.9	27	105.0
36	81.4%	41	0.724	17	88.8	17	105.2
28	80.9%	17	0.724	11	89.9	42	106.2
35	80.9%	1	0.726	1	90.5	11	107.4
19	80.8%	34	0.755	42	91.0	34	107.9
10	80.5%	0	0.757	34	91.7	1	108.3
11	80.4%	42	0.758	26	92.6	26	109.0
1	80.3%	26	0.762	9	93.8	9	110.9
27	80.1%	9	0.767	0	96.4	0	117.0
18	80.0%	18	0.782	18	97.7	18	117.3
0	78.6%	10	0.835	10	103.7	10	124.0

Table 2. Experimental data in Experiment B. ID is region ID. *Cost* 1 indicates calculated *Cost* as $M = 1$, $N = 100$. *Cost* 2 indicates calculated *Cost* as $M = 2$, $N = 100$. These data is sorted from the highest to the lowest performance.

ID	accuracy	ID	time (sec)	ID	Cost 1 (sec)	ID	Cost 2 (sec)
41	61.8%	23	0.696	40	122.0	40	169.1
40	61.5%	22	0.696	32	123.0	41	171.7
33	59.7%	14	0.698	33	123.5	33	173.3
42	59.4%	15	0.699	41	124.3	32	174.0
39	59.0%	24	0.704	25	125.4	39	177.6
32	58.5%	21	0.708	39	125.9	25	178.7
34	57.8%	16	0.708	24	126.3	24	182.2
25	57.5%	30	0.710	31	128.8	7	184.4
8	57.3%	13	0.712	7	129.0	31	186.3
7	57.1%	31	0.713	6	132.1	34	187.9
26	56.1%	29	0.717	34	132.1	42	189.1
24	55.7%	32	0.720	8	132.5	8	189.2
9	55.4%	5	0.721	23	132.9	6	191.5
31	55.4%	25	0.721	26	133.7	26	192.4
38	55.1%	6	0.726	38	133.7	38	193.7
6	55.0%	17	0.726	42	134.5	23	196.2
23	52.4%	20	0.728	5	139.2	9	205.7
5	51.8%	4	0.728	30	140.2	5	206.3
10	50.9%	3	0.731	9	142.2	30	209.3
17	50.9%	28	0.731	17	142.7	17	212.9
30	50.6%	12	0.736	16	143.2	16	215.5
37	50.4%	7	0.736	22	146.1	37	219.8
18	49.9%	38	0.737	37	146.9	22	222.7
16	49.5%	33	0.738	15	150.9	18	229.0
22	47.6%	37	0.740	18	152.6	15	232.0
4	46.9%	39	0.742	4	155.3	4	237.7
15	46.3%	2	0.747	29	157.9	29	244.2
29	45.4%	36	0.750	10	163.9	10	244.4
36	44.8%	26	0.750	36	167.2	36	259.4
21	42.1%	40	0.750	14	167.7	14	265.6
14	41.6%	27	0.756	21	168.3	21	265.8
3	41.3%	19	0.758	3	177.1	3	281.1
28	39.5%	8	0.759	28	185.1	28	297.2
35	39.0%	18	0.762	13	195.3	35	318.9
13	36.5%	34	0.763	35	198.0	13	319.4
20	36.1%	41	0.768	20	201.7	20	330.7
2	34.5%	35	0.772	2	216.5	2	358.2
27	33.7%	1	0.773	27	224.6	27	373.5
12	31.0%	11	0.776	12	237.3	12	400.9
19	30.2%	9	0.787	19	250.8	19	425.9
1	27.9%	42	0.799	1	276.6	1	475.9
11	25.7%	0	0.821	11	302.0	11	526.3
0	21.6%	10	0.834	0	380.2	0	678.2

5.1 Procedure

We asked the participants to input phrases chosen at random from a set of 500 phrases [10]. The length of the phrases ranged from 16 to 43 (mean = 28.61). These phrases have only lowercase characters and no punctuation.

The participants input 5 phrases as a training task. Then, they conducted two parts of the evaluation described below:

Part I - Basic Performance

Part I was a longitudinal study designed in accordance with conventional studies on text input systems [11, 22] to measure the basic performance of the QAZ keyboard. This part consisted of 10 sessions. The sessions were scheduled with one or two sessions per day. The maximum allowable interval between sessions was two days. Each session was divided into 12 blocks with 5 phrases per block. Participants could take a break freely between blocks and sessions.

In order to normalize experimental conditions between participants, we also asked the participants to hold the smartphone without supporting it using a desk or their bodies.

Part II - vs. normal QWERTY keyboard

After Part I, Part II was conducted to compare the performance of the QAZ keyboard and a QWERTY keyboard (Fig. 2). The aim of this comparison was to investigate whether the QAZ keyboard has a comparative performance improvement compared to a QWERTY keyboard. Part II consisted of two extra sessions: one session per keyboard. Specifically, Session 11 was conducted using the QAZ keyboard; Session 12 was conducted using the QWERTY keyboard. In order to normalize experimental conditions between the two keyboards, the two sessions were conducted on the same day. Furthermore, the layout, key size, and shape were equal for both keyboards; only the orientation of the keys and a keyboard were different. In Part II, we used the same set of phrases as in Part I; but they were different phrases between the two sessions to eliminate any learning effect, given that the two sessions were conducted on the same day.

Each session lasted 20–35 min. After Session 12, we asked the participants to complete a questionnaire about usability of the keyboards.

5.2 Results and Analysis

The mean text entry speed in Part I started with 11.4 wpm (SD = 1.4) in Session 1 and ended with 17.8 wpm (SD = 2.1) in Session 10 with an increase of 56 % as shown in Fig. 8. The black line in Fig. 8 is the linear regression (R^2 = .9243). The fastest text entry speed was 19.9 wpm recorded by P3 in Session 7.

The mean error rate over the 10 sessions was 8.7 % (Fig. 9). Error rates slightly increased (R^2 = .0005) over the sessions. The lowest error rate was 2.9 % recorded by P3 in Session 7.

P1 and P2 might have focused on speed rather than accuracy, because P1 and P2 tended to input with a higher error rate than P3 and P4, while P1

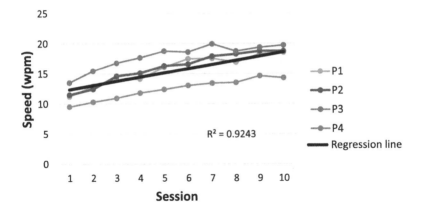

Fig. 8. Text entry speed. (Color figure online)

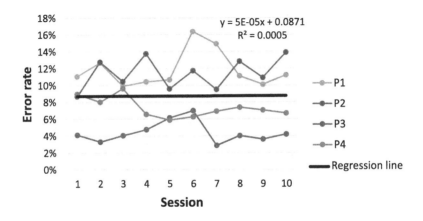

Fig. 9. Error rate. (Color figure online)

and P2 tended to input faster. Similarly, P4 might have focused on accuracy rather than speed, because P4 tended to record lower speeds. However, P3's error rates were lower than other participants' error rates except for Session 5 and 6. Furthermore, P3's text entry speeds were faster than other participants throughout all sessions. These results were supported by P3's comment. In the questionnaire, P3 commented that the size of the keys on the QAZ keyboard was larger than those of the QWERTY keyboard. We thought this subjective evaluation might be caused by the ease of moving the thumb.

The mean text entry speed from Session 11 and 12 were 18.2 wpm (SD = 0.52) and 18.4 wpm (SD = 0.87), respectively. With a paired t-test, there was no significant difference between the sessions ($t_{11} = .728$, $p = 482 > .01$). The mean error rates from Session 11 and 12 were 9.09 % (SD = 0.017) and 13.1 % (SD = 0.015), respectively. With a paired t-test, the QAZ keyboard's error rate was found to be

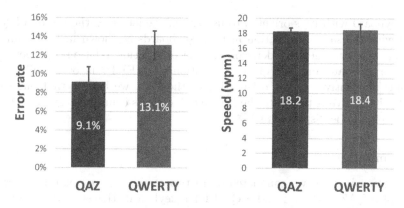

Fig. 10. Left: the mean error rate. Right: the mean text entry speed.

significantly lower than QWERTY keyboard ($t_{11} = 6.046$, $p = .000 < .01$). These results suggest that the QAZ keyboard will perform better than the QWERTY keyboard (Fig. 10).

6 Discussion

6.1 Occlusion

Because a QAZ keyboard is placed near the center of the screen in our current implementation, contents on the screen are occluded by the keyboard. To address this issue, we plan to test the following two design alternatives.

Reduction of Keyboard Size. The first solution is to reduce the size of the keyboard. Since a QAZ keyboard is surrounded by space, flicking or dragging outward from the keyboard can also be used along with tapping. By utilizing this, keys placed outside can be shrunk, because using flick or drag can reduce the number of keys required [3,4]. In this case, however, the optimum region may be different from the one we used in this paper, because the optimum region to tap, flick, and drag would be different. Therefore, it is necessary to investigate performance of flicking or dragging with one-handed thumb input on a large mobile touchscreen.

Semi-transparent Keyboard. The second solution is to make the keyboard semi-transparent. When users input a text, because they do not look at contents except for the input component, they can see only an overview of the contents. Accordingly, reducing the occlusion with an almost transparent keyboard will be feasible.

6.2 Orientation of Keys

Orientation of keys may change the learning cost of the QAZ keyboard, and therefore is to be investigated as future work. Note that this paper presents the

QAZ keyboard with keys oriented to users, i.e., the letter on the top of a key is placed with the same orientation in both keyboards as shown in Figs. 1 and 2. However, this arrangement deteriorates the orientation relationships between the entire keyboard and keys of the conventional QWERTY layout. While there are some alternatives to the orientation of the keys, we believe that one such feasible alternative is to rotate the keys by 90 degrees counterclockwise so that, for example, 'Q' is displayed as 'ⵡ'.

6.3 Limitation

In evaluation Part II, we conducted extra two sessions to compare the performance of a QAZ keyboard and a QWERTY keyboard. However, the results of using the QWERTY keyboard could be disadvantaged due to the fact that all of participants began the evaluation using the QWERTY keyboard. To compare the performances accurately, we will evaluate the two keyboards in a counterbalanced order.

7 Conclusion

In this paper, we presented the QAZ keyboard, a QWERTY keyboard designed for one-handed thumb input on a large touchscreen. To design the keyboard, we first conducted experiments to investigate pointing performance on a large mobile touchscreen using one-hand thumb input. The results showed that vertically long areas around the center of the touchscreen would be suitable to place a keyboard in terms of accuracy and time of pointing. Based on this finding, we designed and implemented the QAZ keyboard on Android-based devices. A longitudinal study with 4 participants showed that the mean text entry speed was 18.2 wpm, and the mean error rate was 9.1 %. Moreover, a comparative study of the QAZ keyboard against a QWERTY keyboard showed that the QAZ keyboard's error rate was significantly lower than when using a QWERTY keyboard.

References

1. Bi, X., Smith, B.A., Zhai, S.: Quasi-Qwerty soft keyboard optimization. In: CHI 2010, pp. 283–286 (2010)
2. Cheng, L.P., Liang, H.S., Wu, C.Y., Chen, M.Y.: iGrasp: grasp-based adaptive keyboard for mobile devices. In: CHI 2013, pp. 3037–3046 (2013)
3. Coskun, T., Wiesner, C., Artinger, E., Benzina, A., Maier, P., Huber, M., Grill, C., Schmitt, P., Klinker, G.: Gestyboard 2.0: a gesture-based text entry concept for high performance ten-finger touch-typing and blind typing on touchscreens. In: Holzinger, A., Ziefle, M., Hitz, M., Debevc, M. (eds.) SouthCHI 2013. LNCS, vol. 7946, pp. 680–691. Springer, Heidelberg (2013)
4. Fukatsu, Y., Shizuki, B., Tanaka, J.: No-look flick: single-handed and eyes-free Japanese text input system on touch screens of mobile devices. In: MobileHCI 2013, pp. 161–170 (2013)

5. Henze, N., Rukzio, E., Boll, S.: 100,000,000 taps: analysis and improvement of touch performance in the large. In: MobileHCI 2011, pp. 133–142 (2011)
6. Karlson, A.K., Bederson, B.B.: Understanding single-handed mobile device interaction. Technical report, Department of Computer Science, University of Maryland (2006)
7. Kimioka, G., Shizuki, B., Tanaka, J.: Niboshi for slate devices: a Japanese input method using multi-touch for slate devices. In: Jacko, J.A. (ed.) Human-Computer Interaction, Part II, HCII 2011. LNCS, vol. 6762, pp. 81–89. Springer, Heidelberg (2011)
8. Kuno, Y., Shizuki, B., Tanaka, J.: Long-term study of a software keyboard that places keys at positions of fingers and their surroundings. In: Kurosu, M. (ed.) HCII/HCI 2013, Part V. LNCS, vol. 8008, pp. 72–81. Springer, Heidelberg (2013)
9. Li, F.C.Y., Guy, R.T., Yatani, K., Truong, K.N.: The 1Line keyboard: a QWERTY layout in a single line. In: UIST 2011, pp. 461–470 (2011)
10. MacKenzie, I.S., Soukoreff, R.W.: Phrase sets for evaluating text entry techniques. In: CHI EA 2003, pp. 754–755 (2003)
11. MacKenzie, I.S., Soukoreff, R.W., Helga, J.: 1 thumb, 4 buttons, 20 words per minute: design and evaluation of H4-writer. In: UIST 2011, pp. 471–480 (2011)
12. MacKenzie, I.S., Zhang, S.X.: The design and evaluation of a high-performance soft keyboard. In: CHI 1999, pp. 25–31 (1999)
13. MacKenzie, I.S., Zhang, S.X., Soukoreff, R.W.: Text entry using soft keyboards. Behav. Inf. Technol. 18(4), 131–144 (1999)
14. Matias, E., MacKenzie, I.S., Buxton, W.: Half-QWERTY: a one-handed keyboard facilitating skill transfer from QWERTY. In: CHI 1993, pp. 88–94 (1993)
15. Park, Y.S., Han, S.H.: Touch key design for one-handed thumb interaction with a mobile phone: effects of touch key size and touch key location. Int. J. Ind. Ergon. 1(40), 68–76 (2010)
16. Park, Y.S., Han, S.H., Park, J., Cho, Y.: Touch key design for target selection on a mobile phone. In: MobileHCI 2008, pp. 423–426 (2008)
17. Perry, K.B., Hourcade, J.P.: Evaluating one handed thumb tapping on mobile touchscreen devices. In: GI 2008, pp. 57–64 (2008)
18. Sax, C., Lau, H., Lawrence, E.: LiquidKeyboard: an ergonomic, adaptive QWERTY keyboard for touchscreens and surfaces. In: ICDS 2011, pp. 117–122 (2011)
19. Sipos, O., Peric, I., Ivetic, D.: Layout proposal for one-handed device interface. In: CEUR Workshop Proceedings, vol. 920, pp. 81–84 (2012)
20. Takahama, K., Go, K.: A software keyboard for small touch screen terminals based on the coming and going movement of the thumb. J. Hum. Interface Soc. 12(3), 269–275 (2010). (in Japanese)
21. Wang, Y., Yu, C., Liu, J., Shi, Y.: Understanding performance of eyes-free, absolute position control on touchable mobile phones. In: MobileHCI 2013, pp. 79–88 (2013)
22. Wobbrock, J., Myers, B., Rothrock, B.: Few-key text entry revisited: mnemonic gestures on four keys. In: CHI 2006, pp. 489–492 (2006)
23. Zhai, S., Hunter, M., Smith, B.A.: The metropolis keyboard - an exploration of quantitative techniques for virtual keyboard design. In: UIST 2000, pp. 119–128, (2000)

Service Modeling for Situation-Aware Communication Method Decision

Jungkih Hong, Scott Song[(⊠)], Minseok Kim, and Wonseok Lee

Samsung Electronics Co., Ltd., Maetan 3-dong, Yeongtong-gu, Suwon-si,
Gyeonggi-do, Korea
{jungkih.hong, sangkon.song, msvic.kim, Wons.lee}
@samsung.com

Abstract. The expansion of wireless communication networks based on the development of diverse device technologies can promote an environment in which smart phones, tablet PCs, cars can be collaboratively communicated with each other anytime and anywhere. To meet such future expectations, communication is growing in order to enhance various possible interactions between smart devices. In the future, we may use truly immersive ways, which may be virtually indistinguishable from face-to-face meetings, to communicate with other people at a distance [1]. Whilst we develop communication technologies toward that vision, the interface between users and communication devices/systems needs to be advanced. In this paper, we discuss human-communication from the perspective of computers that can proactively learn and know about users. In other words, we want computers of communication system and devices that are well aware of users [2]. Therefore, we propose new models and systematic ways to design and implement the user- and situation-aware communication [3].

Keywords: Intelligent system · Context-aware · Situational-aware · Communication channel · Alternative communication

1 Introduction

Today, many computing devices around people are provided with interaction and behavior, which are very similar to human, and can be aware of environments around human. Advances in the technology help users to communicate with each other and share interactions anywhere and anytime.

In this paper, we discuss human-communication system interfaces from the perspective of a system that can anticipate and recognize the environment between users [4]. Most of all, we assert a service modeling, which maintains the effect of delivery for communications, even if different communication channels for different situations are alternatively used. First, we analyzed behavior based on situations and information of users. For example, whether a caller at the sending side has which goal-oriented communication, the other caller at the side is considered for relations between callers like business, family, friend, the situation of the receiver, or what the caller's purpose.

© Springer International Publishing Switzerland 2016
A. Marcus (Ed.): DUXU 2016, Part III, LNCS 9748, pp. 36–44, 2016.
DOI: 10.1007/978-3-319-40406-6_4

Through this consideration, we structuralized situation information of a user based on 5W1H (Five W's and One H). Second, we designed the service modeling for communication with respective to user's communication activities. As a result, we assert the communication service which automatically knows the information and situation of a user, and suggests the good one. Namely, we propose the user-centric communication environment.

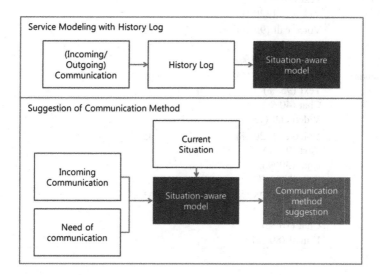

Fig. 1. The concept of the service modeling

Figure 1 describes the overall of our concept. When a caller at the sending side wants one activity for communication, he/she selects an appropriate one like voice/video-call, SNS, Text or e-mail based on situation modeling and history of the other caller at the receiving side.

2 Research Background

The increasing popularity of smart devices and new ways of communication unleash highly upgraded usability and values compared to traditional communication services. For example, Google HangoutTM includes instant messaging and video chat platform, and Skype provides video chat and voice call functions from computers, tablet PCs, and mobile devices to the similar devices, smartphones, and even to regular telephones. It enables users to send instant voice/video messages, exchange images and files, and make conference calls.

Most of these communication channels are provided directly by users' own devices. Especially, the usage of communication channels varies based on the relationship between users and the communication purpose. In order to identify usage behavior of communication channels in everyday life with respect to the type of relationships

Table 1. Communication channel usage behavior with respect to the type of relationships between users

Relationship	Communication	
	Preferred interaction (multiple answers)	Percentage of users using multiple interactions
Family (parents and siblings)	Voice call (95 %) Text (80 %) Video call (20 %)	80 %
Family (spouse and children)	Voice call (95 %) Text (75 %) Video call (25 %)	75 %
Close friends	Voice call (70 %) Text (95 %) Chat (40 %) Video call (15 %)	65 %
Colleagues	Voice call (20 %), Text (95 %), Chat (30 %), E-mail (50 %)	45 %
Others	Voice call (25 %), Text (55 %), Chat (10 %), E-mail (80 %)	35 %

between users, an experience sampling method (ESM) [5] was conducted with 20 participants who were aged between 27 and 45 during two days (Table 1).

In general, families and couples frequently used voice, video calls and texts with each other over e-mail, whereas co-workers more often used e-mails instead. Especially, the participants told that they used more than two different communication channels when communicating with other people. Moreover, we found that people with a more intimate relationship tended to prefer communication channels with quicker feedback like voice or chat. Even though a user uses more than two communication channels with others, the natural flow of communication must be considered. According to the condition for a good communication, an effective communication environment and minimizing the communication preparation time are essential.

In the future, smart devices communication systems and interfaces must proactively understand user's preference and situation rather than a user has to learn some interactions interfaces to manipulate them.

2.1 User Behavior Analysis

In order to achieve the future communication, as mentioned above, we have to analyze user's behavior for communication purposes. However, even though a user focuses on a specific task, it is difficult to examine user's accurate behavior because situation-aware service modeling is not built yet. In order to resolve this problem, we made "user behavior structuring" under environments with smart devices. Through it, we can design the communication service modeling based on situations. These ways are required to consider the preference of communication channels and communication history between people.

Table 2 shows the preference of communications based on user's activities. In addition, this preference can be structured by 5W1H like Table 3.

Table 2. User behavior structuring

Main action (constants)	Situation model (constants)	User behavior (preference)	System action (available candidates)
Meeting	Speak X, Listen O	Send texts back (I'm in a meeting)	Switch SMS/SNS message
Jogging	Read X	Switch to voice call	Switch to voice call
Calling	–	Send texts back (I will call you later)	Automatic sending message
Walking	Read X	Switch to voice call	Switch to voice call
Sleeping	–	Not to disturb	Automatic block
Driving	Speak O, Listen O	Redirect to voice call	Switch to voice call

Table 3. 5W1H factors

WHEN	Date & time	Time, date (weekend, holiday..), celebration day
WHERE	Location	User location info by GPS, Beacon and Wi-Fi
WHAT	Activity & state	Place & activity mapping (ex) Working in the office Guessing the user activity by place, motion and sensors (ex) 100 km/h speed in the highway location → Driving
WHO	Personal information	Communication partner (ex) Friends, Family, Business partners and etc.
WHY	Schedule & event	User activity & status by schedule info. (ex) 10:00 AM, Meeting schedule → Not available call
HOW	Method	Available communication channels

2.2 The Decision Modeling of Communication Channel

In order to provide users with appropriate communication services, the service modeling requires numerical history data. We designed 5W1H graph that is a requisite for the service model to decide which communication channel would be suggested. The most important factors to decide a proper communication channel are how much interaction is concentrated and immediacy of feedback is required. We created the Flow Indicator of Communication (FIC) to evaluate qualitative levels that are difficult to be obtained by the amount of interaction. For instance, since e-mail does not usually require immediate response, it is considered to lead to the lowest FIC, while video chat exposes all users' actions and has therefore the highest FIC.

FIC of non-real time interaction such as e-mail or text message is calculated by the average response period. Real-time chat may have a similar FIC level as with voice call and the FIC of late reply texts may be lower than the FIC of fast reply e-mail (Table 4).

Table 4. Checklist for flow indicator

Factors	e-mail	Text	Chat	Voice	Video call
Immediate take	1	2	2	3	3
Immediate response	1	1	2	3	3
Visual exposure	0	0	0	0	3
Audial exposure	0	0	0	3	0
Requires real time device/service control	0	1	2	1	1

[0 (Not associated) ~ 3 (Highly required)]

Several factors including immediacy of feedback, exposures, and operations are taken into account to evaluate FIC.

FIC is used on five W variables defined as Wn (When), Wr (Where), Wy (Why), Wt (What) and Wo (Who). These variables represent how immediate communication is required in each W. All events from a user activity have their own numerical W values. Situations with higher FIC value require voice or video calls more. As all factors are relative value, we set the minimum and maximum value of those with 0 to 10.

We converted various situations into 5W values. Graphs in Fig. 2 are initiated values that can be changed by new user histories. Whenever a history of situation and chosen communication channel is made, the area of each situation on W graph is adjusted (Fig. 3).

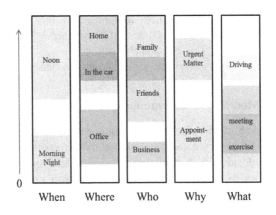

Fig. 2. The 5W graph

Fig. 3. The default H graph

H is a weighted average of W values. All communication channels have their ranges on 5W graphs. Each W value is calculated by two variables, U and F. The variable U is user's weighted value of each W. Another variable F is FIC value of each situation. All situations have their own F value. U values differ from users.

We extracted the following formula.

$$H = U_n F_n + U_r F_r + U_y F_y + U_t F_t + U_o F_o$$

Based on FIC, A history of user communication and communication channel with 5Ws led to the results described below.

By calculating the amount of interaction based on each W graph, 5W1H graph is created for each history, as shown in Fig. 4.

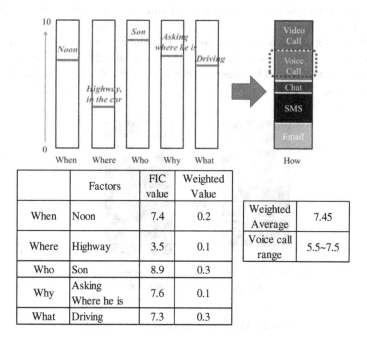

	Factors	FIC value	Weighted Value
When	Noon	7.4	0.2
Where	Highway	3.5	0.1
Who	Son	8.9	0.3
Why	Asking Where he is	7.6	0.1
What	Driving	7.3	0.3

Weighted Average	7.45
Voice call range	5.5~7.5

Fig. 4. An example of communication channel history based on 5W1H

Table 5. Factors defining communication channel area

C_{min}^x	The minimum H (How) value that a user would use the communication channel x
C_{MAX}^x	The maximum H (How) value that a user would use the communication channel x
S_{min}^z	The minimum W (5Ws) value that the communication channel is used in situation z
S_{min}^z	The maximum W (5Ws) value that the communication channel is used in situation z

In W and H graph, situations and communication channels have their own ranges. These ranges are customized for users. Every history of users affects the communication channel(C) and situation(S) ranges.

The greater $(C_{min}^1 - C_{MAX}^1)$ value means that the communication channel is used under various situation. If $(C_{min}^1 - C_{min}^1)$ value is small, it means that the communication channel is used only under very limited situation.

In the manipulation process of 5W1H graph, when user histories are not made enough, initial values are given. The modeling doesn't automatically provide any communication channels until a user creates sufficient history (Fig. 5).

As user history logs are accumulated on the decision modeling, the shape of each graph changes. When the history logs are collected enough, the decision modeling can recommend appropriate communication channels automatically (Fig. 6).

When a user prefers suggestion services, H graph is fully filled with communication channels. On the other hand, if a user doesn't want, H graph has a lot of blank area that doesn't provide any communication channels automatically. Whenever a user denies a proposed communication channel, the area of suggestion shrinks. This step prevents users from receiving unnecessary suggestions.

The following example shows that a voice call is activated outside of the current suggestion area for voice call.

As a new history is created, each area of communication channel must be rearranged. In Fig. 7, after a voice call event occurs, it affects the voice call area of 5W1H graph. The smaller scope is allocated for the communication channels that are rarely used. The cases such as above help devices to provide alternative communication methods or proper feedbacks by understanding the context of user activity or constrains of user situation.

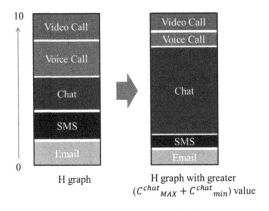

Fig. 5. The process of H graph adjustment

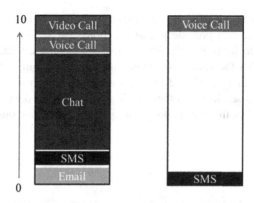

Fig. 6. Comparison of automation-preferred and customization-preferred

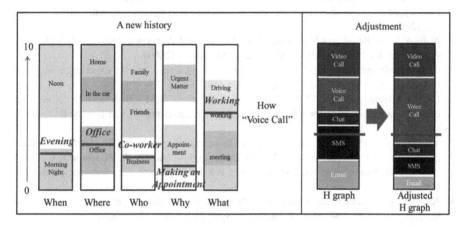

Fig. 7. Adjustment of decision matrix by user history

3   Conclusions

With the introduction of new IT technologies and the emergence of numerous smart devices, complexity of user experience has greatly increased and our everyday life is evolving at a rapid pace. This trend motivated many research institutions [6, 7] and companies [8, 9] to actively study new communication interfaces that can intuitively connect people and support various communication channels as needed based on traditional communication. In this paper, we introduced a new communication service model that can synthetically suggests whichever any communication channel to design and implement user-centric communication instead of the current device-centric communication.

The ultimate purpose of the model is that users can conveniently use an appropriate communication based on user situations. The previous ways of communication have the dependency of device functions and capabilities. For example, a caller in a receiving side has to accept the request from the caller channel in a sending side. Our proposed modeling can consider the caller context in the both receiving and sending side. Furthermore, we can provide useful functions and services to users by using analyzed life-log data from electric devices like smartphones, wearable devices and smart TV devices. It's the change of communication paradigm [10]. Therefore, this study can be immediately deployed in smart devices and can be directly applied to actual communication services. In other words, it will focus on developing user-centric communication services that can build mash-up service and new business models.

References

1. Lyytinen, K., Yoo, Y.: Ubiquitous computing. Commun. ACM **45**(12), 63–96 (2002)
2. Schilit, B., Adams, N., Want, R.: Context-aware computing applications. In: First Workshop on Mobile Computing Systems and Applications, WMCSA 1994, pp. 85–90. IEEE (1994)
3. Endsley, M.R.: Toward a theory of situation awareness in dynamic systems. Hum. Factors **37**, 32–64 (1995)
4. Nofi, A.A.: Defining and Measuring Shared Situational Awareness (No. CRM-D0002895. A1). Center for Naval Analyses Alexandria, Alexandria (2000)
5. Csikszentmihalyi, M., Larson, R.: Validity and reliability of the experience-sampling method. J. Nerv. Ment. Dis. **175**(9), 526–536 (1987)
6. Guye-Vuillème, A., Capin, T.K., Pandzic, S., Thalmann, N.M., Thalmann, D.: Nonverbal communication interface for collaborative virtual environments. Virtual Reality **4**(1), 49–59 (1999)
7. Vanderheyden, P.B., Pennington, C.A.: An augmentative communication interface based on conversational schemata. In: Mittal, V.O., Yanco, H.A., Aronis, J., Simpson, R.C. (eds.) Assistive Technology and AI. LNCS (LNAI), vol. 1458, pp. 109–125. Springer, Heidelberg (1998)
8. Nonaka, H.: Communication interface with eye-gaze and head gesture using successive DP matching and fuzzy inference. J. Intell. Inf. Syst. **21**(2), 105–112 (2003)
9. Eklund, A., Andersson, M., Ohlsson, H., Ynnerman, A., Knutsson, H.: A brain computer interface for communication using real-time fMRI. In: 2010 20th International Conference on Pattern Recognition (ICPR), pp. 3665–3669. IEEE, August 2010
10. Akyildiz, I.F., Brunetti, F., Blázquez, C.: Nanonetworks: a new communication paradigm. Comput. Netw. **52**(12), 2260–2279 (2008)

Aspect-Oriented Approach for User Interaction Logging of iOS Applications

Ilka Kokemor and Hans-Peter Hutter$^{(\boxtimes)}$

Institute of Applied Information Technology (InIT),
Zurich University of Applied Sciences (ZHAW), Winterthur, Switzerland
`hans-peter.hutter@zhaw.ch`

Abstract. Mobile applications that don't meet the users' expectations regarding usability risk bad user feedbacks that lower the application's download rate or the app will just be quietly ignored. In order to identify and improve major usability issues of a mobile application, data about the real user interaction in the actual mobile usage context needs to be gathered without disturbing the interaction environment. This paper presents an aspect-oriented approach for gathering user interaction data for iOS applications without any additional hardware. To that end, two libraries have been developed that track the user and system behavior, take screenshots, record user videos and collect GPS coordinates. The data can later be downloaded from the mobile device to third party tools for further analysis. A usability test with a sample application shows the possibilities of the implemented framework.

Keywords: Mobile human computer interaction · iOS app design and development · Mobile app usability

1 Introduction

This paper shows an approach to gather detailed data about the real user interaction with an iOS application and how to analyze it to improve its usability issues.

1.1 Problem Description

Todays mobile devices not only allow to use an application anywhere anytime but also offer a variety of interaction modalities (touch, gestures, speech) the user can choose from. For usability researchers a lot of new questions therefore arise: How does a user interact with a mobile application? Which combination of modalities does a user use to interact and how does he actually interact in detail with the mobile application? When and where does a user interact with the application and what is the usage context? Which gestures does he use or try to use? Are the basic usability requirements described in ISO 9241-110 [14] fulfilled? For example, the principle about conformity with user expectations:

© Springer International Publishing Switzerland 2016
A. Marcus (Ed.): DUXU 2016, Part III, LNCS 9748, pp. 45–56, 2016.
DOI: 10.1007/978-3-319-40406-6_5

Can the user's expectations about the user interaction with the application, e.g. regarding gesture usage, be met? To answer this kind of questions, it is necessary not only to scrutinize the server logs but also to analyze in detail the mobile user interaction with the application. To get this information one way is to shadow him. But this is very time consuming, and worse, interferes with the real usage context. So to unobtrusively find out, how a user interacts with the application and what he actually intends to do, detailed data about the interaction, the system and usage context, and other sensor data (e.g. accelerometers, gyros) have to be gathered by the device itself without additional external hardware. There are already tools for desktop applications, e.g. [13], but mobile applications need a different approach because they are used in a mobile environment and tests in a laboratory environment cannot simulate how the real world affects the interaction with an application. So there is only the possibility to use the device in use.

1.2 Contributions

In this paper a toolkit that has been developed in our lab is presented which allows the recording of detailed data about the user interactions with an iOS application. The toolkit comprises two static libraries written in Objective-C and in Swift, resp. It logs all user interactions, i.e. view changes, button clicks, and gestures. In addition, it makes screenshots of the application screens and uses the front camera to record a user video while the user is using the application. Additionally, environmental and system information are gathered, including GPS coordinates and internet connectivity. So the usage context in which the user interacts with the application can be analyzed and used for the interpretation of the interaction flow. Often the user changes his or her behavior, because the system environment forces him to (e.g. due to a lost internet connectivity). All log information is stored in a XML file that is saved in the application's directory on the iOS device together with the screenshots and the user videos. For recording the GPS coordinates an additional application called TrackApp has been developed which is to be installed on the iOS device. After the user quits the mobile application TrackApp generates a GPX file that is also stored on the iOS device. All stored data can be uploaded to a usability test server for further analysis and can be synchronized with other recorded data.

The toolkit is based on a general framework of method swizzling that can be used not only for Objective-C but also for Swift in order to gather interaction data for any kind of usability tests, especially for multimodal interactions comprising e.g. gestures.

2 Related Work

Most approaches so far focus on the usability of Android applications and have often implemented a supplement which can be used on mobile devices using Android as operating system.

Balgates-Fernandez et al. presented in [8] the EvaHelper, a framework which logs user interactions with an Android application and stores the data in CSV files. The collected data in the CSV file can then be transformed to a format which can be imported in GraphML [15]. There the user interaction can be visualized as nested directed graphs.

Lettner et al. described in [16,17] their project AUToMAte (Automated Usability Testing of Mobile Applications). For their toolbox they implemented an Android mobile framework, an IDE Wizard and a cloud-based web server. The Android mobile framework can be added to Android applications with aspect-oriented programming measures. After the framework has been integrated into an Android application user interactions can be logged, e.g. changes between views and interactions on the screens. With the also provided web server metrics and statistics are calculated to locate usability issues within the application.

Holzinger et al. [10] presented an approach with an aspect-oriented addition to a sample iOS application which records interface events of keyboard input, context menus and drag and drop actions. The tracked data is logged in a text format. With this approach the quality of the auto-advancing short-key tagging of the sample application was measured by identifying user corrections. Holzinger uses an aspect-oriented approach of method swizzling and categories in Objective-C to gather the described data.

Google Analytics [12] is widely known and used for analyzing web activities. Also frameworks for Android and iOS are available. For that the Google Analytics Framework needs to be downloaded and integrated into the application's source code. This framework does not use an aspect-oriented approach like the one described in this paper. The recorded data cannot be downloaded but Google Analytics reports can be exported in different file types (e.g. CSV, Excel).

The companies Lookback [18] and Appsee [7] provide SDKs which can be integrated in iOS applications. While using the application a user video and a screen video are recorded. Also a timeline is logged showing which views are selected during the application's usage. On the screen video it is shown where the finger is moved. The data is uploaded to the company's servers as soon as there is an internet connection available. Additionally, Appsee provides a platform for further analysis of the interaction data. It is possible to follow the detailed interactions which are logged as well and draw heat maps that show which parts of the screen are used the most on a view. So both companies provide frameworks which can be used for gathering interaction data about applications. However, the data is automatically uploaded to their servers and only the videos can be downloaded after that. All other information about the user interaction cannot be downloaded. With the approach described in this paper, the logged data is stored in XML files which can be downloaded from the iOS device and then used in a tool that can interpret the XML format for further analysis. Also the screenshots and the user videos are stored on the iOS device and can be downloaded as well.

3   Requirements

There are several requirements for collecting information about the usage of an application to improve it's usability. All requirements are build on the prerequisite, that no third party device is necessary. Also all iOS applications should be supported, those written in Objective-C, those with a mix of Objective-C and Swift and those totally written in Swift.

User Activities. The user activities no only comprise the user interactions with the application but also his other activities, e.g. whether his attention is actually focused on the application or distracted by external events.

Screenshots or Screenvideos. Screenshots or screen videos help a lot when reconstructing the details of the user interaction flow. With that it is possible to dive into every detail of successful or unsuccessful interactions.

User Video. If user videos are recorded it is possible to get the user's reaction and emotion while he or she is using the application. Also the environment of the user is recorded. So it is possible to draw conclusions about the usage context as well.

Audio Recording. Audio recording can be added to user video recording. With that is possible not only to get a picture about the user's environment but also about the background noises. Additionally it is possible for the user to comment spontaneously.

Device and System Information. If the application heavily depends on certain device or system features, it is useful to log this information, too. If they are not available and prevent the user from actions he wants to perform, this is an important usability issue. Especially missing internet connectivity is often such an issue.

GPS Coordinates. Applications are normally used in a mobile environment, often while being on the move. Therefore the information where and when the user uses a certain application is important for analyzing it's usability. Recording the GPS coordinates is very helpful in this case.

4   Approach of Aspect-Oriented Programming

The approach for aspect-oriented programming in addition to an object-oriented design is mostly chosen because there are some issues in the system that occur allover the application, e.g. security, logging, or testing. Aspects are properties that tend to cut across functional components [11]. With adding aspects to an application it is possible to avoid restructuring it and just add the required aspect.

4.1   Aspect-Oriented Programming in AUToMAte

Lettner et al. [17] use aspect-oriented programming to add their framework to existing Android applications. They used AspectJ, an aspect-oriented programming framework for Java, to integrate the monitoring framework. With AspectJ the host application does not have and need any connection to the monitoring framework. The monitoring framework can be added easily and fast to the hosting application. Lettner et al. add aspects into applications with join point model (JPM). They use compile-time weaving, which means adding the framework during compilation time. They point out, that post-compile weaving and load-time weaving do not have any advantages to compile-time weaving and load-time weaving does not work with Android applications because of its virtual machine limitations.

4.2   Aspect-Oriented Programming with Objective-C

In the Objective-C Runtime Programming Guide [2] it is pointed out that many decisions are deferred to runtime. For that Objective-C programs interact with the runtime system at three levels: through Objective-C source code, through methods defined in the NSObject class of the Foundation framework, and through direct calls to runtime functions. So in contrast to Lettner et al. who chose compile-time weaving for aspect-oriented programming in Java, adding or changing functionality in an aspect-oriented way in Objective-C programs is done at runtime.

Method Swizzling. In Objective-C the messaging system is used to call methods. The compiler builds a structure for each class which includes the pointer to the superclass and a class dispatch table. While creating a new object, memory is allocated and its instance variables are initialized. The instance variables include a pointer (isa) to its class structure. With this pointer the object gets access to its class and indirectly to all superclasses as well. A class maintains a dispatch table to resolve messages sent at runtime: each entry in the table is a method, which keys a particular name, the selector, to an implementation, i.e. a pointer to an underlying C function. To swizzle a method is to change a class's dispatch table in order to resolve messages from an existing selector to a different implementation, while aliasing the original method implementation to a new selector [20]. Method swizzling used for method interception in Objective-C, since Apple provides the possibility to change the class dispatch table at runtime. For that the original selector shows to a new implementation and a new selector shows to the original implementation, which means swapping selectors. For that either the new implementation of the method is added directly to the original selector and the original implementation is replaced in the swizzled selector, or the methods are just swapped.

Categories. Holzinger et al. [10] use the concept of categories to add methods and functionality to existing classes. Categories are a runtime feature. Apple states, "at runtime, there is no difference between a method added by a category and one that is implemented by the original class" [3]. In our case categories are also used to enhance implementation of certain classes to collect data about the user's interactions. The interface needs not be changed, since the methods are swizzled and no additional methods are added nor their interface is changed.

Holzinger et al. use a property list to configure aspects for certain classes. In our approach classes are extended with categories to add functionality to existing methods which does not require changing or adding property configurations. Since all this is implemented in a static library, we only need to consider that the categories are loaded properly into the used applications by setting the `Other Linker Flags` correspondingly.

4.3   Aspect-Oriented Programming with Swift

Using the Objective-C Approach. Since Swift is based on Objective-C and uses the same runtime environment, all Objective-C features are also available in Swift. That means we can use method swizzling and categories in Swift as well.

Approach of Compile-Time Weaving. In addition to Objective-C, Swift uses virtual method tables (vtables) for method runtime binding. While compiling the Swift Front End translates the code into Swift Intermediate Language (SIL). Then the SIL Optimizer optimizes SIL and generates code in Intermediate Representation (IR) format. Finally, the IR Optimizer transfers the IR format into machine code. In Objective-C the Clang Front End transfers the code directly into IR [9,19]. SIL generates the vtables for the classes, by mapping the method names to their implementations. Final methods are not listed here. They do not need to be mapped, since their implementation always stays the same. So for aspect-oriented programming, static weaving could be used to replace non-final methods in the vtables.

5   Implementation

To log data about user interactions with an application, the above described method swizzling was chosen. The reason for this decision was that the approach and implementation for Objective-C and Swift would be similar and final methods in Swift would be supported as well. To that end, two static libraries have been build to support apps written in Objective-C, Swift, or even a mix of both.

5.1   Methods to Be Swizzled

In our approach specific classes are enhanced that collect data whenever they are called. Whenever the user is moving his fingers over the touch screen, the class

UITouch is involved. The method `locationInView` of UITouch is central for that. It returns the location of the touch in the receiving view [5]. So whenever the user interacts with the screen, even when the application does not respond to the user's touch, the method `locationInView` is called. Therefore also unrecognized gestures, e.g. the user unsuccessfully tries to zoom in, can be recognized. The property `gestureRecognizers` in class UITouch holds an array of instances of class `UIGestureRecognizer`, which is the super class of all gesture recognizers. The array holds all gesture recognizers who would respond to the given touch of the user, even if it triggers no action. This feature can be used to find out if there are user gestures the app hasn't implemented.

All visual control elements are derived from UIControl. It includes the method `sendAction` which is called when there is an action triggered because the visual control element is activated. The method `endTrackingWithTouch` is called when the recording of a touch gesture is stopped [4]. Especially with the method `sendAction` it is possible to log control elements. However, in some cases the method `sendAction` does not include any implementation and is therefore not called, even if there are visual control elements.

All view controllers are derived from class `UIViewController`. This class is responsible for the view management. So when the user changes the view, e.g. through forward navigation, the `UIViewController` changes as well and another view will be displayed. The methods `viewDidAppear` and `viewWillDisappear` can be used to log this information. The first one notifies when a new view is shown, the other one triggers when the view is about to be shut down [6].

Normally the class `CLLocationManager` is used to collect GPS coordinates. There the method `didUpdateLocations` is called regularly to get new GPS coordinates [1].

5.2 Static Libraries

Method swizzling works a little different in Objective-C than in Swift. In Objective-C methods are normally overwritten in the function `load`. In Swift this must happen in the function `init`. Also it is necessary that the classes are swizzled in the according language. So classes in Objective-C need to be swizzled in Objective-C, Swift classes have to be swizzled in Swift. However, it is not possible to swizzle the same class twice in one library. Therefore two libraries were developed, one swizzling in Swift and one swizzling the same classes in Objective-C.

5.3 Functionality

To enhance an existing iOS application in order to log interaction data, one of the libraries need to be integrated into it. The following functionalities are currently implemented in both static libraries:

– For each user interaction a screenshot with a timestamp is taken and stored in the iOS device's file system.

- Start and end of the usage of the application is marked. For that the appropriate functions needs to be included in methods of the class `AppDelegate` of the monitored application.
- When the usage or observation is finished an XML file is created and stored in the iOS device's file system.
- GPS coordinates are tracked.
- System data are recorded, especially internet connectivity.
- A user video is recorded and stored in the iOS device's file system while the user uses the application.
- Easy integration into the existing application: for that the Apple standard of static libraries has been chosen.

6   Usability Analysis of a Sample Mobile Application

In ISO 9241-110 [14] seven general usability principles are listed which are important guidelines also for analyzing the usability of mobile applications. Conformity with user expectation and self descriptiveness e.g. is important for mobile applications because users will try to use common gestures to control the application and use hints within the application for its usage but they rarely read a handbook. The application must also be error tolerant, which means the system must help the users if there is a problem with the system or with the usage of the application. The user also wants to know why an error has occurred and how to avoid or solve the problem. As mobile users often try to perform a specific task, the principle "suitability for the task" is specially important for mobile applications.

In this case study a usability test of the ZHAW Engineering CampusInfo App [21] was conducted. The main functionality of this iOS application includes timetables for students, professors, classes, rooms and courses. The application also shows the actual menu and opening times of the canteens, the administration contact information, the campuses schematic maps and social media links. It also lists events and news of the ZHAW School of Engineering department. The application only exists in German language, therefore all given screenshots show German labels. For the usability test, the application was enhanced with the described Objective-C library. Users were recruited do use the application in their daily routine. After the tests the data was downloaded from their iOS phones and analyzed.

6.1   Evaluation Example

With the gained logs and videos, different evaluations are possible. A general statistic of the usage of the different functionalities for 3 users is shown in Fig.1. The overall time ratio spent in a functionality, however, does not tell us whether the functionality was actually used. If a user spends much time within one functionality, there could be times of inactivity which then can be analyzed using user videos and GPS logs. Or the user could spend much time within one functionality because he or she searches for something and cannot find it.

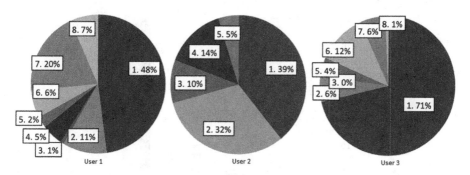

Fig. 1. Percent of time of functionality usage of the example application with three users (1. Timetable, 2. Cafeteria, 3. News and Events, 4. Settings, 5. Public Transport, 6. Location, 7. Contacts, 8. Social Media)

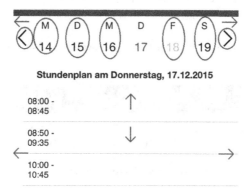

Fig. 2. Possible gestures and buttons to change the day or week, marked with red arrows and circles (Color figure online)

Figure 1 shows how much time three users spend within the functionalities of our example application. Users were given the task to use the example application during some days in their daily routine. In Fig. 1 the percentage of usage time within the functionalities of the application of different users is shown. As expected all users spent most of their time with the timetable functionality: User 1 48 %, User 2 39 %, and User 3 71 %. In the next important features the users start to defer: while User 2 spent 32 % of his time in Cafeteria, User 1 switched between Contacts and Cafeteria, and User 3 spent it in Locations. The overall time ratio spent in a functionality, however, does not tell us whether the functionality was actually used. The recorded user videos revealed, e.g., that User 3 put his mobile device into his pocket while the mobile application was still running in the timetable functionality.

Since all users spent most of their time within the timetable functionality, we continue our investigations there. In Fig. 2 the time table overview is shown. There are different possibilities to use gestures and buttons there. If the swiping

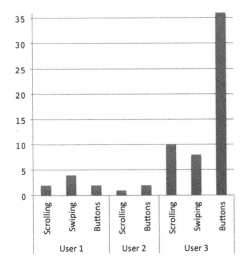

Fig. 3. Gestures and buttons used in timetable overview, focussing on changing the day or week

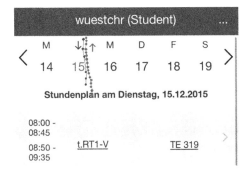

Fig. 4. Scrolling gesture in timetable overview

gesture is used in the table, the day is changed forward or backward depending on a left or right swipe. Swiping in the list of days view results in changing the week, forward or backward depending on a left or right swipe. But also buttons can be used here, either one of the day buttons to change the day of the current week, or the arrow buttons on the lift and right side to change the week. The possible gestures and buttons are marked with red arrows and red circles, resp.

With the interaction log it is possible to figure out, if the users used the swiping gestures or used the buttons to change the day or week. Figure 3 shows which gestures the users used in the given view and how many times they used the buttons for changing the day or week. User 1 changed the day or week using swiping gestures and buttons while User 2 used buttons only. User 3 largely used the buttons but also the swiping gestures from time to time. All users used scrolling gestures as this is the only way to scroll through the time slots of a day.

The interaction log also provides the information, where the user touched the display during a gesture interaction. The coordinates of the gesture movement are logged and can be exported later to draw the gesture into the screenshot. In Fig. 4 a scrolling gesture is shown where first the user scrolled down the timetable and then up again.

7   Conclusion

In this paper we have shown how detailed interaction logging of an iOS application can be performed with method swizzling. To that end, two libraries for iOS applications were developed. We chose method swizzling and categories as an aspect-oriented approach to gather those data. The two libraries provided support applications written in Objective-C as well as in Swift. The interaction data is available in form of user videos and screenshots as well as different XML files recorded on the mobile device. These can be downloaded and used in third party usability research tools for further analysis and synchronization with other external recordings. With this setup detailed analysis of mobile usability issues can be performed in order to optimize the usability and user experience of a given mobile application.

References

1. Apple: CLLocationManagerDelegate, 11 November 2015. Website: https:// developer.apple.com/library/prerelease/ios/documentation/CoreLocation/ Reference/CLLocationManagerDelegate_Protocol
2. Apple: Objective-c runtime programming guide, 11 November 2015. Website: https://developer.apple.com/library/ios/documentation/Cocoa/Conceptual/ ObjCRuntimeGuide/Introduction/Introduction.html#apple_ref/doc/uid/ TP40008048-CH1-SW1
3. Apple: Programming with objective-c - customizing existing classes, 11 November 2015. Website: https://developer.apple.com/library/ios/documentation/Cocoa/ Conceptual/ProgrammingWithObjectiveC/CustomizingExistingClasses/ CustomizingExistingClasses.html
4. Apple: Uicontrol, 11 November 2015. Website: https://developer.apple.com/ library/ios/documentation/UIKit/Reference/UIControl_Class
5. Apple: Uitouch, 11 November 2015. Website: https://developer.apple.com/library/ ios/documentation/UIKit/Reference/UITouch_Class/#apple_ref/occ/instm/ UITouch
6. Apple: UIViewController, 11 November 2015. Website: https://developer.apple. com/library/ios/documentation/UIKit/Reference/UIViewController_Class
7. Appsee: Appsee, 11 November 2015. Website: https://www.appsee.com/
8. Balagtas-Fernandez, F., Hussmann, H.: A methodology and framework to simplify usability analysis of mobile applications. In: IEEE/ACM International Conference on Automated Software Engineering, pp. 520–524 (2009)

9. Borzym, K.: Swift method dispatching a summary of my talk at swift warsaw, 11 November 2015. Website: http://allegro.tech/2014/12/swift-method-dispatching. html

10. Brugger, A.H.M., Slany, W.: Applying aspect oriented programming in usability engineering processes: on the example of tracking usage information for remote usability testing. In: 2011 Proceedings of the International Conference on e-Business (ICE-B), pp. 1–4, Jul 2011

11. Fayad, C.: Designing an aspect-oriented framework in an object-oriented environment. ACM Comput. Surv. (CSUR) **32**(41), 1–12 (2000)

12. Google.org: Google analytics, 11 November 2015. Website: https://developers. google.com/analytics/

13. Hilbert, D.M., Redmiles, D.F.: Extracting usability information from user interface events. ACM Comput. Surv. **32**(4), 384–421 (2000)

14. Ergonomics of human-system interaction Part 110: Dialogue principles, 11 November 2015. http://www.iso.org/iso/iso_catalogue/catalogue_tc/catalogue_ detail.htm?csnumber=38009

15. Konstanz, U.: graphdrawing.org, 11 November 2015. Website: http:// graphdrawing.org/

16. Lettner, F., Holzmann, C.: Automated and unsupervised user interaction logging as basis for usability evaluation of mobile applications. In: Proceedings of the 10th International Conference on Advances in Mobile Computing and Multimedia, pp. 118–127 (2012)

17. Lettner, F., Holzmann, C.: Sensing mobile phone interaction in the field. In: 2012 IEEE International Conference on Pervasive Computing and Communications Workshops (PERCOM Workshops), pp. 877–882 (2012)

18. Lookback: Lookback, 11 November 2015. Website: https://lookback.io/

19. Siracusa, J.: OS X 10.10 Yosemite: The ars technica review, 11 November 2015. Website: http://arstechnica.com/apple/2014/10/os-x-10-10/22/

20. Thompson, M.: Method swizzling, 11 November 2015. Website: http://nshipster. com/method-swizzling/

21. ZHAW School of Engineering: ZHAW Engineering CampusInfo, 11 November 2015. Website: https://itunes.apple.com/ch/app/zhaw-engineering-campusinfo/ id715684381?mt=8

Comparing Android App Permissions

Jason K. MacDuffie$^{(\boxtimes)}$ and Patricia A. Morreale

Department of Computer Science, Kean University, Union, USA
{macduffj,pmorreal}@kean.edu

Abstract. With increasingly more apps added to the Google Play Store, the security of those apps is a concern. Users cannot sort apps based on their expected permissions. An interface was designed that allows users to specify their ideal permissions for an app. The ideal permissions are used to evaluate a list of apps based on proximity to that ideal. Apps are presented to indicate greater or less security using cues of color and presentation order. A survey was conducted to see whether the interface discouraged users from downloading an app that requires many permissions when compared to information provided by the Google Play Store. Most users showed significant concern towards their mobile app security, with 50 % of the users responding to the interface with greater concern over the app requiring many permissions. The research concludes that increasing user awareness of security increases user selection of more secure apps.

Keywords: Human-computer interaction · Android · Permissions · Security

1 Introduction

Currently, the only convenient way to make choices about what Android app to use based on permissions settings is to cycle through the most popular apps on the Play Store to decide which app requires the fewest permissions (Fig. 1). This process can clearly be automated, and the results of such a process can be presented in an informative way.

The number of apps in the Google Play Store continues to grow. As of January 2015, there were 1.43 million apps [1] and as of May 2013 there were 48 billion app downloads [2]. When examining the twelve most downloaded apps in the Google Play Store as of July 2015 [3], adding together the permissions each app required, as represented by a bullet point on the list of permissions, the average number of permissions required is 28, and the total number of permissions required ranges from 6 to 52. In response to this approach, an alternative user interface to the Google Play Store's permissions view is presented, which consolidates an app's permissions settings based on user preference. The interface presented here uses visual cues such as color and presentation to influence user behavior [4], and also provides a quantitative score for each app.

© Springer International Publishing Switzerland 2016
A. Marcus (Ed.): DUXU 2016, Part III, LNCS 9748, pp. 57–64, 2016.
DOI: 10.1007/978-3-319-40406-6_6

Fig. 1. An example of a typical permissions info page

2   Related Work

Prior research concerning how to analyze apps and give users better information based on their subjective expectations about the app [5] showed that influencing user behavior to be more privacy-focused can be done through the use of nudges [6]. Presentation order has been demonstrated to be an effective cue in influencing user perception of security [4]. Color coding using a gradient from green to red, where green is "good" and red is "bad" has also been shown to be an effective cue [4]. Nudges can influence users to interact with their privacy settings [6].

Previous research has also looked at the API-side of the security issue [7] which tried to influence developer behavior by granting more granular information about the user's location. However, with so many incentives to track users such as advertising, the approach presented here focused on being more productive by empowering users to control their privacy.

3   AppRater

An initial comparison of static and dynamic analyzers was done to see strengths and weaknesses (Table 1).

Almost all of the analyzer tried had serious problems. The static analyzers often did not provide useful information other than the permissions manifest, and the dynamic analyzers were challenging to install.

The permissions manifest is a list of all the permissions an app can access. This information is not very helpful because the user already sees the list of permissions when they first install the application. However, since that was the most readily available information with respect to an app's security, it was worthwhile to present the same information available from the manifest to the user in a more helpful interface.

Table 1. Static and dynamic analyzers tested

Static analyzers	Dynamic analyzers
APKInspector (Python)	Taintdroid
Androwarn (Python)	ASEF (Java)
CFGScandroid (Java)	Decaf
ApkAnalyser (Java)	AMAT
DidFail (Python, Java)	DroidBox
FlowDroid (Java)	Drozer
Amandroid (Scala)	Appie
Smalisca (Python)	AndroidHooker
Maldrolyzer (Python)	CobraDroid (Java)
DroidSafe (Java)	

Users could select which permissions were acceptable or unacceptable, and a score is produced based on how an app agrees with a user's permissions preferences.

Two algorithms were experimented with while building the new interface. Both algorithms work similarly, but were based on two very different input types.

The first algorithm (Fig. 2) displayed the options on a Likert scale from 0 to 5, where 5 meant "no opinion about this permission" and 0 meant "strongly negative opinion about this permission." Algorithm 1 associated with this scale would give an app an "absolute score" based on how many unwanted permissions were in the app. This "absolute score" would then be divided by the worst possible score; that is, the score an app would have if it had every unwanted permission. The result would be subtracted from 100 % to produce a final score.

The other algorithm, Algorithm 2, is the one used for the scores shown in the actual survey. This other interface distinguishes "tier" permissions, such as no location, coarse location, or fine location and "boolean" permissions, such as no network access or network access allowed. The motivation for this new interface was that a user seems unlikely to want coarse location when they do not want fine location, so whether an app compared well to a user's location preferences was given double the weight compared to other permissions if the user does not want their fine location shared. The second algorithm compared the actual permission to the worst possible score per permission and took the average of those scores. This had the unexpected effect of putting a lower boundary on the score an app could have. This was considered acceptable for the initial effort, but eventually it would be good to reconsider the algorithm.

3.1   Upload Interface

Several benefits with Androwarn analyzer included the software being easy to set up, easy to use, and the results could be output as plain-text or html. The only severe problem is that Androwarn failed to accept some apps as input. Because of these benefits, Androwarn was a good candidate for extracting the permissions manifest from the apps, a script was written to call Androwarn when the user uploads an app.

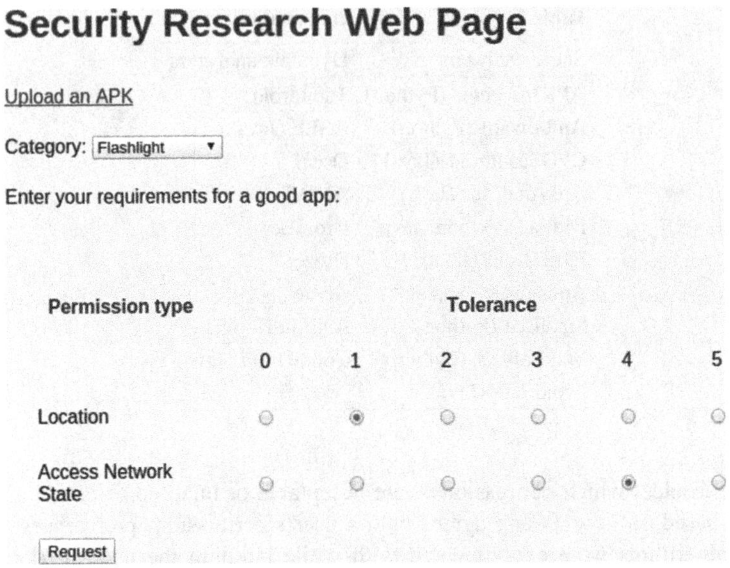

Security Research Web Page

Upload an APK

Category: [Flashlight ▼]

Enter your requirements for a good app:

Permission type	Tolerance					
	0	1	2	3	4	5
Location	○	◉	○	○	○	○
Access Network State	○	○	○	○	◉	○

[Request]

Fig. 2. Likert scale for user responses related to user tolerance for app permission request indicated (Algorithm 1)

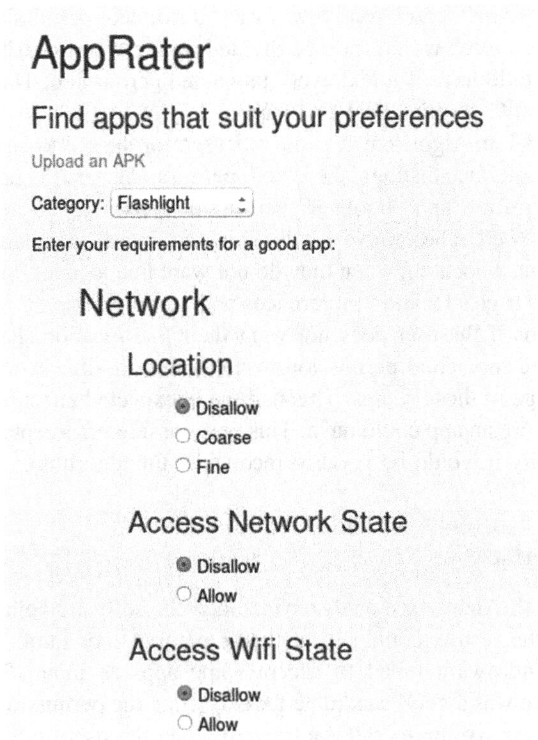

AppRater

Find apps that suit your preferences

Upload an APK

Category: [Flashlight ▲▼]

Enter your requirements for a good app:

Network

Location

◉ Disallow
○ Coarse
○ Fine

Access Network State

◉ Disallow
○ Allow

Access Wifi State

◉ Disallow
○ Allow

Fig. 3. AppRater menu - user view

3.2 Selection Interface

An interface was written in Gauche Scheme which uses a simple algorithm to compare apps. Each app is evaluated and compared with the user's requested behavior. First the user is presented with an interface to select which permissions are important to them (Fig. 3).

3.3 Results Interface

Using the Algorithm 2 described earlier, a score from 0 to 100 percent is produced, where 100 indicates an app that agrees with the user's preference and 0 indicates an app that disagrees with the user's preference. The results are then displayed to the user. Highest rated apps are displayed at the top, with lower rated apps placed at the bottom. As an additional visual cue, apps change color based on their score: a score below 60 is red, with the scale progressively turning yellow then green, which is the color for a score above 90 (Fig. 4).

Fig. 4. App rate results view, as presented to user (Color figure online)

4 Methods

A survey of five questions, designed to evaluate the effectiveness of the new interface to influence the user was distributed by e-mail to a community of university students. It was hypothesized that the interface will make users more concerned about app security because it provides a clear feedback comparing the apps, instead of displaying a long list of permissions which the user may not be concerned with. Rather, it allows the user to select which permissions matter and consolidate the results based on that information.

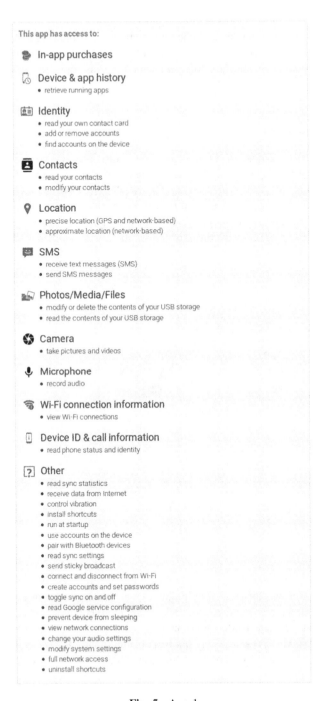

Fig. 5. App 1

5 Results

Responses to the survey (n = 58) were interesting. First, users were asked which app they preferred when given the following choice and were only shown the permissions manifest from the Google Play store.

- *App 1* used the manifest from WhatsApp, a well-known messaging app, and was meant to resemble a typical app that requires many permissions (Fig. 5).
- *App 2* used the manifest from Xabber, a less-known messaging app, and was meant to resemble a typical app that does not require many permissions (Fig. 6).

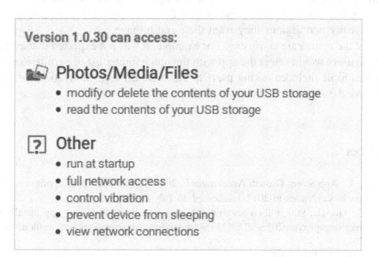

Fig. 6. App 2

The majority of participants (64 %) preferred App 2 when presented with the permissions interface. A significant portion of users (22 %) said they preferred App 1. This was not expected given the contents of the permissions list, considering that the permissions for App 1 are much broader than the permissions given to App 2. This may be a topic for future research.

Half of the participants felt less comfortable after seeing the new interface. 36 % of participants had no change of opinion. This indicates that the developed interface was effective at influencing user opinion of the apps.

There were only very weak linear correlations between the answers given. The questions for awareness and concern had a positive correlation of 0.219. It makes sense that those people who are more concerned with app security will also be more aware.

More significantly, the linear correlation coefficient of the question for concern and reaction to the permissions settings had a positive correlation of 0.293. It also makes sense to suppose that respondents who were more concerned about privacy would be more taken aback by App 1's permissions screen.

Therefore, while nothing conclusive can be said about the correlations observed, there is some evidence that users who are concerned about mobile app security do make choices based on the broadness of permissions.

6 Conclusion

In conclusion, this research indicates that users are concerned about their privacy, and, as a result of their concern, will make decisions based on the broadness of permissions when given a side-by-side offering. In addition, when information about permissions is presented in a simple way, users may form new opinions about the app. By refining the algorithm in this interface, users can search for new apps using specific guidelines about how many permissions they want their app to have.

Some of the results are confusing. For example, it was not expected that as many as 22 % of the users would select the app with the much longer list of permissions. Future work on this topic includes asking users to elaborate on their motivation for selecting one app over the other.

References

1. Michaeli, A.: App Stores Growth Accelerates in 2014 (2015). http://blog.appfigures.com/app-stores-growth-accelerates-in-2014/. Accessed 28 July 2015
2. Welch, C.: Google: 900 million android activations to date, 48 billion app installs (2013). http://www.theverge.com/2013/5/15/4333584/total-android-activations-900-million. Accessed 30 July 2015
3. Android App Ranking (2015). http://www.androidrank.org/. Accessed 30 July 2015
4. Turland, J., Coventry, L., Jeske, D., Briggs, P., van Moorsel, A.: Nudging towards security: developing an application for wireless network selection for android phones. In: Proceedings of the 2015 British HCI Conference (British HCI 2015), pp. 193–201 (2015)
5. Lin, J., Amini, S., Hong, J.I., Sadeh, N., Lindqvist, J., Zhang, J.: Expectation and purpose: understanding users' mental models of mobile app privacy through crowdsourcing. In: Proceedings of the 2012 ACM Conference on Ubiquitous Computing (UbiComp 2012), pp. 501–510 (2012)
6. Almuhimedi, H., Schaub, F., Sadeh, N., Adjerid, I., Acquisti, A., Gluck, J., Cranor, L., Agarwa, Y.: Your location has been shared 5,398 times! A field study on mobile app privacy nudging. In: Proceedings of the 33rd Annual ACM Conference on Human Factors in Computing Systems (CHI 2015), pp. 787–796 (2015)
7. Jain, S., Lindqvist, J.: Should i protect you? Understanding developers' behavior to privacy-preserving APIs. In: Workshop on Usable Security (USEC 2014) (2014)

Touch Zone Sizing for Mobile Devices in Military Applications

Jerry Ray[(⊠)], Stuart Michelson, Chandler Price, and Cara Fausset

Georgia Tech Research Institute, Atlanta, GA, USA
{jerry.ray,stuart.michelson,chandler.price,
cara.fausset}@gtri.gatech.edu

Abstract. Of late, the desire to adopt devices such as Apple iPads for use in military cockpits (for example, as "electronic flight bags" to replace paper-based reference materials) has increased. Two sources for touch screen design guidance for military applications are MIL-STD-1472 and manufacturer (e.g., Apple) interface style guides. However, minimum touch zone size and separation recommendations vary considerably between these sources. This study assessed the impact of manipulating touch zone size and separation in ungloved and gloved conditions. Despite a small sample size (n = 6), significant main effects of gloves and sizing guidelines were found. Unsurprisingly, participants were less accurate hitting targets on the first try when wearing gloves. Participants made no errors (i.e., activating a button other than the target) in the MIL-STD-1472 sizing condition irrespective of gloves. These results indicate that following MIL-STD-1472 guidelines reduces the likelihood of activation errors at the cost of decreased information density.

Keywords: Touch screen · Mobile · UI design · Design guidelines · Aviation · Gloved operation · Electronic flight bags

1 Introduction

1.1 Background

Mobile computing devices have become ubiquitous in everyday life. The average American spends nearly three hours per day on smartphones and tablets for business, entertainment, and other activities [1], interacting with touch screen interfaces while on foot, in cars, on airplanes, and in any other circumstance imaginable. These devices provide access to a wealth of information in a compact, portable format. Unsurprisingly, there is an increasing desire to adopt tablets (such as Apple iPads, Android tablets, or Microsoft Surface tablets) for use in aviation [2]. Tablets are becoming prevalent in military cockpits as "electronic flight bags" that replace paper-based reference materials and support flight management tasks such as fuel calculations.

Designers of mobile apps intended for use in military cockpits must design user interfaces that are compatible with this unique environment. Conditions in the cockpit that can interfere with touch screen operation include motion, vibration, and unexpected acceleration (due to turbulence); flight gloves commonly worn by aviators;

© Springer International Publishing Switzerland 2016
A. Marcus (Ed.): DUXU 2016, Part III, LNCS 9748, pp. 65–76, 2016.
DOI: 10.1007/978-3-319-40406-6_7

placement of devices in locations (such as on the aviator's thigh) that are awkward for interaction; and divided attention due to multitasking. However, designers are faced with conflicting guidance regarding such fundamental design features as the size of touch screen active areas.

1.2   Touch Zone Size and Separation Guidelines

For user interfaces designed for military use, MIL-STD-1472 is the prevailing source of human engineering requirements, including detailed guidelines for the size and separation of touch screen active areas [3]. The MIL-STD-1472 touch screen guidelines originally evolved from recommended dimensions for physical buttons and were first published in their current form in 1999, well before the advent of modern touch devices. MIL-STD-1472 specifies a minimum touch zone size of 15 mm (0.6 in) square, with 3 mm (0.12 in) separation between zones for ungloved operation. The minimum touch zone size increases to 20 mm (0.8 in) square for gloved operation (as is common in military cockpits).

Tablet manufacturers also provide guidelines for designing user interfaces for their devices (for example, the iOS Human Interface Guidelines published by Apple). These "style guides" include guidance on touch zone size and separation. The manufacturer recommendations for size and separation tend to be significantly smaller than those in MIL-STD-1472. Apple's iOS guidelines specify a touch zone sizing of 44 × 44 points (a device-independent size measurement to account for varying pixel densities across iOS devices), which translates to a physical size of 8.5 mm (0.3 in) square [4]. The Apple guidelines do not specify a minimum separation between adjacent touch zones.

Increased touch zone size and separation can reduce selection errors, and may be warranted in cockpit environments due to such factors as motion, vibration, and unfavorable viewing and reach angles that can induce errors [5–7]. However, meeting the MIL-STD-1472 guidelines while also achieving desirable information density on a tablet screen can be challenging. Figure 1 shows the difference in vertical sizing between a standard Apple-developed iPad screen and a simple table of contents for an electronic flight bag app developed in accordance with MIL-STD-1472 touch zone sizing guidelines.

The disparity between the manufacturer style guides and the military standard raises several questions. Are the smaller touch zone sizes and separations specified in the manufacturer style guides suitable for applications for use in military cockpit environments (particularly for gloved operation), or are the larger MIL-STD-1472 guidelines still necessary for modern tablets? What effect does touch zone sizing and separation have on touch screen error rates in a moving vehicle? Could smaller touch zone sizing and separation be used to achieve higher information density on modern touch devices without an undesirably large increase in error rate? This technical examination presents the results of a study of human performance under various touch zone sizing and operation (ungloved versus gloved) conditions.

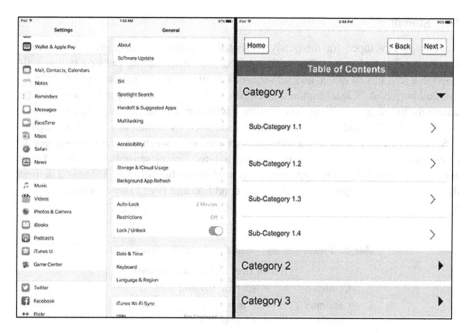

Fig. 1. G. Vertical sizing and separation for iPad screen (left) versus MIL-STD-1472-compliant screen (right).

2 Method

2.1 Design

Touch zone size and separation guidelines (Apple, MIL-STD-1472) and operation condition (ungloved, gloved) were manipulated within participants in a 2 × 2 repeated measures design. Each participant completed four experimental conditions, each consisting of fifty trials in which a specified target button was activated by the participant. To account for practice effects, the order of the conditions was randomized for each participant. The conditions are defined in Table 1.

Table 1. Guideline source and operation condition for each study condition

	Guideline source	Operation condition
Condition 1	Apple	Ungloved
Condition 2	MIL-STD-1472 (Normal sizing)	Ungloved
Condition 3	Apple	Gloved
Condition 4	MIL-STD-1472 (Gloved sizing)	Gloved

2.2 Stimuli

A web app developed for this study presented participants with a grid of numbered buttons on the iPad screen. To facilitate researcher observations, the first button activated in a trial turned green, and subsequent activations turned buttons yellow, orange, red, and purple. A "Clear" button located below the grid of numbered buttons reset the screen for the next trial. Three sets of stimuli with varying button sizing and separation were used for the study; the same stimuli were used for conditions 1 and 3. Apple's iOS guidelines do not specify a minimum separation between touch zones. Inspection of common iOS interface screens revealed a 1 to 2 pixel separation between touch zones, so a 2 pixel (0.4 mm) separation was used in conditions 1 and 3. Table 2 defines the button size and separation used in each condition and Fig. 2 shows resulting button layouts.

Table 2. Button size and separation for each study condition

	Button size	Button separation
Condition 1	8.5 × 8.5 mm	0.4 mm
Condition 2	15 × 15 mm	3 mm
Condition 3	8.5 × 8.5 mm	0.4 mm
Condition 4	20 × 20 mm	3 mm

Each set of fifty trials was structured so that each button in the grid was used as the target at least once. The buttons were subdivided into three categories: corners, with adjacent buttons on two sides; edges, with adjacent buttons on three sides; and middles, with adjacent buttons on four sides. Placement distinction was made in order to assess possible screen position effects on accuracy, as described by Henze et al. [6]. Each set of trials included twelve corner targets, nineteen edge targets, and nineteen middle targets. To achieve these numbers, some edge and middle targets were randomly selected to serve as targets a second time, and all four corner buttons were targeted three times each. The target order was randomized within each condition but was held constant across all participants. Table 3 shows the composition of stimulus items by grid location for each condition.

Table 3. Composition of stimulus items by grid location

	Conditions 1–3			Condition 4		
	Unique	Repeat	Total	Unique	Repeat	Total
Corner	4	8	12	4	8	12
Edge	16	3	19	14	5	19
Middle	15	4	19	12	7	19

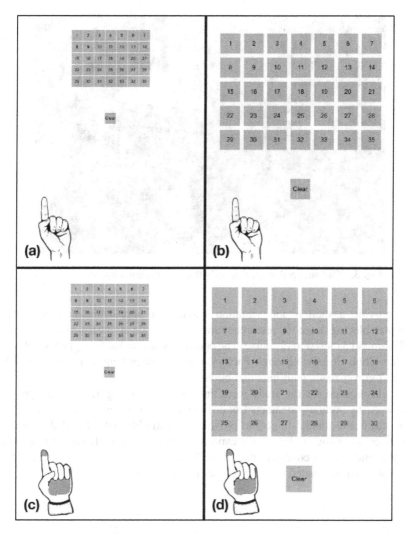

Fig. 2. Illustration of (a) condition 1, (b) condition 2, (c) condition 3, and (d) condition 4. Stimuli are presented to scale

2.3   Materials and Environment

Participants were seated in the back seat of an SUV for the duration of the study. A third-generation Apple iPad was strapped to the participant's thigh using a pilot's kneeboard mount as shown in Fig. 3. If the participant was right-handed, the iPad was mounted on the right leg and the participant was seated in the left seat; if the participant was left-handed, the iPad was mounted on the left leg and the participant was seated in the right seat. The researcher was seated beside the participant, on the same side as the iPad to facilitate observation of the participant's iPad interactions.

Fig. 3. iPad strapped to participant's thigh with pilot's kneeboard mount

To provide a motion and vibration component approximating conditions for in-cockpit tablet use, a second researcher drove the vehicle at low speed (approximately 5 MPH) around a closed road course. The course, located at the Georgia Tech Research Institute's Cobb County Research Facility, was 1.5 miles long and consisted of both paved and gravel roads with hills and curves.

The gloves used for the study were fire-resistant flying gloves of the type commonly worn by military aviators. Conductive fabric was sewn into the tips of the thumb, index, and middle fingers to provide compatibility with the iPad's capacitive touch screen. As shown in Fig. 4, the capacitive material primarily covered the pads of the fingers and did not cover the fingertips. Three sizes of gloves were available, and participants were instructed to select gloves that fit snugly.

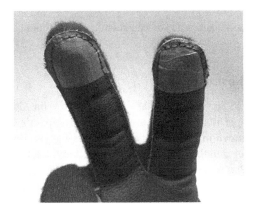

Fig. 4. Flying gloves used in the study, with conductive fabric on index and middle fingers

2.4   Task

To begin each trial, the researcher announced the target button number. The participant was instructed to press the target button as soon as he or she located it, without rushing – accuracy was emphasized over speed. Participants were also instructed to use the index finger on the dominant hand to activate buttons, and to avoid steadying the iPad with the non-dominant hand. The researcher observed participant actions and recorded hits, misses, and errors, asking the participant for verbal clarification if necessary. The researcher then said "OK," which signaled the participant to press the Clear button to reset the screen for next trial. The researcher recorded misses for the Clear button in a separate data category.

2.5   Dependent Variables

The dependent variables for the study are defined below:

- *Hit.* The participant accurately selected the target button on the first try.
- *Miss.* The participant touched the screen but did not activate a button (neither the target button nor any other button). Multiple misses could occur within a trial.
- *Error.* The participant activated a button other than the target button. Multiple errors could occur within a trial.
- *"Clear" Miss.* Misses that occurred when the participant attempted to press the "Clear" button at the end of the trial. A "Clear" miss did not count against target accuracy for the trial – the participant could score a hit and "Clear" miss in the same trial.

2.6   Procedure

Upon their arrival to the study site, participants were given an overview of the task and the structure of the study, and written consent was obtained. Participants were then seated in the left or right back seat of the vehicle, based on whether they were right- or left-handed, and fastened their seatbelt. The researcher occupied the opposite back seat in the vehicle. Basic demographic data (gender, age, dominant hand, touch screen experience) were collected, and participants selected the appropriately-sized glove for the dominant hand from the three sizes available. Participants then strapped the iPad to their leg and were given a moment to become familiar with the web app stimuli. After any participant questions were addressed, the driver began driving and the first condition began.

Each condition took approximately six to eight minutes to complete. At the end of each condition, the vehicle was stopped for two to three minutes to allow participants to rest and to reset for the next condition. The total session took approximately 45 min per participant. As the vehicle returned to the parking lot at the conclusion of the session, participants were given an opportunity to make any additional comments on the study and were then dismissed.

3 Results

Six participants took part in the study. Five participants were right-handed (two females, three males) and one male was left-handed. Participant ages ranged from 25 to 42 (M_{age} = 37.2; SD = 6.8). All six participants responded to the question, "How experienced are you with using touch screen devices (like tablets or smartphones)?" with a response of "5 – extremely experienced" on a five-point scale ranging from "1 – not experienced" to "5 – extremely experienced."

The study used a 2 × 2 within-subjects design with Latin square counterbalancing to control for order effects. The two independent variables were touch zone size and separation (Apple guidelines, MIL-STD-1472 guidelines), and operation condition (ungloved and gloved). The dependent variables were hits, misses, errors, and "Clear" misses, as defined above. Grand means and standard deviations for each experimental condition, reported as number of times in fifty trials that each dependent variable was observed, are shown in Table 4.

Table 4. Grand means and standard deviations for each experimental condition (n = 6)

Condition	Hits (SD)	Misses (SD)	Errors (SD)	"Clear" misses (SD)
1 Apple, no gloves	43.67 (4.97)	6.83 (6.31)	3.67 (3.14)	6.67 (5.05)
2 1472, no gloves	46.33 (2.25)	5.00 (3.69)	0.00 (0.00)	3.00 (3.58)
3 Apple, with gloves	37.33 (3.83)	12.00 (5.40)	6.33 (3.67)	12.67 (6.41)
4 1472, with gloves	42.00 (4.34)	13.33 (8.55)	0.00 (0.00)	11.17 (5.74)

A repeated measures analysis of variance was conducted. The results indicate a statistically significant main effect of gloves and sizing guidelines. No significant interaction of sizing guidelines by operation condition was revealed.

A main effect of operation condition on hits was identified, $F(1, 5) = 12.67$, $p = .016$. Participants' accuracy on touching the target on the first attempt decreased when they had to perform the task with gloves. A main effect of gloves on misses, $F(1, 5) = 9.37$, $p = .028$, and "Clear" misses, $F(1, 5) = 32.93$, $p = .002$, was also revealed. Participants missed the target without selecting anything on the screen and missed the "Clear" target significantly more when wearing gloves. There was no main effect of gloves on errors, $F(1, 5) = 6.40$, $p = .053$. Figure 5 shows the mean performance for each dependent variable in the ungloved and gloved operation conditions.

A main effect of sizing guidelines was revealed for errors, $F(1, 5) = 15.00$, $p = .012$. Participants made no errors in the MIL-STD-1472 conditions, whereas participants did make errors in the Apple conditions. No main effects of sizing guidelines were found for hits, misses, or "Clear" misses. Figure 6 shows the mean performance for each dependent variable in the Apple and MIL-STD-1472 sizing guideline conditions.

To understand the effect of target position on participant accuracy, a 2 (Sizing: Apple, MIL-STD-1472) × 2 (Gloves: no, yes) × 3 (Position: corner, edge, middle) repeated measures analysis of variance was conducted. Percent accuracy was used as the dependent measure because there were an unequal number of trials for each

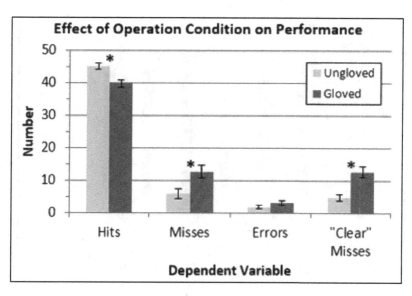

Fig. 5. Mean performance in the ungloved and gloved operation conditions. Bars represent standard error of the mean. * indicates statistically significant difference.

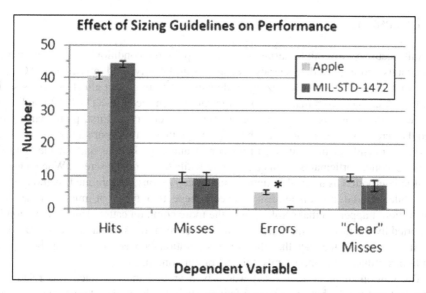

Fig. 6. Mean performance in the Apple and MIL-STD-1472 sizing guideline conditions. Bars represent standard error of the mean. * indicates statistically significant difference.

position: 12 corner, 19 edge, 19 middle. No significant main effects or interactions with target position were identified. Figure 7 shows the mean accuracy for each target position in the Apple and MIL-STD-1472 sizing guideline conditions and for ungloved and gloved operation.

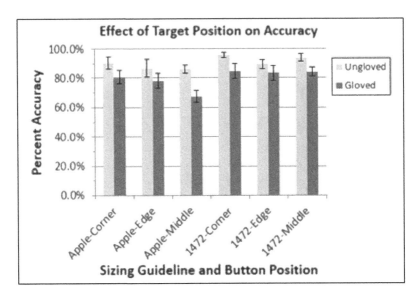

Fig. 7. Mean accuracy for each target position in the Apple and MIL-STD-1472 sizing conditions and for ungloved and gloved operation. Bars represent standard error of the mean.

4 Discussion

Overall accuracy was high during ungloved operation conditions. However, when participants wore gloved, accuracy declined significantly, and misses and "Clear" misses increased significantly. Sizing guidelines had a significant effect on errors such that there were no errors made for the larger buttons in the MIL-STD-1472 condition.

Two sources of misses and "Clear" misses were observed. First, participants touched the screen outside of the active button areas, either in the separation zone between buttons or outside of the button grid for corner and edge buttons and for the "Clear" button. Second, participants initiated scrolling while touching the screen. When a touch event is interpreted as a scroll initiation, button activations are inhibited. Although the data collected did not distinguish between these two types of misses, based on observation it appeared that scrolling was the more common cause. This observation is supported by the fact that miss rates are similar between the Apple and MIL-STD-1472 conditions, despite the fact that the small separation between buttons in the Apple conditions reduces the opportunity for separation zone misses.

The motion of the vehicle as it was driven around the test track was relatively consistent and gentle, but there were a few points in the loop (e.g., transitions between paved and unpaved segments) where the amount of motion made it difficult to accurately operate the touch screen. Vehicle motion contributed to misses and errors in two ways. First, gross movements of the vehicle occasionally disrupted accurate targeting by causing relative motion between the participant's hand and the iPad. Second, even minor vehicle movements at the moment the participant touched the screen caused hand movements that resulted in initiation of scrolling rather than activation of controls.

The effect of gloves on misses and errors can be attributed to two factors. First, the touch screen-compatible area of the gloves was on the pads of the fingers and did not cover the full tip of the finger. This required users to adopt a different method of activating targets when wearing gloves, using the pad of the finger, which had a larger contact area with the screen and also visually obscured more of the target compared with fingertip activation. A glove design that allows use of the fingertip for selection could reduce errors and misses. Second, the smallest gloves that were available were too large for two of the participants, so loose glove fabric sometimes made contact with the screen prematurely, throwing off targeting and occasionally inducing scrolling. The participants for whom the gloves were too large were observed manipulating the gloves frequently to keep the material as tight as possible around the fingertips. In a real-world situation, aviators would likely choose from a wider range of available glove sizes to obtain a better fit, potentially reducing scrolling-induced misses.

5 Conclusion

The results of this study indicate that following the larger MIL-STD-1472 sizing and separation guidelines reduces the likelihood of activation errors; however, this comes at the cost of decreased information density. As decreased information density can result in an increase in the number of control actions (e.g., scrolling to view additional content) and therefore in the number of error opportunities, additional research is needed to investigate the tradeoffs between touch zone sizing and information density.

Future research studies should increase the number of participants and the number of trials for additional statistical power. An effect of target location (corner, edge, middle) is expected such that more errors will occur for middle targets, which provide more opportunity for accidental activation of surrounding buttons. A wider range of glove sizes should be made available to eliminate problems with fit. Data collection should be expanded to distinguish targeting misses and scrolling-induced misses, and also to collect timing data to support consideration of Fitts' Law. Additional sizes of targets and separation distances should also be manipulated to identify optimal user performance with respect to the trade-offs between accuracy, misses, errors, response time, and information density. These data are necessary to understand for critical aviation situations in which time is short and accuracy is required.

References

1. Flurry Analytics. http://flurrymobile.tumblr.com/post/115194107130
2. Barstow, D.: The aviation iPad revolution. J. Air Traffic Control **54**(2), 4 (2012)
3. U.S. Department of Defense: MIL-STD-1472G: Department of Defense Design Criteria Standard – Human Engineering. U.S. Government Printing Office, Washington DC (2012)
4. Apple iOS Human Interface Guidelines. https://developer.apple.com/library/ios/documentation/UserExperience/Conceptual/MobileHIG

5. Azenkot, S., Zhai, S.: Touch behavior with different postures on soft smartphone keyboards. In: 14th International Conference on Human Computer Interaction with Mobile Devices and Services, pp. 251–260. ACM (2012)
6. Henze, N., Rukzio, E., Boll, S.: 100,000,000 taps: analysis and improvement of touch performance in the large. In: 13th International Conference on Human Computer Interaction with Mobile Devices and Services, pp. 133–142. ACM (2011)
7. Sears, A.: Improving touchscreen keyboards: design issues and a comparison with other devices. Interact. Comput. **3**(3), 253–269 (1991)

Applying Flow Theory to Predict
User-Perceived Performance of Tablets

James Scovell[✉] and Rina Doherty

Intel Corporation, Platform Evaluation and Competitive Assessment,
Hillsboro, OR, USA
{James.J.Scovell,Rina.A.Doherty}@intel.com

Abstract. A users' perception of interactive device performance is influenced by their feeling of being *in control* and that there is a sense of constant progress. A system will be able to keep users in the flow by meeting expectations and keeping up with their inputs and commands. The concept of flow has been discussed since the 1960's and has been used in the context of computing devices; however, the ability to operationally define and quantitatively measure this construct is limited. This paper describes a study that tested a new framework for measuring flow as it relates to User-Perceived Performance (UPP) of tablets.

Keywords: User-perceived performance · Severity-Duration · Mean Opinion Score (MOS) · User experience (UX) · Flow · Tablet · Computer performance

1 Introduction

Technological advances over the last several years have shifted the way in which humans interact with computing devices. One major shift has been in the use of touchscreens as a primary means of interaction. However, the software and hardware that enables this input modality has created complexities that challenge engineers to maintain the instant response a user has come accustom to like with a mouse and keyboard. New challenges like this have impacted the utility of computer performance measurement techniques and their relevance to user experience. Traditional performance metrics are primarily designated for compute intensive operations as opposed to the shorter, more interactive exchanges. As such, the aspects that largely shape how an end-user perceives the performance of a touchscreen device cannot be measured using these customary methods. Comprehending this distinction has taken time and being able to quantify and rate the perceived performance of a touch interactive device poses many exciting challenges. This paper discusses the use of a new user-centric approach to measuring computer performance developed from a distillation of user research studies, along with a review of published literature. A comparison of the average participant ratings from a tablet study is presented as they compare with predicted average ratings derived from this new approach.

© Springer International Publishing Switzerland 2016
A. Marcus (Ed.): DUXU 2016, Part III, LNCS 9748, pp. 77–87, 2016.
DOI: 10.1007/978-3-319-40406-6_8

2 Background

2.1 Flow

Keeping users in the flow is a key to end-user satisfaction with highly interactive devices like tablet computers. The theory of flow was first introduced in the 1960's and started to be discussed in the literature more in the 1980's when Csikszentmihalyi described the concept as the state of being fully absorbed and motivated toward an activity where a person's attention is so narrowly focused on an activity that time can seem to fade away [1]. Flow is sometimes interchanged with the notion of immersion or being *in the zone*. According to Csikszentmihalyi, flow has four preconditions; (1) goals, (2) clear rules to obtain those goals, (3) clear and immediate feedback to provide certainty, and (4) skill level must be appropriate to achieve a balance of control and challenge [1]. Amongst the different categories that flow has been examined, it has also been studied as it relates to computer performance and user satisfaction; specifi-cally, how poor computer performance impacts flow [2–4]. Especially in the case of highly interactive devices like tablets, poor responsiveness violates the last two pre-conditions of flow; it creates uncertainty and it diminishes a users' sense of control. Depending on the user request, dissatisfaction can be the result of sub-second latencies or much longer processing delays [4–8]. This unique dimension of time perception increases the challenge associated with determining how to measure user satisfaction. As such, research on how users perceive computer performance has a long history.

2.2 User-Perceived Performance (UPP)

Mangan has been credited with first describing the term, "perceived performance", in a white paper he published in 2003 [10]. He recommended that practitioners shift their focus away from only relying on traditional computational performance measurement and scoring practices to those aspects of system behavior that impact end-users more saliently. Prominent researchers such as Miller [11], Shneiderman [2], Card et al. [12], and Seow [4] have proposed taxonomies of system response requirements centered on memory, task type, user expectations, and task complexity. For a more in-depth understanding, these contributions are described in Anderson et al. [13], Doherty and Sorenson [9], and Dabrowski and Munson [3].

Largely influenced by Mangan and the other researchers noted above, Verheij published a white paper in 2011 describing an approach to quantifying and rating perceived performance of a virtual desktop system application [14]. The goal of his process was to give an indication of how an average user would rate responsiveness. It includes what he calls an ARI (Application Responsiveness Index) and a PPI (Per-ceived Performance Index). In this approach, the rating of response times is determined by the type of user action. User actions are categorized in three ways and each have a corresponding threshold of time as seen in Table 1. An Apdex [15] calculation is used to quantify the level of perceived performance and maps back to one of these five qualifiers: excellent, good, fair, poor, and unacceptable. The PPI adds an additional weighting function based on the variability of response times; the less variability the

Table 1. Ingmar's response time rating categories and time thresholds

Category name	Threshold
Acknowledgement of command	0.1 s
Simple task	1 s
Complex task	10 s

better the perceived performance rating. He believed this added a good indication of the perceived performance of an application over time.

There have also been other approaches presented in the literature to quantify perceived performance. For example, Tolia et al. [16] described a technique they used to quantify the impact of network latency on what they called "interactive experience" using thin clients (i.e., all application and operating system code is executed on a server). Thin client computing is particularly challenged with providing crisp responses to the basic (but common) interactions like menu navigation and mouse tracking. As such, their quantification and rating categories focused solely on these shorter interactions and system responses that require limited processing. The categories that they placed response times into can be seen in Table 2 below.

Table 2. Tolia et al.'s response time categories

Category name	Time
Crisp	<150 ms
Noticeable to annoying	150 ms to 1 s
Annoying	1 to 2 s
Unacceptable	2 to 5 s
Unusable	>5 s

In 2015, Doherty and Sorenson presented another categorization mapping system response time (SRT) to user satisfaction. Their categorization was an extension of Shneiderman and Seow's work that combined the influence of user expectations and complexity of tasks and added human perceptual limits as a third factor for determining appropriate categories. They also went beyond the attentive (10 s) time frame to include those more compute intensive operations that require SRTs beyond users' attention span to provide a more comprehensive set of SRT ranges to account for any user task flow (see Table 3).

In addition, they proposed that it is necessary to go beyond this simple mapping in order to quantify and rate users' perception of flow. A more comprehensive mapping includes predictive models that quantitatively define how user experience ratings change as a function of SRT changes so that instead of just being able to report if a SRT fell within a given range of user satisfaction, it is possible to calculate a quantifiable rating on a continuous scale. This can provide more robust data for practitioners to make informed decisions around design trade-offs, but also affords the ability to 'add

Table 3. Doherty and Sorenson's SRT framework with category names, time range, and descriptions.

Attention	Category name	SRT range	Category description
Attentive	Instantaneous	<300 ms	User feels like they are in a closed-loop system; as if they are in direct control
	Immediate	300 ms–1 s	Processes perceived by user as easy to perform
	Transient	1 s–5 s	Perceived by user as requiring some simple processing but user feels that they are making continuous progress (appropriate feedback required). It is unlikely a user would disengage from task flow
	Attention span	5 s–10 s	Perceived by users as requiring more processing/wait time but user needs useful and informative feedback to stay closely engaged.
Non-attentive	Non-attentive	10 s–5 min	Perceived by users as requiring more complex processing. Users would be likely to disengage and multi-task during this process. Feedback of progress is necessary
	Walk-away	>5 min	Perceived by users as requiring intensive processing. Users would not stay engaged with this task. Feedback of progress is necessary

up' or aggregate a sequence of interactions and calculate an overall responsiveness experience rating.

A similar example of this can be seen from a study conducted by Anderson et al. [13] where participants were asked to carry out several tasks and then rate the satisfaction of the response times on a five point scale. Participants repeated the tasks and ratings under varying levels of computer performance and as a result the researchers presented trend lines depicting the user ratings as a function of SRT (Fig. 1). These, in fact, represent the early stages of a collection of predictive models that can populate the Table 3 SRT framework.

In past research there has been a strong emphasis on total system response time from the start of a user input to the end (completion) of the system response. However, the type and stages of feedback given can impact a user's perception of being in control and the feeling that constant progress is being made. For example, recognition of a user input and progressive loading can reduce participant anxiety and set expectations as to how long the interaction will take to complete [17].

There are other factors that can degrade user-perceived performance (UPP) while using an interactive device, such as the interface and/or graphics quality, the smoothness of content, or the accuracy of responses to user inputs. Display smoothness and/or poor frame delivery can greatly impact a user's perception of performance, especially for high motion interactions such as gaming and watching videos. Similarly,

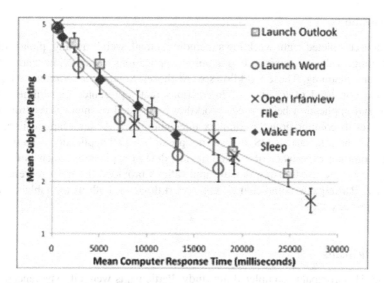

Fig. 1. Mean rating by duration for launching Outlook, Word, an IrfanView file, and wake from sleep. Reprinted from "Diminishing Returns? Revisiting Perception of Computing Performance" by G. Anderson, R. Doherty, E. Baugh, 2011, Proceedings of CHI, p. 2073.

inaccuracies related to touch interactions affect user's performance when she or he is forced to repeat a selection and/or correct an unintended input. Consideration of smoothness and accuracy variables is necessary to predict tablet UPP since they impact users' sense of certainty and control.

The study presented below was designed to collect participant ratings of tablet performance from realistic use cases and interactions. Measures of responsiveness, feedback, smoothness, and accuracy were used to predict overall UPP ratings for each workflow on each device tested. These overall predicted ratings were compared to the average participant ratings to determine if the predicted formula was a good approximation for UPP. By developing representative workflows and measuring multiple stages of feedback it was hypothesized that it would be possible to utilize predictive models to more holistically quantify UPP.

3 Research Methods

3.1 Devices

A total of six tablets of similar screen size were included in this study, two from each of the three common operating systems (iOS, Android, and Windows). Each pair of operation system (OS) devices included one high-end system and one system that had been on the market for two to three years. These devices were selected to understand participant expectations of best in class tablets and ensure there would be variation in the performance of the devices.

3.2   Workflows

Participants completed eight workflows including; email, web browsing, photo editing, video editing, video streaming, two gaming applications (Fruit Ninja and Jetpack Joyride), and mapping. These workflows were chosen to represent common usages of tablets and consisted of a series of interactions that represented capabilities of the software and application being used. Workflows consisted of interactions from basic system level to computationally complex interactions. While some applications, like games, were the same across OS this was not possible for all applications. To represent the most common experience of a given device, default applications such as for email and mapping were used. Using default applications provided the most representative experience. Participants completed all eight workflows on both of the tablets of their personal, primary OS.

3.3   Participants

A total of 51 participants completed the study. Participants were all experienced tablet users who used one or more tablets for more than five hours per week. Participants were screened in an attempt to get an equal number per OS (19 iOS, 16 Windows, 16 Android) and a good distribution across age, gender, and income. Test sessions lasted about one hour and participants were compensated accordingly.

3.4   Procedures

The experimental design and rating procedures followed the MOS (Mean Opinion Score) ITU standards for measurement of subjective assessment [18]. Participants received instructions on how to complete the eight workflows to ensure each participant completed the same interactions. While completing the workflows participants were asked to focus on the device performance and ignore extraneous variables such as comfort of the chair or room environment. A five point scale (5 = excellent, 4 = good, 3 = fair, 2 = poor, 1 = bad) was presented to participants to rate the performance of the device. Participants were asked to give a rating at the end of each workflow and provide an overall rating when they completed all eight workflows on a device. In addition, participants were asked to provide a rating any time they felt the system was not performing at a 5 (excellent). In order to gather more insights into what variables impacted UPP, participants were also asked to comment on what aspects impacted their ratings. These participant comments were transcribed for later analysis.

Participants were presented with one device of their personal, primary OS. Participants were then instructed to complete all eight workflows, one at a time. Upon completion of all eight workflows the participant was given a short break then completed all eight workflows on the other device of the same OS (in the same order as the first device). Participants only interacted with devices that had the OS they were most familiar with to reduce potential learning effect confounds. Device order was counterbalanced between participants to minimize order effects.

All participant sessions were recorded with the device display as the focal point of the camera. These recordings were used to capture the interactions with the device to observe any discrepancies/errors, to capture participant comments, and capture the device latency to participant inputs. The tablet devices were held in place at a 45 degree angle to the participant on a tablet stand. The participants did not hold or pick up the devices during the study.

3.5 Analysis

Quantifying Subjective Comments. SRT was captured during the study objectively using the video capture content. However, video/gaming smoothness and input accuracy issues were collected subjectively. In an effort to quantify these metrics, participant comments were documented and categorized to understand their contribution to negative UPP. Subjective comments were quantified by dividing the number of negative comments in a given category (i.e. input accuracy issues) by the number of participants who completed the given workflow on a given device. This calculation was completed for each device workflow combination so each workflow had a percentage associated with input accuracy and smoothness issues for each device. These percentages were then converted to a five point scale by correlating them with the average participant ratings. This provided an estimation in the absence of objectively measured feasibility at the time of this study.

System Response Time. The video recordings were analyzed to collect the latencies of each participant interaction. Multiple stages of loading were captured for each interaction to capture the aspect of feedback. There were two stages of loading that were measured, start of load (first indication to participant that the system is executing the intended interaction) and end of interaction (load is complete and ready for further input). Average system response times were taken across participants for each phase of load and of each interaction for all eight workflows per device. This provided the average response time for each interaction within each workflow on each device. Doherty and Sorenson's [9] framework was used to categorize each SRT measurement into a perceptual category. Proprietary mathematical models were assigned to each stage of load for each interaction according to human perceptual limits, perceived complexity, and user expectations. Calculating a range of response times across devices provided an indication of what users expect for each interaction. Using these models, a UPP was calculated for each interaction and stage of feedback.

The predicted UPP's were then aggregated according to a concept called Severity-Duration (Fig. 2). Severity-Duration penalizes for the severity of degradation when interactions do not meet user expectations. There is also a penalty for duration (or consecutiveness) of interactions that did not meet user expectations. An example of this can be seen in Table 4. This concept was implemented into the aggregation methodology since using a straight average was not believed to capture the impact of these negative contributors to UPP over the duration of a workflow. Evidence of this has been seen in the literature where negative experiences outweigh positive when reporting overall impressions [19–22].

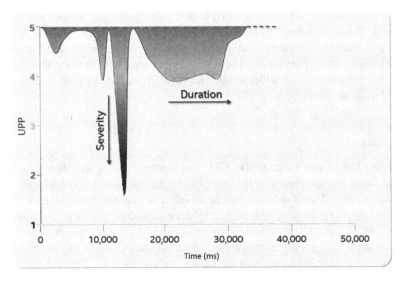

Fig. 2. Severity-Duration concept

Table 4. Severity-Duration example calculation

	SRT	SRT MOS	Severity-Duration MOS
	A	B	C
1	Time (ms)	y = m(A1) + B	=B1
2	Time (ms)	y = m(A2) + B	=(C1 + B2)/2
3	Time (ms)	y = m(A3) + B	=(C2 + B3)/2
4	Time (ms)	y = m(A4) + B	=(C3 + B4)/2
			Average

Metric Aggregation. The overall predicted UPP rating was calculated by averaging the SRT Severity-Duration MOS with relevant subjective variables, depending on the workflow. Gaming and video streaming workflows equally weighted the SRT Severity-Duration MOS, accuracy subjective rating, and smoothness rating. The other five workflows did not include significant video or animation so overall predicted ratings were simply an average of the SRT Severity-Duration MOS and accuracy subjective ratings.

4   Results

Results of a correlational analysis show the overall predicted UPP ratings were highly correlated with the average study participant ratings r(46) = .783, p < .001 with an average absolute delta of 0.14. Figure 3 shows the results of the regression analysis for each workflow on each device. Although there was an effort to include tablet devices

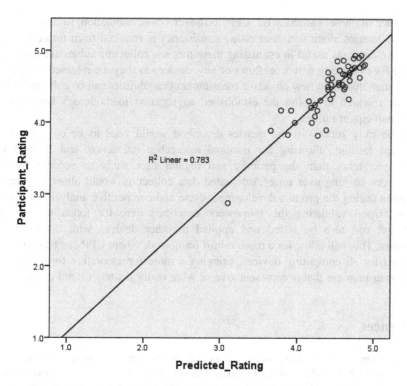

Fig. 3. Correlation of overall predicted ratings with average user ratings

with a range of perceived performance, the results show that the majority of average participant and predicted ratings fell above the 3.5 range.

5   Discussion

The study described in this paper adds to the evolution of flow theory as it relates to computer performance. It provides a new user-centric approach for calculating UPP of tablet devices. This new approach also expands upon traditional UPP metrics by incorporating touch accuracy and video/gaming smoothness metrics. A new aggregation concept was introduced, called Severity-Duration, to provide an alternative approach to simply *averaging* multiple interactions within a workflow to calculate an overall UPP. This methodology was able to accurately predict participant UPP ratings within 0.14, on average (range 0.0–0.47). It should be noted that while an effort was made to get a wide range of UPP tablets, ratings were almost entirely above 3.5. Future research is necessary to expand this range to ensure accuracy across the full ratings scale.

It is critical to develop methodologies that can collect objective metrics for both perceived touch accuracy issues and video/animation smoothness. The transformation of subjective comments to a percentage and then to a five point scale helped confirm the impact of these variables on UPP; however, more validation from objectively measured metrics along with user rating consistency is required from future research. Subjective data was useful in estimating these metrics, collecting subjective data is not scalable for evaluating new workflows or new devices as they are released. It will also be important that these new objective measurement capabilities can be collected during live user research to ensure the established aggregation methodology holds true to predict participant ratings.

To be truly successful the metrics described would need to be collected in an automated fashion, allowing for minimal researcher interaction and no end user involvement other than the periodic and regular user study to account for user expectations shifting over time. Automated data collection would allow for iterative evaluation during the product development cycle and competitive analysis on existing devices. Upon validating the framework described here for touch devices, this framework can also be tested and applied to other devices with different input modalities. This will allow for a more robust framework where UPP can be objectively measured for all computing devices, bringing a more representative form of performance measurement that is representative of what really matters to end-users.

References

1. Csikszentmihalyi, M.: The flow experience and its significance for human psychology. In: Csikszentmihalyi, M., Csikszentmihalyi, I.S. (eds.) Optimal Experience: Psychological Studies of Slow in Consciousness, pp. 15–35. Cambridge University Press, Cambridge (1988)
2. Shneiderman, B.: Designing the User Interface: Strategies for Effective Human-Computer Interaction, 1st edn. Addison-Wesley, Reading (1987)
3. Dabrowski, J., Munson, E.: 40 Years of searching for the best computer system response time. Interact. with Comput. **23**, 555–564 (2011). Elsevier B.V
4. Seow, S.C.: Designing and Engineering Time: The Psychology of Time Perception in Software. Addison-Wesley, Amsterdam (2008)
5. Zakay, D., Hornik, J.: How much time did you wait in line? A time perception perspective. In: Time and Consumer Behaviour (1991)
6. Angrilu, A., Cherubini, P., Pavase, A., Manfredini, S.: The influence of affective factors on time perception. Percept. Pyschophys. **59**, 972–982 (1997)
7. Goldstein, B.E.: Sensation and Perception, 5th edn. University of Pittsburg, Pittsburg (1999)
8. Jota, R., Ng, A., Dietz, P., Wigdor, D.: How fast is fast enough? A study of the effects of latency in direct touch pointing tasks. In: Proceedings of S1GCHI Conference on Human Factors in Computing Systems (CHI 2013), pp. 2291–2300. ACM, New York, NY, USA (2013)
9. Doherty, R., Sorenson, P.: Keeping users in the flow: mapping system responsiveness with user experience. Procedia Manuf. **3**, 4384–4391 (2015)
10. Mangan, T.: White paper perceived performance. Tuning a system for what really matters. TMurgent Technologies (2003). http://www.tmurgent.com/WhitePapers/Perceived Performance.pdf
11. Miller, R.B.: Response time in man-computer conversational transactions. In: International Business Machines (IBM) Corporation, Fall Joint Computer Conference, Poughkeepsie, New York (1968)

12. Card, S.K., Moran, T.P., Newell, A.: The Psychology of Human-Computer Interaction. Lawrence Erlbaum Associates, Hillsdale (1983)
13. Anderson, G., Doherty, R., Baugh, E.: Diminishing returns? Revisiting perception of computing performance. In: Proceedings of CHI, pp. 2703–2706 (2011)
14. Verheij, I.: White paper quantifying and rating perceived performance of a virtual desktop system application (2011). http://www.ingmarverheij.com/wp-content/uploads/downloads/2011/09/Whitepaper-Quantifying-Perceived-Performance-v1.0.pdf
15. Apdex (2007). http://apdex.org/overview.html
16. Tolia, N., Andersen, D.G., Satyanarayanan, M.: Quantifying interactive user experience on thin clients. In: Proceedings of the IEEE. Carnegie Mellon University (2006)
17. Norman, D.: The Design of Everyday Things. Basic Books, New York (2002). ISBN 978-0-465-06710-7
18. ITU-R.: Methodology for the subjective assessment of the quality of television pictures. Recommendation BT.500-13, Geneva (2012)
19. Mittal, V., Ross Jr, W.T., Baldasare, P.M.: The asymmetric impact of negative and positive attribute-level performance on overall satisfaction and repurchase intentions. J. Mark. **62**, 33–47 (1998)
20. Oliva, T.A., Oliver, R.L., Bearden, W.O.: The relationship among consumer satisfaction, involvement, and product performance. Behav. Sci. **40**(April), 104–132 (1995)
21. Oliver, R.L.: Cognitive, affective, and attribute bases of the satisfaction response. J. Consum. Res. **20**(December), 418–430 (1993)
22. Peeters, G., Czapinski, J.: Positive-negative asymmetry in evaluations: the distinction between affective and informational negativity effect. Eur. Rev. Soc. Psychol. **1**, 33–60 (1990)

"One Doesn't Fit All": A Comparative Study of Various Finger Gesture Interaction Methods

Tiffany Y. Tang[✉], Maldini Yifan He, and Vince Lineng Cao

Media Lab, Department of Computer Science,
Wenzhou Kean University, Wenzhou, China
{yatang,heyif,caolin}@kean.edu

Abstract. Thanks to the increasing popularity of mobile applications, finger gesture interactions are prevalent; evaluation studies of finger gesture interaction for these devices also gain attention recently. However, prior studies fail to examine users' interaction preferences and performance of three most popular mobile interaction patterns in mobile games (Tap, Swipe, and Tilt) and link their usage appropriateness with different operation settings (such as lying on the bed, running in a treadmill, etc.), which motivate our study here. In particular, in this paper we offer a comparative study of the three popular finger interaction types under different operation modes in terms of users' performance accuracy and experiences. Experiment results were mixed, which lead us to suggest that designers should consider users' most common operation mode before determining interaction styles. We are currently modifying the testing user interfaces and simplifying the testing tasks so as to investigate how children with autism tend to respond to these various interaction styles as we had observed that Chinese children with Autism Spectrum Disorder (ASD) are more inclined to interact with the touch-screen-enabled applications; and to the best of our knowledge, such research is under-explored and yet key to inform the development of appropriate interactions for these children.

Keywords: Mobile application · Swipe · Tap · Tilt · Finger gesture · Experiment · Autism

1 Introduction

Largely thanks to the introduction of iPhone in 2007, the landscape of HCI for mobile and ubiquitous computing has been shifted. Such finger gesture interactions as swiping, pinching, tapping have pushed away the traditional and dominant 'non-smart' phone inputs–pressing key on small keyboards), which in turn generate a lot of interests among the evaluation of such interactions (Browne and Anand 2011; Findlater et al. 2013; Fitton et al. 2013; MacKenzie et al. 2012; Negulescu et al. 2012; Stößel and Blessing 2010a, b; Teather and MacKenzie 2014; Tran et al. 2013; Trewin et al. 2013; Shi et al. 2008; Gilbertson et al. 2008). However, as much as the appealing features mobile phones can bring, they often pose considerable challenges for game developers, especially regarding user interface design and game control (Gilbertson et al. 2008; Fishkin et al. 2000). Among the many primitive and innovative interface mechanism,

© Springer International Publishing Switzerland 2016
A. Marcus (Ed.): DUXU 2016, Part III, LNCS 9748, pp. 88–97, 2016.
DOI: 10.1007/978-3-319-40406-6_9

tilt, in particular, has been dominantly adopted in mobile games, due to its minimal signal processing and light-weight external references. The interaction is made ascertain with the phone's built-in accelerometers so as to allow players to incline or tip the device so as to control the game (Lane et al. 2010). Other popular and affordable (in terms of the control's programmability) mobile game interactions include swipe and tap which have been extensively examined in applications other than mobile games (Fitton et al. 2013; Findlater et al. 2013; Browne and Anand 2011; MacKenzie and Teather 2012; Motti et al. 2014; Negulescu et al. 2012; Volker and Turner 2009; Stößel and Blessing 2010a, b; Teather and MacKenzie 2014).

When it comes to unite and examine users' interaction preferences and performance of these three most popular mobile interaction patterns in mobile games (Tap, Swipe, and Tilt), there are very few studies here, which motivate our study here. Our study is the first and only an initial comparative study of three popular finger interaction types in mobile games: Tap, Swipe and Tilt under different operation modes.

The rest of the paper is organized as below. Section 2 presents and discusses prior studies on evaluating the usability of swipe, tap and tilt interactions. Our study design will be presented in Sect. 3, followed by experiment results. We conclude this paper by pointing to the limitations of our study as well as show the interesting research paths we will follow.

2 Related Work

2.1 Finger Gesture Interactions

Due to an increasing popularity of mobile touchscreen devices, evaluation studies of finger gesture interaction for these devices also gain attention recently. Shi et al. (2008) designed a set of both single and double finger gesture interaction techniques for digital document sharing on large tabletop; although the result sheds light on the general learnability, usability and naturalness of these finger interaction types, it is not applicable in our study since we focus on exploring the comfort and naturalness of them in a mobile game. A couple of other similar studies on the usability of finger gesture interaction techniques focus on the comparative studies of psychomotor performance between older and younger users (Findlater et al. 2013). In summary, general findings in these studies are consistent in terms of the significant slower performance for older adults than younger ones (Stößel and Blessing 2010a, b; Findlater et al. 2013). Findlater et al. (2013) further reported that when compared with younger adults, older ones showed quicker movement in touchscreen devices. (Stößel and Blessing 2010a) offered gesture design recommendations based on their comparative studies. Results showed that there is a difference between younger and older users on the gesture type they chose. For younger group, 86 % participants chose direct manipulation gesture and only 14 % chose symbolic gesture. It revealed that the symbolic gesture is easier to memorize and therefore easier to be used for the old. When comparing between one-finger and multiple-finger interactions, both two age groups prefer the former over the latter. But older users are not less comfortable with two-finger action than their younger counterparts (Stößel and Blessing 2010a). Motti et al. (2014) focused on the accuracy of drag-and-drop interaction for older adults in tactile puzzle games on two different screen sizes, tablet and smartphones.

Other studies explored the various interactions in mobile devices in general. For instance, Tran et al. (2013) conducted an exploratory study of two prevent gestures (pinch and spread) with seated participants on a tablet and smartphone device; the results revealed that most of the pinch and spread tasks can be finished on an average of 0.9–1.2 s. The study fail to find any significant association between device orientation and gesture performance, One surprising finding did report a good fit to a simple Fitts's Law model as determined by varying target width and gesture size (Tran et al. 2013).

Although tilt interaction has predominantly been explored in game research, a couple of others have focused how it can help enhance human performance in general. (MacKenzie et al. 2012) employed a mixed methodology to explore the adoption of tilt interaction for mobile users: survey questions were used to obtain users' subjective evaluation over the usability of tilt; while quantitative methods are used to measure accuracy, maximum tilt, and moving time. (Trewin et al. 2013) compared swipe and tap inputs in the context of smartphone's physical assess to participants with dexterity impairment, and concluded that swipe input has a better flexibility than tap one due to the latter's requirement of find finger positioning, which in turn contributed to a higher accuracy rate than tap input. Other similar studies include Teather and MacKenzie (2014), Teather and MacKenzie (2014).

2.2 Swipe, Tap and Tilt in Mobile Games

Evaluating finger gesture interactions in game research is predominantly on tilt control, and the majority of them are qualitative in nature. For instance, mobile phone tilt and the traditional button input were evaluated in a driving game Gilbertson et al. (2008); user experiences such as fun were focused in the testing (informal). Valente et al. (2009) examined tilt interactions for a mobile accessible game for the visually impaired; qualitative measurement was employed via observations and interviews. Participants preferred tilt-based interactions since they are more natural. More recently, evaluation has been shifted to employ some quantitative methods as well. For example, Browne and Anand (2011) examined tilt, gesture and buttons in a shooting game, and reported a similar result as tilt interaction is preferred (Valente et al. 2009). In addition, the results revealed that participants who used tilt can play significantly longer than those who did not.

When it comes to unite and examine users' interaction preferences and performance of three most popular mobile interaction patterns in mobile games (Tap, Swipe, and Tilt) there are very few studies.

To the best of our knowledge, our study is the first and only an initial comparative study of three popular finger interaction types in mobile games: tap, swipe and tilt. Unique to smartphones and tablet devices is tilt interaction pattern which has primarily been deployed in games (Fitton et al. 2013), particularly, tilt operations can be mapped to specific game inputs and recently has been used in motion sensor-based devices such as Nintendo Wii and Sony PlayStation 3.

3   Our Experiment and Brief Analysis

3.1   Participants and Apparatus

17 participants aged between 18 and 20 are selected from Wenzhou Kean University where the three authors are. The experiment was performed using a Nokia Lumia 730 and a Nokia Lumia 530 running on Windows Phone 8.1.

3.2   Study Design and Testing Applications

We followed recommendations from (Stößel and Blessing 2010b) that the usability of the three types of interaction patterns can only measure realistically in real interactive scenarios. The interface design in this experiment followed two rules proposed in (Negulescu et al. 2012) which centers on the prevention of user distraction should be limited:

1. the need for visual attention during interaction should be limited;
2. the need for more streamlined commands for common tasks;

Following the two principles, we designed four types of interfaces — three as testing applications and one as a testing game.

The Tap Testing Application. In the Tap applications (known as **Tap I, II** and **III**), the interfaces are shown in Fig. 1a. The differences among the three testing interfaces are the size of the active areas (Tap I > II > III). Users can tap the button. Once the user taps on the button, it will be recorded in the upper number and if the user taps out of the button, it will be recorded in the other number.

The Swipe Testing Application. In the Swipe applications (known as **Swipe I, II** and **III**), the interfaces are shown in Fig. 1b, with the main difference on the size of the white rectangles (Swipe I > II > III). Users can swipe the rectangle to the right and it will come back to the initial position once the user's finger released from the screen. If the user swipes the rectangle, it will be recorded in the number on the right down corner.

The Tilt Testing Application. In the Tilt application (known as **Tilt I, II, III**), the interfaces are shown in Fig. 1c. User can use the tilt action to move the screen object to the left and right. Once the user tilts to the left or to the right, it will be recorded in the numbers on the left or the right side of the interface. The sensitive of the accelerometer in the three applications are different (known as Tilt I > II > III).

The Game Application. The last testing environment was implemented as a simple game (Fig. 1d). Users can choose different types of interaction techniques to play the game: — for tap, users can tap the button L, R, U and D; for swipe, users can swipe the rectangle in the middle; and for tilt, users can tilt the phone. The game will randomly make the upper (lower, left and right) half two of the four squares white and the other gray. Once the user provides a correct reaction, he or she can get one point. For example, swipe the rectangle to the right when the right two squares are white. Otherwise, the game will stop.

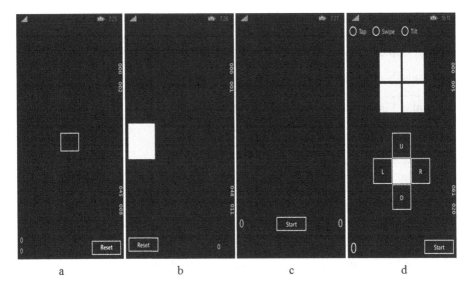

a   b   c   d

Fig. 1. The three testing environment with Tap (a), Swipe (b) and Tilt (c) interaction and a testing environment implemented as a game (d).

3.3 Experiment Procedure and Evaluation Protocol

We follow prior study of similar nature on the experiment procedure and evaluation protocol (Negulescu et al. 2012; Stößel and Blessing 2010a, b): both quantitative and qualitative data had been collected. The former includes task completion time, and performance quality; while the latter data examining player experiences and preferences regarding the three interaction techniques. We report the result of our quantitative analysis.

Before the testing, an experimenter provides detailed description on the experiment procedure. They were then asked to fill in a survey and then start the experiment. In the experiment, first, the participants perform the **Tap** tasks — tap on the button for ten times as fast as possible (in the order: Tap I, II, III). Second, participants will focus on the **Swipe** tasks — swipe the rectangle for ten times as fast as possible (in the order: Swipe I, II, III). Third, they were asked to manipulate using the **Tilt** interaction — tilt the phone to the left and back to the right for ten times (in the order Tilt I, II, III). Each task has to repeat for three times in the selected scenarios. At last, the participant plays the testing game. Use different input ways (in the order: Tap, Swipe, Tilt) to play the games three times (30 s per play) in the selected scenarios and playing scores are recorded accordingly. At the end of each task, each participant rates his/her user experiences on the interaction on a 5-point Likert scale where "1" indicates the worst user experience and "5" indicates the best user experience. Figure 2 shows the testing moment when the participant was running on a treadmill.

Fig. 2. The participant is testing the application while running in a treadmill

3.4 Experiment Mode

We posit that when users may prefer one interaction over another when in different operation mode, therefore, we invite participants to perform the tasks in the following four modes in our lab and the gym:

- Standing — interacting while standing
- Sitting — interacting while sitting on the chair
- Walking — interaction while walking on the running machine with a comfortable but constant speed in the gym
- Running — interacting while running on the running machine in the gym
- Lying — interacting while lying on the sofa

In all scenarios, the participants can choose to finish the task with either one hand or both. The experiment was conducted in the same room or gym (see Fig. 2).

3.5 Experiment Result and Discussions

In this section, we discussed the results of the experiment both the testing environment and the testing game. In each part, we discussed the results in five different scenarios and compared them with each other.

The Testing Environment. The result of the experiment has been shown in Fig. 3a, b, c respectively. We found no significant difference for tap and swipe operations with a 'big' object. In the Sitting mode, the average performance is 10.07 ($SD = 1.29$) for Tap and 9.80 ($SD = 0.48$) with Swipe. In the Standing scenario, participants averaged 10.00 ($SD = 0.33$) using tap and averaged 9.56 ($SD = 0.61$) with Swipe. In Walking scenario, participants averaged 10.03 ($SD = 0.18$) using Tap and averaged 9.73 ($SD = 0.81$)

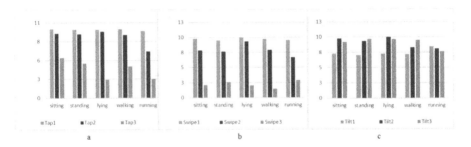

Fig. 3. Experiment results in three testing mode with Tap, Swipe and Tilt operations respectively. (Color figure online)

using Swipe. In Lying mode, participants averaged 10.00 (SD = 0.00) with Tap and Swipe. In Running MODE, participants averaged 9.78 (SD = 0.42) with Tap and 9.56 (SD = 0.68) with Swipe. Interestingly, the difference between the results in Running mode when using Tilt is significant. Though the program had the largest fault-tolerance rate, participants only averaged 7.67 (SD = 3.53).

However, when the object or the fault-tolerance gets smaller, we obtained more significant differences across these modes with different manipulation types. In Sitting scenario, participants scored an average of 5.90 (SD = 2.53) using Tap and 7.83 (SD = 1.61) when Swiping. In Standing scenario, participants obtained an average score of 5.10 (SD = 3.70) with Tap and 2.56 (SD = 2.70) with Swipe. In Walking scenario, participants averaged 4.60 (SD = 2.72) in Tap operations and 1.47 (SD = 1.48) in Swipe. But the difference is not significant in both Lying and Running modes despite that the object is small. Particularly, in Lying mode, participants averaged 2.70 (SD = 1.25) using Tap and averaged 2.00 (SD = 0.00) with Swipe. In Running scenario, participants averaged 2.78 (SD = 2.20) using tap and 2.89 (SD = 2.02). When in the Running mode, using Tilt manipulating a small object also lead to a large performance difference between Tap and Swipe operations.

The Testing Game. In the experiment, participant played a game using three input techniques: Tap, Swipe and Tilt in all modes. In Sitting scenario, participants scored the lowest in Tilt operations (M = 21.74, SD = 13.60), and the highest in Swipe (M = 40.00, SD = 9.00). In Standing mode, participants averaged 40.28 (SD = 9.67) with Swipe mode as the highest score and 9.00 (SD = 9.57) with Tilt mode as the lowest score. In Lying mode, participants scored the highest in Tilt (M = 20.33, SD = 17.52), and the lowest in Tap (M = 16.00, SD = 20.12). In Walking mode, participants averaged 38.63 (SD = 13.00) with Tap mode as the highest score and 19.30 (SD = 13.90) with Tilt mode as the lowest score. In Running mode, the highest performance was received in the Tap manipulations (M = 42.56, SD = 14.46), and the lowest in Tilt operations (M = 4.83, SD = 3.81).

Discussion. On one hand, if operating in the same mode and with only one input style, especially with Tap or Swipe, the bigger size of a bottom or a control interface can offer a friendlier input experience for the participants. On the other hand, for different input operations' quality in each mode, using Tap, Swipe and Tilt operations lead to similar performance. For example, in the testing application on relatively stable mode including Sitting, Standing and Lying, operations with Tap and Swipe can help the player obtain a steady improving score. However, in the Walking and Running mode, it is Tilt and Swipe that can achieve most users' input requirement. For Tap, Swipe and Tilt input styles, we can divide them into three different levels: Level I is entirely static and motionless when the user need to input something, such as in Tap; Level II is a combination of motion and movement, such as in Swipe; as in Level 3, it require a large amount of amplifying motion, like Tilt. It is obvious that in Level I and Level II, Tap and Swipe operations can fulfill most of the basic input requirements in the simple testing environment. However, in the context of the game, interestingly, we obtained some opposite results. We believe that the complexity of the game itself and participants' limited familiarity contributed to lower and unstable performances. In fact, the game itself poses an intrinsic requirements when compared with the elementary instructions in the simple testing environments. Therefore, we suggest that designers should consider users' most common operation mode before determining interaction styles.

4 Future Study: Touch-Screen Interaction Styles for Children with ASD

We had observed that Chinese children with ASD are more inclined to interact with the touch-screen-enabled applications during the testing of other applications in a large children's autism educational development; that is, when given the computer-based application, the majority of children's first attempt is to touch and tap the screen-objects. This important observation leads us to ponder how our current research can be extended to investigate the interaction styles preferred by these children. To the best of our knowledge, such research is under-explored and yet key to inform the development of appropriate interactions for these children.

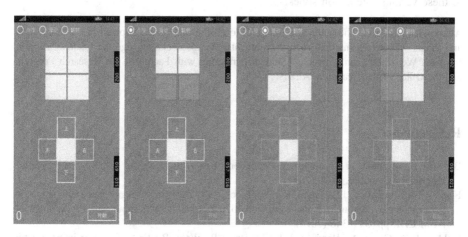

Fig. 4. New Testing Environment to be tested with Children with ASD: from left to right, the initial environment and the Tap, Swipe and Tilt mode respectively.

We are currently modifying the testing user interfaces and simplifying the testing tasks in order to investigate how children with autism tend to respond to these various interaction styles. Figure 4 below shows the simplified and enhanced testing screens after various interaction styles. Note that we will simplify the testing tasks by only requiring the children to tap, swipe or tilt the screen blocks in order to preclude the learning component of the task.

5   Concluding Remarks

Thanks to the increasing popularity of mobile applications, finger gesture interactions are prevalent; evaluation studies of finger gesture interaction for these devices also gain attention recently. However, prior studies fail to examine users' interaction preferences and performance of three most popular mobile interaction patterns in mobile games (Tap, Swipe, and Tilt) and link their usage appropriateness with different operation settings (such as lying on the bed, running in a treadmill, etc.), which motivate our study here. In particular, in this paper we offer a comparative study of the three popular finger interaction types in mobile games under different operation modes in terms of users' performance accuracy and experiences.

Our experiments revealed that in relatively stable operating environment such as Walking, Lying and Sitting, Type and Swipe input styles are preferred over Tilt; however, in such operating modes as Walking and Running, Tilt is preferred. However, when testing these input styles in a game, due to the complexity of the game itself and participants' limited familiarity, lower performance has been observed. It leads us to believe that the game itself poses intrinsic requirements when compared with the elementary instructions in the simple testing environments. Therefore, we suggest that designers should consider users' most common operation mode before determining interaction styles. We are currently modifying the testing user interfaces and simplifying the testing tasks in order to investigate how children with autism tend to respond to these various interaction styles.

Acknowledgements. The authors are grateful to all the players participated in our user study and Pinata Winoto for his constructive comments. We also acknowledge the financial support from the Wenzhou Kean University Student Partnering with Faculty (SpF) Research Program and the Office of the Academic Affairs.

References

Browne, K., Anand, C.: An empirical evaluation of user interfaces for a mobile video game. Entertain. Comput. **3**, 1–10 (2011)

Findlater, L., Froehlich, J.E., Fattal, K., Wobbrock, J.O., Dastyar, T.: Age-related differences in performance with touchscreens compared to traditional mouse input. In: Proceedings of ACM CHI, pp. 343–346 (2013)

Fishkin, K.P., Gujar, A., Harrison, B.L., Moran, T.P., Want, R.: Embodied user interfaces for really direct manipulation. CACM **43**(9), 74–80 (2000)

Fitton, D., MacKenzie, I.S., Read, J.C., Horton, M.: Exploring tilt-based text input for mobile devices with teenagers. In: Proceedings of BCS-HCI 2013, p. 25 (2013)

Gilbertson, P., Coulton, P., Chehimi, F., Vajk, T.: Using "tilt" as an interface to control "no-button" 3-D mobile games. Comput. Entertain. (CIE) 6(3), 38 (2008)

Lane, N.D., Miluzzo, E., Lu, H., Peebles, D., Choudhury, T., Campbell, A.T.: A survey of mobile phone sensing. IEEE Commun. Mag. 48(9), 140–150 (2010)

MacKenzie, I.S., Teather, R.J.: FittsTilt: the application of Fitts' law to tilt-based interaction. In: Proceeindgs of NordiCHI 2012, pp. 568–577 (2012)

Motti, L.G., Vigouroux, N., Gorce, P.: Drag-and-drop for older adults using touchscreen devices: effects of screen sizes and interaction techniques on accuracy. In: Proceedings of IHM 2014, pp. 139–146 (2014)

Negulescu, M., Ruiz, J., Li, Y., Lank, E.: Tap, swipe, or move: attentional demands for distracted smartphone input. In: Proceedings of AVI 2012 (2012)

Volker, R., Turner, T.A.: Bezel swipe: conflict-free scrolling and multiple selections on mobile touch screen devices. In: Proceedings of ACM CHI 2009 (2009)

Stößel, C., Blessing, L.: Tap, swipe and pinch: designing suitable multi-touch gestures for older users. In: Proceedings of DESIGN 2010, pp. 463–472. Design Society (2010a)

Stößel, C., Blessing, L.: Mobile device interaction gestures for older users. In: Proceedings of NordiCHI 2010, pp. 793–796 (2010b)

Teather, R.J., MacKenzie, I.S.: Position vs. velocity control for tilt-based interaction. In: Proceedings of GI 2014, pp. 51–58 (2014)

Tran, J.J., Trewin, S., Swart, C., John, B.E., Thomas, J.C.: Exploring pinch and spread gestures on mobile devices. In: Proceedings of MobileHCI 2013, pp. 151–160 (2013)

Trewin, S., Swart, C., Pettick, D.: Physical accessibility of touchscreen smartphones. In: Proceedings of ASSETS 2013, Article 19, 8 pages (2013)

Shi, Y., Yu, C., Shi, Y.: Finger gesture interaction on large tabletop for sharing digital documents among multiple users. In: Proceedings of 2008 1st IEEE International Conference on Ubi-Media Computing, pp. 8–13 (2008)

Valente, L., de Souza, C.S., Feijo, B.: Turn off the graphics: designing non-visual interfaces for mobile phone games. J. Braz. Comput. Soc. 15, 45–58 (2009)

Study of Smart Watch Interface Usability Evaluation Based on Eye-Tracking

Yixiang Wu$^{(\boxtimes)}$, Jianxin Cheng, and Xinhui Kang

School of Art, Design and Media, East China University of Science
and Technology, No. 130, Meilong Road, Xuhui District,
Shanghai 200237, China
{wuyixiang_15,nbukxh}@163.com, cjx.master@gmail.com

Abstract. Nowadays the intelligence of watches brings users brand new experience, and at the same time it makes human-watch interaction relationship becomes more and more complicated, therefore the design of smart watch interface faces greater challenge. As the interface of smart watches delivers more and more information, how to guarantee favorable usability of smart watch interface becomes the focus of designers. Designers need more objectively evaluate the reasonableness of smart watch interface layout and the visibility of interface elements. But traditional evaluation indexes can't intuitively reflect whether the system structure conforms to the thinking mode of users; and traditional evaluation indexes can't reveal the strategies employed on interface by users.

In this study smart watch interface user performance test is carried out and eye movement tracking technology is introduced into usability evaluation of smart watch interface to measure the usability level of smart watch interface and quantity analysis on internal differences among smart watch interfaces is conducted. It is founded from task test result that eye movement data can well compare internal differences among watch interfaces and reveal how users search their target options and information on smart watch interface. Compared with the previous studies, in this study the author proposes smart watch usability evaluation method based on eye movement, applies eye movement data in usability evaluation index system to reveal users' thinking for the designer and provide the clue of solving usability problems. These results have great significance in guiding the practice of smart watch usability evaluation and further perfecting usability evaluation index system.

Eye movement tracking technology is used in this study so that it can comprehensively and objectively evaluate usability level of smart watch interface and provide objective evidence for designer to improve the interface of smart watch and improve the usability level. The following results are obtained from the study: 1 Eye movement data such as fixation time and fixation point number are used as quantified indexes to evaluate interface information structure and interface element representation˙meaning. And the eye movement data can effectively evaluate the internal differences of watch interfaces and measure usability level of watch interfaces. 2 Fixation time hot spot diagram obtained from graphic eye movement data can intuitively reflect the attention layout of tested users on interface and provide objective evidences for experimenter to analyze interface problems. 3 Eye movement video can reappear the activity of sight line when tested users use the smart watch interface. Many interface

© Springer International Publishing Switzerland 2016
A. Marcus (Ed.): DUXU 2016, Part III, LNCS 9748, pp. 98–109, 2016.
DOI: 10.1007/978-3-319-40406-6_10

problems at deep levels can be found using the analysis method of combining eye movement video and graphic eye movement data. 4 Interface usability evaluation method based on eye movement tracking applies in early and middle stage of smart watch design and provide objective evidences for designers to understand users' thinking and improve interface design.

Keywords: Usability evaluation · Eye movement tracking · Smart watch · Interface design

1 Introduction

For a smart watch, a smart system installed in a watch can piggyback on a smart mobile phone system and connect to internet to realize multi-functions. It can synchronize calls, messages, e-mails, photos and music etc. in a mobile phone. And data shows that the year of 2013 is a smart watch year, because technology giants such as Apple, Samsung and Google etc. all released smart watches in 2013. These two years the relation between smart watches and users are closer and closer so that users can enjoy the convenience of intelligent era more.

The screen of a smart watch is limited by size. Therefore the interface must be displayed directly and effectively. Information should be arrayed effectively. And interface should display contents to users by reasonable interface layout. Favorable interface layout can lead the visual behavior of users therefore it is important to improve the interface of a smart watch. Apple Company overcomes the limit that screen of a smart watch is too small and sets a digital wheel. Pictures are zoomed or moved by rotating the digital wheel. Apple Company also designed the interface newly. Users can see APP list on a dial plate, which makes users have a whole new experience. Good user experience embodies in good man-machine interaction, and most information of human is obtained from their own eyes, thus studying on the performance of visual search for information can make interface interaction more fast and convenient.

An eye tracker is a high technology instrument which records the eye movement track characteristics when a man is managing visual information. Eye trackers are widely used in the study of visual perception, reading and etc. When people are attracted by stimulation objects or search a target object, people's eyes will stare at received information a little while, and people will make response, make decision and deal with it. When sight line stays at a fixed point temporarily, it is called visual focus or fixation point. The period during gazing is called fixation time. The image is formed at the center of retina when gazing.

When eyes stare or run down at something, it is a particularly important part for visual attention. Fixation time, fixation location, eye track and other eye movement process can be used as evidence basis to judge if a product is noticed. An eye tracker is used as an auxiliary mean of interface design, committing to making users feel more smooth and comfortable and producing largest vision and psychological effects on users.

2 Evaluation Method

Interface design is an important key point to decide whether users will be successful in operation and study. If the design is not appropriate, it will result in a series of problems such as users' slow operation and learning frustration and so the use willing of users will be reduced. Eye movement track technology uses eye movement of users as standard and it can improve the operation mode of interface and enhance the use willing of users.

During usability evaluation test for interface of a smart watch, eye movement of testers are recorded by the eye tracker, the eye movement data is introduced into usability evaluation index system, intuitive and graphic eye movement data and eye movement video are evidences for analyzing interface of the smart watch and user strategies. This evaluation method is called usability evaluation method of a smart watch based on eye movement track. Simply, this study defines representation meaning of interface element and search index of interface as fixation time and fixation point, and analysis evidence is defined as fixation time hot spot diagram and eye movement video.

2.1 Fixation Time

Fixation is a relative static state of eyes. Long time fixing represents interest or confusion. Fixation time means the duration time of observing visual stimulation objects and keeping visual focus.

In this study fixation time is used to test users spend how much fixation time during the process from the operation beginning to typical task completion. Longer fixation time means that the representation meaning is worse. After experimentation, questionnaire survey is conducted to determine the implication of users' fixation.

2.2 Fixation Point Number

Each staring means a fixation point. In this study fixation point number means total number of fixation points when users view interfaces during tasks. The number of fixation points represents cognitive process number of human for graphic interface. If the data number is big, it means testers' absolute attention for this region or misunderstanding at a certain degree. Larger number of fixation points represents a low performance of search; and it shows that perhaps there is some problem existing in the smart watch interface.

2.3 Fixation Time Hot Spot Distribution Diagram

The hot spot diagram shows which region spends more time of the testers. In the fixation time hot spot distribution diagram more bright color represents more fixation time. It is drawn by counting sight line movement data of many testers.

2.4   Scanned Path Diagram

Space distribution of a series of fixation points and twitching of the eyelid is called scanned path diagram. Scanned path diagram provides a snapshot of tested users' attention. But if in the test scan path is recorded long time, image will turn to be in disorder. If it is needed to record sight line movement long time, adopting hot spot diagram is appropriate.

2.5   Movement Video

Movement video can reappear sight line movement process and operation path of users during using process of smart watch. An experimenter can use eye movement data to analyze thinking process and operation behavior of users.

3   Experimental Method

3.1   Testing Users and Testing Products

There are totally 10 tested users in this experiment. They are undergraduate and graduate student from Shanghai universities. Among them 10 students are female and other students are male. Participants' ages are between 22 and 32. Tested smart watch is Moto360. The positioning of this type of watch is an auxiliary alarm of mobile phone. Dial plate interface of Moto360 is very beautiful. It can satisfy the requirement of social communication, can also be a good accompany of sports and involves various aspects of life. Among the tested users, two used Moto360 and 6 of them have never used it.

3.2   Experimental Device

Experimental device is head-mounted eye tracker produced by German SensoMotoric Instruments Company. Its sampling frequency is 50 Hz. It mainly includes a light weight helmet and a testing computer. A camera device for photographing eyes and a camera device for photographing field are mounted on the light weight helmet. The camera device for photographing eyes is infrared camera used to photograph infrared pictures of testers' ocular pulse. The camera device for photographing field is mainly used to photograph field images. The testing computer is mainly used to system control and record and process of data. Experimental materials are interfaces of smart watch Moto360. Experiment Center and BeGaze softwares are used to record and analyze experimental data.

3.3   Experimental Task Design

Experimental tasks of tested users are operating specified typical tasks of the smart watch. Detailed typical tasks seen in Table 1.

Table 1. Typical tasks

	Typical tasks
1	Look for a countdown icon
2	Set a countdown alarm of 1 min and 3 s
3	Look for an alarm icon and set it as an alarm of getting up at seven o'clock
4	Look for a pedometer icon
5	Look for an icon of setting
6	Send a sound message to a WeChat friend
7	Look for an icon of raising a wrist and an icon of lighting screen of the smart watch

3.4 Evaluation Index

Fixation time means the fixation time of all interfaces during the process from operation beginning to typical tasks operation completion for tested users. The fixation time of failure task operation for tested users is not within statistic range. Typical failure task operation includes two aspects: 1 If tested users don't finish the typical task operation within 2 min, then typical task operation is failure. 2 If tested users don't complete typical task operation as required, then typical task operation is failure.

Fixation point number: fixation point number of all interfaces during the process from operation beginning to typical task completion for tested users. The fixation point number of failure task operation for tested users is not within statistic range.

Task completion ratio: for each operation task, the ratio of successful typical task operation for tested users.

3.5 Experimental Procedure

Experiment Preparation and Introduction. At the stage of experimental preparation, the experimenter checks if experimental materials, questionnaires, experimental equipments and experiment environment are all prepared. The experimenter tells the tested users the main procedure of the experiment, answer the questions proposed by tested users, and let the tested users fill in registration forms.

Eye Tracker Calibration and Eyeball Correction. Before beginning the experiment, explain procedures and aims of the experiment to testers first, then please testers adjust position and height of a seat and sitting posture. Sight distance of testers (from eyes to screen) is kept at 60 cm. And the correction for eyeballs of testers is conducted. First determine how system detects eyeballs. Adjust the position, focus, brightness and contrast ratio of photographer to obtain optimal experimental effect (Fig. 1).

After position of head and eyeball is adjusted to an appropriate position, 5 points eye movement position calibration procedure is conducted. A cross mark will appear at the middle, upper right, lower right, upper left and lower left positions in order. Testers stare at the mark stably one by one. If there is no obvious mistake, the eye tracker will count the correspond function of screen and eyeball movement during 5 points

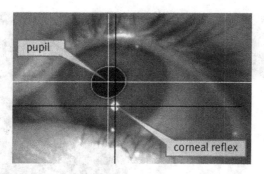

Fig. 1. Eye correction for the tester

calibration and directly convert the movement amount of eyeballs to displacement of screen coordinate (Fig. 2).

Validation affirmation procedure is to affirm difference of the converted cross point position and the real cross point position. If the difference is within the tolerable error range that was presupposed and then experiment can be started.

Fig. 2. Five point eye movement position correction

Test Period. The testers prepare for the test after understanding the experiment. Experimenters let testers know well of Moto360 smart watch interface within specified time to meet experiment requirements. Testers start test according to test instruction; testers turn on record switch. Test users start to operate the first typical task. Testers finish each task in order; and experimenters close the record switch and save (Fig. 3).

Interview After Test. Experimenters communicate the problems, inconvenience or wrong operation users encountered during the test with testers, so that problems are found and solved.

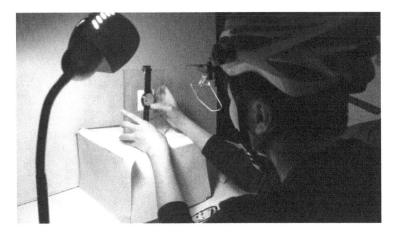

Fig. 3. The tester is conducting usability test experiment of Moto360 smart watch interface

4 Analysis on Experiment Result

4.1 Comparison of Evaluation Index

In this experiment, data process is conducted by using dedicated software of eye tracker to obtain the data of fixation time, fixation point number, average fixation time and hot spot diagram.

The following diagrams are statistic result of fixation time and fixation point number for typical tasks of smart watch interface. Compare test results combining with eye movement video and find that there is significant difference between testers in using Moto360 smart watch to finish tasks. When finishing Task3 and Task6, the average time and average fixation point number of testers using Moto360 are no different than test data of users with experienced operation, testers finish the tasks smoothly. It shows that in Moto360 smart watch interface, the representation meaning of interface element related to these two tasks is superior to others (Figs. 4 and 5).

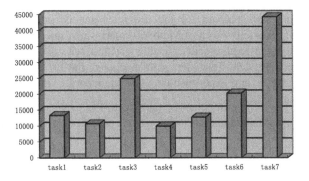

Fig. 4. Average fixation time of smart watch interface

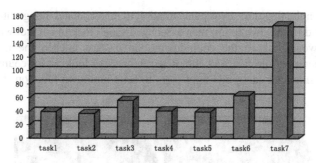

Fig. 5. Average fixation point number of smart watch interface

The table shows the task completion rate of Moto360 interface. It is seen from the table that completion rate of Task4 and Task7 is less than 100 % and the completion rate of Task7 is only 20 %, which shows that there is serious usability problem in the interface design of this task (Table. 2).

Table 2. Task completion rate of smart watch Moto360 interface

	Task1	Task2	Task3	Task4	Task5	Task6	Task7
Moto360	100 %	100 %	100 %	90 %	100 %	100 %	20 %

4.2 Analyze Usability Problem and Causes of Interface Using Eye Movement Data

There is a bigger difference in fixation time, fixation point number and task completion rate evaluation index for finishing 7 tasks of Moto360 from above 3 dimensions of evaluation indexes. It is divided into 4 categories: the first category is that tasks are completed normally, the second category is that there are some obstacles during completion but relatively smooth, the third category is that there are some difficulties in completion process, and the fourth category is that completing task is very difficult. Above tasks are analyzed by combining with fixation time hot spot distribution diagram and eye movement video of tested users. It is found that big difference of performance in completing tasks is caused by different interface elements (Table. 3).

Average fixation time of looking for countdown icon is 13317.64/ms, and average fixation point number is 39.6 each one. It is found by observing eye movement video that testers regarded an alarm clock icon as a countdown icon mistakenly. Testers'eyes stared at it temporarily because the alarm clock picture contains the meaning of time, which is known by deep understand and questionnaire after test. When testers saw the

Table 3. Task completion category of smart watch Moto360 interface

	Task1	Task2	Task3	Task4	Task5	Task6	Task7
Moto 360	Relative difficult	Relative smooth	Completed normally	Relative difficult	Relative difficult	Relative smooth	Very difficult

countdown icon the first time, eyes paid attention to this icon and thought it temporarily after fingers slid from down to up; then associated sand clock to countdown, slid down quickly and went back to the countdown icon, at last clicked the icon to enter countdown operation interface and completed the task of looking for countdown icon. It is seen that this icon can guide the testers to set countdown function (Fig. 6).

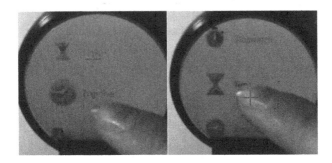

Fig. 6. Find countdown icon

Task2 is to set a countdown alarm of 1 min and 3 s, testers need to slide screen left and right to know well of setting dial plate interface of hour, minute and second. Because of the limitation of dial plate screen, one time unit can be set once; hour, minute and second can not be seen at the same time, left and right arrow need to be added for users to provide guidance for operation.

Task4 is to look for a pedometer icon, the average fixation time is 9933.257/ms, average fixation point number is 40.71429 each one, and task completion ratio is 90 %. It can be found by path scan diagram and hot spot analysis diagram that testers hesitate between a heart shape picture and a ladder shape icon. Individual testers regarded the heart rate measuring icon as the pedometer icon mistakenly thus clicking the heart rate measuring icon mistakenly. When testers saw pedometer the first time, their eyes stared at it temporarily, and most of testers clicked the pedometer icon after observing it repeatedly. Later it was understood by questionnaire and deep study that testers hesitated between heart picture and ladder icon and so it was difficult to find the pedometer icon (Fig. 7).

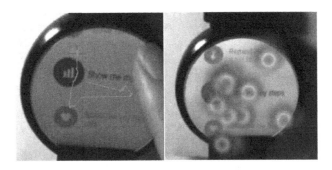

Fig. 7. Path scan diagram and hot spot analysis diagram

Task5 is to look for the icon of setting, the average fixation time is 12744.16/ms and average fixation point number is 39.25 each one. During the process of looking for the icon of setting, wrong operation is caused by brighten and setting icons are similar, fingers slide from right to left in the middle of screen habitually, theater mode is started and so wrong operation is caused. If testers' fingers slide at the bottom of screen, then operating icons in the middle can be avoided. It gives an inspiration to designers that visual center of the smart watch is in the middle of the dial plate. Important icons and characters should be designed according to this rule (Fig. 8).

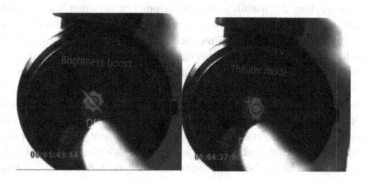

Fig. 8. Causing wrong operation

Task7 is to look for the raising wrist icon and screen brightening icon and task completion ratio is 20 %. 2 of 10 testers completed the tasks very difficultly. This icon lies in the setting. When environmental mode is "on" started, you raise a wrist, eyes stare at Moto360, at this time, screen lights up, and the screen gets dark gradually after a few seconds, but keeps lighting up all the time, the screen turned off after a time. Testers do wrong operation when they see Wrist gestures icon; Wrist gestures icon is clicked to turn pages by the action of overturning wrist when another hand is busy. It is understood by combining questionnaires after test that testers regarded the implication of a double-headed arrow as raising a wrist wrongly and testers can't understand the implication of eyes so they don't understand the function of this icon (Fig. 9).

Fig. 9. Causing wrong operation

5 Conclusion

In this study the user test was conducted for smart watch interface. Eye movement track technology is introduced to usability evaluation of smart watch interface to measure usability level of smart watch interface. It is found from task test results that eye movement data can well evaluate smart watch interface icons and can reveal how users search their target items and information on smart watch interfaces. In this study usability evaluation method of a smart watch based on eye movement track is proposed and eye movement data is introduced to usability evaluation index system, and they are significant for guiding the usability evaluation practice of smart watch, further perfecting usability evaluation index system of smart watch and providing objective evidence for improving smart watch interface and improving usability level. The following conclusions are obtained from this study: 1 Eye movement data such as fixation time and fixation point are used as quantitative index for evaluating representation meaning of interface information structure and interface elements. 2 Eye movement data is shown by fixation time hot spot diagram which can reflect the attention distribution situation of users on interface intuitively and provide objective evidence for experimenters to analyze interface problems. 3 Eye movement video can reproduce the sight line movement situation when testers use smart watch interface. A lot of interface problems at deep levels can be found using the analysis methods of combining eye movement video and graphic eye movement data. 4 The interface usability evaluation method based on eye movement track is applied to early and middle stage of smart watch design, and the interface usability evaluation method provides objective evidence for designers to understand users' thought and improve interface design.

References

1. Yuan, L.: A new visual testing instrument: infrared helmet eye movement. J. Beijing Univ. Aeronaut. Astronaut. **2**, 200–203 (2007)
2. Rayner, K., Rotello, C.M., Stewart, A.J., Keir, J., Duffy, S.A.: Integrating text and pictorial information: eye movements when looking at print advertisements. J. Exp. Psychol. Appl. **7**(3), 219–226 (2001)
3. Rayner, K.: Eye movements in reading and information processing: 20 years of research. Psychol. Bull. **124**(3), 372–422 (1998)
4. Rayner, K., Reichle, E.D., Stroud, M.J., Williams, C.C., Pollatsek, A.: The effect of word frequency, word predictability, and font difficulty on the eye movements of young and older readers. Psychol. Aging **21**(3), 448–465 (2006)
5. Shih, Y.-F.: The effects of layout design of mobile advertisement on eye movement and aesthetic emotion. Master thesis, National Chiao Tung University (2013)
6. Zhang, G., Shen, M.: Eye tracking technology in usability testing. Chin. J. Ergon. **7**(4), 9–13 (2001)

7. Zhuang, W.: A study of evoking visual fixation by pleasure product shapes - using kettles as examples. Master thesis, Chang Gung University (2011)
8. Newman, W.M., Lamming, M.G.: Interactive System Design. Addison-wesley, Harlow (1995)
9. Manllartsberger, M., Zellhofer, N.: Eye tracking in usability research: what users really see. In: Usability Symposium, vol. 198, pp. 141–152. OCG Publication (2005)

DUXU in Information Design
and Visualization

Balancing Tradeoffs in the Design of an Interactive Art Installation on Surveillance and Big Data

Simone Ashby[1(✉)], Julian Hanna[1], Katie Ramp[2],
and Jennifer Baranoff[2]

[1] Madeira-ITI, University of Madeira, Caminho da Penteada,
9020-105 Funchal, Portugal
{simone.ashby, julian.hanna}@m-iti.org
[2] Human-Computer Interaction Institute, Carnegie Mellon University,
Pittsburgh, PA 15213, USA
http://www.m-iti.org

Abstract. North Circular is an interactive public art installation that invites participants to navigate a fictional urban environment built from data fragments. This paper asks how best to design for ambiguity and critique while balancing aesthetic considerations against complex ideas about big data and surveillance. We describe the results of a cultural probe aimed at understanding user thresholds for minimal specification and ambiguity in design in interactive installations, as well as our efforts to model interactions and design two prototypes. We conclude by presenting five insights and design recommendations for balancing complex themes with minimal specification in the design of interactive installations and displays.

Keywords: Ambiguity in design · Complex themes · Mass surveillance · Big data · Interactive installations · James Joyce's Ulysses

1 Introduction

'If James Joyce were alive today he'd be working for Google' [1].

James Joyce's *Ulysses* (1922) is often referred to as a hypertext or proto–hypertext because it demonstrates qualities such as non-linearity, interconnectivity, and synchronicity [2]. This is particularly true of the central chapter, 'The Wandering Rocks', which follows nineteen different characters as they circulate through the streets of Dublin, each lost in an interior monologue of thoughts and impressions. The characters in 'The Wandering Rocks' interact with each other as their paths cross, and they observe and are observed by one another in the social fishbowl that was Dublin a century ago. But they are also seen from above, by a more omniscient form of authorial surveillance. As one scholar describes it: '"Wandering Rocks" is a chapter that can be played as a board game on a map of Dublin and that employs surveillance from a vertical perspective as its narrative metaphor' [3]. Joyce's painstakingly mapped and detailed central episode, presenting both an omniscient bird's eye view of Dublin and

A. Marcus (Ed.): DUXU 2016, Part III, LNCS 9748, pp. 113–123, 2016.
DOI: 10.1007/978-3-319-40406-6_11

its inhabitants and a multiplicity of subjective views of the city, in turn makes an apt metaphor for the heavily surveilled and data rich 21st century metropolis.

In a remark to a friend, Joyce is famously quoted as having said: 'I want to give a picture of Dublin so complete that if the city suddenly disappeared from the earth it could be reconstructed out of my book' [4]. Drawing on various aspects of Joyce's Dublin as represented in *Ulysses* and more recent (and ominous) plans for a digital 'social credit system' in China [5], our project encourages participants to consider what 21st century Dublin – the multilayered, hyperconnected, datafied city of the present and near future – would look like if we could hear and see the city as it is constructed from our own data artefacts and traces. But how best to design for ambiguity while balancing aesthetic considerations against complex ideas about big data and surveillance?

'North Circular' is a design fiction project and future scenario–based interactive public art installation that invites participants to navigate an urban environment built from big data fragments exposing the political, social, and consumer behaviour of a fictitious populace. The goal of North Circular is not to reconstruct Dublin as it was, but rather the current lives of Dubliners from their own online data presence. We want participants to hear and see, in an abstract manner, the data layer that underlies the city, henceforth known as the datasphere. The emergence of big data can be interpreted in a number of ways: on the positive end of the spectrum, open data can be an enjoyable way of exploring a city and its people; on the negative end, however, data can equate to heavy surveillance, influencing behaviour and interfering in citizens' private lives. It is this duality that we aim to highlight in our installation.

In this paper, we describe the results of a cultural probe aimed at understanding user thresholds for minimal specification and ambiguity in design in interactive installations. In the initial sections of this paper, we describe our efforts to model the interaction between participant and system, and design prototypes. Through these efforts we explore the limits of minimalism and underspecification in the design of an interactive installation that deals with complex issues surrounding big data and surveillance. This paper asks: How can artists and designers open a meaningful dialogue on the vast complexities of, for example, the datasphere or mass surveillance (not to mention *Ulysses*) using a minimum of text, image, and sound? Drawing on ideas around productive ambiguity in design [6] and affordances [7, 8], we investigate the tradeoffs between clarity and ambiguity, and functionality vs. aesthetics.

2 Related Work

We position our project as an interactive digital art installation with an analogue heart ('The Wandering Rocks') and a particular emphasis on designing for ambiguity, subtlety, and minimalism. On one hand, the ubiquity of data in our 21st-century cities has seen the production of innumerable data-driven art projects that both explore the expressive potential of these new resources and reflect on the rich and challenging experience of life in the digital datasphere [9]. On the other hand, much effort, funding, and research in the digital humanities has sought to preserve, adapt, and reinvigorate analogue works of previous eras to the digital world we now inhabit [10]. As in the case of North Circular, combining these two broad aims has sometimes taken the form of digital projects based on the complex and highly suggestive works of the Irish modernist author James Joyce as they intersect with the topography of Dublin. Three examples of Joycean projects, all of which are based around mapping, include: JoyceWalks[1]; the Walking Ulysses project at Boston College[2]; and Dislocating Ulysses at the University of Victoria[3]. All of these examples use geospatial data to help users explore the densely multilayered city.

Interactive installations and displays that address themes of big data and surveillance are becoming increasingly common in the art world. This is evident for example in the Big Bang Data exhibition (2016) at Somerset House in London, which gathers together a diverse array of projects[4] exploring aspects of the boom in publicly available data. These projects invite visitors to reflect on how we generate and contribute to the growing mass of data, not only actively through social media but passively through our always on mobile devices. Using cutting-edge techniques in data sifting and visualization, the exhibition explores the quantification of individual lives and whole populations, changing forms of communication, ideas of privacy and piracy, consumption and commodification, and so on - often promoting interaction through the unsettling use of visitors' own data.

In terms of engaging visitors, designers of interactive installations and displays often cite the importance of ambiguity, such as that described in [6], as a means of arousing intrigue, mystery and delight in onlookers [e.g. 11]. Other designs rely on more explicit indicators for drawing in visitors, arguing the need for clear, unambiguous affordances that people can easily identify and relate to [12]. One recent example of an installation that makes productive use of ambiguity and a minimalist aesthetic to engage users with themes around big data, surveillance, and hidden systems is *Familiars* (2015)[5] by Georgina Voss and Wesley Goatley. Using intercepted communication signals, the installation maps the trajectories of cargo vessels as they move across the globe by land, sea, and air. Visuals are kept to a minimum of suggestive white tracking numbers and red pathways; the audio soundtrack consists of a cacophony of overlapping radio navigation communications. As in North Circular, *Familiars* aims to transform the immaterial world of raw data into something material, while leaving room for reflection on the part of users about the potential impact this data and these unseen systems have on their daily lives.

With these considerations in mind, we recognize that there is room for deeper investigation. The tension between ambiguity and more overt physical affordances, for example, remains a relatively unexplored area of research. Through this paper we hope to bring greater attention to the use of ambiguity in the context of ambient displays. We also hope to go beyond the more conventional digital humanities approaches to exploring Joyce's works. Projects that simply map Joyce onto the topography of Dublin are interesting but limited; they miss the playful, challenging, and capricious spirit of the

---

[1] http://www.joycewalks.com.

[2] Accessed from http://ulysses.bc.edu.

[3] Accessed from http://web.uvic.ca/~achris/zaxis/index.html.

[4] E.g. LONDON DATA STREAMS (http://www.tekja.com/project-big-bang-data.html).

[5] Accessed from http://www.familiars.org.

author, who resisted easy formulas and narrative enclosures. Mobile applications such as Walking Ulysses do not go much further than attaching key passages from Joyce's writing, along with corresponding historical data, to points on a Google Map. While enhancing an existing map in this way was groundbreaking a decade ago, such projects now appear reductive and literal in their treatment of Joyce's vision. We instead aim to use Joyce's vision of the modern metropolis (circa 1904) - heavily surveilled, data rich, a jumble of interactions and crossed paths - as a jumping off point to explore the 21st century urban space in all its post-digital complexity. 'Post-digital' in this context suggests a point beyond the digital revolution, where immersion in the datasphere is taken for granted and the interaction and overlap between human and digital worlds becomes a primary focus of artistic investigation [13].

3   The North Circular Project

The North Circular project employs metaphors from Joyce's *Ulysses* to look at surveillance but more specifically at voyeurism, creating a space in which the participant is both the observer and the observed. Nearly everyone who uses social media admits to lurking – the practice of using your account to 'spy' on others without actually posting. So-called 'lurkers' are a majority faction in interactive situations of all types [14]. Participation inequality, described by Nielsen's '900-9-1 principle' [15], is a defining characteristic of most online communities. This, in a sense, is what the experience of reading the 'Wandering Rocks' episode of *Ulysses* feels like. The reader is given privileged access to bits and pieces of Dubliners' everyday lives, silently observing their private thoughts and public behaviour, and witnessing the gap between the two, as they traverse the city.

In the installation, we aim to create an immersive, thought-provoking experience of voyeurism. When the interactant enters, they will get the sense of being in a bustling city center, with ambient sounds of the city filling the room. We are exploring the use of sound as minimally as possible, while still conveying these complex ideas, namely, making one's interior monologue external. As we browse the internet, we are, in essence, internalizing others' thoughts. What feelings emerge when instead those fragments are spoken aloud? Is it strange to hear vocalizations of text features such as emojis or hashtags? Whose data are we listening to? We plan to gather a limited set of personal information from the visitors and include some of their own public data in the installation. When they hear their own comments, photo captions, tweets, etc. voiced back to them, does it spark reflection on what they are putting into the data-sphere? Do they question whether the other fragments they hear belong to the other participants in the room? Will they talk to each other about it?

3.1   Cultural Probe

To explore the thresholds for minimal specification, we conducted a cultural probe focusing on interactive art installations in London. Two exhibits in particular provided us with relevant content from which to obtain user feedback, each representing a different end of the spectrum in terms of the affordances they offer to convey specific ideas to an audience.

The first was *Empty Lot*, an interactive living sculpture commissioned by Hyundai for the Tate Modern museum and designed by Abraham Cruzvillegas. The large-scale piece filled the Turbine Hall; it consisted of wooden scaffolding, similar to that of a ship, holding over 100 boxes of dirt taken from various parks around London. The artist described the living sculpture as a whole as being 'made out of hope' (Fig. 1).

Fig. 1. Empty lot exhibit (Cruzvillegas) in the turbine hall of the tate modern museum

The exhibition text suggested hidden layers of meaning - social, personal, and cultural - beneath the simple concept of waiting for something to grow. The idea was that with daily watering and sunlight, organic material would start to grow out of whatever was in the dirt. The space was so large, however, that many visitors did not read the instructions and therefore did not realize that they were being encouraged to throw objects into the dirt.

During two hours of observation of visitors' reactions, the average amount of time each person spent looking at the piece was only three minutes. There was some confusion among visitors who claimed they 'just don't get [this] sort of thing', i.e. putting empty planters in a museum space. Several people we interviewed brought their own background to their interpretation: a landscape architect told us that nothing was likely to germinate in December; another visitor said that it reminded her of what she learned in school about explorers bringing seeds home from the New World.

The second exhibition we observed was *States of Mind* by Ann Veronica Janssens at the Welcome Collection. There was so much interest surrounding this exhibition that a long queue had formed, with only ten visitors admitted at a time to ensure that each person could experience the room properly. The installation played on individual perception: the room was filled with multi-coloured mist and was intentionally disorienting. Visitors could see only one meter or so ahead. We were interested in the fact that visitors knew exactly what to expect based on widespread publicity, but they came anyway. In the queue, iPads were given out that provided demonstrations of famous perception experiments, but these visuals sparked only minimal conversation. Visitors tended to stick together while inside, which somewhat undermined the goal of challenging individual perception of time and space. Visitors seemed to treat the exhibition almost like an amusement park, complete with rules and regulations to guide enjoyment.

3.2 Defining the Concept

Our cultural probe findings led us to strive for an adequate balance between minimal specification and ambiguity on one hand, and clear affordances and specificity on the other. We started with a vision for North Circular (Prototype I) in which we attempted to synthesize a number of divergent strands on the main themes of Joyce, big data, and surveillance. We later devised a simpler, more site-specific model (Prototype II) wherein we sought to avoid overburdening the visitor with too many stimuli. We also tried to avoid some of the pitfalls observed in the *States of Mind* exhibit (see Sect. 3.1) by ensuring that the experience left space for exploration and discovery.

In the initial prototype we conceived of two separate rooms, one for the observer ('outside') and one for the observed ('inside'). The observed participant was immersed in the subjective experience of the digital datasphere, while the 'outside' observer enjoyed a more omniscient, godlike view of the 'inside' room. In the second prototype, we refined the concept to require a single room - a long corridor with elevators at both ends for descending to and ascending from the space - in order to combine the passive experience of being 'spied on' with the active voyeurism of observing and consuming others' data traces. Both prototypes are further elaborated below.

Prototype I. Our initial concept invited participants to assume a surveillance role in which they observed the principal interaction taking place inside the exhibit's central space. The first stop was a surveillance area, which gave users a chance to understand what was happening inside; the second stop was a larger main room for exploring and interacting with the visually minimalist and binaural urban social space.

The main room was dimly lit and featured brightly coloured floor projections and multiple soundtracks played through a wireless headset. Circles containing basic personal data (age, sex) and a three–digit citizen score were seen moving around the space. Meanwhile, through kinetic typography, blue lines of objective data (e.g. headline and financial news, transportation check–ins, census figures) suggested paths through the city. Four separate binaural audio loops represented subjective data streams (e.g. a telephone conversation, text–to–speech enabled tweets, private thoughts, missed connections). Every crossed path and data stream encounter appeared to impact the citizen score shown inside the moving circles. The participant could traverse this urban labyrinth and reflect on how their decisions, as well as chance encounters, might affect their own individual status in this heavily surveilled environment (Fig. 2).

Joyce does not represent Dublin visually in *Ulysses*, argues one critic, but 'through the minds of the Dubliners we overhear talking to each other' [3]. We do not see the

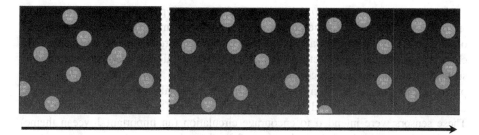

Fig. 2. North circular prototype I depicting participants' surveilled movements, interactions and citizen scores over time

city directly; we soak it up indirectly, through surveillance. Outside the main room, on the other side of the surveillance partition, a row of screens and headsets could be found, enabling the participant to listen to the conversations and other personal material on the audio channels being played inside and watch a live video feed of the interactions occurring in the main space, as the names and scores of fictitious citizens scrolled rapidly down the right-hand panel.

Prototype II. We refined our concept with a particular testing environment in mind, i.e. the corridor that runs through our institute. The space needed to be confined enough to draw visitors past the simple, motion-activated speakers, but large enough to encourage circulation. The space we chose had elevators at either end of the hallway, thus allowing for a staging area upstairs where we could take time to scrape the internet for visitors' public web data. The elevator itself served as a transitional space with an information card describing North Circular. The series of rooms opening onto the corridor held projectors, which were placed to display abstract visualizations of data on the walls (Fig. 3). This was intended to give the visitor a preliminary sense of what the exhibit was about, i.e., comprehending and reflecting on all the 1s and 0 s we create in our everyday lives.

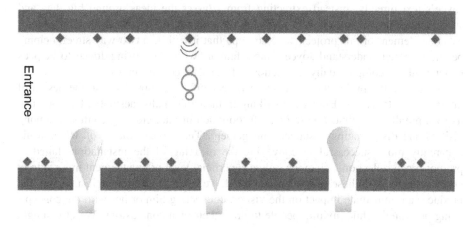

Fig. 3. North circular prototype II depicting an aerial view of the installation space

One question that came up in the design of this prototype was: Which types of data are interesting to listen to? The point was not to overwhelm the user with the enormity of all the data out there, but rather give them a chance to reflect on how decisions and chance encounters might affect their data, personal interactions, etc. Using data sources such as Craigslist's 'missed connections' would lead the user to reflect on the ways people try to connect in the modern age. On the technical side, motion sensors were used to activate Irish accented text-to-speech fragments of real Dubliners' online data. These sensors were intended to encourage circulation (an important Joycean theme) around the space to simulate exploration of the datasphere.

We also experimented with ways of gathering visitor data. For testing purposes, it had to be flexible enough to perform a Wizard of Oz experiment using people's names and postal codes or other commonly accessible information. Once we knew what kind of information was easily and quickly available, we would be able to devise a way to automate the process. The correct ratio of personal data to random data fragments also had to be achieved. If there were 19 snippets (reflecting the 19 characters in 'The Wandering Rocks'), we hypothesized that four should be enough to be certain a user would hear something from his or her own life and therefore be encouraged to further explore the space. The data snippets should also be banal enough that only the interactant knows who created the comment, thus avoiding violation of privacy by revealing actual addresses, phone numbers, etc.

4   Discussion

At this stage in our project we believe that the union of *Ulysses* with themes of big data and surveillance is one worth pursuing. Yet these rich and complex themes require significant unpacking. Without proper handling there is a danger that the weight of these themes could potentially overwhelm the visitor and make for a poor interactive experience, obscuring rather than illuminating the topics at hand. So the question arises: how to winnow the content to a manageable, comprehensible package? In our attempts thus far we have tried to avoid overwhelming users with the complexities of Joyce's text directly, instead extracting from *Ulysses* the ideas around big data and surveillance that are still relevant today. While interpreting Joyce for the 21st century was one element of this project, we also hope that it will be a two-way street: helping people to better understand Joyce's most famous work, and using Joyce to help us understand the complex daily interactions of our 21st century cities.

In our cultural probe, we witnessed two very different approaches to the design of interactive installations. Both were striking in their minimalist aesthetic, but each had its own pitfalls. The first, *Empty Lot*, left too much unsaid, creating confusion among visitors and discouraging sustained engagement. The second, *States of Mind*, while apparently more successful in conveying the meaning of the installation, failed to promote deep reflection, achieving only a superficial level of engagement more akin to entertainment. With these experiences in mind, we sought to design an installation that produces an immediate impact on the visitor, connecting him or her with the concepts being presented, while inviting people to draw their own conclusions. We also sought to create a personalized experience by employing users' own data as part of the installation.

Our prototypes I and II show a progression in the visioning of North Circular from an overly complex tangle of ideas, stimuli, and role playing (observer, observed) to a more simplified, streamlined concept whose spatial characteristics give the installation a clear start and end point (missing from Prototype I, which lacked a defined path). Prototype II also jettisoned as too heavy-handed the motifs of citizen scores and an external surveillance control room, replacing them with a less narrativized, less explicitly dystopian experience. We aimed for an experience that opens up space for reflection on themes of big data and surveillance without prejudicing the user's response. We achieved this by: focusing the visitor's attention on motion sensor activated audio while reducing visual cues; inviting interactants to take notice of their contribution to the data layer by uncovering minor data fragments that were forgotten or even unknown to the user; and relying on wall displays only to afford a general contextual understanding of data immersion. The decision to use visitors' own data fragments to personalize the engagement was inspired by *Empty Lot* and the possibility of allowing visitors to bring their own seeds to plant. We posited that interactants would be met with surprise when they heard their contributions to the datasphere as synthesized utterance fragments, and this would provoke a shock of recognition and a deeper level of engagement.

With these decisions in mind, we present five insights and design recommendations for balancing complex themes with minimal specification in the design of interactive installations and displays.

- Tailor content to the user to make it relevant.
- Create a clear path through the installation space.
- Encourage active engagement and reflection through a combination of playful ambiguity and affordances that interactants can recognize and relate to their own experiences.
- Don't inhibit reflection by telling interactants what to think. Instead, allow interactants to muse freely on complex themes.
- Create a clear signal by reducing noise from competing modalities.

5 Conclusions and Future Work

Returning to the quotation at the start of this paper, Tom McCarthy wrote of *Ulysses* that Joyce's ambition was 'to make a whole culture, at micro- and macro-level, from its advertising slogans or the small talk in bars to its funerary rituals and the way the entire past and future are imagined'. In other words, constructing *Ulysses* was a bidirectional process: in one direction, building a text, city, and culture out of data fragments; in the other, making it possible to reconstruct that city and culture from the text (should anything happen to 'dear dirty Dublin').

This was our initial inspiration for North Circular, which seeks to apply the insights and provocations of Joyce's text to similar but evolving concerns raised by big data and surveillance in the data rich 21st century city. When we looked at previous attempts to use digital technology to in some sense 'update' Joyce, we found them to be overly literal in a way that goes against the playful, experimental, endlessly inventive nature of Joyce's writing. Using digital technology to update analogue texts without exploring contemporary parallels - Joyce's Dublin to the digital datasphere - is a missed opportunity to 'make it new', in the words of fellow modernist Ezra Pound.

On the issue of ambiguity, we observed in our cultural probe the fine line between the kind of productive ambiguity posited by Gaver et al. [6] and the baffling ambiguity that causes visitors to turn away from art installations. Once again, Joyce's novels - not only *Ulysses* but also *Finnegans Wake* (1939) - show us the way forward, the means of achieving an appropriate balance. Joyce uses rhetorical devices such as omission and paronomasia to add layers of ambiguity to his otherwise highly structured texts. (In *Finnegans Wake*, for example, a typical instance of wordplay is: 'they were yung and easily freudened' [FW 115.21-23].) In this way Joyce's writing simultaneously reflects the intricate systems underpinning nature and human society, and the unpredictable, serendipitous, infinite possibilities of everyday life.

Finally, our future work involves testing the current prototype and experimenting with different types of data fragments. The goal will be to assess which data sources interactants find to be most compelling and thought provoking, and to determine how well our curation of audio and visual elements enhances the experience. We will also explore interactants' privacy and security concerns in the use of their personal data fragments.

References

1. McCarthy, T.: The death of writing - if James Joyce were alive today he'd be working for Google. The Guardian. http://www.theguardian.com/books/2015/mar/07/tom-mccarthy-death-writing-james-joyce-working-google
2. Bolter, J.D., Joyce, M., Smith, J.B.: STORYSPACE: Hypertext Writing Environment for the Macintosh. Eastgate Systems, Cambridge (1990)
3. Voelker, J.C.: Clown meets cops: comedy and paranoia in under the volcano and Ulysses. In: MacCarthy, P.A., Tiessen, P. (eds.) Joyce/Lowry: Critical Perspectives, pp. 21–40. University Press of Kentucky, Lexington (1997)
4. Budgen, F.: James Joyce and the Making of 'Ulysses', and Other Writings. Oxford University Press, Oxford (1972)
5. Schiller, B.: China is Building the Mother of All Reputation Systems to Monitor Citizen Behavior. Fast Company. http://www.fastcoexist.com/3050606/china-is-building-the-mother-of-all-reputation-systems-to-monitor-citizen-behavior
6. Gaver, W., Beaver, J., Benford, S.: Ambiguity as a resource for design. In: Proceedings of CHI, pp. 233–240. ACM Press, New York (2003)
7. Norman, D.A.: Affordance, conventions, and design. Interactions 6(3), 38–42 (1999)
8. Gibson, J.J.: The Ecological Approach to Visual Perception. Houghton Mifflin, Boston (1979)
9. Hansen, M.: Data-Driven Aesthetics. Bits Blog. http://bits.blogs.nytimes.com/2013/06/19/data-driven-aesthetics
10. Burdick, A., Drucker, J., Lunenfeld, P., Presner, T., Schnapp, J.: Digital_Humanities. MIT Press, Cambridge (2012)

11. Vogel, D., Balakrishnan, R.: Interactive public ambient displays: transitioning from implicit to explicit, public to personal, interaction with multiple users. In: Proceeding of the UIST, pp. 137–146 (2004)

12. Brignull, H., Rogers, Y.: Enticing people to interact with large public displays in public spaces. In: Proceeding of Interact, pp. 17–24 (2003)

13. Kulle, D., Lund, C., Schmidt, O., Ziegenhagen, D.: Welcome to Post-Digital Culture: A Short Introduction. Post-Digital Culture. http://www.post-digital-culture.org

14. Muller, M., Shami, N. S., Millen, D. R., Feinberg, J.: We are all lurkers: consuming behaviors among authors and readers in an enterprise file-sharing service. In: Proceeding of 16th ACM International Conference on Supporting Group Work, pp. 201–210. ACM Press, New York (2010)

15. Nielsen, J.: Participation Inequality: Encouraging More Users to Contribute. http://www.nngroup.com/articles/participation-inequality

Learning from the Users for Spatio-Temporal Data Visualization Explorations on Social Events

Damla Çay and Asım Evren Yantaç[(✉)]

KUAR - Koç University Arçelik Research Center for Creative Industries,
Istanbul, Turkey
{dcayl3,eyantac}@ku.edu.tr

Abstract. The amount of volunteered geographic information is on the rise through geo-tagged data on social media. While this growth opens new paths for designers and developers to form new geographical visualizations and interactive geographic tools, it also engenders new design and visualization problems. We now can turn any kind of data into daily useful information to be used during our daily lives. This paper is about exploration of novel visualization methods for spatio-temporal data related to what is happening in the city, planned or unplanned. We, hereby evaluate design students' works on visualizing social events in the city and share the results as design implications. Yet we contribute by presenting intuitive visualization ideas for social events, for the use of interactive media designers and developers who are developing map based interactive tools.

Keywords: Geographical information visualization · Volunteered geographical information · Event-maps · Spatio-temporal data · Interaction · Visualization · Design ethnography

1 Introduction

Volunteered geographical data opened cartographers and mapmakers a path of many possibilities of creating meaning out of different datasets from different sources [1]. Now, with the help of social media applications like Foursquare or Facebook, we can reach the metadata of events' location, time and topic, volume of the event that is happening in the city or comment and media of them with Twitter or Instagram. And since we can also reach the data from remote sources like weather data or traffic data, now it is the time that new questions arise. How can we visualize all this multi-layered live data in a legible way so that people can read them together, to create meaning for public to make decisions, plan, act or react about any kind of activity in the city?

The amount of spatio-temporal data has raised, causing the only field that is related to visualize spatio-temporal data, cartography, to evolve into something more interdisciplinary, mapmaking. This new field has its roots from cartography, but with the common use of interactive maps, it is now more interdisciplinary including disciplines like interactive media design, graphic design and software development, city planning.

© Springer International Publishing Switzerland 2016
A. Marcus (Ed.): DUXU 2016, Part III, LNCS 9748, pp. 124–135, 2016.
DOI: 10.1007/978-3-319-40406-6_12

It is now an open area for more people to create new meanings and new ways to present this widely available spatio-temporal data.

Now we are at a point in time where we try to represent new types of data that we would not achieve before, using the old ways to visualize. This might cause the map makers to create maps that are less engaging and harder to read. This paper is our way of exploring spatio-temporal data visualization ideas and intuitive visual patterns for spatial movement and event data. Presenting movement and event data in the city in a legible way might be a very challenging task for a designer. Yet, it also can be highly useful for supporting daily decision making processes of public (Fig. 1).

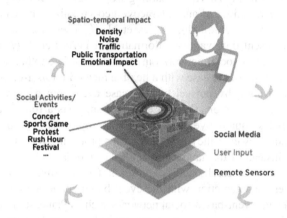

Fig. 1. Diagram of our motivation, sources and visualization layers of a hypothetical interactive tool

In our research, we had two goals; (1) finding interesting visualization ideas and (2) intuitive visualization patterns for representing movement and spatio temporal event data in a multi-layered format. To achieve this, we used an exploratory design research method, a participatory design workshop as a part of the basic design class. Then we evaluated the outcomes, using analysis criteria that we borrowed from the information design field.

2   Literature Review

In this section, we briefly summarize related work on event-based data visualization, spatio-temporal data visualization, participatory design methods, and the use of cultural probes as an ethnographic research tool in this context.

Location based data is an increasingly critical topic which has been studied in detail under the field of geographical information systems (GIS). As MacEachren [2] suggests, most of the digital data we produce, comes with geospatial information like coordinates, postal codes. When we add every other geo-tagged data like photos, videos from social media applications or when we semantically analyze the content of messages and their relation with location, we can understand the potential of spatial information analysis in terms of decision making. Today, every specific coordinate in the cities holds a lot of valuable data which can be turned into useful information. Bertrand et al. [3] argues that the increasing amount of measurable public sentiment, allows more of the timely and geographically precise data.

Studies on visualizing geo-spatial information include static, animated and interactive visualizations. O'Madadhain [4] expresses that research on data analysis is very much focused on static visuals. Geo-visualization has also its roots coming from semiology of cartographic visualization studies. Bertin [5] classified and identified the visual elements and diagrams that are used in the cartography field which forms a basis for geographical visualizations. While learning from Bertin is crucial, there is a need for researching modern animated and interactive geo-visualization methods for a case like urban event-maps. Accordingly, Eccles et al. [6] uses story as an element in visualization to represent time varying information or Ferrari et al. [7] presents urban patterns using the data of social networks in their studies. In another study, Tominski [8] solves the complexity of the case with a flexible method for user-driven event-based concepts for visualization by not selecting a case event, but a more general event definition and its representation. Quercia et al. [9] suggests a route-planning service model that includes qualitative and emotional opinions by making use of crowd-sourced data. However they use the data for proposing routes according to the user preferences, instead of displaying this multi-layered data.

While such recent research studies, question the information architecture and visualization issues for interaction with the event-based spatio-temporal data, we can also see some relevant event-based social networks such as Plancast or Meetup [10, 11] for the end-user, but none of these use a geographical visualization approach but a list based interface design. Yet, it is obvious that there is still need for research in the field for novel, effective and sophisticated representation and interaction methods.

3   Methodology

This research study is a part of an ongoing wide research interest on exploring novel ways of visualizing and interacting with the multi-layered urban data. We have been making use of several different ethnographic methods and user research studies. However, this paper is concentrated on spatio-temporal data visualization explorations on event-based urban data. Here, in this section, we present our process of previous studies related to event-based urban data visualization, and how we conducted the whole iterative process (Fig. 2).

3.1   Previous Studies on Spatio-Temporal Data Visualization

We started this research by conducting a set of participatory design workshops about spatio-temporal data visualization and we also conducted a diary study. Our goal in these studies was to find qualitative user needs by discussing through participatory design and finding novel spatio-temporal visualization explorations which has been previously presented [12]. Below we briefly explain how the previous studies are related to this paper.

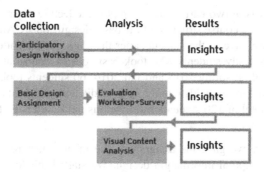

Fig. 2. Diagram showing the connection between our previous studies

After the first PD workshop and the diary studies, we conducted a more focused workshop on the specific topic of visualizing events in the city. We developed user scenarios based on the user needs from previous studies. In this workshop, our first aim was to find patterns on what types of information users choose to visualize and how they visualize them, which would lead us to understand user needs of a hypothetical interactive event map while a second aim was to explore novel visualization ideas in the context of social events. The PD workshop was held on a Saturday for a total of 8 h. It required volunteered participation by the people who were interested in the topic of spatio-temporal visualization and living in the same city. We sent an invitation to the network of people who attended at least one of our previous studies and are interested in the topic. The workshop had 10 participants who were mainly senior design students from interactive media design department and media and visual arts department. In the workshop, we presented them the scenarios we prepared and asked participants to visualize the activities and possible data that would have been created in such a scenario. Later on, the visualizations were presented by participants and we closed the session.

Basic Design Lecture and Assignment. Building up on our previous experience with the diary and the workshops, we decided that we needed a more structured visualization user research for collecting intuitive and creative ideas. With this perspective in mind, we prepared a presentation and gave an assignment to the basic design students of a media and visual arts department, two terms in a row. The basic design course is a one term class about the foundations of art and design. It is an introductory course to the principles and elements of design. Interdisciplinary seminars and discussions are held with a wide range of issues about art and design, design thinking, visual arts, plastic arts, moving image, photography, interdisciplinary relations with philosophy, psychology, and math. This study of giving spatio-temporal data visualization as an assignment to the students in the basic design course is a valuable idea because throughout the term, students learn the fundamental elements (line, shape, direction, size, texture, color) and principles (balance, proximity, alignment, repetition, contrast and space) of design and the assignment provides a challenging task that requires students' to apply the skills they gained.

Our study consists of two parts. The first part is the lecture on spatio-temporal data visualization within the course structure of the basic design course. And the second part is the assignment we gave to the students after the class, for the following week. The participants are university students who took basic design course at spring 2015 and fall 2016 terms. Both at spring 2015 and fall 2016, 60 students took the class. These students come from various fields mainly from media and visual arts, engineering and social sciences. A total of 120 students from various fields, attended to the lecture and made the assignment.

Presentation. Before we gave the assignment, we made a lecture about information design and spatio-temporal information design. We started this lecture with the basic principles of information design and then later on started discussing about what spatio-temporal data is, how it can be an asset in our daily lives for observing, understanding or planning needs.

Assignment. After the lecture, we gave an assignment to the students. We asked the students to visualize a social event or an incident they observe or experience in the city from bird's eye view, in an abstract way. They can use color. And we informed them that it is important that their work should be original, different than existing examples, and intuitive. One other thing that is important for the works is which data types they will include in their visualizations. We briefed them that the data types could include, but are not limited to: (1) time (date/time/duration); (2) movement (i.e. people/vehicle); (3) population (i.e. people/vehicle); (4) important elements about the space; (5) other data types you think are relevant with the event/incident (i.e. weather, sound). They are free to decide on the scale, whether it will be a city, region, or neighborhood. They had 2 weeks to finish the assignment.

Analysis and Evaluation. In this process, first we collected the assignments and separated the ones that were off brief and we scanned all the assignments and created a visual board using Pinterest [13] (Fig. 3). Later on, we went through an iterative analysis process. As a first iteration, we prepared a survey with quantitative and qualitative items and organized an analysis workshop where participants completed the surveys individually and evaluated the works through group discussion, explained below. But not feeling content about the outcomes of this first iteration, we then we conducted content analysis to code the visual data as a second and final iteration, of which we share the results below Sect. (4.2).

Survey and Analysis Workshop. We prepared a survey to evaluate the works. In the survey, we borrowed design analysis criteria from the cartography field, to evaluate how well the students' works fitted basic cartography design principles. These principles are, visual contrast, legibility, figure-ground organization, hierarchical organization and balance. [14] We used a likert scale from 1 to 5 for the items. Next section included three open ended questions and one multiple choice question. First question asked the users the types of data that they can read from the visualization. Second question asked if they can locate the main subject (locator) on the visualization and where is it. Third question asked if the viewer can see the effects of the environment through the event and how was it visualized. The last multiple choice question consists of two parts, first part asked the participants if the visualization is overall intuitive or

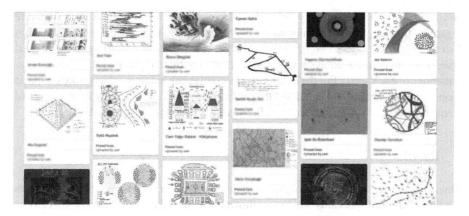

Fig. 3. Examples from student works

mediated, the second part asked if the visualization overall is interesting or ordinary. At the final part of the analysis, there is a section where we wanted the participants to redraw the interesting visual elements individually and write the data type they think it represents.

We announced the evaluation workshop to our network of participants who have participated in previous workshops. The workshop had 5 participants. (Fig. 4) 3 from various design backgrounds and 2 senior interactive media design students. The workshop lasted for 5 h. First we briefed the participants on the aim and structure of the workshop and we went through the survey structure. The participants selected works from our visual board and completed the evaluation survey individually. After this, they did a group discussion on each work.

Visual Content Analysis. The experience we had through the analysis workshop led us to revise our analysis method. One of the main problems with the workshop was that, participants had to select works to analyze, since there was insufficient time to analyze all of the results. Another problem was that, most of the student visualizations were too abstract to be evaluated as maps. This caused us to eliminate the set of criteria that we

Fig. 4. A photo from the analysis workshop and survey

borrowed from the cartography field. We added another set of criteria from literature regarding how engaging and informative each visualization was, using likert scale from 1 to 5 [15]. Two experienced designers rated 80 visualizations according to the revised criteria we used in the analysis workshop. Raters qualitatively coded the visual representations in each work. For the coding of representations, raters used keywords of basic shapes like dot, arrow, and spiral and they noted down the data type they think the visual element represents. After the analysis finished, we used inter-rater reliability check.

4 Results

Finally here, we share our insights throughout the whole design research process starting from our previous studies, followed by our data collection and analysis methodology and our insights from the process.

4.1 Previous Studies

As mentioned about, we started with a series of participatory design workshops and a diary study in combination. Since the time and effort the participants spent on the study was very limited, the visualization results were unsophisticated. Even though we can say that these methods were successful in terms of collecting user needs, they were insufficient for us to make a visual content analysis in terms of quantity. We leave the results of this study to another paper.

4.2 Data Collection

For collecting visual data, we conducted two studies, design workshop and assignment. The main reason that led us to use the assignments (student works) for data collection in this paper rather than design workshop, was that volunteered participants of design workshop had limited time to execute their ideas. This caused the workshop results to be unsophisticated and less detailed while this research interest is all about detail. This led us to change our method and try a data collection method that could have more detail in the visual data. The differences between basic design assignment and the workshops that might lead the assignments to be more successful are;

- Time: The workshop's time span was limited to 8 h, while the students had two weeks to finish their assignments.
- Discussion: After the lecture prior to the assignments, we spent enough time discussing on visualization examples so that students were able to create more original results.
- Motivation: The grading motivation in the basic design course assignment created a more limited space for the participants of the study. Students' previous studies on visual representation, ways of seeing and observation studies provided a background for the hard problem of visualizing complex information.

4.3   Analysis

Our process of analyzing the results was an iterative process and had several challenges. Through the process we realized that some of the analysis criteria did not serve our purposes related to the context and we revised the criteria. As mentioned before, we started off by borrowing design analysis criteria from related fields like cartography and information design literature. We realized that most of the results were too abstract to be evaluated as maps and all of them were hypothetical maps, in terms of the data they represent.

The first method to analyze the results, the analysis workshop was ineffective in a couple of ways. We planned the workshop in a way that participants both analyzed each work individually via analysis survey and made a group discussion at the end of survey, on each work. This caused the analysis process to be very slow. Therefore, only some selected works were analyzed through workshop. Another obstacle that we realized during the workshop was that, some of the works had metaphorical expressions like icons, while the brief told the students to use abstractions. This caused us to eliminate the works that were off brief and left us with 80 works. Among these 80 works that we will discuss, some had a more abstract language while others didn't had. So for the visual content analysis, we added an abstraction criteria, and raters rated the level of abstraction from 1 to 5. In this rating 1 is more metaphorical and using more concrete geographical elements and 5 is less metaphorical and visually most abstract. In the last analysis section where raters coded the data types that they recognize, we added another item regarding how many data types can raters recognize to understand how having more data together in one work effected other parameters.

4.4   Evaluation and Discussion

In this section, we will share our insights on event visualization. We conducted a content analysis study on spatio-temporal data visualizations created by basic design students to find out what they prefer to include on these maps, how they visualize them, patterns on what kind of visual elements are used for which information and criteria such as engaging, informative, abstract, intuitive/mediated. According to the content analysis, we reached the following results that we will present in three sections, first one is the visual representation patterns that we encountered in the works. Second one is the relationship of abstraction and other elements. Third one is about how the amount of data types effects other parameters.

Common Data Types. Here we will present two outcomes. First one is the most encountered data types from the works. (Fig. 5) 40 % of the students chose to visualize people individually (Person) when describing an event visually. 30 % visualized the movement path of people or vehicles (Path). 14 % visualized direction of moving elements (Direction). 12.5 % visualized moods or feelings (Mood). The works we wanted from students were static, so most of the works were showing a certain point in time when visualizing an event, but 10 % of the students, still visualized time in different ways. 7.5 % of the students represented people not individually, but as a whole.

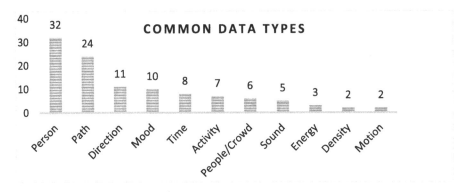

Fig. 5. Common data types that students chose to represent on their works

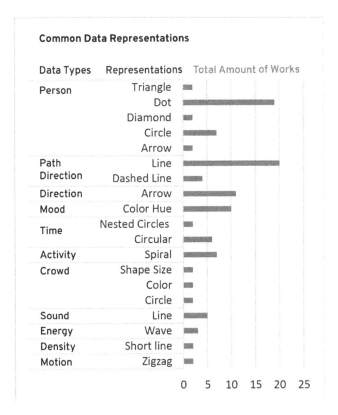

Fig. 6. Common data representation patterns on each data type

Visual Representation Patterns for Event Maps. Our second outcome is about the
visual element that were used while visualizing the data types above. (Fig. 6) 59 % of the
students who visualized people individually, used dot while others used circle, diamond,
arrow and triangle. 83 % of the student who visualized path used line including curved or

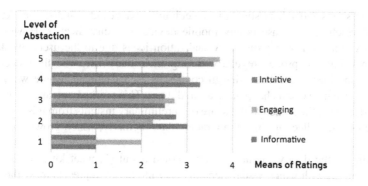

Fig. 7. Relationship between level of abstraction and intuitiveness, engaging and informative (Color figure online)

straight lines and the rest used dashed lines. Students used arrow to visualize direction, color hue to visualize feelings or mood. The students who wanted to represent a period of time, used clock-like circular shapes while others used nested circles.

Abstraction. We are interested in how the level of abstraction effected other parameters like engaging, informative and intuitiveness. To see the relationships more clearly, we compared means of four parameters which were rated from 1 to 5 (level of abstraction, informative, engaging, and intuitive) (Fig. 7). Even though we cannot say that we see a consistent correlation between abstraction and intuitiveness or abstraction and informative, but the ratings show that as the level of abstraction increases, the visual works become more engaging. This relationship might help designers in early design stages, keeping in mind that this is a case study related to visualizing events in the city and might not be applicable for every other design case.

Multi-layerability. Even though we told the students that they are free to combine as many type of data as they choose, most of them chose to have fewer data types on their work. 35 % of the students had one type of dominant visual representation. 31.25 % had two, 27.5 % had three and only 5 % of the students had four type of data representations in one work. This downside prevents us from interpreting how having more data type effect other criteria in a visualization.

5 Conclusion

Here in this paper, we share our preliminary insights from our exploratory user studies on how people visually represent event-based urban stories or situations in an intuitive way. This is a part of an ongoing study, where we are exploring novel ways of providing interactions between the things happening in a city and its dwellers. We envision bringing together different (both needed and also unexpected) urban data in a crowd-sourced event-based interactive tool. The way how these complex, unrelated, live data can come together on such a multi-layered tool while still being self-expressive, is still an open research question. With this motivation, we first conducted participatory design workshops and a diary study to collect intuitive data and visualization ideas from the users which in this case is any mobile device user city dweller. However, our preliminary studies lacked profound visualization ideas due to the users' weak motivation on using the probes regularly during their daily life. We then decided to implement the idea into a basic design course, as an assignment, where we asked to students to visualize events happening around them. This worked out, and we collected valuable data from the students. We share our preliminary insights from this study while we still continue collecting this ethnographic data regularly, which grows the data we have.

Looking at the data we collected, we learned about (1) what kinds of data users prefer to see; (2) with which visual elements they intuitively represent these data types; (3) some creative visual elements and representations to be used; (4) and some criteria (such as abstraction, intuitiveness, engagement) that teaches us about each visual element – data matching. Even though these are very valuable feedbacks for our ongoing research, we haven't yet reached significant information regarding the multi-layerability of the data types and how an interactive tool would benefit from the use of which types of visualization methods in terms of multi-layerability. While starting to work on the design of the visualization, based on the findings of this study, we will continue collecting intuitive user data to further learn how different layers can be brought together in an easy to read manner.

Acknowledgements. We would like to thank all participants at PD workshops and three important women in this project. Özge Genç for helping with the workshops; Ayşe Özer and İdil Bostan for their contributions on analysis and evaluation process.

References

1. Craig, W., Harris, T., Weiner, D. (eds.): Community participation in geographic information systems. Taylor & Francis, London (2002)
2. MacEachren, A.M., Kraak, M.J.: Research challenges in geovisualization. Cartography Geogr. Inf. Sci. **28**(1), 3–12 (2001)
3. Bertrand, K.Z., Bialik, M., Virdee, K., Gros, A., Bar-Yam, Y.: Sentiment in New York City: A high resolution spatial and temporal view (2013)
4. O'Madadhain, J., Hutchins, J., Smyth, P.: Prediction and ranking algorithms for event based network data. ACM SIGKDD Explor. Newslett. **7**(2), 23–30 (2005)
5. Bertin, J.: Semiology of Graphics: Diagrams, Networks, Maps (1983)
6. Eccles, R., Kapler, T., Harper, R., Wright, W.: Stories in geotime. Inf. Vis. **7**(1), 3–17 (2008)
7. Ferrari, L., Rosi, A., Mamei, M., Zambonelli, F.: Extracting urban patterns from location-based social networks. In: Proceedings of the 3rd ACM SIGSPATIAL International Workshop on Location-Based Social Networks, pp. 9–16. ACM (2011)
8. Tominski, C.: Event-based concepts for user-driven visualization. Inf. Vis. **10**(1), 65–81 (2011)
9. Quercia, D., Schifanella, R., Aiello, L.M. The shortest path to happiness: recommending beautiful, quiet, and happy routes in the city. In: Proceedings of the 25th ACM Conference on Hypertext and Social Media, pp. 116–125. ACM (2014)
10. Plancast. http://plancast.com/

11. Meetup. http://www.meetup.com/
12. Genç, Ö., Çay, D., Yantaç, A.E.: Participatory explorations on a location based urban information system. In: Marcus, A. (ed.) DUXU 2015. LNCS, vol. 9188, pp. 357–367. Springer, Heidelberg (2015)
13. Pinterest board. https://tr.pinterest.com/damlacay/spatio-temporal-movement-and-events-evaluation/
14. Make Maps People Want to Look at Five Primary Design Principles for Cartography by Aileen Buckley, Esri. http://www.esri.com/news/arcuser/0112/make-maps-people-want-to-look-at.html
15. Blackler, A.: Using a visually-based assignment to reinforce and assess design history knowledge and understanding. Design Big Debates: Pushing the Boundaries of Design Research, pp. 1244–1259 (2014)

Data-Intensive Analytics for Cat Bonds by Considering Supply Chain Risks

Linda Eggert[1(✉)], Yingjie Fan[2], and Stefan Voß[2]

[1] Institute for Risk and Insurance, University of Hamburg,
20146 Hamburg, Germany
linda.eggert@uni-hamburg.de
[2] Institute of Information Systems (IWI), University of Hamburg,
20146 Hamburg, Germany
{fan.yingjie,stefan.voss}@uni-hamburg.de,
http://www.uni-hamburg.de

Abstract. Catastrophe (cat) bonds are securities that transfer catastrophic risks to capital markets. From a macroscopic perspective, cat bonds provide a way to extend insurance capacities in catastrophic environments. Financial flows are the focus of most cat bond related articles. This paper will focus on information flows. The first contribution of this paper is to provide an extended cat bond structure and analyze catastrophic risk from a systematic perspective. Policyholders of catastrophe insurances are classified into different categories according to their roles in supply chains and analyzed distinguishingly. Due to uncertainties of natural catastrophes and the diversification of policyholders, data-intensive analysis is not only required for setting and calibrating cat bond policy values, but also required for providing decision support for investors and potential policyholders. The second contribution of this paper is to propose an idea of utilizing a data-intensive analysis platform to provide decision support for all participants of the cat bond structure, including investors, potential policyholders, the insurer and reinsurer. Furthermore, we identify more factors that will impact the price of a cat bond and catastrophe insurance.

Keywords: Data-intensive analytics · Cat bonds · Loss probability · Prediction · Supply chain risk

1 Introduction

The number of catastrophic events has increased during the last decades which induces a need for an extension of insurance capacity in terms of risk capital [25]. Economic losses caused by natural disasters are USD123 billion in 2015, but only 28 percent of global economic losses (USD35 billion) were covered by insurance [4]. Since the early 1990s, the market for cat bonds has grown steadily providing an additional source of risk capital to insurance and reinsurance companies. Cat bonds are alternative risk transfer instruments used to lay off natural

© Springer International Publishing Switzerland 2016
A. Marcus (Ed.): DUXU 2016, Part III, LNCS 9748, pp. 136–147, 2016.
DOI: 10.1007/978-3-319-40406-6_13

disaster risk in the capital markets and meet funding demands following natural catastrophes. Cat bonds offer regular coupons to the investor and refund of the principal at maturity unless the predefined catastrophic event occurs, leading to a full or partial loss. For insurers and reinsurers, cat bonds are hedging instruments that offer protection without the credit risk by using the principal as full collateral to cover the losses if the trigger condition is fulfilled. The complexity of the impact factors specifying the structure and terms of cat bonds and the scarcity of information and historical data about extreme events in the past results in unpredictable loss probabilities, especially for catastrophic events with low probability and high impact. Although the body of literature on cat bonds is growing continuously, it seems that there is a lack of research about how to implement data-intensive analytics to improve loss prediction and adequate risk premium calculation. Besides, data-intensive analytics should also be used for pricing cat bonds. To some extent, the sustainable growth of the cat bond market depends on cat bond pricing techniques. When there is a diversity of cat bonds in the capital market, data-intensive analytics could be used to provide decision support for investors.

In this paper we first present a comprehensive literature review of the relevant data-intensive analytics for the optimization of the cat bond policy values. We focus on how related methods revise the management of handling increasing additional information to make prediction more precise. Additionally, data-intensive analytics leads to less dependence on not sufficiently available historical data. Our purpose is to provide an idea of a data-intensive analytics platform using advanced modeling, computing, and database techniques to provide decision support for potential policyholders, investors, the insurer and reinsurer. With more precise prediction, insurability of low probability high impact risks will be enhanced. To the best of our knowledge, this is the first approach to incorporate data-intensive analytics and alternative risk transfer. This is also the first paper focusing on information flows of an extended cat bond structure. As such, the paper is a first step towards a new research direction in alternative risk transfer and related fields.

Our paper is organized as follows. Section 2 introduces a typical cat bond structure. A review of the literature on data-intensive analytics to classify and compare the methods is presented in Sect. 3. Afterwards, we provide a classification of policyholders of catastrophe risks and provide an extended structure of cat bonds. Information flows are analyzed and indicated on the extended cat bond structure. An idea of a data-intensive analytics platform is proposed to provide decision supports for all participants of the extended cat bond structure. Finally, a conclusion of our contribution and future research direction is presented.

2   Cat Bond Structure

Catastrophic risks (e.g. earthquake or flood) have extraordinary loss potential inherent and the high correlations of the losses constitute high risks for the

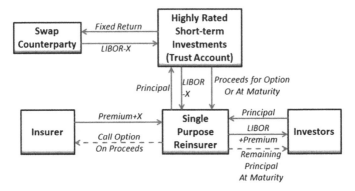

Note: X=the fee of the swap conterparty. LIBOR=London inter-bank offer rate.

Fig. 1. Financial flows for a cat bond (see Sect. 2 for detailed notation) (Source: [9])

insurer and reinsurer [6]. Up to the 1990s there was no alternative to classic reinsurance. However, the high losses from Hurricane Andrew in 1992 which exceeded many times the loss sizes caused by a natural disaster that were considered plausible up to that moment drove the developments in financial instruments for hedging catastrophic risks [25]. Covering the high layers of reinsurance protection, cat bonds offer coverage for layers that are difficult to insure. The high layers often go uninsured for two reasons. On the one hand primary insurance companies are concerned about the credit risk of the reinsurance company in the case of a catastrophic event; on the other hand high pricing spreads and reinsurance margins that are put on high layers by reinsurance companies result in high costs for the primary insurer [7]. Thus, cat bonds being fully collateralized eliminate the concerns about credit risk and offer insurance for a lower spread [8].

The covered territory is the geographic area in which catastrophes need to occur to be relevant under the bond contract and are usually defined in terms of countries, regions or states. The type of catastrophe covered by a cat bond, normally earthquakes, windstorms or multiple perils, is called the reference peril. The most common combinations of territory and peril are as follows [14]:

(a) US wind: Bonds that reference severe windstorms in the United States in particular Florida and Gulf Coast hurricane risk
(b) US Earthquake: Seismic events most focused on California
(c) Europe Wind: Cover extratropical cyclones that affect Northern and Western European countries
(d) Japan Earthquake: Due to the rifts of the tectonic plates earthquakes occur and could also lead to damage by a subsequent Tsunami

A typical cat bond structure is shown in Fig. 1 [9, 14]. The transaction starts from a single purpose reinsurer (SPR), who issues bonds to investors. The principals from the investors are put in highly rated short-term investments by the SPR. A call option, which is embedded in the cat bonds, is triggered by a predefined catastrophic event. Once the predefined catastrophic event occurs, principals are released from the SPR to help the insurer pay claims arising from the event [8]. In this case, the principal will be lost entirely or partly. If no predefined catastrophic event occurs during the term of the cat bonds, the principal is returned to the investors upon the expiration of the bonds. In return for the risk that the investors take, the insurer pays a premium to the investors. The fixed returns on the securities held in the trust are usually swapped for floating returns based on LIBOR or another widely accepted index. The reason for the swap is to immunize the insurer and the investors from interest rate risks and also default risks [9].

In [9], cat bonds have been structured to pay off on basic types of triggers:

(a) indemnity triggers, where the bond payoffs are determined by the event losses of the issuing insurer

(b) industry-index triggers, where the bond payoffs are triggered by the value of an industry loss index

(c) modeled loss triggers, the payoff is determined by simulated losses generated by inputting specific event parameters into the catastrophe model maintained by one of the catastrophe modeling firms

(d) parametric triggers, a parametric trigger pays off if the covered event exceeds a specified physical severity level

(e) hybrid triggers, which blend more than one trigger in a single bond [8]
The choice of trigger type has an important impact on the cat bond structure, e.g. indemnity trigger can induce information asymmetry.

3   Literature Review

Numerical analysis methods have been used for pricing cat bonds in [15,18, 26,32]. In [18], a model to price default-free and default-risky cat bonds with a simple form of payoff function is proposed with consideration of default risk, basis risk, and moral hazard that are associated with cat bonds. Default risk is the risk that the insurer becomes insolvent and defaults. Basis risk refers to the risk that the losses that insurers incur will not have an anticipated correlation with the underlying loss index of the cat bond. Moral hazard issues need to be taken into account because economic losses are determined by the cat bonds issuing firm when the losses incurred approach the trigger level. The moral hazard behavior occurs when the insurer's cost of loss control efforts exceeds the benefits from debt forgiveness. Cat bonds with stepwise and piecewise payoff functions are developed in [26]. An arbitrage approach is applied to cat bond pricing in [32]. From the case study about cat bonds for earthquakes sponsored by the Mexican government, cat bonds proved to be a good choice to provide coverage for a lower cost and lower exposure at default than reinsurance itself [15]. Hybrid cat bonds, combining the transfer of cat risk with protection against a stock market crash, are proposed to complete the market in [3]. According to the authors of [3], replacing simple cat bonds with hybrid cat bonds would lead to an increase in market volume.

Natural catastrophes include hurricanes, earthquakes, severe thunderstorms, floods, extratropical cyclones, wildfires, winter storms, and etc. Prediction of a catastrophe is important to reduce economic losses for local residents and companies. For instance, long-term (one year or longer) catastrophe prediction provides support for firms and insurers to hedge low-loss frequency, high-loss severity catastrophe risks. Short-term catastrophe prediction provides decision support for firms to make preparations before catastrophes, evacuate efficiently once a catastrophe happens and recover fast after the catastrophe. Economic losses of a firm after a catastrophe are relevant with catastrophe prediction accuracy. Natural disaster prediction is a typical data-intensive scientific application. Predictive modeling is at the intersection of machine learning, statistical modeling, and database technology [2]. Corresponding prediction tools or methods are developed for different kinds of catastrophes.

According to [1], hurricane prediction models should consider about temperature and wind observations near the center of the storm, as well as specific humidity observations. The record of net hurricane power dissipation, which is related with the severity of the hurricane, is found to be highly correlated with tropical sea surface temperature, including multi-decadal oscillations in the North Atlantic and North Pacific, and global warming [12]. A variety of effects premonitory to earthquakes such as crustal movements and anomalous changes in such phenomena as tilt, fluid pressure, electrical and magnetic fields, radon emission, the frequency of occurrence of small local earthquakes, and the ratio of the number of small to large shocks have been observed before various earthquakes [28]. According to [22], a large amount of seismological data is required for earthquake hazard assessment and earthquake prediction. Data mining techniques which are used for the prediction of earthquakes are reviewed in [27]. Machine learning techniques are applied in the field of forecasting frequently, such as [19,21]. In [21], the Support Vector Machine (SVM) concept which is based on statistical learning theory is explored for flood prediction. The Geospatial Stream Flow Model (GeoSFM) is applied in [11] for flood forecasting and stream flow simulation with remotely acquired data. New techniques emerge for data-intensive scientific discovery. In [20], two kinds of typhoon rainfall forecasting models, SVM-based and BPN (backpropagation network)-based models, are investigated. Compared with BPNs, which are the most frequently used conventional neural networks (NNs), SVMs have advantages on their generalization ability. In the investigation of [20], the proposed SVM-based models are more accurate, robust and efficient than existing BPN-based models. Furthermore, the proposed modeling technique is also expected to be helpful to support flood, landslide, debris flow and other disaster warning systems and should therefore be considered amongst other methods for the prediction in our case.

The increasing volume of additional information available from internal and external sources (e.g. weather forecasts, seismic monitors, and satellite data) improves the predictability of loss probabilities to set up beneficial cat bond structures. In recent years, advanced data processing methods for handling data-intensive applications have become available. These applications are usually associated with the execution of computations on large data sets or large data structures [29]. It is beyond the capability of any individual machine and requires clusters—which means that large-data problems are fundamental regarding organizing computations on dozens, hundreds, or even thousands of machines.

Since prediction of loss probabilities in catastrophic environments involves large-scale data, predictive modeling requires high performance computing platforms. Three classes of platforms are mainly used to deal with large-scale data, namely, batch processing tools, stream processing tools, and interactive analysis tools [5]. With batch processing tools, multiple jobs can be processed simultaneously. Most batch processing tools are based on the Apache Hadoop infrastructure, such as Mahout, which is an Apache project for building scalable machine learning libraries [30]. MapReduce is a programming model and an associated implementation for processing and generating large datasets that is amenable to a broad variety of real-world tasks [10]. The MapReduce programming model has been used at Google for many different purposes. Stream processing platforms are necessary for real-time analytics for stream data applications. S4 (Simple Scalable Streaming System) is a distributed stream processing engine inspired by the MapReduce Model [24]. S4 is designed for solving real-world problems in the context of search applications that use data mining and machine learning algorithms. For example, in order to provide personalized search advertising for millions of unique users, thousands of queries per second are needed to be processed in real-time. There is a clear need for highly scalable stream computing solutions, such as S4. Another application of stream processing is Twitter Storm, which is a distributed, fault-tolerant, real-time large-scale streaming data analytics platform [31]. The interactive analysis processes the data in an interactive environment, allowing users to undertake their own analysis of information [5]. For instance, Dremel is a distributed system that supports interactive analysis of very big datasets over clusters of machines [23]. Apache Drill is designed to handle up to petabytes of data spread across thousands of servers; the goal of Drill is to respond to ad-hoc queries in low-latency manner [16].

Big data analytics require innovations of both hardware and software. Future hardware innovations will continue to drive software innovation [17]. The authors of [17] propose that minimizing the time spent in moving the data from storage to the processor or between storage/compute nodes in a distributed setting will be the main focus.

4   Data Intensive Analytics

4.1   Classification of Policyholders of Catastrophe Risk

Economic losses after a catastrophe are relevant with the severity of the catastrophe and catastrophe prediction in advance. To some extent, the role of a firm on a supply chain impacts economic losses of the firm after a catastrophic event. In addition, the flexibility of the policyholder, as well as policy values of cat bonds will also impact economic losses of the policyholder in case of a catastrophe. According to the role of a firm on a supply chain, policyholders are classified

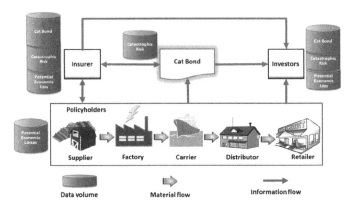

Fig. 2. Information flow for a cat bond (see Sect. 4.2 for detailed introduction)

into raw material suppliers, manufacturers, carriers, distributors, retailers, etc. (see Fig. 2)

From a farmer's perspective of view, the main concern of catastrophes comes from extreme weathers. The economic losses mainly depends on the scale of the insured farm and the severity of the catastrophe. Economic losses of a manufacturer in case of a catastrophe comes from two sides: Direct losses from rebuilding or repairing destroyed facilities; indirect losses related to business interruptions and to temporary relocation and/or rerouting of materiel. In this case, the amount of economic loss depends on the prediction and flexibility of the manufacturer, especially for indirect losses. Economic losses of a carrier company in case of a catastrophe rely on the accuracy of catastrophe prediction. For instance, with detailed and accurate weather prediction, the carrier company will be able to modify transport planning to avoid economic losses from extreme weathers. Once a distributor is attacked by a catastrophe, facilities and inventories at the distribution center may be ruined. Comparing with the manufacturer of the supply chain, the function of a distributor is more replaceable. The indirect economic losses of a retailer due to lost customers and unsatisfied demand are crucial to a whole supply chain. A fast replenishment of final products will effectively reduce negative impacts to a supply chain. Whereas the replenishment speed after a catastrophe depends on the flexibility of a supply chain.

4.2 Information Flow for an Extended Cat Bond Structure

Cat bond structures usually display the cash flows and the risk transfer. In Fig. 2, an extended cat bond structure with information flows is provided.

If all participants on the extended cat bond structure are seen as a interconnected system, the external risks is derived from potential economic losses of policyholders caused by natural catastrophes. According to the analysis in Sect. 4.1, economic losses of policyholders depend on the severity and probability of catastrophes, the prediction techniques, the role of the policyholder in a supply chain, as well as the flexibility of the supply chain. In the process of transferring catastrophic risk from policyholders to investors via capital markets, the credit and behavior of the insurer and the reinsurer influences the risks that investors take.

The price of a cat bond is influenced by a series of factors e.g.:

(a) The probability and severity of the catastrophe/catastrophes,
(b) policyholder's role in a supply chain,
(c) policyholder's response speed once the catastrophe occurs,
(d) catastrophe prediction and the accuracy of the prediction that the policyholder can receive in advance,
(e) the credit and behavior of the insurer and the reinsurer involved in the cat bond structure.

Policyholders possess all the information about their own and potential economic losses from catastrophes. However, the insurer can't get all the information, especially policyholders' commercial confidential information. However, policyholders only hold parts of the insurer's knowledge about evaluating catastrophic risk. The information asymmetry occurs in every interface of this extended cat bond structure. The insurance companies have an information advantage about the policyholders and the potential risk compared with the investors due to their business model.

As the final undertaker of risks, investors have the least information about catastrophes and policyholders.

Due to information asymmetry among policyholders, the insurer, the reinsurer and investors, the price for cat bonds may not reflect the real value of the risk. Without a proper price for cat bonds, basis risk and moral hazard cannot be reduced. Basis risk might reduce the hedging effect of cat bonds and increase the default probability of the issuing firm [18]. Enhancing the information flow with more appropriate methods can lead to less information asymmetry and therefore to a better pricing and more efficient risk sharing [13].

4.3   Data-Intensive Analytics for Cat Bonds

Due to all participants in Fig. 2 take catastrophe prediction into account, data-intensive analytics is required by all participants.

For a company in a environment with possible catastrophic disruptions, data-intensive analytics is required to provide the company with strategic decision support. Strategies, such as purchasing catastrophe insurance and/or keeping a high flexibility of the company, can be chosen to reduce economic losses once a catastrophe occurs. Factors, including the moment of occurrence and the severity of the catastrophe, should be taken into account by the company. However, from our literature review, these factor cannot be predicted accurately and precisely yet. The best information that people can obtain from the current catastrophe prediction techniques is the probability distribution for the severity and occurrence moment of a catastrophe. In this case, stochastic programming will help to make a beneficial decision for the company. Stochastic programming has been applied in a broad range of areas from finance to production and transportation planning. In order to get a high quality solution for a stochastic programming problem, high performance computing platform (HPC) is required.

For an insurer, before making decision on transferring catastrophic risk to the capital market, data-intensive analytics is also required. Two crucial questions are needed to be clear for the insurer: (1) based on all risk that the insurer holds, which catastrophic risk should be transferred to the capital market through cat bonds, and (2) how much the insurer would like to pay for transferring the risk. In order to answer these questions, the following information is needed: the most precise and accurate prediction of all catastrophes that the insurer hold, each related policyholder's economic loss once the corresponding catastrophe occurs, the inter-dependency of risks that the insurer holds. Here comes with another stochastic programming problem due to the lack of accurate and precise catastrophe prediction techniques.

For a reinsurer, constructing the cat bond structure and pricing cat bonds also requires data-intensive analytics. Because the prediction information about the related catastrophe and the possible economic losses of the policyholder are needed to be taken into account in designing the cat bond structure.

For a investor, before the decision of investing in a specific cat bond, the investor should check the dependencies between the risk behind the cat bond and the risk of the investor's own as well as the risks of capital products that the investor has already held. Cat bonds should be used to provide investment diversification and balance catastrophe risks, but it should not act as an evil that aggravates the tragedy. To avoid double tragedies from purchasing the wrong cat bonds, data-intensive analytics is necessary for investors.

Based on analysis above, catastrophe prediction information is required for all participants, an innovative idea is to design a data-intensive analytics platform, which can make use of catastrophe prediction information as well as analytic tools for all users(Fig. 3). The idea of the data-intensive analytics platform is to provide a common application to users for catastrophe related decision support. The database of catastrophe prediction is provided by professional catastrophe prediction organizations, which can be a government department or a third party data analytic company. The database of catastrophe prediction should always incorporate with the latest information.

Users will get decision supports by providing required parameters to the platform. For instance, a company gets to know whether they should buy a catastrophe insurance or not by providing its location, its supply chain partners (for calculating indirect economic losses) and costs parameters. According to the location, the prediction of catastrophes in this area will be selected from the catastrophe prediction database. With the information of costs and supply chain partners, economic losses in case of a catastrophe will be calculated. By further incorporating the probability and severity of possible catastrophes, a better strategy will be selected for the company. A insurer will obtain decision supports on which catastrophe risk should be transferred to the capital market as the insurer may hold diversity of catastrophe risks from policyholders. A reinsurer can get a suggestion on cat bond price based on the evaluation of catastrophe risk of the policyholder. The data-intensive analytics platform will help a investor to make the right decision on which cat bond is better for the investor to obtain investment diversification.

Based on this idea, the latest catastrophe prediction information will be saved in a database which provides valuable real-time and historical information to all users. On the one hand, by using a common database, single users don't need to save copies which will save a big amount of data storage space. On the other hand, with real-time renewing catastrophe prediction information, it will help to reduce economic losses for the platform users in case of a catastrophe. Besides, due to the insurer and reinsurer have their own advanced data analytic techniques, once they get the latest prediction or real-time warning about catastrophes, they should immediately inform relevant policyholders. With the latest more precise and accurate catastrophe prediction, policyholders will be able to reduce economic losses effectively once a catastrophe occurs.

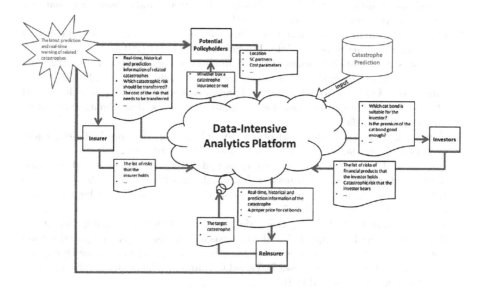

Fig. 3. Data-intensive analytics structure (see Sect. 4.3 for detailed introduction)

5   Conclusion

Cat bonds are attractive to investors for diversification purposes. Catastrophe insurance has a wide future market. The insurer and reinsurer are able to meet both policyholders and investors' demand through issuing cat bonds and pricing them at the proper levels. Unlike existing articles about cat bonds and catastrophe insurance, this paper provides an extended structure of cat bonds and analyzes risk from a systematic perspective. Based on the situation that catastrophe prediction information and data-intensive analytics are required by policyholders, investors, the insurer and reinsurer, an idea of a common Data-Intensive Analytic Platform is proposed in our paper. The extended cat bond structure and the Data-Intensive Analytic Platform are two main contributions of this paper. A further contribution is that we identify more factors which will impact pricing cat bonds and catastrophe insurance. Further research should focus on how to realize such a common data-intensive analytic platform.

References

1. Anthes, R.A.: Data assimilation and initialization of hurricane prediction models. J. Atmos. Sci. **31**(3), 702–719 (1974)
2. Apte, C., Hong, S.J., Natarajan, R., Pednault, E.P., Tipu, F., Weiss, S.M.: Data-intensive analytics for predictive modeling. IBM J. Res. Dev. **47**(1), 17–23 (2003)
3. Barrieu, P., Loubergé, H.: Hybrid cat bonds. J. Risk Insur. **76**(3), 547–578 (2009)
4. Benfield, A.: Annual global climate and catastrophe report (2015). http://thoughtleadership.aonbenfield.com/Documents/20160113-ab-if-annual-climate-catastrophe-report.pdf. Accessed 19 Feb 2016
5. Chen, C.P., Zhang, C.Y.: Data-intensive applications, challenges, techniques and technologies: a survey on big data. Inf. Sci. **275**, 314–347 (2014)
6. Cummins, J.D.: Convergence in wholesale financial services: reinsurance and investment banking. Geneva Pap. Risk Insur. Issues Pract. **30**(2), 187–222 (2005)
7. Cummins, J.D.: Reinsurance for natural and man-made catastrophes in the United States: current state of the market and regulatory reforms. Risk Manag. Insur. Rev. **10**(2), 179–220 (2007)
8. Cummins, J.D.: Cat bonds and other risk-linked securities: product design and evolution of the market. The Geneva Reports, pp. 39–61 (2012)
9. Cummins, J.D., Weiss, M.A.: Convergence of insurance and financial markets: hybrid and securitized risk-transfer solutions. J. Risk Insur. **76**(3), 493–545 (2009)
10. Dean, J., Ghemawat, S.: Mapreduce: simplified data processing on large clusters. Commun. ACM **51**(1), 107–113 (2008)
11. Dessu, S.B., Seid, A.H., Abiy, A.Z., Melesse, A.M.: Flood forecasting and stream flow simulation of the upper Awash river basin, Ethiopia using geospatial stream flow model (GeoSFM). In: Melesse, A.M., Abtew, W. (eds.) Landscape Dynamics, Soils and Hydrological Processes in Varied Climates. Springer Geography, pp. 367–384. Springer, Switzerland (2016)
12. Emanuel, K.: Increasing destructiveness of tropical cyclones over the past 30 years. Nature **436**(7051), 686–688 (2005)
13. Finken, S., Laux, C.: Catastrophe bonds and reinsurance: the competitive effect of information-insensitive triggers. J. Risk Insur. **76**(3), 579–605 (2009)
14. Frey, A., Kirova, M., Schmidt, C.: The role of indices in transferring insurance risks to the capital markets. Sigma **4**, 2009 (2009)
15. Härdle, W.K., Cabrera, B.L.: Calibrating cat bonds for Mexican earthquakes. J. Risk Insur. **77**(3), 625–650 (2010)
16. Hausenblas, M., Nadeau, J.: Apache drill: interactive ad-hoc analysis at scale. Big Data **1**(2), 100–104 (2013)
17. Kambatla, K., Kollias, G., Kumar, V., Grama, A.: Trends in big data analytics. J. Parallel Distrib. Comput. **74**(7), 2561–2573 (2014)

18. Lee, J.P., Yu, M.T.: Pricing default-risky cat bonds with moral hazard and basis risk. J. Risk Insur. **69**(1), 25–44 (2002)
19. Lessmann, S., Voß, S.: A reference model for customer-centric data mining with support vector machines. Eur. J. Oper. Res. **199**(2), 520–530 (2009)
20. Lin, G.F., Chen, G.R., Wu, M.C., Chou, Y.C.: Effective forecasting of hourly typhoon rainfall using support vector machines. Water Resour. Res. **45**(8), 1–11 (2009)
21. Liong, S.Y., Sivapragasam, C.: Flood stage forecasting with support vector machines. J. Am. Water Resour. Assoc. **38**(1), 173–186 (2002)
22. Liu, D., Wang, J., Wang, Y.: Application of catastrophe theory in earthquake hazard assessment and earthquake prediction research. Tectonophysics **167**(2–4), 179–186 (1989)
23. Melnik, S., Gubarev, A., Long, J.J., Romer, G., Shivakumar, S., Tolton, M., Vassilakis, T.: Dremel: interactive analysis of web-scale datasets. Proc. VLDB Endowment **3**(1–2), 330–339 (2010)
24. Neumeyer, L., Robbins, B., Nair, A., Kesari, A.: S4: distributed stream computing platform. In: 2010 IEEE International Conference Data Mining Workshops (ICDMW), pp. 170–177. IEEE (2010)
25. Nguyen, T., Lindenmeier, J.: Catastrophe risks, cat bonds and innovation resistance. Qual. Res. Financ. Markets **6**(1), 75–92 (2014)
26. Nowak, P., Romaniuk, M.: Pricing and simulations of catastrophe bonds. Insur. Math. Econ. **52**(1), 18–28 (2013)
27. Otari, G., Kulkarni, R.: A review of application of data mining in earthquake prediction. Int. J. Comput. Sci. Inf. Technol. **3**(2), 3570–3574 (2012)
28. Scholz, C.H., Sykes, L.R., Aggarwal, Y.P.: Earthquake prediction: a physical basis. Science **181**(4102), 803–810 (1973)
29. Słota, R., Król, D., Skałkowski, K., Kryza, B., Nikołow, D., Orzechowski, M., Kitowski, J.: A toolkit for storage QoS provisioning for data-intensive applications. In: Bubak, M., Szepieniec, T., Wiatr, K. (eds.) PL-Grid 2011. LNCS, vol. 7136, pp. 157–170. Springer, Heidelberg (2012)
30. Taylor, R.C.: An overview of the Hadoop/MapReduce/HBase framework and its current applications in bioinformatics. BMC Bioinform. **11**(Suppl. 12), S1 (2010)
31. Toshniwal, A., Taneja, S., Shukla, A., Ramasamy, K., Patel, J.M., Kulkarni, S., Jackson, J., Gade, K., Fu, M., Donham, J., et al.: Storm@Twitter. In: Proceedings of the 2014 ACM SIGMOD International Conference on Management of Data, pp. 147–156. ACM (2014)
32. Vaugirard, V.E.: Pricing catastrophe bonds by an arbitrage approach. Q. Rev. Econ. Finan. **43**(1), 119–132 (2003)

A Framework to Evaluate User Empowerment in Decision-Making Experiences with Participatory GIS

Elizabeth Sucupira Furtado[1], Lara Furtado[2(✉)], and Vasco Furtado[1]

[1] University of Fortaleza (Unifor), Fortaleza, CE, Brazil
elizabet@unifor.br, vasco@gmail.com
[2] University of Massachusetts Amherst, Amherst, MA, USA
larasfur@gmail.com

Abstract. This paper describes a framework to guide designers on how to investigate UX empowerment by using PGIS to support the decision making process. Investigative questions are proposed and aligned with UX elements in order to facilitate the access to information and its discussion within a community, as well as empower users (decision makers) to act not just as consumers of information and systems, but also as creators of new knowledge. The goal was to guarantee an appropriate gathering and observation of the questions in order to evaluate how particular users tasks can be accomplished in a PGIS while complying with requisites that promote empowerment.

Keywords: User experience · UX · Interdisciplinary · Empowering · PGIS

1 Introduction

When developing a software, it may be competitively advantageous to attract early-adopters [1] and maintain them as returning users by providing a pleasant user experience with the software. A common practice among developers is primarily to share the basic features and tools of a software and provide additional more advanced resources as the user interacts with it. This method is justified by user's behavior studies, which reveal that the user's empowerment capacity increases as he acquires technological skills and does not depend on him being an expert.

In this paper, we examine users' empowerment based on the User eXperiences (UX) while making use of a Participatory Geographic Information System (PGIS). GIS provides vast commands, which allow the user to manipulate large volumes of information through "systems for positioning, data acquisition, data dissemination, and analysis" [2]. It also enables graphical display of complex spatial information, deemed beneficial in decision-making processes [3]. Scenarios of local decision-making can be the following: land use/resource development negotiations, choices of feasible alternatives for environmental management, changes in traffic regulations etc. The increasing demand for the involvement of stakeholders that represent diverse areas of competence in order to reach more comprehensive decisions has been supported by PGIS [4]. This demand extends the use of the tool to non-experts from the initial stages

A. Marcus (Ed.): DUXU 2016, Part III, LNCS 9748, pp. 148–158, 2016.
DOI: 10.1007/978-3-319-40406-6_14

of group decision-making in order to empower users by incorporating local-level processes and knowledge [5–7].

Advanced interactive solutions are increasingly identified in GIS (Multimodality [8, 9] and Multiple viewing screens [10]) to provide resources (e.g. pre-determined database of elements, filters) that improve the usability and utility of GIS. Such tools are valuable since GIS is often reported as difficult to maneuver and as an exclusionary technology. The evaluation of users' empowerment levels should not be limited to usability requisites, but also regarding the user's perception of individual empowerment[1] in his UX [11].

Some works explore the users' empowerment in their experiences with GIS for group decision-making. In [4], the feature that is related to user empowerment refers to the laws and regulations that interest the participating groups. Corbett and Keller [5] combine four catalysts of empowerment (information, process, skills, and tools) with two social scales (individuals and community). This combination allows to identify which aspects of change in the condition of an individual or community have an influence on their empowerment. In this paper, the empowerment notion is referred to as the "empowerment capacity" of users, which originates from their interactions, whether they be with the PGIS and/or socially with the community from the study area. This capacity is evaluated based on some UX elements (e.g. the user's role, his acquired technological skill, his successful actions, his shared opinions, and so on), which are collected throughout a group decision-making process.

This paper aims at investigating the existing PGIS solutions that address the following question: Is the geographic information technology ready to empower people without overwhelming/excluding a non-expert user during such process? To answer this question, we analyzed some works that present GIS interaction aspects, collected social and design recommendations from other related disciplines and grouped them to a new framework with UX elements. Subsequently, we elaborated some investigative questions to guide designers when elaborating these types of systems.

The results of those studies reveal that the purpose of promoting a non-expert user's empowerment in the decision-making process before, during and after their UX with GIS is a subject not yet sufficiently explored. We expect this framework to be useful for designers, as it presents requisites for a process that empowers the UX, and indicators that evaluate the non-users ability to manipulate and generate information in GIS.

This article initiates with a short review of the literature on GIS and its fundamental aspects. Then, it presents a survey of the participatory making decision theory in order to identify the key elements needed to elaborate our proposal. Finally, it provides an approach to illustrate the application of such elements.

2 Background in GIS and Problematic in UX with GIS

The main goal of this paper was to investigate how the interaction design of a GIS favors the user's perception of their level of empowerment. Specifically, we have sought to evaluate which items impact the UX of the system analyzed. Some comments regarding those items are reported as we present the works studied.

---

[1] Individual empowerment is a perceived feeling of greater competence or power [12].

It is worth noting that UX and Usability are not the same concept, even though the former encompasses the latter. The Usability Framework focuses on the interaction factors, and is still clearly task-oriented, which turns out to be a restriction in terms of human factors. The UX is defined by the ISO standard 9241:210 [13] as a "person's perceptions and responses resulting from the use and/or anticipated use of a product, system or service." It includes all the users' emotions, preferences, motivations, and accomplishments that occur before, during and after usage [11]. Of the items investigated in this research, the initial four are closely related to GIS usability while the last focuses on emotional aspects related to the UX. They consist of: (i) Graphic resources to explore information (such as Filters, Dashboards); (ii) The method by which the resources are visually available (e.g. Multiple viewing screens, Multimodality); (iii) Tools that enable the generation of new data and/or information (e.g. templates, Knowledge Discovery tools); (iv) Tools that support decision making (e.g. Integration with Collaborative Social Systems (SS) and Decision Support Systems (DSS)) and; (v) Support for users with different skill and technical levels to engage with UX (e.g. practical examples, perceptions, explanations).

Several PGIS requisites for HCI are reported in a multidisciplinary literature as being useful to support user empowerment. [14] Provides a practical example of how a DSS was used to help stakeholders make better informed decisions regarding housing funding policies, and adjusting housing to a consumer profile by incorporating GIS to facilitate dialogue and produce information. Other sources report on requisites that aid the user in various GIS tasks. In the fields of Artificial Intelligence and Cognitive Science, GIS tools are knowledge based due to their capacity to capture decision-makers' knowledge and perform automated predictive processes (i.e. Cellular Automata [15]; Fuzzy Concepts [16]; Expert and Knowledge Based Systems [17, 18]). In the fields of HCI and GIS, the requisites evolve around the tool's capacity to sort through non-deterministic criteria and its usability (i.e. providing user-friendly resources such as Virtual Reality [19] and Multimodality [8, 9]). In HCI and Digital Graphics, tools also seek to facilitate the display of information (i.e. Multiple viewing screens [10] and Mobile 3D architecture [20]).

Even though such examples illustrate the potential of GIS interface to support a variety of disciplines, [4] point out that its effective use still requires a considerable knowledge and is compromised by the "multiple realities" that the technology tries to depict. The poorly integrated and exhaustive amount of operations available makes GIS a complex interface and difficult for non-specialists to navigate outside of a technical setting [21]. Therefore, design recommendations related to the investigated items may assist users to filter the vast expanse of information and maximize the chances that any information they come across is valuable [4].

The simple combination of interdisciplinary requisites and recommendations in one tool is not sufficient to guarantee users empowerment from their experiences with GIS. In order to do so, HCI designers must first understand which elements can enhance the UX, in order to define requisites that allow the stakeholders to effectively manipulate information (interacting with community through GIS, SS, directly face-to-face) and achieve status equal to experts'. In [22], the authors define empowerment as providing users with tools to use and transform information according to their needs. One example of such tool is Approach End-User Programming, which allows users to build new functions in a system from existing resources to CATER to new demands [23]. In Co-design approach, empowerment is reported as when the user becomes the co-author of a system interaction [24].

None of the studies examined have presented a framework for HCI designers to reflect on the necessary resources (personal, informational, technical) to empower users in their UX while using GIS. This shift in power dynamic is enabled by the knowledge obtained from the user interaction with the system, from her/his relations with the context in study to obtain and generate information and her/his participation in collaborative decision processes.

3 Participatory Decision Making with GIS

According to [4], Participatory GIS have all of the capabilities of GIS, with additional features that support group decisions. This section describes three elements that were considered for the proposed framework as they impact the users' empowerment from UX with PGIS: People, Information and Decision-making Process.

3.1 The Profile of the User

When individuals need to make decisions influenced by geography, they take into account the realities of a specific geography. Decisions can be made ad hoc, based on a formal analysis, and/or with the collaboration of others who live in and/or know of the local reality. Independent of how a problem is solved, technology may increase the Decision Makers' (DM) abilities to formulate, frame or assess decision situations. Spatial decision making problems commonly involve three categories of DM stakeholders [4]: a specialist in the subject domain, who usually does not use GIS (known as DM), a technical specialist, who has experience in interaction with GIS (e.g. he is able to elaborate complex queries, to use commands) and a non-specialist user, who uses just macros elaborated by a technical user, for instance. In this text, we will call any of them as user.

3.2 Accessing and Sharing of Information - A Perspective of User Empowerment from HCI

During GIS usage, different scenarios of access to information and communication take place via interfaces, which are investigated in the field of HCI. Information refers to the object that is discussed such as features of the environment, communities' and individuals' needs, objectives by which to measure the successful resolution of an issue, impacts of alternatives and the selection of a preferred alternative option, etc. In such systems, the sharing of relevant information is important to consolidate a community. As the user notices his increased knowledge of certain object, it consequently influences his personal perception of empowerment.

To make better-informed decisions and reduce the complexity of the problem, users must take some actions *before* starting these scenarios. Some actions may include the following: to treat the information to be discussed from the understanding of initial assumptions; to motivate specialists in the subject domain in order to also engage in experiences with GIS; to provide individuals or communities that need to understand geographic information with technological means to access resources (such as internet, open source software, databases); and to promote the accessibility and digital inclusion for individual who is not capable of reading, interpreting data, understanding a map, etc.

Users' actions must also take place *after* use scenarios, in order to evaluate the accuracy of a decision achieved according to users' preferences, regarding how effective and equitable it is. Some actions may include the following: at the end of a session of GIS use, but constantly during a decision process, users must apply strategies in order to raise individual participatory behavior; to measure the perception of personal knowledge building; to communicate widely in the community the results of final decision (as of a voting process); etc.

The HCI researcher can become more sensitive to different issues and solutions by understanding how the user accesses information, makes decisions, communicates, and establishes priorities. The view advocated in this article requires solutions that go beyond the choice of graphics, sounds, gestures, etc. as it considers new factors to measure an increase in user empowerment such as [22]:

- Their role in their community, which becomes more prominent as they transmit knowledge to others;
- Their UX with the technology; which can be measured according to their individual perception of knowledge as they use basic and advanced GIS resources and generate new information, (such as if it is "desirable", "useful", "attractive design" and "valuable") [11];
- Their ability to communicate; which increases as they use new solutions (devices, artifacts, modalities) to express their opinions and feelings in order to achieve a decision. Users' participation usually leads them to engage more in UX.

3.3   Process of Spatial Decision Situations

In Spatial Decision Situations (SDS), one user or a group of users composed of various stakeholders should communicate, identify, explore and solve problems through human–computer dialogue [25]. We define SDS as problems related to the knowledge available, which is usually collected from databases (using data mining algorithms, for instance), but also directly from people (through personal posts, answers to question-naires, etc.).

This paper presents three stages of the decision-making process, defined by [26], to illustrate the relation of DSS and PGIS. Regarding PGIS, they consist of:

- An Intelligence stage, in which users establish the technologic-socio-economic values, objectives and decision criteria for a determined geography;
- A Design stage, in which users generate a set of feasible solutions about the subject domain; and
- A Choice stage, in which users research and evaluate the option set(s) then select and communicate the final solution.

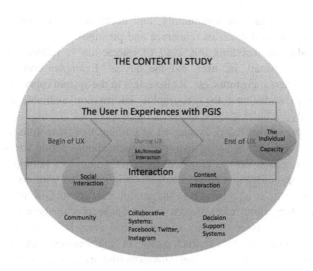

Fig. 1. UXP Framework

4 Proposed Framework

4.1 Characteristics for Empowerment of a UX Through GIS

The framework proposed in this paper is called UXP, which is focused on the design of UX with PGIS to attain individual empowerment. The UXP is formed by characteristics to evaluate user empowerment before, during and after a UX with PGIS (Fig. 1). The initial characteristics (user capacity building and interaction, including social interaction), have an impact on UX hedonic aspects which are related to social-emotional behavior [27] and the latter characteristics (Multimodal, Social Interaction and Content Interaction) are related to the system's pragmatic aspects.

In further detail, the characteristics consist of:

- **Building user capacity;** they refer to the measure (quantitative) or specification (qualitative) of individual knowledge and of the user's perception of individual empowerment resulting from UX. The individual knowledge variable can be measured considering the following variables: the user's perception of his knowledge increasing and his technological skill [11]. The user's perception of individual empowerment variable can be measured considering his role in the community, among other variables;
- **Interaction:** refers to the importance of design to generate, decide and communicate options to achieve collaborative decisions. The occurrence of the interaction is defined by the presence and attributes of the GIS itself (its usability, aesthetics, interoperability with other systems, etc.):
  - **Content Interaction:** refers to the value of GIS information, which may originate from several sources. In interacting with GIS, users absorb, create and modify content (which is when they take ownership of information and engage in experiences). When such interaction takes place without GIS, the information

may originate from the community, and depends on the users role within a context to access it (such as relevance and prestige).

– **Multimodal Interaction:** this kind of interaction is related to the physical interaction between the user and the device. Examples consist of touching interface patterns, gestures, etc. It also refers to the system capacity necessary for the user to understand the geographic information available and explore it accordingly;

– **Social Interaction:** refers to support to participation, therefore, user's motivation should be a matter of concern. Designers should define social and content interactions based on the knowledge of what motivates people towards community engagement, and consequently their interactions within such community [11]. This stage is also related to the interoperability of GIS and SS;

• **Context of Interaction:** refers to socio-cultural aspects of the community as well as its information and usage of other social networks and DSS. In HCI studies [13], this variable refers to the characteristics of the environment (Office, Home, Out-of-doors, etc.) and/or ongoing situation (the experience occurring in quiet place, or in a stressful, etc.).

4.2   Investigative Questions of Empowerment

This paper presents a non-preemptive list of questions, which are associated to each framework characteristic. This list originated from our research investigations involving UX in decision-making supported by PGIS, GIS interactive aspects, uses behavior, and users' empowerment capacity [22].

User Capacity Building

• Who is this individual?
• Does the user consider that an increase in knowledge when using the system results in his personal empowerment perception?
• Which factors affect the user's perception of personal empowerment?
• Does users' face-to-face interaction with the community affects such perception of personal empowerment?
• Does the generation of new information, which is based on queries set by the user, consist of an index of increasing personal knowledge and/or empowerment?
• Does the user think that a decision-maker can be independent from an expert?

Content Interaction

• How is information important for the individual? And for the community?
• Who/what is the holder of the information valuable for the community?
• Who/what is the holder of the information about the community?
• Which information and information technology does/don't the community have access?
• How is information assimilated, transmitted and stored in the community?

- How could new technology information be adapted, transformed and used to empower the group?
- How do users appropriate of information?
- How does a subject exchange information with his group and others and what is his role in the process?
- How difficult is it to generate content with GIS information?

Context and Social Interaction

- Who holds the power within a community?
- How does this individual exchange information with her/his group? With other groups?
- How does society interact with this group?
- How organized is the social structure of the community?
- Does access to information poses a threat to one's power?
- Has the group established any rapport or connection with other groups (teachers, researchers, technicians, etc.)?
- Does the group have any rejection or fear of other groups (politics, bureaucrats, etc.)?
- Does any group (terrorists, drug dealers, public authorities, rival tribes, etc.) exert any kind of violence or oppressive power over the community?
- How does the user collect and organize information in partnership with the community to establish queries and take actions in GIS?
- Is the information broadly shared and communicated?
- How does a non-expert user feel while taking part in a group decision-making process?
- When is it possible to state that a decision has been achieved through community consensus?

Multimodal Interaction

- Is this individual full with her/his basic needs?
- How oppressive is the technology for the group?
- How accessible, usable and valuable is the technology for the users?
- How difficult is it for users to understand maps, context, direction and reference points?
- How difficult is it to make use of basic and/or advanced resources in different scenarios while using GIS?

5 Application of the Framework

This paper described an empirical approach to illustrate how designers can apply the questions proposed in the design process of a PGIS. We considered the stages presented in Sect. 3.3 as a part of the integration between the DSS and the GIS being designed, and the social interactions that take place within the system.

Initially, the designer must identify the users' tasks in order to solve group problems accordingly. For instance, on a certain scenario, the user can specify objectives and decision criteria for a determined geography during the intelligence phase; select which of those are feasible during the decision phase; and communicate the final decision in the choice phase [26]. Subsequently, the designer must define UX requirements and information necessary before, during and after the experience with PGIS. Examples of UX requirements consist of: i) a DM stakeholder must be capable of using PGIS (before UX); ii) the user must be able to elaborate as many feasible options as possible from GIS information (during UX); and iii) the user must be able to verify if the final choices are in accordance with the values, objectives and criteria desired by the group (end of UX). One example of information requirement to support the intelligence stage is when information comes from multiple sources: some from the end user (from social and face-to-face interaction) and others from the system (based on knowledge).

However, before defining UX requirements, the designer should analyze the user's behavior and the study context to understand whether it is viable to implement a system with such requisites. In order to do so, the designer should use the list of questions related to UXP characteristics. For instance, the definition of the user profile and context can be based on questions 4.1.1 and 4.1.2. A questionnaire can be given to DM stakeholders and results may validate potential requisites and the appropriate context to use a system in order to empower the UX. During validation, new requisites may arise, such as usability and social requisites, which may be more successfully investigated with questions presented in items 4.1.4 e 4.1.3, respectively. We provide an example of the application of the framework to validate a PGIS system that is defined with MD stakeholders (users).

When the system is being continuously used, the analysis of empowerment involves exploring how these different aspects influence the individual's perception of empowerment considering that they are (or have been) in collaborative decision scenarios. For example, the UX requirement regarding the choice phase, that was previously mentioned, can be evaluated by analyzing the empowerment aspect *User capacity building*.

This analysis can be made based on a user's social interaction within PGIS, his perception of empowerment and from answers obtained with DM stakeholders from an investigative question, such as *When is a decision achieved via community consensus*. Results may present evidence that will allow the designer to verify whether the user feels confident that the final choices he identified are in accordance with the desired preferences agreed on by the majority of stakeholders.

6   Conclusion

This works established a framework to structure an UX evaluation of personal perception of empowerment. In the example provided of its application, we showed an approach to define and validate requisites of a PGIS that support group decision-making in order to the understand user's perception of individual empowerment. In the approach, designers can use UX aspects (divided in pragmatic and emotional aspects) aligned with stages involved in decision-making regarding GIS. At the intersection of those two dimensions, the framework presents multidisciplinary investigative questions regarding user's behavior, information and interaction with GIS tools and the community in study.

Future work will consist of an empirical analysis of UX when using such PGIS to test whether the UXP characteristics related to social values of the proposed framework change based on which communities are involved in decision-making situations.

References

1. Norman, D.A.: The Invisible Computer: Why Good Products can Fail, the Personal Computer is so Complex, and Information Appliances are the Solution. The MIT Press, Cambridge (1999)
2. Goodchild, M.: Geographic information systems and science: today and tomorrow. Ann. GIS **15**, 1 (2009)
3. Crossland, M.D., Wynne, B.E., Perkins, W.C.: Spatial decision support systems: An overview of technology and a test of efficacy. Decis. Support Syst. **14**(3), 219–235 (1995)
4. Jankowski, P., Nyerges, T.: GIS for Group Decision Making, p. 296. CRC Press, Boca Raton (2001)
5. Corbett, J.M., Keller, C.P.: An analytical framework to examine empowerment associated with PGIS. Cartographica: Int. J. Geogr. Inf. Geovisualization (2005)
6. Craig, W.J., Harris, T.M., Weiner, D. (eds.): Community Participation and Geographic Information Systems. Taylor & Francis, London (2002)
7. McCall, M.: Seeking good governance in participatory-GIS: a review of processes and governance dimensions in applying GIS to participatory spatial planning. Habitat Int. **27**(4), 549–573 (2003)
8. MacEachren, A.M., et al.: Enabling collaborative geoinformation access and decision-making through a natural, multimodal interface. IJGIS **19**, 3 (2005)
9. Jeong, W., Gluck, M.: Multimodal geographic information systems: Adding haptic and auditory display. J. Am. Soc. Inform. Sci. Technol. **54**(3), 229–242 (2003)
10. Butkiewicz, T., et al.: Multi-focused geospatial analysis using probes. IEEE Trans. Visual Comput. Graph. **14**, 1165–1172 (2008)
11. Carvalho, R., Furtado, E., Furtado, V.: Does content categorization lead to knowledge building? An experiment in a social bookmarking service. In: Computing for Human Learning, Behaviour and Collaboration. 51, Part B, pp. 1177–1184, October 2015
12. Dubois, B., Miley, K.: Social Work: An Empowering Profession. Allyn Et Bacon, Boston (1992)
13. ISO 9241-210:2010(E). Geneve: International Standardization Organization (2010)
14. Natividade-Jesus, E., et al.: A multicriteria decision support system for housing evaluation. Decis. Support Syst. **43**, 338–349 (2007)
15. Wu, F.: SimLand: a prototype to simulate land conversion through the integrated GIS and CA with AHP-derived transition rules. IJGIS. **12**, 1 (1998)
16. Benedikt, J., Reinberg, S., Riedl, L.: A GIS application to enhance cell-based information modeling. Inf. Sci. **142**, 1–4 (2002)
17. Sikder, I.: Knowledge-based spatial decision support systems: An assessment of environmental adaptability of crops. Expert Syst. Appl. **36**, 3 (2009)

18. Tang, C., Xu, L., Feng, S.: An agent-based geographical information system. Knowl.-Based Syst. **14**, 5–6 (2001)
19. Huang, B., Jiang, B., Li, H.: An integration of GIS, virtual reality and the Internet for visualization, analysis and exploration of spatial data. IJGIS **15**, 5 (2001)
20. Noguera, J., et al.: A mobile 3D-GIS hybrid recommender system for tourism. Inf. Sci. **215**, 37–52 (2012)
21. Goodchild, M.: Spatial thinking and the GIS User interface. Procedia – Soc. Behav. Sci. **21**, 3–9 (2011)
22. Chagas, D.A., Maia, C.L.B., Furtado, E., de Carvalho, C.R.: Prospecting HCI challenges for extreme poverty communities: redefining and optimizing user experiences with technology. In: Kurosu, M. (ed.) Human-Computer Interaction. LNCS, vol. 9171, pp. 281–290. Springer, Heidelberg (2015)
23. Lieberman, H., et al.: End-User Development: An Emerging Paradigm. Human-Computer Interaction Series, vol. 9, Chap. 1, pp. 1–7. Springer Netherlands (2006)
24. Baranauskas, C.: Codesign de Redes Digitais. Ed. Penso (2013)
25. Turban, E.: Decision Support and Expert Systems. Macmillan, New York (1993)
26. Simon, H.A.: The New Science of Management Decision. Harper and Row, Prentice Hall (1960)
27. Roto, V., Väänänen-Vainio-Mattila, K., Law, E., Vermeeren, A.: User experience evaluation methods in product development. In: Workshop in INTERACT 2009 (2009)

Robust Design: An Image Analysis Tool for Analyzing Information Loss Caused by Viewers and Environments

Sung Soo Hwang[✉]

School of Computer Science and Electronic Engineering,
Handong Global University, Pohang, Republic of Korea
sshwang@handong.edu

Abstract. For the efficient expression of information, graphic designers utilize colors or various combinations of colors. Unfortunately, the information expressed by colors may be lost depending on the characteristics of viewers and environment. This paper presents an image analysis algorithm which informs designers of these information losses and helps them to produce graphic designs that are robust to various situations. The proposed method first generates the simulated model of the design and applies the equivalent segmentation algorithm to the original design and the simulated model. As a result of segmentation, each image is partitioned into several groups. And by measuring the ratio between the number of groups in the original design and that in the simulated model, the information loss can be estimated. With the proposed algorithm, designers can easily perceive that the use of certain colors or combination of colors should be avoided to minimize the information loss.

Keywords: Universal design · Information loss measurement · Image segmentation

1 Introduction

For the efficient expression of information, graphic designers utilize colors or various combinations of colors. Utilizing colors is a reasonable choice, because for general users in general environment, it gives a large amount of information and insight. Unfortunately, the information expressed by colors may be lost depending on the characteristics of viewers and environment. This can happen when viewers are color blind, colored graphic designs are printed in gray-scale, and designs are displayed in colored illumination, and so forth. Figure 1 shows several examples of these information losses. When it is viewed by a person with protanopia, a graphic design which is easy to notice such as Fig. 1(a) becomes a vague one. Similarly, a graphic design which contains lots of information such as Fig. 1(c) becomes meaningless when it is printed as in gray-scale. Even though a certain amount of information loss is inevitable, it can cause serious problems if the information expressed by colors is critical. Hence, it is desirable, during the design process, to notify designers that the use of certain colors should be avoided to minimize the information loss.

© Springer International Publishing Switzerland 2016
A. Marcus (Ed.): DUXU 2016, Part III, LNCS 9748, pp. 159–166, 2016.
DOI: 10.1007/978-3-319-40406-6_15

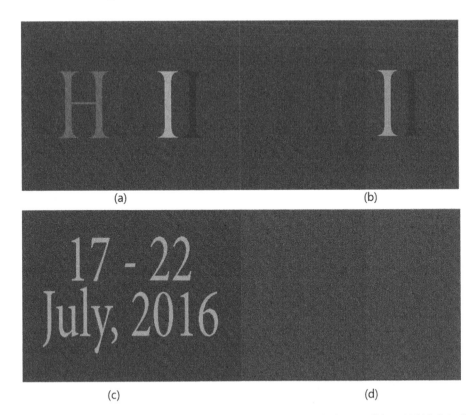

Fig. 1. Examples of information losses caused by viewers and display condition. (a)(c)Original graphic design (b) Graphic design (a) viewed by a person with protanopia (d) Graphic design (c) when printed in gray-scale

In order to prevent graphic designers from using several colors or combinations of colors that causes serious information losses, the information loss depending on the characteristics of viewers and environments should be estimated beforehand. This can be achieved by generating the simulated models of an original graphic design first, and visually checking each simulated model. A similar platform is currently provided by Adobe Systems Inc. [1]. They only consider the information losses caused by color blindness, and they let graphic designers preview their arts in the same way that a colorblind individual would see it. They also let graphic designers adjust colors in their original arts while seeing how the changes impact the color blindness view. However, information loss can happen not only when viewers are color blind but also when display environment is unusual. Hence, it can be tedious to test every graphics designs since there can be lots of cases graphics designers should consider. Moreover, the platform provided by [1] does not measure the quantitative information loss. Thus, among several graphic design candidates which are designed to minimize information losses, a graphic designer should subjectively select one.

To deal with these problems, this paper proposes an image analysis tool which estimates information losses caused by viewers and display environments. In many cases, the impression of colors is related with providing subjective feelings to viewers, whereas the contrast of colors is related with providing objective information. Hence, when the contrast of colors in a graphic design is reduced, it usually causes information losses. Therefore, the proposed method measures information loss by measuring the reduction of color contrast. The main characteristic of the proposed method is that it automatically and quantitatively estimates information losses caused by various situations. For these reasons, the proposed method can help graphics designers achieve *robust design*: a graphic design that critical information is preserved regardless of viewers and environments.

This paper is organized as follows. In Sect. 2, the proposed method is explained. In Sect. 3, the proposed method is evaluated by several graphic designs. And I conclude in Sect. 4.

2 The Proposed Method

2.1 System Overview

Figure 2 illustrates the overview of the proposed method. The proposed method first generates a simulated model of the design. Thereafter, the equivalent image segmentation algorithm is applied to the original design and the simulated model. As a result, the original design and the simulated model are partitioned into several regions. Finally, the number of groups in the original design and that in the simulated design are compared to estimate the information loss.

Among a variety of situations which leads to information loss, I focus the case when viewers are protanopic, and color graphic designs are printed in gray-scale (gray-level printing). To generate the simulated model in case of users being color blind, simulation model proposed by H. Brettel *et al.* is used [2]. Gray-level image is generated by taking the average of R, G, B color components.

2.2 Simulated Model Generation

As mentioned, simulated model for protanopia is generated by using the method proposed in [2]. For the completeness of the paper, I briefly explain the method. Normal color vision is trichromatic and it is initiated by the absorption of photons in three classes of cones. The peak sensitivities of each cone is different, i.e., one type of cones is sensitive to long-wavelength (L), one type of cone is sensitive to middle-wavelength (M), and the other is sensitive to short-wavelength (S). Therefore, any color stimulus can be specified by three cone responses and all colors visible to the color-normal observer are included in a three-dimensional color space. For dichromatic observers, however, any color stimulus is initiated by two cone responses, and all colors that they can discriminate are included in a two-dimensional color space.

Based on this fact, H. Brettel et al. proposed an algorithm to imitate for the normal observer the appearance of colors for the dichromat. First, they represented a color

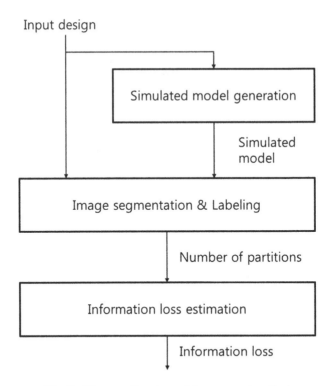

Fig. 2. The overall system of the proposed method

stimuli as vectors in a three-dimensional LMS space, *i.e.*, a color represented in RGB color space is represented in LMS space. Then, the algorithm replaces each stimulus by its projection onto a reduced stimulus surface defined by a given type of dichromat. Finally, the reduced stimulus surface is again transformed into RGB color space.

For instance, to imitate color appearance for a person with protanopia, a color stimulus Q represented in RGB color space is transformed into LMS space as (1).

$$
\begin{pmatrix} L_Q \\ M_Q \\ S_Q \end{pmatrix} = \begin{bmatrix} 0.1992 & 0.4112 & 0.0742 \\ 0.0353 & 0.2226 & 0.0574 \\ 0.0185 & 0.1231 & 1.3550 \end{bmatrix} \begin{pmatrix} R_Q \\ G_Q \\ B_Q \end{pmatrix} \tag{1}
$$

Then by using Eq. (2), a color stimulus Q in LMS space is projected onto the reduced stimulus surface for protanopia.

$$
\begin{pmatrix} L'_P \\ M'_P \\ S'_P \end{pmatrix} = \begin{bmatrix} 0 & 2.02344 & -2.52581 \\ 0 & 1 & 0 \\ 0 & 0 & 1 \end{bmatrix} \begin{pmatrix} L_Q \\ M_Q \\ S_Q \end{pmatrix} \tag{2}
$$

Finally by using Eq. (3), it is again transformed into RGB color space.

$$\begin{pmatrix} R' \\ G' \\ B' \end{pmatrix} = \begin{bmatrix} 0.0809 & -0.1305 & 0.1167 \\ -0.0102 & 0.0540 & -0.1136 \\ -0.0003 & -0.0041 & 0.6935 \end{bmatrix} \begin{pmatrix} L'_P \\ M'_P \\ S'_P \end{pmatrix} \tag{3}$$

To generate a simulated model for gray-level printing, the intensity of each color component is generated as (4).

$$Y = \frac{R+G+B}{3} \tag{4}$$

Figure 3 illustrates simulated models for protanopia, and gray-level printing. Even though this paper deals with protanopia and gray-level printing, generating simulated models for another types of dichromat is straight-forward by using the method proposed in [2].

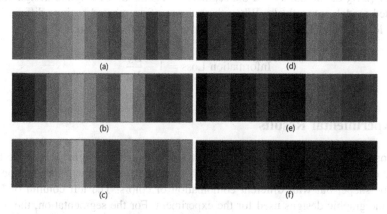

Fig. 3. Simulated model generation and segmentation results. (a) original graphic design (b) simulated model for protanopia (c) simulated model for gray-level printing (d) segmentation result of original design (e) segmentation result of (b) (f) segmentation result of (c)

2.3   Image Segmentation and Labeling

As a second step, the original graphic design and the simulated model is partitioned into several regions. A variety of researches have been conducted on image segmentation and arbitrary segmentation can be used. However, color thresholding is used in this paper for the simplicity of the algorithm. First, we uniformly quantize each color component into multiple levels. When a quantization step is set to 8 and the range of the intensity of each color component is 256, then each color component is divided into 32 levels. As a normal color consists of three color components, this makes 32,768 levels. And a color in a pixel is assigned to a certain level depending on its color components. Hence, colors that fall into the same level are considered as the same color.

For labeling (i.e., counting the number of regions in a design), a blob counting method proposed in [3] is used. Figure 3 also illustrates the result of segmentation for the original design and the simulated model.

2.4   Information Loss Estimation

Finally, the information loss of the original graphic design is estimated. As a result of segmentation, each image is partitioned into several groups. Even though equivalent segmentation method is used, as Fig. 4 illustrates, the number of groups is different and the number of groups in the simulated model tends to be smaller than that in the original design. This is because some colors become undistinguishable to protanopic, and in gray-level printing. Thus, by measuring the ratio between the number of groups in the original design and that in the simulated model, the information loss can be estimated.

Let N_O, N_S be the number of the segmented regions in the original design and the simulated model, respectively. When the number of segmented regions differs, information loss is estimated to be occurred, and it is computed by Eq. (5).

$$\text{Information Loss} = 1 - \frac{N_S}{N_O} \qquad (5)$$

3   Experimental Results

The proposed method is evaluated by two types of graphic designs. Each type has 3 graphic design candidates, and each candidate contains the identical information with the same shape, but with different combination of colors. The left column of Fig. 4 shows the graphic designs used for the experiment. For the segmentation, the quantization step size was set to 8.

Figure 4 also shows the generated simulated model for each graphic design; the middle column for a person with protanopia and the right column for gray-level printing. And Table 1 describes the information loss for each graphic design estimated by the proposed method. As Fig. 4 and Table 1 indicates, the quantitative measurement of information losses estimated by the proposed method is coherent with the subjective measurement of information losses. For instance, the letter 'H' and the letter 'I' in design 1 becomes invisible when it is viewed by a person with protanopia and gray-level printing, respectively. In this case, the proposed method informs the designers that the possible information loss for each case is 0.25. In case of design 2, it is still distinguishable when it is viewed by a protanopic person, but it loses whole information when it is printed as gray-level. The proposed method still shows coherent results, i.e., it analyzes that information loss for protanopia and gray-level printing is 0 and 1, respectively. Based on this information, designers can choose one design among several candidates that is robust to various viewers and environments, without personally checking the simulation results. In this experiment, choosing deigns 3 and design 5 is reasonable.

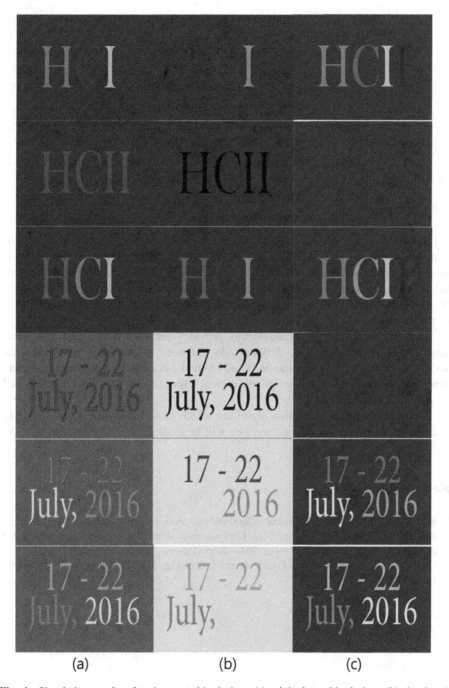

Fig. 4. Simulation results of various graphic designs (a) original graphic designs (b) simulated models for a person with protanopia (c) simulated models for gray-level printing

Table 1. The estimated information loss of each graphic design

		Information loss	
		Protanopia	Gray-level printing
Type 1	Design 1	0.25	0.25
	Design 2	0	1
	Design 3	0	0.25
Type 2	Design 4	0	1
	Design 5	0.3	0
	Design 6	0.8	0

4   Conclusion

In this paper, an image analysis algorithm is proposed which informs the designers of information loss of their design when viewed by certain viewers and certain environments. Simulated models of the original design are generated and a simple segmentation algorithm is applied to the simulated models and the input graphic design. By analyzing the number of segmented groups in each image, the information loss is finally estimated.

As the proposed method automatically provides designers with quantitative measurement of information loss, designers do not need to personally simulate their designs. Hence, I believe that the proposed method can ease the difficulties of generating robust design; a graphic design that critical information is preserved regardless of viewers and environments.

As future works, a suggestion algorithm which provides designers with possible solutions to minimize the information loss will be studied.

References

1. http://blogs.adobe.com/adobeillustrator/2009/04/new_tools_for_color_making_you_1.html
2. Brettel, H., Viénot, F., Mollon, J.D.: Computerized simulation of color appearance for dichromats. J. Opt. Soc. Am. **14**(10), 2647–2655 (1997)
3. Gonzalez, R.C., Woods, R.E.: Digital Image Processing, 3rd edn. Pearson, Upper Saddle River (2008)

Systematic Application of Circle-Similar Shapes to Visualize Database-Homogeneity in a Big Data Environment

Verena Lechner[(⊠)], Karl-Heinz Weidmann, and Isabella Hämmerle

Research Center for User Centered Technologies, University of Applied Sciences Vorarlberg, Hochschulstrasse 1, 6850 Dornbirn, Austria
uct@fhv.at

Abstract. Creating a useful visualization of database-homogeneity in a big data environment contains the task to present the underlying data in a perceivable way to the human observer. This paper provides a deep insight into the results of a research project commissioned by Crate Technology GmbH, where the before mentioned task was tackled by using a modified method of radar charts. A novel visualization tool to observe database-homogeneity was created with the aim to integrate it into the UI of the massive scalable elastic SQL Data store developed by Crate. The results of the formative usability test of this tool showed that the principle is understood intuitively by almost all test subjects already during the first task without any briefing about how to identify the problematic state of the single nodes of the database cluster. The results showed that this tool is expedient to visualize database-metadata in a big data environment.

Keywords: Database visualization · Big data · Form perception · Shape perception · Radar chart · Visualization · User interface · Formative usability test · Homogeneity

1 Introduction

Visualizing homogeneity in the area of database-metadata in a big data environment holds several challenges, as for example the amount of data to be displayed is not only huge but also changes during time [1, 2], therefore a good visualization should offer these data in an easily perceivable way to the human observer. For the research project with Crate Technology GmbH, who developed an elastic SQL Data Store that is massively scalable [3], the task was to develop such a visualization combining these already mentioned challenges with the precondition, that the observer doesn't necessarily has to be a highly professional database specialist. Moreover, as the databases of Crate are massively scalable, a broad variety of number of nodes has to be included into the visualization. This paper will first provide an insight into the development of a new visualization tool for database homogeneity. Then, an overview is given about the results of a formative usability test with the resulting tool that has been carried out at the Research Institute for User Centered Technologies (UCT). One of the main objectives was to explore whether the potential users are able to use the developed

© Springer International Publishing Switzerland 2016
A. Marcus (Ed.): DUXU 2016, Part III, LNCS 9748, pp. 167–179, 2016.
DOI: 10.1007/978-3-319-40406-6_16

visualization system intuitively, i.e. without prior instruction, for the observation of the database-homogeneity and to find potential improvable aspects.

2 Structure of the Visualization

2.1 Data to Be Represented

The visualization to be developed should enable the users to observe the database-homogeneity, for which we used a combination of four types of database metadata as the basic data set. Basically, database metadata can be defined as "data about database data", so it's not the data in the database itself, database metadata rather has the task to describe the database [4]. The four types of database metadata used for this tool are the average load for the last minute[1], the used disk (data size)[2], the used heap[3] and the number of shards[4]. These four data types are considered per node, the number of which may vary considerably, depending on the configuration of the database setup. As the visualization should enable an overview about the database-homogeneity, it's not expedient to visualize the absolute values of each node, but the difference of these four data types of each node to the completely homogeneous cluster – so it's the difference to the average of all nodes, which defines a relative measure.

2.2 Basic Concept of the Visualization

For the development of the visualization tool of metadata that should be applicable not only for highly professional database specialists, basic principles of human perception of shapes [5–9] were combined with the information visualization method of radar charts [10, 11]. The four types of database metadata we used for this visualization are available on the level of a single node. Therefore the basic element of the visualization is the node itself, which is (in its ideal state) represented as a circle[5]. Invisible in the overview mode of the visualization are the four circular arranged axes of the radar chart that lie behind the apparent circle-similar shape. In contrast to the radar chart first described by Georg Mayr in 1877 [10], the data points on the circular-arranged axes

---

[1] The arithmetic mean of all ethernet traffic (in bps) calculated over the last minute per node.

[2] The quotient of secondary-storage (disk) usage (blocks) in relation to the total available secondary-storage per node.

[3] The quotient of heap storage usage (bytes) in relation to the total available heap storage per node.

[4] The number of database shards (a horizontal partition of data in a database) per node.

[5] The reason why the form of a circle was chosen to represent a node in its ideal state has been investigated during an earlier stage of the research project. A detailed description of the form perception principles with regard to this project can be found in the proceedings of the HCI2015 [12]. Furthermore, an online web-survey with 399 test persons has been carried out in March 2015 in order to investigate the differences between the perception of polygons, circles and circle-similar shapes. The results of this survey as well as an analysis of comparable tools on the market have been published in January 2016 [13].

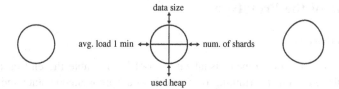

Fig. 1. Principle of the representation of a single node. 1. node in an ideal state (left circle); 2. with the axes labeling (middle circle); 3. inhomogeneous node (right deformed circle).

aren't connected with straight lines (resulting in a polygon) but with curves, that create a regular circle if the data points have the same distance from the center (which is the case when it has the ideal value) and a deformed circle-shape in the other case (cf. Fig. 1). So every node of the visualized database is represented as such a shape, the axes represent the four values "average load", "used disk", "used heap" and "number of shards". The ideal value of these metrics (observing cluster homogeneity) has been determined by Crate as the average of the single values of these metrics of all nodes. Therefore, if the observer of the database visualization perceives all the nodes as regular circles (and thus can assume that the cluster homogeneity is in the ideal state), depends on whether the values of these four axes of all nodes are the same. As soon as the values of one or more nodes deviate from the average, the forms of all other nodes of the cluster are modified as well to a lesser extent. Throughout this paper, only the nodes that deviate at least 15 % from the regular circle are stated as "inhomogeneous nodes".

The single nodes of a database running on Crate are arranged in a dark blue filled circle, which represents a whole cluster. The space between each node is 1,1 times larger than the radius of the ideal circle. That ensures that even if the maximum deviation of the data point on the axes is achieved with two adjacent nodes (50 % of the radius of the ideal circle), the outer edges don't touch each other. In order to make it easier for the user to interpret the deformations of the single circles, a legend is provided on the upper right corner. A white tooltip-box on single nodes shows the exact values of the four axes of the selected node as well as the exact average value of the whole cluster. Clicking on one of the nodes triggers a zoom into the selected node and shows also the axes (labeled with the underlying data type, the exact values of the enlarged node as well as the average value) and the ideal circle to compare the curves (cf. Fig. 2).

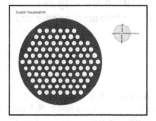
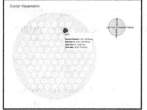
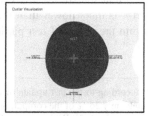

Fig. 2. Overview of the interface in its basic state with 100 nodes (left picture); in the mouse-over mode (middle picture); while zoomed in to a single node (right picture).

3 Testing of the Prototype

3.1 Objectives

The main aim of the developed visualization tool is to enable the end users to intuitively decide if the cluster running on Crate is in a homogeneous state and if not, to identifiy (not necessarily the whole number, but at least some of) those nodes that are inhomogeneous. Thus the observer may decide what problem could lie behind the deformation of the nodes and try to solve it. Therefore, the main objective of the testing was to evaluate if the test participants recognize that the shape of the nodes represents the status of a node and if they are capable to identify them in different settings with cluster sizes. The result should show if it's expedient to visualize database homogeneity through shapes as described earlier in this paper. Furthermore, questions such as which strategy was applied to scan through the clusters or whether the direction in which the circular shape is deformed (either inwards or outwards the center of the circle) have any impact on the simplicity of detection should be answered.

3.2 Method

Formative Usability Test. Due to the fact that the interface is still under development, carrying out a formative usability test was the chosen method to scrutinize it for potential points for improvement [14]. As the visual elements shown on the screen needed to be perceived with the same attributes (such as size, color, position), the test has been carried out under repeatable conditions between 14 to 20 October 2015 in the UCT in Dornbirn, Austria. Moreover, relevant data (as described later) wouldn't be possible to gather if the tests would have been carried out locally independent, as the technical systems have to be installed in a fix setup. Recording the comments of the test participants given through using the thinking aloud approach is also simplified by having a unified locality of the test.

Test Participants. The test has been carried out with 12 (graduated and undergraduated) computer science students of the University of Applied Sciences in Vorarlberg (who according to Crate are potential users with at least the minimum of required prior knowledge). Three test participants were studying in the fifth semester of the bachelor of computer science and nine participants were students of the master of computer science. The age of the test persons ranged between 22 and 56 (median 32). Two of them were women, thus the gender ratio is unbalanced. But considering that according to current statistics of the U.S. and the U.K. the number of women working in the IT sector is much lower than the number of men[6], therefore the unbalanced gender ratio within the group of test participants seems appropriate.

---

[6] According to the last update of the National Center for Women & Information Technology women held only 26 % of the computing occupations in the U.S. in 2014, taking into account 500 U.S. based companies [15]. With view on Europe, in the UK the percentage of women being employed as IT and Telecommunications Professionals was at 12.2 in 2013 [16].

Structure and Procedure. The test consisted of 12 different tasks the participants had to process. Each task showed a cluster that contained 8, 50 or 100 nodes with 1 to 10 inhomogeneous nodes. The testing was structured into two parts, the first offered only static pictures of the cluster as shown in Fig. 2 to solve the eight given tasks. In the second part, the test users had to interact with the visualization (cf. Fig. 2) and therefore got additional information and other views of the cluster.

As shown in Tables 1 and 2, the tasks 2, 6, 7 and 8 (static part of the test) contained the same number of nodes in a cluster and the same number of inhomogeneous nodes with the same percentage of deformation as tasks 9, 10, 11 and 12 (interactive part). Besides the fact, that in the second part of the test the earlier described interactive elements have been offered, the only difference between these two groups of tasks was the positioning of the modified nodes. Thereby it's important to emphasize that the changes of the positions have been altered only very slightly, that on the one hand the positions can't be memorized, but on the other hand the single tasks still stay comparable.

Before each task, the test participants got a written task description on the screen, instructing them to identify the node/s in a problematic state. For tasks 1, 2 and 9 they additionally had to tell the test leader the reason why they thought the selected nodes are in a problematic state. (How the problematic state of a node is represented and subsequently how the test persons should define the nodes that are in a problematic state wasn't explained at all.) After task 10 and 11 of the interactive part, an online questionnaire had to be filled out.

Used Software and Measurement Parameters. Five methods of data collection have been used for the testing:

- As a basis for all the analyses the screen (including the mouse positions) has been recorded during the whole test sessions.
- In order to gain precise data about where the test participants were looking at, the eye movements have been recorded with an eye tracking system.
- To collect the data of the think-aloud method the test participants have been filmed.
- Further information about the subjective evaluation of the participants has been gathered with a short online questionnaire. The questions concerned the easiness to identify the inhomogeneous nodes, the helpfulness of the arrangement of the nodes, the similarity of the inhomogeneous nodes to the homogeneous ones, the number of nodes displayed and if the size of the nodes enabled a comfortable perception. The questions had to be rated on a 5-point semantic differential (-2 to $+2$). Participants also had to answer how the ideal values of the single axes of a node have been developed (two answer options were given).

Data Analysis. The data of all 12 participants were included in the statistical analysis. The amount of errors made was determined by measuring firstly how many deformed circles in each task were not identified as inhomogeneous nodes (hereinafter "error type 1") and secondly how many almost regular circles were classified mistakenly as inhomogeneous nodes (hereinafter "error type 2"). The relation of identified inhomogeneous nodes to the amount of inhomogeneous nodes in each task was also calculated and is displayed in percentage. The deformations of the inhomogeneous nodes were

Table 1. Overview of the tasks of the static part of the test

Task numbers	Number of nodes in the cluster	Number of inhomogeneous nodes	Position of the inhomogeneous node/s	Percentage of deformation in comparison with the radius of the ideal value
task 1	8	1	left horizontal axis: value below average	30 %
task 2	8	1	left horizontal axis: value above average	40 %
task 3	8	2	bottom vertical axis: value above average	20 %
task 4	8	2	bottom vertical axis: value below average	20 %
task 5	8	3	bottom vertical axis: value above average	20 %
task 6	50	6	3 nodes: right horizontal and upper vertical axis: value above average; 3 nodes: right horizontal and upper vertical axis: value below average	25 %
task 7	100	10	5 nodes: right horizontal and upper vertical axis: value above average; 5 nodes: right horizontal and upper vertical axis: value below average	25 %
task 8	100	2	right horizontal and upper vertical axis: value below average	50 %

Table 2. Overview of the tasks of the interactive part of the test

Task numbers	Number of nodes in the cluster	Number of inhomogeneous nodes	Position of the inhomogeneous node/s	Percentage of deformation in comparison with the radius of the ideal value
task 9	8	1	left horizontal axis: value above average	40 %
task 10	50	6	3 nodes: right horizontal and upper vertical axis: value above average; 3 nodes: right horizontal and upper vertical axis: value below average	25 %
task 11	100	10	5 nodes: right horizontal and upper vertical axis: value above average; 5 nodes: right horizontal and upper vertical axis: value below average	25 %
task 12	100	2	right horizontal and upper vertical axis: value below average	50 %

classified in hereafter so called "too small nodes", which included the nodes that had at least one value of the four axes below the average, and in hereafter so called "too big nodes", which had at least one value of the four axes above the average of the whole cluster (cf. Tables 1 and 2).

To identify the strategy used to search for the inhomogeneous nodes eye tracking data were analyzed. The results lead us to the two categorizations: The test participants used either a "chaotic" or "line-based" strategy (cf. Fig. 3). The category "chaotic" contained all participants who didn't use an explicit line-based strategy. The categorisation was done for each task with at least 50 nodes.

The answers of the questionnaire were transformed to values from 1 to 5, where 1 represented the positive end and 5 the negative end.

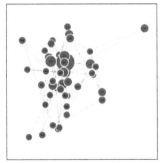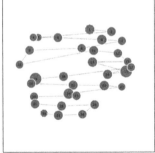

Fig. 3. Exemplary eye tracking data: chaotic (left square) and line-based strategy (right square)

Not all tasks were included in every analysis, since the percentage of deformation of the problematic nodes wasn't the same for all clusters as well as the ratio of inhomogeneous nodes to the total amount of nodes in a cluster differed (cf. Tables 1 and 2). Which tasks are included is therefore stated for each step of analysis.

Statistical Analysis. Descriptive statistics was used to describe the amount and types of errors the participants made. Independent Student's t-tests were calculated to determine if there are any differences between the cluster sizes (only 50 or 100 nodes) regarding the subjective evaluation of the visualization system with the questionnaire.

A Pearson's chi-square test was conducted to test for a relationship between the size of the cluster and the method used to scan the cluster. Furthermore, Pearson's chi-square tests were calculated to test if there is a relationship between the cluster size and the amount of identified inhomogeneous nodes as well as if there is any relationship between the size of the inhomogeneous node (too small or too big) and the probability that the problematic node is identified.

The significance level was fixed at the 5 % level. The statistical analysis was performed using IBM SPSS Statistics Data Editor Version 23.0.

3.3   Results

Correct Identification of the Inhomogeneous Nodes. The average percentage of all identified inhomogeneous nodes (ratio of detected inhomogeneous nodes to the amount of inhomogeneous nodes per task) and of all too small and too big inhomogeneous nodes were calculated once for all tasks and once for the tasks 6, 7, 10 and 11. If all tasks were included in the analysis the participants identified 86 % of all inhomogeneous nodes compared to 75 %, if just the tasks 6, 7, 10 and 11 were considered. If the type of deformation was regarded separately it can be seen that the percentage of identified inhomogeneous too big nodes was 90 % (for all tasks) resp. 87 % compared to 77 % resp. 62 % for the nodes that were too small.

After the first, the second and the ninth task, the test persons were asked to describe orally, why they thought that the nodes they selected in the previous task are in a problematic state. As shown in Table 3, the answers were classified in three categories. For the right answers two categories were defined: If the test participants named the axis (as described in the legend in the right upper corner) where the deformation took place, the answer was right because it was the most precise answer they could give (named as "right answer type 1" in Table 3). The second type of right answers contains all answers where the test participants only named the deformation of the single circles representing a node as the indicating parameter for the problematic state (named as "right answer type 2" in Table 3). If a test participant didn't name one of the previous reasons, the answer was wrong (named as "wrong answer" in Table 3).

Table 3. Oral answers to the question why the test persons thought that the before selected nodes are in a problematic state.

Answer	Num. of persons that selected that answer after task 1 (n = 12)	Num. of persons that selected that answer after task 2 (n = 10)	Num. of persons that selected that answer after task 9 (n = 11)
right answer type 1	3	2	8
right answer type 2	8	8	3
wrong answer	1	0	0

Pearson's chi-square test revealed a significant association between the type of deformation and whether the nodes were identified or not, χ^2 (1) = 30.76, $p < .001$ as well as for the size of a cluster and whether the nodes were identified or not, χ^2 (1) = 3.88, $p < .05$. Based on the odds ratio, the odds of nodes to be identified as inhomogeneous nodes were 3.92 times higher if they were too big than if they were too small and 1.63 times higher if they were in a cluster with 50 nodes than if they were in a cluster with 100 nodes. Tasks included in the analysis were task number 6, 7, 10 and 11 since they had the same amount of too big and too small nodes within each task and all nodes had the same degree of deformation.

Error Rates. The average of the absolute value of errors of all 12 participants of type 1 and type 2 per task is displayed in Table 4. These results have been calculated once for all tasks as well as just for tasks with a cluster size of at least 50 nodes and a uniform deformation of 25 % (tasks 6, 7, 10, 11).

Table 4. Comparison of the error rate of error type 1 and type 2 of two different task groups

Tasks included in the analysis	Error type 1 per task	Error type 2 per task	Error type 1 per person per task	Error type 2 per person per task
all tasks	9.8	8.5	0.8	0.7
tasks 6, 7, 10, 11	25.5	9.8	2.1	0.8

Table 5. Absolute values of used search strategies per cluster size (n = number of tasks)

Cluster size	Chaotic	Line-based
50 nodes (n = 2)	21	3
100 nodes (n = 4)	27	21

As can be seen in Table 4 the error rate of type 1 increased from 0.8 per person per task to 2.1 if not all tasks but just the more complex ones (min. 50 nodes, deformation value 25 %) were included. This rise in mistakes wasn't observed for errors of type 2 (0.7 to 0.8).

Half of the participants (6 persons) answered the question (of the questionnaire) how the ideal values of the single axes have been developed correctly (through the average of all nodes displayed at the same time) and five persons had chosen the wrong answer (through a fixed value). One person thought that none of the two answers is correct.

Strategy Used to Scan Through the Clusters. Table 5 shows how often the two scanning strategies (chaotic or line-based) were used for different cluster sizes. All tasks that had a cluster size of at least 50 nodes were included in this analysis (cf. Table 5).

Pearson's chi-square test to conduct if there is a relationship between the size of the cluster and the strategy used to scan a cluster was significant, χ^2 (1) = 7.03, $p < .01$. Based on the odds ratio, the odds of using a chaotic search strategy were 5.4 times higher for 50 node clusters than for 100 node clusters.

Table 6. Means, standard errors and p-values of the t-tests to compare different questions depending on the cluster size

Question (categorisation of the answer)	Cluster size	M	SE	p
It was difficult /easy for me to detect the problematic nodes. (1 = easy, 5 = difficult)	50 nodes	2.83	0.83	1
	100 nodes	2.83	0.83	
The presentation of the single nodes was too small /too big for a comfortable perception. (1 = too big, 5 = too small)	50 nodes	3.12	0.58	.058
	100 nodes	3.92	1.16	
The presentation showed too many /too less nodes to compare. (1 = too less, 5 = too many)	50 nodes	3.83	0.94	.65
	100 nodes	4.00	0.85	
The problematic nodes have been too similar to the not problematic ones /the difference was large enough to easily distinguish. (1 = large enough, 5 = too similar)	50 nodes	3.50	0.67	.67
	100 nodes	3.67	1.15	

Results of the Subjective Evaluation of the Visualization System. The t-tests revealed only a significant difference between 50 node clusters and 100 node clusters for the question, if the arrangement of the nodes was confusing or helpful, $t(22) = -2.11$, $p < .05$. On average, participants rated the arrangement of the 50 node clusters less confusing ($M = 2.75$, $SE = 0.22$) than for the 100 node clusters ($M = 3.42$, $SE = 0.23$). The means, standard errors and p-values for the other questions can be seen in Table 6.

4 Discussion

The results showed that all participants but one understood the visualization system intuitively already in the first task in terms of recognizing that the shape of the nodes represents the status of a node. After the 9th task eight participants answered the open question why they thought that the nodes they have selected in the previous task were in a problematic state totally correct (answers referred to the axis of the nodes). The other three participants just mentioned the deformation of the nodes, which is also a right answer, but not as precise as the other one. On the other side the question how the ideal values of the single axes have been developed was just answered right by six participants. This indicates, that the system can be operated by users even if they don't know how the ideal values of the nodes are developed, but recognizing the deformation of the nodes is sufficient.

If all tasks were considered, 86 % of all inhomogeneous nodes were identified to be in a problematic state but just 75 % if only the more complex tasks (at least 50 nodes and more than two inhomogeneous nodes per cluster) were included in the analysis. Interestingly was the result, that the type of deformation (too small or too big) seems to be important for the identification of the inhomogeneous nodes, since 90 % (87 % for the complex tasks) of the nodes that were too big were identified compared to just 77 % (62 % for the complex tasks) of the nodes that were too small. This indicates that - at least for our specific setting (regarding distance between the nodes, colours and display size of the nodes) - too big nodes are easier to identify than too small nodes.

The analysis of the error types also revealed impressive results. If all tasks were considered in the error rate analysis each participant didn't identify 0.8 inhomogeneous nodes per task as problematic ones (error type 1) and rated 0.7 of the circular shaped nodes mistakenly as problematic ones (error type 2). If just the complex tasks were considered, the amount of not identified inhomogeneous nodes rose from 0.7 to 2.1 per task. This high increase of errors wasn't observed for the circular shaped nodes that were rated as problematic ones (increase from 0.7 to 0.8). Based on this results it can be concluded that with increasing complexity more inhomogeneous nodes are overlooked but not more homogeneous nodes are rated mistakenly as inhomogeneous.

For the subjective evaluation where the participants rated different aspects of the visualization we expected some differences depending on the cluster size. The results showed just a significant difference between the cluster sizes for the arrangement of the nodes. The smaller cluster was rated less confusing. The easiness to identify homogeneous nodes was rated exactly the same for 50 and 100 nodes, it was neither perceived as very easy nor as very difficult. The problematic nodes were neither rated as too similar to the problematic ones to easily identify them nor was the difference rated as large enough. The participants rated the nodes as rather too small for a comfortable perception and as rather showing too many nodes per cluster. On the one hand it seems like the participants weren't really satisfied, but also not extremely dissatisfied with the visualization. But on the other hand, the dissatisfaction didn't increase significantly from 50 nodes to 100 nodes, even not for the statement if the visualization showed too many nodes. The question arises, how the ratings would be if the clusters were even bigger.

The analysis of the search strategy showed that a line-based search strategy is more often applied for clusters with 100 nodes than for clusters with just 50 nodes. This indicates that with a rising number of nodes the participants started to use a strategic approach, probably because with a higher number of nodes the chance to overlook an inhomogeneous node is bigger. The question arises, if a visualization tool that is developed to give a quick overview of the cluster homogeneity should be scanned line-based. It has to be said that the arrangement of the nodes in the clusters supported a line-based strategy, since the nodes were arranged not totally chaotic but in horizontal lines. It would be interesting, if a line-based strategy would also be used if this isn't the case. Further research is necessary to gain better insights which search strategy should be applied to fulfil the task best and what kind of node arrangement best supports that the users apply this particular strategy.

5   Conclusion

The test of the prototype implementation confirmed the usefulness of the selected approach. Participants didn't have problems to understand the developed visualization tool intuitively without any explanation and performed at a reasonable well level for all selected tasks. They performed even better compared to their subjective judgement. Certainly, there is room for improvement of the presentation of the visualization e.g. the users rated the nodes as rather too small for a comfortable perception. Further research is necessary to confirm our findings and to see if our findings are also applicable for bigger clusters.

References

1. Cox, M., Ellsworth, D.: Managing big data for scientific visualization. In: Siggraph 1997, Computer Graphics Annual Conference Series, Course 4, Exploring Gigabyte Datasets in Real-Time: Algorithms, Data Management, and Time-Critical Design. Assn for Computing Machinery, Los Angeles (1997)
2. Illingworth, J.A., Lippstreu, M., Deprez-Sims, A.-S.: Big data in talent selection and assessment. In: Big Data at Work. The Data Science Revolution and Organizational Psychology. p. 368. Routledge Taylor & Francis Group, New York (2016)
3. CRATE Technology GmbH: Crate. Your Elastic Data Store. https://crate.io/
4. Parsian, M.: JDBC Metadata, MySQL, and Oracle Recipes: A Problem-Solution Approach. Apress, Berkeley (2006)

5. Bernhard, T.: Wahrnehmung der Schönheit in der Architektur. epubli, Berlin (2012)
6. Naumann, A.: Raimer Jochims: FarbFormBeziehungen: Anschauliche Bedingungen seiner Identitätskonzeption. Königshausen & Neumann, Würzburg (2005)
7. Arnheim, R.: Art and visual perception: a psychology of the creative eye. In: 50th Anniversary Printing. Original edition: Art and Visual Perception: A Psychology of the Creative Eye. Universitiy of California Press, Berkeley and Los Angeles 1954. University of California Press (2004)
8. Pizlo, Z.: 3D Shape: Its Unique Place in Visual Perception. MIT Press, Massachusetts (2008)
9. Alexander, K.: Kompendium der visuellen Information und Kommunikation. Springer-Verlag, Berlin (2013)
10. Mayr, G.: Die Gesetzmäßigkeit im Gesellschaftsleben. Statistische Studien. Oldenbourg, München (1877)
11. Takezawa, K.: Guidebook to R Graphics Using Microsoft Windows. Wiley, Hoboken (2013)
12. Lechner, V., Weidmann, K.-H.: Visualizing database-performance through shape, reflecting the development opportunities of radar charts. In: HCI International 2015 Conference Proceedings. Springer, Los Angeles (2015)
13. Lechner, V., Weidmann, K.-H., Mayer, H.O.: Visualisierung der Datenbank-Performance durch die methodische Verknüpfung von Grundlagen der Formwahrnehmung mit den Prinzipien des Radardiagramms. In: design2product. Beiträge zur empirischen Designforschung. Band 5 - Methoden der Designforschung, pp. 148–168. Bucher, Hohenems (2015)
14. Nielsen, J.: Usability Engineering. Morgan Kaufmann, San Francisco (1994)
15. National Center for Women & Information Technology: Women in IT: The Facts Infographic. https://www.ncwit.org/resources/women-it-facts-infographic-2015-update
16. Baker, C., Cracknell, R.: Women in Public life, the Professions and the Boardroom. House of Commons Library, London (2014)

The Exploration of User Knowledge Architecture Based on Mining User Generated Contents – An Application Case of Photo-Sharing Website

Nan Liang, Jiaming Zhong, Di Wang, and Liqun Zhang[✉]

Institute of Design Management, S.J.T.U., Shanghai, China
zhanglq@sjtu.edu.cn

Abstract. Traditional methods to obtain user needs, such as interview, have exposed the increasingly serious problem of bias and inefficiency when meeting the blooming of users. This research tried to ameliorate the situation by mining user-generated data and constructing corresponding user knowledge systems with the help of modern technologies. With a photo-sharing website as a study case, several techniques have been implemented, including image feature extraction, content analysis and statistical calculation, to analyze users' characteristics and preferences. The results indicated that many of these techniques are practical and effective for future research in user experience design. It is foreseeable that the domain of this research can be expanded to text and voice to construct a synthesis approach for ultimately understanding users.

Keywords: Image · Content analysis · User knowledge · Experience · Photo sharing site

1 Introduction

In view of the considerable improvement of material living standard in recent years, designers begin to pay more attention to emotional and spiritual elements in their products and services. The major consideration of user experience design, or UED, is to create satisfying, aesthetic and innovative products which constantly meet user's needs and even lead the trend of modern lifestyle. Therefore, it is important for designers to understand user needs and further translate them into appropriate products. In the age of the Internet, the presence of blogs, forums, wiki, SNS and RSS combining with newly developed theories such as Six Degrees of Separation and the Long Tail, has made user knowledge into an open, complex and adaptive system. In the current web environment, there is an increasing diversity in the representing forms of user knowledge, while users usually feel easy to accommodate this situation. The problem is left to designers on both acquiring user knowledge and constructing corresponding systems.

The key of user research is mining the needs buried deeply in users' mind through their language and daily behavior. Traditional methods, including questionnaire, interview, observation, focus group and persona, achieve the goal through behavior

© Springer International Publishing Switzerland 2016
A. Marcus (Ed.): DUXU 2016, Part III, LNCS 9748, pp. 180–192, 2016.
DOI: 10.1007/978-3-319-40406-6_17

observation and carefully designed conversation. Designers are required to have empathy and an open mind throughout the process. Otherwise, bad expressions may lead to different or even opposite answers, deviating from user's reality.

To certain extent, traditional methods reveal user needs, but suffer from poor efficiency and non-negligible influence of mood and environment. Hence, they are not suitable for researching on massive users. On the other hand, the original knowledge produced by users themselves better expresses their real thought. Big data technology has made it possible and cheaper to study large groups of users. Till now, it is frequently used in many fields like finance, online business, healthcare, social security and smart city, comparatively rare in that of design.

Data mining can be a new aspect for extending the study of user experience and user knowledge. This paper describes how to dig for user knowledge and understand their needs by large-scale data searching and image content analysis technologies and finally construct user knowledge system which ensures excellent user experience. The methods described in this paper are also good references to other design research.

2 Methodology Description

2.1 Overview

This paper mainly elucidate how we apply image feature recognition and content analysis technologies to obtain research variables, which are later estimated by statistical calculation, in order to acquire user knowledge and construct corresponding system. The detailed research process is as follows:

- **How to acquire user knowledge?** When using certain products or services, users would exchange information (namely words, images and voice) and this information could be recognized as "user knowledge" since they directly reflect users' demands. For instance, users of photo sharing social websites interact with each other by uploading images, clicking "like", commenting and reposting. In the process of this type of interactions, users undoubtedly leave "internet footprints" as a part of user knowledge, which manifest their attention and preference.
- **How to acquire users' footprints?** In short, one could apply respective techniques to figure out the footprints left by users. For example, equipped with public programming interfaces exposed by relevant websites (e.g. WeChat API) and web crawler programs, one is able to get users' information such as images, texts, and voice, under certain agreement of privacy. The emerging of new technologies fulfills the purpose of image analysis, broadening the area of information capture and analysis.
- **Analysis methodology and tools.** Three main methods have been exploited, including image feature identification, content analysis and statistical calculation.

2.2 Details of Three Methods

Image Feature Recognition. Three particular tools fall into this category.

Analyzing tools for color spatial distribution. Based on pixel RGB values of sample images, this tool generates color spatial points and conducts clustering and dimension-reduction processing through vector calculation and principal component analysis. The result can help researchers analyze variation in color characteristics of samples from different users.

Extracting tools for sample dominant color tone. Based on the calculation of pixel color features, this tool respectively generates the entire color constitution, by which the dominant 80 % colors of raw samples can be represented (Fig. 2). After that, it will conduct batch processing analysis and generate a form for each sample, manifesting its dominant color tone for following analysis of multi-dimensional color deviation (Fig. 1).

Fig. 1. Extracting tools for sample dominant color (Color figure online)

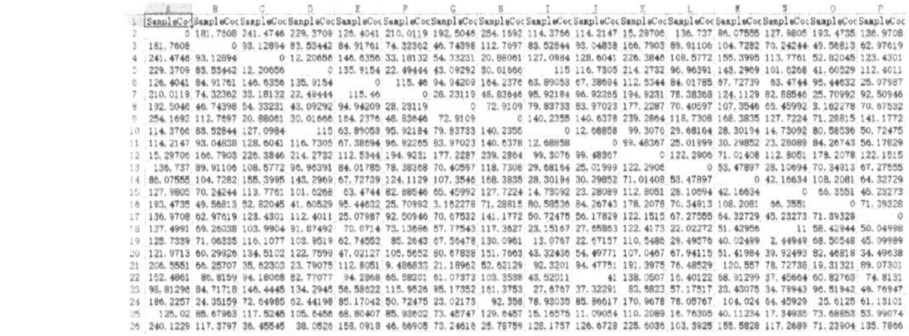

Fig. 2. Analyzing tools for the similarity of sample dominant colors (themeDistComputing Tool_v1).

Analyzing tools for the similarity of sample dominant color tone. Depending on sample dominant color tone data, this tool calculates the dominant color tone similarity between each pair among 574 samples and generates csv format files as the input of statistical calculations in MDS analysis.

Content Analyzing Technology. Content analysis is a technology which analyzes the content of samples and generates a structured variable system to describe these samples by means of tags. The tags demonstrate the category and order description of the samples, in order to support future statistical analysis and search for similarity or differences.

Base on the overall analysis of samples, several descriptive variables have been proposed and labeled. In the scope of this research, all labels fall into one of the following six categories: picture type, picture theme, composition, means of expression, light and shade, image style.

Next, we introduce the notion of matrix of metrical data which is by definition a table for managing samples and corresponding variable labels. All assignment of values to variables results from combination of image feature and artificial labeling. Based on this matrix, all data is imported into SPSS after necessary normalization for next descriptive statistical analysis and advanced calculation.

Statistical Calculation. Statistical calculation provides a way to discover the internal relation between objective elements shown by pictures and subjective recognition of users, by means of clustering, multi-dimensional analysis and some other tools.

Correspondence analysis is the main statistical method used in this research. The connections between variables are represented graphically by interaction summary table. This analysis technique is suitable for situations with many qualitative variables in which connections between these variables of different categories is to be established. SPSS is a prevalent software for this kind of analysis.

Nowadays correspondence analysis is widely used in early-stage concept designing, in areas of developing new product, market positioning and advertisement. It has become an important tool for designers and market researchers to solve the problem of evaluating product property, competitor and targeting market.

3 Case Study of Photo Sharing Websites

Benefited from massive data mining technology, we selected a popular use case to launch our study which concentrated on constructing user knowledge of photo sharing websites and further analyzing the needs and psychological features of their active users.

Many user actions can be regarded as the process of producing user knowledge, including uploading photos and social operations such as clicking a like, commenting and reposting. In this scenario, user knowledge lies in the images, text and user actions. Although text usually indicates the exact thought of users, understanding the meaning by programming is very hard and most importantly text cannot reflect the relation between the image itself and users' judgement on it.

After careful consideration, the popular images in photo-sharing websites were chosen as the main object for studying, fulfilling the purpose of mining information apropos to images itself, user preferences and their relation.

3.1 Selecting Target Website

There are many well-known photo-sharing websites including Instagram, Lofter and Flickr by Yahoo. We finally chose Flickr after comparing the foundation date, number of users and some other aspects. Flickr is an image hosting and video hosting website and the web services suite was created by Ludicorp in 2004, acquired by Yahoo in

2005. It offers preeminent services including picture uploading and storing, classification, tagging and searching. Users need to fill in their profiles after registration and the profiles can help us in future study.

In the uploading process, users are required to give the picture a title, a description and some tags. For managing photos more effectively, users can create "set", which is similar to a photo album.

Users of Flickr have various background, from professional photographers to PS amateur. All of them enjoy uploading their favorite photos, adding tags and descriptions and creating sets for them. Social operations are even more popular since everybody loves discovering beautiful pictures and grabbing attention of others reflected by the number of like

Fig. 3. Flickr website

and comments. The feature of a particular user can be revealed by the pictures s/he likes and hottest pictures manifest the inclination of most users. As a result, these hottest pictures provide us an effective way of getting the features we are studying, analyzing user disposition and finally construct user knowledge system of the website. The purpose of this study is exploring the type and features of popular pictures shared by Flickr users and describing their behaviors in Flickr (Fig. 3).

3.2   Process of Research

Flickr holds an annual show named "best shot", selecting the most popular pictures of that year. We selected pictures from "2015 best shot" to narrow down the sample domain. Totally 574 pictures were filtered out through our crawler programs because they receive more than 99 comments or likes.

Based on previous state-of-the-art studies, we divided all labels into 6 categories.

- **Picture type:** daily; documentary; black and white; art; portrait; landscape; abstract; report;
- **Picture theme:** natural scenery; animals and insects; flowers and plants; still-life objects; character portrait; cultural construction; scene of stories; light rhythm;
- **Composition:** nine-squared; diagonal; symmetry; frame; guide line; dynamic; triangle; photographic subtraction; special angle; repetition; vertical; curve; slash; centripetal; change; S-shape; open type; balance;
- **Means of expression:** simplification; choice; comparison; contrast; scenery depth; background; lines; balance; motion; perspective; reflection;

- **Light and shade:** backlight; soft light; capture light; appropriate exposure; contrast of exposure level; low angle light source; regional exposure; multicolor contrast;
- **Image style:** traditional nostalgic, romantic, solemn and elegant, deep and solemn, easy dial, decorative arts, comparison of cool & warm, open magic, scarce unique, novel and creative, human sensations, rhythm, non-mainstream

In order to synthesize tag information, the matrix should be transformed into questionnaire. Some experts in both design and photography assigned the tags shown above to the 574 samples based on certain principles explored in previous studies.

With the 574 samples and their tags, the matrix of metrical data was established, a measure method previously mentioned. The matrix was being imported to SPSS latter (Fig. 4).

Matrix of Metrical Data – 574 Sample

No.	Pic	Picture Type	Picture Theme	Composition	Means of Expression	Light and Shade	Image Style
		daily; documentary; black and white; art; portrait; landscape; abstract; report;	natural scenery; animals and insects; flowers and plants; still-life objects; character portrait; cultural construction; scene of stories; light rhythm;	nine-squared; diagonal; symmetry; frame; guide line; dynamic; triangle; photographic subtraction; special angle; repetition; vertical; curve; slash; contrapotal; change; S-shape; open type; balance;	simplification; choice; comparison; contrast; scenery depth; back-ground; lines; balance; motion; perspective; reflection;	backlight; soft light; capture light; appropriate exposure; contrast of exposure level; low angle light source; regional exposure; multicolor contrast;	traditional nostalgic; roman-tic, solemn and elegant, deep and solemn, easy dial, decorative arts, comparison of cool & warm, open magic, scarce unique, novel and creative, human sensations, rhythm, non-mainstream
F-001							
F-002							
......							
F-574							

Fig. 4. Matrix of metrical data

4 Result

4.1 Result Evaluation of Image Feature Identification

According to the design of research previously described, the research of image features mainly involves feature extraction of the samples. The extraction job includes:

Make quantitative analysis based on color attributes of the sample (sample pixel RGB value). The main research steps include extracting the dominant color tone. According to the specific features of samples, the composition of the picture usually differs in many ways. Some of them possess a conspicuous dominant color tone while others are composed of many colors. Whatever, the number of dominant color tones of certain sample is able to represent 80 % of its color information.

The representative color tone of samples is evolved from all dominant color tones, which is used to analyze similarity between samples.

The distance between the color tones, which occupies relatively larger proportion of dominant color tones, is calculated based on the composition of each sample.

Figure 5 illustrate the similarity of the positioning of color space, based on our calculation and analysis.

Figure 6 illustrate the similarity analysis of dominant color tones, by the MDS multidimensional scaling function of themeDist ComputingTool_v1.

In Fig. 7, it is obvious that all of the samples shows remarkable patterns on positioning distribution of dominant color tone similarity. Based on the distribution of scattered plots, a two element regression equation is obtained by two order curve fitting:

Fig. 5. The similarity of the positioning of color space. (Color figure online)

$$y = -0.2 + -0.27 * x + 0.53 * x^2$$

To make the distribution pattern of the result more easily determined, researchers supplement information for Fig. 8 and 574 dominant color tone palette which are also positioned to the corresponding scattered positions.

We found that despite the differences in properties and content among the 574 samples, a significant pattern exists in the features of visual cognition of dominant color tones. The pattern was represented by the mild gradient of brightness from darkness on the left to brightness on the right. However, no obvious pattern was recognized in vertical dimension. In addition, the significance of saturation in center and center-right areas in the U-shape curve area is higher than that in other areas.

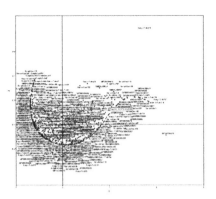

Fig. 6. Theme Color Position-1.

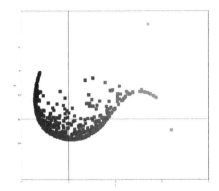

Fig. 7. Theme Color Position-2 (Color figure online)

To sum up, it is convincing that the 574 samples primarily reflects differences in saturation and color temperature in terms of color properties, based on the result of color space positioning analysis and dominant color tone similarity MDS analysis.

4.2   Result Evaluation of Statistical Calculation

Recall previous discussion, correspondence analysis is the main method in this research. The location map analysis, resulting from 574 samples in all dimensions, is discussed below. Among all the dimensions, abundance of color tones is particular interesting so that the first part of this section makes a comparison between it and other dimensions while the second part discusses results within the other dimensions.

Abundance of Color Tones Compare to Other Dimensions

Picture Theme. Picture Theme The sig value is 1.000a, which indicates that there's no significant relation between picture theme and tone abundance. No typical pattern is recognized in the distribution of the sample from different topics. In addition, the theme of still life objects is rare in the sample.

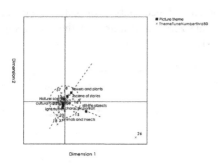

Fig. 8. Picture theme   **Fig. 9.** Composition

Composition. The sig value is 1.000a, one can see that most types of the composition is in a relatively concentrated manner while the diagonal type and curves type are relatively rare (Fig. 9).

Means of Expression. In this figure, excepting the line type, the performance is similar in the majority of the sample (Fig. 10).

Light and Shade. The sig value is 1.000a. There is no obvious correlation between lighting and tone abundance in this dimension. Meanwhile, low angle light source is more unique due to the special angle (Fig. 11).

Image Style. The sig value is 1.000a. Image style and tone abundance have no significant correlation. However, the rhythm is relatively rare (Fig. 12).

Results Within Other Dimensions. Overall, three common features were found through all 574 samples. Firstly, in terms of the type, pictures about scenery or daily lives ranked the highest; then follows art, documentary and portrait; report and abstract had the least quantity. Secondly, for the composition, most samples were showed in a

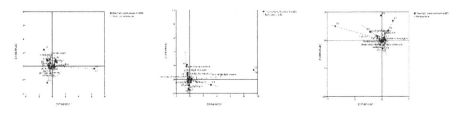

Fig. 10. Means of expression   **Fig. 11.** Lights and shade   **Fig. 12.** Image style

way of nine-squared or symmetry, which is associated with human aesthetic physiological characteristics. People like pictures which are concisely composed with a certain guidance or restriction, such as radial line, leading line, diagonal, or frame. The third common feature lies in image style. The most popular pictures are usually unique and relaxing. Nostalgic, romantic, solemn, aesthetic and novel ingredients are welcome as well. In contrast, popular pictures are scarcely in themes of rhythm, contrast or humanity.

The four results of specific analysis are shown in following figures.

Picture Type Compare to Image Style. The correspondence analysis of picture type and styles, with 574 effective samples and Sig value zero, indicating that there is a significant correlation between the type and the style.

The common aesthetic taste of inclining scenery and daily type of pictures was very likely being developed along with the evolution of human beings. Analysis of this type indicates that ancient prairie scenery, composed by fresh grass, low jungles and winding streams, gives comfortable and congruent feelings to people living in nearly all places. People often find senses of identity from documentary and portrait paintings, making it the second popular type. Abstract pictures are only appreciated by a small group of people (Fig. 13).

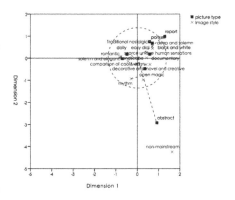

Fig. 13. Picture type&Image style

The result also shows that there's a common mapping between image content type and means of expression. Sceneries are normally expressed through romantic, solemn, elegant or temperature contrasting styles, portraits by nostalgic and black-white ways and artistic pictures by decorating, novel, open magical ones.

Composition Compare to Image Style. In the correspondence analysis of this comparison, 562 effective samples leaded to a sig value of 0.005, suggesting a significant connection between image style and composition (Fig. 14).

In the history of human aesthetic, nine-squared and symmetric have occupied their place in composition. Famous historical buildings, from Gothic to Chinese style, are

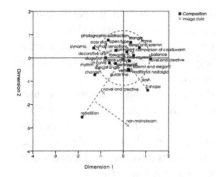

Fig. 14. Composition&Image style

designed to be strictly symmetric. Centripetal, guide-line, diagonal and frame are also prevailing metamorphism of symmetric.

The paring of romantic with symmetric, traditional with vertical, nine-squared with temperature contrast, can serve as a good reference for future composition designing.

Light and Shade Compare to Image Style. Scarce unique and easy dial are the two most welcome styles. The pessimistic nature of deep and solemn and the direct definition of non-mainstream causes the lack of attraction to the majority (Fig. 15).

Considering both dimensions, there's significant relation between backlight and solemn, capture light and temperature contrast, regional exposure and elegant. Appropriate exposure is suitable for many styles, including romantic, human sensations, traditional nostalgic and easy dial.

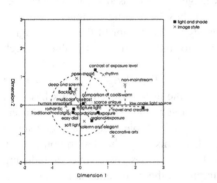

Fig.15. Light and shade&Image style

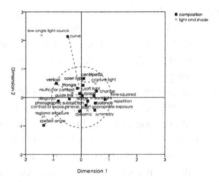

Fig. 16. Composition&Light and shade

Composition Compare to Light and Shade. Soft light pictures typically adopt expressions of S-shape, triangle, open type and centripetal. Diagonal and guide-lines are mostly used in photographic subtraction, while appropriate exposure in balance. Soft light and contrast of exposure level are totally opposite shown in the figure, indicating the thorough difference (Fig. 16).

5   Conclusion

By extracting features of the sample images, analyzing the contents of semantic tags, looking for common features in popular images which hold relatively high degree of users' attention, and studying the corresponding relationship between each label; this essay tends to figure out why users are paying more attention to landscape images. In addition, users favor composition balance, nine-squared format, with proper exposure, backlight or the way of capturing light. Besides, users also prefer the traditional nostalgia, deep dignified black and white photos or portraits; Photos they like range from lyrical romantic, lively, unique landscape to the daily theme; Over and above, users are also interested in innovative photos as well as open magic art photos.

These findings are significant for the construction of photo sharing site user knowledge. In the future, against such users who like sharing photos on these photos sharing websites, you can understand the relationship between the key themes of their favorite pictures, the composition and expression, light and shadow, style and tone. Designers can learn the preferences and needs of such users through first-hand detailed and reliable data to apply to other designs designed for this kind of user.

In this study, the method used is construction of user knowledge system by analyzing user behavior among those who like sharing pictures. This method can also be used in many other aspects of the behavior of keywords. For example, in the field of advertising communication, product packing design and all other users knowledge mining areas related to pictures.

In this study, the construction of the user knowledge mining method is different from the traditional method of user experience. As a result, it can be used in many aspects and fields to establish the user knowledge system based on general characteristics of different users' needs, concerns, and thus facilitating designers' working process. When identified certain feature of the keyword behavior of the user, designer can quickly draw from the user knowledge bank to find effective and usable research data for reference to aid their design decisions.

Mining and Construction of such a user's knowledge system can be time-consuming in the early stage. However, once the user knowledge bank has been set up, it will not only facilitate the designer to effectively understand the needs of users and help decision-making, but also makes it easier for multiple designers in one single design projects to understand the common goal. In this way, the design consistency among several designers can be ensured and it saves designers time in reducing communication costs and in the end largely improves the communication quality.

This study mainly introduces the user knowledge, image mining method. What remains to be analyzed is the construction of other points of the user knowledge, such as text and sound. It is an area which still worth further studying and forms general research methods and theories. These aspects can be used as subsequent supplementary research for user's knowledge system construction.

A well-established user database is built on both the traditional method and the innovative new one. Getting to understand users' need from multi-dimensional perspective of big data method as well as the traditional way of conducting interview, survey and focus group seems to be the new trend. However, this essay deems that the new method of construction is fundamental to this trend while combined with the traditional method will make it better.

References

1. McDonald, J.E., Schvaneveldt, R.W.: The application of user knowledge to interface design. In: Cognitive Science and its Applications for Human-Computer Interaction, pp. 289–338 (1988)
2. Blandford, A., Young, R.M.: Specifying user knowledge for the design of interactive systems. Softw. Eng. J. 11(6), 323–333 (1996)
3. De Rosis, F., Pizzutilo, S., Russo, A., et al.: Modeling the user knowledge by belief networks. User Model. User-Adap. Inter. 2(4), 367–388 (1992)
4. Tesch, D., Sobol, M.G., Klein, G., et al.: User and developer common knowledge: Effect on the success of information system development projects. Int. J. Project Manage. 27(7), 657–664 (2009)
5. Bevan, N.: What is the difference between the purpose of usability and user experience evaluation methods. In: Proceedings of the Workshop UXEM, 9, pp. 1–4 (2009)
6. Vermeeren, A.P.O.S., Law, E.L.C., Roto, V., et al.: User experience evaluation methods: current state and development needs. In: Proceedings of the 6th Nordic Conference on Human-Computer Interaction: Extending Boundaries, pp. 521–530. ACM (2010)
7. Law, E.L.C., Roto, V., Hassenzahl, M., et al.: Understanding, scoping and defining user experience: a survey approach. In: Proceedings of the SIGCHI Conference on Human Factors in Computing Systems, pp. 719–728. ACM (2009)
8. Hassenzahl, M., Tractinsky, N.: User experience-a research agenda[J]. Behav. Inf. Technol. 25(2), 91–97 (2006)
9. Väänänen-Vainio-Mattila, K., Roto, V., Hassenzahl, M.: Towards practical user experience evaluation methods. In: Law, E.L.-C., Bevan, N., Christou, G., Springett, M., Lárusdóttir, M. (eds.) Meaningful Measures: Valid Useful User Experience Measurement, pp. 19–22 (2008)
10. Obrist, M., Roto, V., Väänänen-Vainio-Mattila, K.: User experience evaluation: do you know which method to use? In: CHI 2009 Extended Abstracts on Human Factors in Computing Systems, pp. 2763–2766. ACM (2009)
11. Maguire, M.: Methods to support human-centred design. Int. J. Hum. Comput. Stud. 55(4), 587–634 (2001)
12. Fan, W., Bifet, A.: Mining big data: current status, and forecast to the future. ACM sIGKDD Explor. Newsl. 14(2), 1–5 (2013)
13. Fisher, D., DeLine, R., Czerwinski, M., et al.: Interactions with big data analytics. Interactions 19(3), 50–59 (2012)
14. Sarmento, L., Carvalho, P., Silva, M.J., et al.: Automatic creation of a reference corpus for political opinion mining in user-generated content. In: Proceedings of the 1st International CIKM Workshop on Topic-Sentiment Analysis for Mass Opinion, pp. 29–36. ACM (2009)
15. Graham, J.: Flickr of idea on a gaming project led to photo website. USA Today, 27 (2006)
16. Miller, A.D., Edwards, W.K.: Give and take: a study of consumer photo-sharing culture and practice. In: Proceedings of the SIGCHI Conference on Human Factors in Computing Systems, pp. 347–356. ACM (2007)
17. Liu, S.B., Palen, L., Sutton, J., et al.: In search of the bigger picture: The emergent role of on-line photo sharing in times of disaster. In: Proceedings of the Information Systems for Crisis Response and Management Conference (ISCRAM) (2008)
18. Sigurbjörnsson, B., Van Zwol, R.: Flickr tag recommendation based on collective knowledge. In: Proceedings of the 17th International Conference on World Wide Web, pp. 327–336. ACM (2008)

19. Mislove, A., Koppula, H.S., Gummadi, K.P., et al.: Growth of the flickr social network. In: Proceedings of the First Workshop on Online Social Networks, pp. 25–30. ACM (2008)

20. Kennedy, L., Naaman, M., Ahern, S., et al.: How flickr helps us make sense of the world: context and content in community-contributed media collections. In: Proceedings of the 15th International Conference on Multimedia, pp. 631–640. ACM (2007)

21. Yongchang, J.: Knowledge architecture based on user experience: a review of the basic principles for knowledge architecture in web 2.0. J. China Soc. Sci. Techn. Inf. **5**, 018 (2010)

22. McGinn, J., Kotamraju, N.: Datadriven persona development. In: Proceedings of the SIGCHI Conference on Human Factors in Computing Systems, pp. 1521–1524. ACM (2008)

Open Data Evolution in Information Systems Research: Considering Cases of Data-Intensive Transportation and Grid Systems

Frederik Schulte[1], Hashim Iqbal Chunpir[2,3,4(✉)], and Stefan Voß[1]

[1] Institute of Information Systems, University of Hamburg, Hamburg, Germany
{frederik.schulte,stefan.voss}@uni-hamburg.de
[2] Department of Computer Science, Universidade Federal de São Carlos,
São Paulo, Brazil
[3] Faculty of Informatics, University of Hamburg, Vogt-Kölln-Street 30,
Hamburg, Germany
[4] German Climate Computing Centre (DKRZ), Bundesstraße 45a,
Hamburg, Germany
chunpir@dkrz.de

Abstract. Open data (OD) use and the opening of data have become major strategic objectives in different communities. Nevertheless, the potential of OD is still not leveraged in many areas. In this work, we focus the OD impact information systems research. We review the respective literature for different domains of OD research and analyze cases of data-intensive decision support systems in transportation as well as open research grid systems. The resulting changes, challenges, and opportunities that OD causes are categorized according to different OD activities in IS research. Hence, they may serve as an agenda to foster OD practices, platforms, and administration in the area.

1 Introduction

In research, open data (OD) is considered as a transitional term in the process of defining how scientific data may be published and re-used without price or permission barriers [16,18]. Technological development has made it increasingly convenient to share even big and dynamic data in various relations between individuals and organizations under the OD paradigm. Companies share data with customers and developers, governments share data with citizens, researchers work on OD and share data they created, and many more examples can be observed. Applications are documented in transport [13,20], health care [12], e-government [14], and other domains. In contrast, an OD movement in science claims that information processing habits of scientists dramatically lag this development [5] and wants science to be understood as a public enterprise with open doors. The mounting presence of open data poses the question how research practices will change when data is on the edge from proprietary good of single researcher or research group to free public resource. Molloy [17] and Vision [24] explicitly address this question. While Molloy discusses specific principals for OD

A. Marcus (Ed.): DUXU 2016, Part III, LNCS 9748, pp. 193–201, 2016.
DOI: 10.1007/978-3-319-40406-6_18

in science, Vision points out that open data may alter centuries-old social contract governing scientific publishing. In general, literature provides a significant body of theoretic foundations on the topic. However, there is little work that evaluates the impact based on cases. In this paper, we make use of the theoretical hypotheses and evaluate them for the case of OD based research on decision support for data-intensive vehicle sharing systems. In the following, we present relevant literature on OD research, three distinct cases of OD use in IS research, a discussion on OD shifts in information systems (IS) research, and conclusions drawn from the study. After the literature review in Sect. 2, we introduce cases of data-intensive systems in decision support research and open research grids in Sect. 3. On this foundation, Sect. 4 discusses changes, challenges, and opportunities arising with OD emergence. Finally, Sect. 5 concludes the study and gives an outlook on future research.

2   Open Data in Research

Research on OD can be classified in four major domains. First, studies that apply OD to develop methods, approaches, and generate results that fundamentally depend on the usage of OD are observed. These studies often do not explicitly discuss the contribution of OD for their research, but still provide significant insights on the value and importance OD in science. Second, research that focuses on the development of platforms, communities, systems to gather and provide OD for their users. These endeavors also cover the challenge to link OD on the Internet. Third, studies that examine the use of OD in different communities and institutions such as science, government, or enterprises. Fourth, endeavors that examine social and technological impediments of OD implementations. In the first domain, a plenty of studies can be found in decision support systems (DSS), public systems, and research systems. OD use cases in respective systems are discussed in detail in Sect. 3. A vivid example for related research is provided by the smart* project [2]. This project is based on a system that gathers data from three real homes to enable an in-depth data analysis, e.g., time-dependent electricity usage for every plug load, rather than collecting abstract data for a larger set of households. Both, the tools for data collection and the generated data sets, are made openly available to encourage the design of future sustainable homes.

In the second domain, the OD project DBpedia stands out [1]. The project uses Wikipedia articles and data tables to generate structured OD available on the Web. This enables all kinds of users to perform sophisticated queries on the generated datasets. Another glaring example for OD platforms is the cBio cancer genomics portal [6]. The portal provides access to more than 5000 tumor samples and enables cancer researchers to use the complex genomics data for their studies. To multiply the positive effects of OD on the Internet, researchers are engaged to link OD platform and portals [3,4]. Bizer et al. [4] describe the application of semantic Web techniques to interlink OD on the Internet. These techniques enable an automated linking process of OD sets on the Web. Bauer and Kaltenböck [3], on the other hand, provide a guide with case studies of linked open data. A semantic Web approach for linked open geographical data based on OpenStreetMap is introduced by [23].

In the third domain, OD use in science and public administration are the dominating topics. Boulton et al. [5] frankly lament that research habits in dealing with data dramatically lag behind the information technology progress made to improve science by means OD. The authors describe a kind of protectionism of researchers in dealing with data stating: "Scientists have tended to regard their data as personal property. After all, it is they who worked hard to generate it and ownership has never been seriously challenged." Next to this work, there are numerous other studies that claim a new research culture around OD. Murray-Rust [18] reviews the need for OD in science and discusses examples of OD use as well initiatives to formalize the right to access and re-use scientific data. In the same realm, Molloy [17] is convinced the more data becomes openly available the more efficient the scientific process will be to serve the society. The author discusses the so called Panton principles for OD in science. On the other side, public administration OD is discussed for e-government [14] and health care [12]. These studies also take a critical perspective on the ethics, economics, social, and political effects of OD use.

In the fourth domain, social and technological obstacles as well as opportunities of the OD movement are discussed. Zuiderwijk et al. [27] provide an overview of socio-technical impediments of OD. Based on literature, interviews, and workshops the authors derive 118 OD adoption issues. Reichman et al. [19] examine the potential of open data for ecology and distinguish technological challenges like heterogeneous data and sociological challenges, e.g., adequate rewards to encourage data sharing. Janssen et al. [15] gather qualitative data based interviews and workshops to analyze benefits and adoptions barriers of OD. This work reveals wrong views and myths on OD.

3 Open Data Use Cases

As shown in Sect. 2, OD is viewed from different angles in research. Subsequently, we discuss cases of data-intensive decision support systems (Sect. 3.1) and research grid systems (Sect. 3.2) to shed some light on different domains.

3.1 Decision Support Systems in Transportation

Major applications of public and commercial OD are examined by research on DSS in transportation. For instance, free-floating car-sharing systems (FFCS) face a rapid growth, making car sharing an attractive alternative to a self-owned car. Literature has furthermore demonstrated that, like in bike-sharing, FFCS tend to get imbalanced and system providers are challenged to reposition vehicles in an economic and eco-friendly fashion. The business model and related decision support research make use of OD provided by the system provider. To encourage app development and to enter social network (SN) communities, system providers, such as car2go, started to provide web based interfaces that offer comprehensive real-time OD from their systems. This creates new opportunities for researchers to develop smart strategies and optimization algorithms to guide relocation and balancing attempts in car sharing [13,20]. In addition, access to SNs enables new forms of sharing. In FFCS, SNs can, e.g., connect users, combine trips, help to share demand, and relieve high demand areas in car sharing systems. Thus, OD enables an integrated approach for decision support in balancing FFCS and evaluating user-orientated relocation strategies based on SNs. A Facebook-based app may facilitate ride sharing based on open provider data and user-based relocations. For the demand analysis, a clustering approach may be used to model car2go demand data and support effective relocation plans. Furthermore, demand forecasts and real-time data from the system provider can serve in an integrated decision support approach to control the application of relocation strategies. For the evaluation, a simulation study may use booking and availability data from a provider like car2go [13]. This paves the way for new approaches towards short term forecasting of FFCS demand and an integrated decision support approach for relocation in FFCS with a quantitative analysis of costs and emissions for various relocation strategies using real-time data. The case study clearly demonstrates that the OD based car sharing provides more options for decision support research. Here, forecasts could be improved significantly based on extensive real-time data, and a potential app could be interfaced for future ride-sharing. Moreover, the data availability also grants that researchers can easily replicate the conducted studies and enrich them with their own ideas.

While FFCS may be an obvious application of OD based DSS research, there are more cases in the transportation area in which DSS leverages new OD availability. For instance, airport emissions have recently received plenty of attention by regulators, airport operators, and researchers developing approaches for environmental sustainability. Empirical research has shown that airside or ground operations form a significant percentage of overall airport related emissions [25]. Among those operations, taxiing is one of the most emission-intensive processes, closely related to the initiating pushback process – that in many cases determines the taxiing duration [22]. Thus, various approaches to reduce taxiing emissions have been introduced recently [22,26]. Possible approaches to tackle this problem are simulation and optimization models for an effective management of pushbacks as a resource at the airport. Promising relocation models [13] and adoptions of the vehicle routing problem [21] have been proposed for related problems in different domains. To produce realistic results, such approaches need realistic data on airside operations such as pushback movements and aircraft movements during taxiing. Other than that, proposed approaches are not able to model a comprehensive planning environment for airside operations and pushback availability would rather be understood as an input for taxiing planning. Fortunately, OD on airport ground movements became available for various airports [11]. It is proposed to plan taxiing in order to minimize waiting times and emissions and to schedule pushbacks on that basis. For this approach, pushback vehicles need to be relocated according to their position and the position of the aircraft scheduled for taxiing. This data is also available as OD. Respective algorithms are applied in a realistic simulation environment for airside operations with probability distributions derived from OD and evaluated for real-world cases of various airports. In this case, OD allows easy real-time data access for airside operations visualized in a map. Based on this information, comparisons between different airports can be conducted easily.

3.2   Open Research Grid Systems

Distributed data grids enable users to store, access, and download large amounts of data for research purposes as open research data. These data grids serve OD using open technologies that constitute an e-research platform for open use of data. Distributed data grids are also linked to each other in the form of a network to form larger federations. They mainly serve research communities interacting with distributed data grid federations. These communities include biology, physics, earth system modeling (ESM) and other research areas. The researchers or the end-users interact with the data grids for research purposes. The end-users perform operations such as finding data, downloading data, visualizing data and processing of data amongst other operations. Interaction of the end-users with the data grid interfaces is not always smooth; generally users face various problems while interacting with data grids [7].

These systems have been evolving from the technical test-bed to service oriented systems [9]. The organization, function, technical-architecture, data management, high performance computation facilities, usability, and level of inclusion of users have been constantly on a change. In order to meet the change, there have been numerous challenges that span from technical impediments to political problems. At the same time, there are number of opportunities of improvement and further development that are associated to challenges and changes. In this paper, we take an example of a well-known e-research facility called Earth System Grid Federation (ESGF) that is serving data projects in climate science domain. ESGF facilitates to study climate change and impact of climate change on human society and earths eco system. It has currently 27000 users, mainly researchers [8]. There have been organizational changes proposed in ESGF that facilitate collaboration amongst partners such as user support working team. It is evident from the observations that the aspects of usability and user experience within e-research facilities especially in climate science need improvement [8]. Moreover, ESGF needs to scale with big data produced by higher resolution models, satellites, and instruments [9]. The server side functionality is expected to be expanded. Server side processing through WPS (climate indexes, custom algorithms) is needed and computer scientists are working on that as well as expanding the GIS mapping services for climate change impact studies at regional and local scale. ESGF is making advances to facilitate a model to observations, inter-comparisons, and expand direct client access capabilities. The need for increased support for OpenDAP based access is felt by the ESGF development team and it is expected to meet this need in the next few years

[9]. Tracking provenance of complex processing work flows for reproducibility as well as the origin of data sets is a major challenge and ESGF has some top scientists working on that [9]. At the same time, ESGF intends to package virtual machines for cloud deployment and instantiate ESGF nodes on demand for short life-time projects. As the data demands increase, ESGF is creating an environment with elastic allocation of back-end storage and computing resources. In the future, ESGF will cover other scientific domains such as health sciences, biology, chemistry, energy as well radio-astronomy [10]. With these additions of domains more users will be using the ESGF e-research facility, making usability and user experience very important. Consequently, there are opportunities to invest to enhance the user experience and customized interfaces to attract not only more and more researchers, but also other interested public who want to know and contribute to climate science by accessing or modifying climate open data.

4   Evolution of Open Data in Information Systems Research

Based on the literature review in Sect. 2 and the use cases in Sect. 3, we derive changes initiated by emerging OD and discuss challenges and opportunities that go along with it. Table 1 lists those items and distinguishes OD practice, provision, and administration in IS research.

Changes in OD practice predominantly relate to an equal right of access that goes a long with fact that pure data will no longer perceived as the property or achievement of a researcher or a research group. Also the validation and replication of academic work is eased, creating opportunities as transparency and transforming data into a public resource or infrastructure. Furthermore, efficiency in scientific work may benefit from data re-use, simplified collaboration, real-time data access, and pre-processed data. Nevertheless, successful OD applications have to overcome a number of challenges. Data availability depends on the development of the right incentives for data sharing and breaking habits of data protection as well as finding publisher agreements data sharing. Moreover, data quality assurance needs to grant data validity and complete information about the data sets. Further challenges relate to data pre-processing that often requires sound statistical skills. OD provision, on the other hand, is characterized by connected data structures and Web-based access. This goes along with opportunities for combination of data, data re-use, and standards development. Furthermore, users may generate data structures and enrich data using apps or social networks. On the contrary, challenges are created by data acquisition, opening data, infrastructure costs, and establishing the OD network. Especially, for the discussed data-intensive systems, a scalable server architecture is needed. This also entails indexing, meta-data generation, and semantic Web approaches. Finally, OD enables an administration with simplified knowledge transfer, additional user services, and accountability. This may also lead to improved visibility and user services for the administrating organization, triggering participation

Table 1. Development of OD practice, provision, and administration in research

Category	Changes	Opportunities	Challenges
OD practice	equal right data access	more efficient science	incentives for sharing
	data no longer property	transparency	habits of protectionism
	data no longer achievement	eased collaboration	publisher restrictions
	eased replication	data re-use	data quality assurance
	eased validation	pre-processed data	incomplete information
		real-time data access	data validation
		data as infrastructure	data pre-processing
			statistics often required
OD provision	connected data structures	combination of data	opening data
	Web-based access	data re-use	organizing OD network
		standards development	data acquisition
		user based structures	infrastructure costs
		data enrichment	indexing
			meta-data development
			semantic Web
OD administration	eased knowledge transfer	improved visibility	definition of OD rules
	additional user services	improved user service	data governance
	accountability	trust generation	user support
		participation	privacy legislation
		triggering innovation	security
			data ethics

and innovations as well as generating trust. On the side of challenges, nonetheless, the definition of OD rules is a major issue that also needs to capture data governance, privacy legislation, data ethics, and security. Moreover, user support needs to be taken into account.

5 Conclusion

The general benefits of OD use in science and other domains are widely acknowledged. Nevertheless, OD is still far from being a standard in information systems research. We have reviewed the OD literature and analyzed three cases of data-intensive systems to organize changes, challenges, and opportunities that OD generates in the field. We found that, despite the widely accepted immense potential, there are still some significant challenges to overcome until open data becomes an IS research standard and its prefix may be abolished. Though, OD is often seen as temporally limited expression that will vanish as soon as related practices have become standard. Hence, future work may also include an analysis of open science – where not only data, but also analyses and methods are shared to provide better transparency and reproducibility of results.

References

1. Auer, S., Bizer, C., Kobilarov, G., Lehmann, J., Cyganiak, R., Ives, Z.G.: DBpedia: a nucleus for a web of open data. In: Aberer, K., Choi, K.-S., Noy, N., Allemang, D., Lee, K.-I., Nixon, L.J.B., Golbeck, J., Mika, P., Maynard, D., Mizoguchi, R., Schreiber, G., Cudré-Mauroux, P. (eds.) ASWC 2007 and ISWC 2007. LNCS, vol. 4825, pp. 722–735. Springer, Heidelberg (2007)
2. Barker, S., Mishra, A., Irwin, D., Cecchet, E., Shenoy, P., Albrecht, J.: Smart*: An Open Data Set and Tools for Enabling Research in Sustainable Homes. University of Massachusetts Amherst, Amherst (2012)
3. Bauer, F., Kaltenböck, M.: Linked Open Data: The essentials. Semantic Web Company, Vienna (2011)
4. Bizer, C., Heath, T., Ayers, D., Raimond, Y.: Interlinking open data on the web. In: 4th European Semantic Web Conference on Demonstrations Track, Innsbruck, Austria (2007)
5. Boulton, G., Rawlins, M., Vallance, P., Walport, M.: Science as a public enterprise: the case for open data. Lancet **377**(9778), 1633–1635 (2011)
6. Cerami, E., Gao, J., Dogrusoz, U., Gross, B.E., Sumer, S.O., Aksoy, B.A., Jacobsen, A., Byrne, C.J., Heuer, M.L., Larsson, E., et al.: The cBio cancer genomics portal: an open platform for exploring multidimensional cancer genomics data. Cancer Discov. **2**(5), 401–404 (2012)
7. Chunpir, H.I.: Enhancing User Support Process in Federated e-Science. University of Hamburg, Hamburg (2015)
8. Chunpir, H.I., Ludwig, T., Badewi, A.A.: Using Soft Systems Methodology (SSM) in understanding current user-support scenario in the climate science domain of cyber-infrastructures. In: Marcus, A. (ed.) DUXU 2014, Part III. LNCS, vol. 8519, pp. 495–506. Springer, Heidelberg (2014)
9. Chunpir, H.I., Ludwig, T., Williams, D.N.: Evolution of e-research: from infrastructure development to service orientation. In: Marcus, A. (ed.) DUXU 2015. LNCS, vol. 9188, pp. 25–35. Springer, Heidelberg (2015)
10. Chunpir, H.I., Moll, A.: Analysis of marine ecosystems: usability, visualization and community collaboration challenges. Procedia Manuf. **3**, 3262–3265 (2015)
11. Flightradar24: (2016). https://www.flightradar24.com/52.31,4.78/14
12. Gurstein, M.B.: Open data: empowering the empowered or effective data use for everyone?. First Monday **16**(2) (2011). http://firstmonday.org/article/view/3316/2764. (Last Retrieved) Dec 19 2015
13. Herrmann, S., Schulte, F., Voß, S.: Increasing acceptance of free-floating car sharing systems using smart relocation strategies: a survey based study of car2go Hamburg. In: González-Ramírez, R.G., Schulte, F., Voß, S., Ceroni Díaz, J.A. (eds.) ICCL 2014. LNCS, vol. 8760, pp. 151–162. Springer, Heidelberg (2014)
14. Huijboom, N., Van den Broek, T.: Open data: an international comparison of strategies. Eur. J. ePractice **12**(1), 4–16 (2011)
15. Janssen, M., Charalabidis, Y., Zuiderwijk, A.: Benefits, adoption barriers and myths of open data and open government. Inf. Syst. Manag. **29**(4), 258–268 (2012)
16. Kitchin, R.: The Data Revolution: Big Data, Open Data, Data Infrastructures and their Consequences. Sage, London (2014)
17. Molloy, J.C.: The open knowledge foundation: open data means better science. PLoS Biol. **9**(12), e1001195 (2011)
18. Murray-Rust, P.: Open data in science. Serials Rev. **34**(1), 52–64 (2008)

19. Reichman, O., Jones, M.B., Schildhauer, M.P.: Challenges and opportunities of open data in ecology. Science **331**, 703–705 (2011)
20. Schulte, F., Voß, S.: Decision support for environmental-friendly vehicle relocations in free-floating car sharing systems: the case of car2go. Procedia CIRP **30**, 275–280 (2015)
21. Schwarze, S., Voß, S.: A bicriteria skill vehicle routing problem with time windows and an application to pushback operations at airports. In: Dethloff, J., Haasis, H.-D., Kopfer, H., Kotzab, H., Schönberger, J. (eds.) Logistics Management. Lecture Notes in Logistics, pp. 289–300. Springer, Heidelberg (2015)
22. Simaiakis, I., Balakrishnan, H.: Impact of congestion on taxi times, fuel burn, and emissions at major airports. Transp. Res. Rec. J. Transp. Res. Board **2184**, 22–30 (2010)
23. Stadler, C., Lehmann, J., Höffner, K., Auer, S.: Linkedgeodata: a core for a web of spatial open data. Semant. Web **3**(4), 333–354 (2012)
24. Vision, T.J.: Open data and the social contract of scientific publishing. BioScience **60**(5), 330–331 (2010)
25. Winther, M., Kousgaard, U., Ellermann, T., Massling, A., Nøjgaard, J.K., Ketzel, M.: Emissions of no x, particle mass and particle numbers from aircraft main engines, apu's and handling equipment at Copenhagen airport. Atmos. Environ. **100**, 218–229 (2015)
26. Wollenheit, R., Mühlhausen, T.: Operational and environmental assessment of electric taxi based on fast-time simulation. Transp. Res. Rec. J. Transp. Res. Board **2336**, 36–42 (2013)
27. Zuiderwijk, A., Janssen, M., Choenni, S., Meijer, R., Alibaks, R.S., Sheikh_Alibaks, R.: Socio-technical impediments of open data. Electron. J. eGovernment **10**(2), 156–172 (2012)

Multisensory Physical Environments for Data Representation

Patricia Search(✉)

Rensselaer Polytechnic Institute, Troy, NY, USA
searcp@rpi.edu

Abstract. This paper reviews theoretical research and projects in data representation that use different sensory modalities, embodiment, physical objects, and immersive environments. Other topics include the impact of cross-modal perception on data representation and the role audiovisual aesthetics play in the interpretation of data. Research has shown that cross-modal perception enhances sensory stimuli. Sound, touch, gesture, and movement engage the user and create holistic environments that provide multi-dimensional representations of complex data relationships. These data representations include data sculptures, ambient displays, and multisensory environments that use our intuitive abilities to process information from different sensory modalities. By using multiple senses, it is possible to increase the number of variables and relationships that can be represented simultaneously in complex data sets.

Keywords: Multisensory data representation · Cross-modal perception · Information aesthetics

1 Introduction

There are numerous visualization tools that make it possible to represent complex data sets using two-dimensional diagrams, animations, and virtual models. Interactive functions allow users to filter, sort, and compare different sets of variables to highlight specific relationships. Microsoft Excel, Tableau, and Google chart tools and Fusion Tables are just a few of the tools users can access to visualize and share data. Programming environments for data representation include Processing (http://procssing.org/), which designers and artists favor for creating animated visualizations that exist outside the browser, and D3.js (http://d3js.org/), which was launched in 2011 by the Stanford Visualization Group and includes a JavaScript library for creating web-based interactive data visualizations.

However, three-dimensional data visualizations that incorporate tactile objects, physical spaces, and blended spaces (that integrate virtual and physical data representations) can enhance our understanding of data relationships by tapping into our intuitive abilities to process data by using multiple senses. These representations use symbolic, iconic, and indexical references to data which may be defined by different sensory modalities [1]. Three-dimensional models incorporate interaction, kinesthetic design, embodiment, cross-modal perception, and multimodal semantic structures that define a new type of information aesthetic.

© Springer International Publishing Switzerland 2016
A. Marcus (Ed.): DUXU 2016, Part III, LNCS 9748, pp. 202–213, 2016.
DOI: 10.1007/978-3-319-40406-6_19

2   Three-Dimensional Data Representation

There are several forms of three-dimensional data representations that incorporate physical objects or physical space. Data sculptures are data-based, physical objects that signify data relationships [2]. They can range from three-dimensional extensions of two-dimensional graphs to unique abstract forms and metaphorical representations.

Research has shown that external representations can enhance our understanding of numerical tasks [3]. Vande Moere and Patel [4] demonstrated that physical data sculptures create dynamic narratives that illustrate process as well as outcomes. Data sculptures can represent quantitative relationships and qualitative information such as emotion and context. Physical materials or objects can represent literal connections with the data variables. For example, one of the data sculptures cited by Vande Moere and Patel [4] uses different types of cables (electric, electronic, headphone, phone, coaxial, and network cables) to construct a physical timeline that represents an individual's daily activities that use cables (pp. 10–11).

In interaction design, interfaces that use tangible connections to the physical world engage the senses and augment the learning experience [5, 6]. Dourish [6] noted that interaction with physical objects enhances cognition because tangible computing "is a physical realization of a symbolic reality, and the symbolic reality is, often, the world being manipulated." [p. 207]. Tangible interface designs can be applied to three-dimensional models and metaphorical references for data representation. For example, haptic interfaces can use inertia, force, torque, vibration, texture, and temperature to represent data variables and relationships in the physical world. Haptic interfaces enable users to interpret spatial relationships through the sense of touch. Palmerius [7] pointed out that "our sense of touch and kinesthetics is capable of supplying large amounts of intuitive information about the location, structure, stiffness and other material properties of objects" (p. 154).

Three-dimensional virtual models can be integrated into the surrounding physical space, allowing users to move in and around data representations projected into the environment. These environments may include ambient displays that turn elements in the surrounding architectural space, including physical objects, gases, and liquids, into "interfaces" that represent data [8]. Ambient displays communicate specific details as well as general information about the data variables and relationships. Data can be represented by different forms of sensory stimuli and create multiple levels of perception that lead to alternative perspectives and a holistic understanding of the information. Visual data representations can be augmented by auditory displays. For example, weather data might be enhanced by ambient sounds of rain or wind that reflect the force and velocity of these elements. The temperature of the room can mirror the actual outside temperature. With ambient displays, users can employ multiple senses to analyze relationships that might otherwise be missed [8].

However, the use of many different media and types of data representation can be distracting and overload the user with too much information. Current research is investigating the thresholds for ambient data designs to determine when there are too many media and data representations and how these thresholds transition from background (ambient) data to foreground data during different tasks [8].

Physical and virtual three-dimensional representations of data also provide another axis for mapping relationships, including dynamic changes over space and time. Three-dimensional models generate alternative perspectives and angles for viewing information. These different perspectives can highlight unexpected data relationships that might not be visible with two-dimensional representations.

Ameres and Clement [9], researchers at Rensselaer Polytechnic Institute (Troy, NY), have developed a unique three-dimensional computing interface call Campfire that allows a small group of users to collaborate on information analysis. The platform is a three-dimensional projection device, about six feet in diameter and two feet high, that allows participants to view data projected onto the walls and flat circular floor of the device (Fig. 1). Additional information can also be projected onto the walls in the room that houses the device. The goal is to expand the power of computers in collaborative decision-making by allowing users to intuitively share and manipulate data. Ameres [9] feels Campfire has the potential to enable users to "look inside the data" (para. 8) and expand data exploration beyond three-dimensional representations and traditional "one-to-one correlations between dimensionality and presentation" (para. 7).

Fig. 1. The Campfire technology allows researchers to project data onto the walls and floor of a three-dimensional display. The goal is to provide a collaborative space that encourages new perspectives that expand beyond traditional 2D and 3D representations of data relationships (from research by E. Ameres and G. Clement; photo credit: G. Clement).

3   Kinesthetic Design and Embodiment

Three-dimensional models invite interaction and exploration which can also lead to new insights about the data [4]. This type of interaction design, called kinesthetic design, helps the user understand the visual and cognitive relationships in the spatial representation of the information [10]. Berkeley [11] demonstrated that kinesthetic and tactile experiences shape our perception of space. Klemmer, Hartmann, and Takayma [5] noted that "our bodies play a central role in shaping human experience in the world, understanding of the world, and interactions in the world" (p. 140). When we physically interact with models or other tactile representations of data, we use reflective practice to work through ideas rather than just think about them [5].

Physical interaction is defined as an epistemic action that helps us understand relationships [12, 13]. Researchers have documented the significance of "drawing" relationships in physical space with hand and arm movement to clarify conceptual relationships and enhance memory and recall [14, 15]. Haptic interfaces and interactive hardware use physical movement to augment our understanding of information by leveraging "body-centric experiential cognition" [5, p. 144].

Vande Moere and Patel [4] used the term "embodiment" to describe the physical materialization of the data relationships in data sculptures. Embodiment also refers to the viewer's interpretation of the data through the perception of the data in the physical world. Researchers have noted that we perceive information in relation to our orientation [16]. We intuitively learn about audio, visual, spatial, and temporal relationships by moving in physical environments and touching objects. Piaget [17] noted that logic and the cognitive processing of information are derived from physical and mental interaction, and it is the coordination of action that leads to reflective abstraction.

The cognitive semantics theory of conceptual metaphor states that logic and reasoning are founded on image schemas formed by "patterns of our bodily orientations, movements, and interaction" that we develop into abstract references [18, p. 90]. As a result, physical movement through space and interaction with tangible objects leads to symbolic representations and quantitative analyses [19, p. 2]. As we use gestures and objects, we gain new perspectives and see additional relationships based on our physical interaction with the objects. Abrahamson and Lindgren [19] noted that "we develop the skill of controlling and interpreting the world through the mediating artifact" (p. 4).

Gestures and bodily movements are also intuitive ways of learning and communicating because they constitute a universal visual language that is based on shared and tangible experiences [20]. LeBaron and Streeck [20] pointed out that gestures provide a bridge between tactile experiences and the abstract conceptualization of the experiences. They highlighted the work of the French philosopher Condillac who felt gestures "constituted the original, natural language of humankind" because they formed symbols and a social language based on common experiences [20, p. 118]. Condillac [21] called these symbols or signs *sensations transformées* or transformed sensations (p. 61) because they referred to "the entire complex of affect, desire, sensory perception, and motor action that makes up what nowdays we might call 'embodied experience'" [20, p. 118].

Gestures can play an important role in kinesthetic design for multisensory data representation. Research has shown that gestures increase creativity [22], reduce cognitive overhead [23], and help us translate our experiences with objects into cognitive interpretations [24, 25]. We have already seen how interactive phones and tablets make use of our intuitive understanding of gesture to facilitate interaction with mobile devices and engage us in the communication process.

4   Cross-Modal Perception

Research has shown that we intuitively integrate stimuli from different sensory modalities. The multisensory integration of audio and visual stimuli is a physiological process that takes place within the neurons in the brain [26–28]. Researchers have identified enhanced activity in the visual cortex in congenitally blind people when they analyze speech [29], moving sounds [30], or localized sounds [31].

Research has shown that cross-modal perception heightens perceptual awareness and enhances our ability to process information from individual sensory modalities when the combinations of stimuli are organized or random [32–35]. Freides [36] concluded that perception that involves more than one sensory modality is more accurate than information that is represented with one sense. This is especially true if the cross-modal perception involves the integration of visual or audio information with haptic and kinesthetic stimuli.

There has been extensive research on cross-modal perception that involves the integration of audio and visual stimuli. Research has shown that the perception of visual information is altered when sound is added to the visuals [37–40]. Vroomen and de Gelder [37] also demonstrated that the temporal organization of auditory stimuli impacts visual perception. A random high tone (in a sequence of low tones) improved the perception of a visual target when the tone and the visual stimuli were presented synchronously. However, there was no effect when the high tone was presented before the visual information. The effect was also reduced when there was less contrast between the high and low tones, and when the high tone was part of a melody.

Sound can enhance the detection of specific individual visual elements as well as improve the detection of motion [28, 37]. Beer and Watanabe [28] demonstrated that visual motion detection improved when sounds were paired simultaneously with the visual stimuli. Chen and Yeh [41] discovered that the addition of repetitive sounds to visuals alleviated "repetition blindness" which is the failure to perceive visuals that repeat in rapid succession.

Visual and auditory stimuli can also impact the perception of spatial location. Audio and visual stimuli that are synchronized, but exist in different spatial locations, may appear to come from the same location [42–45]. In addition, research has shown that visual and auditory stimuli that come from the same location seem to emanate from the same source if the visual stimuli precede the sound by 50 ms [46, 47]. Talsma, Senkowski, and Woldorff [48] concluded that this timing difference is due to the different velocities of light and sound, which have caused the brain to develop a higher neural transmission rate for auditory stimuli to compensate for the fact that sound reaches the auditory nerve approximately 50 ms after visual stimuli.

The different velocities of auditory and visual stimuli also impact the perception of time and whether or not sounds and visuals appear to be synchronized. There has been conflicting research in this area with some research showing the auditory stimuli must come first in order for sounds to appear to be simultaneous with visual stimuli [49], while other research indicated that the visual stimuli must come first [50–52]. These different findings suggested that other variables, in addition to velocity, impact how we perceive the temporal order and synchronicity of auditory and visual stimuli. Research had indicated that the relative intensities of sensory stimuli effect the perception of temporal order by showing that a stimulus with a higher intensity was perceived before a stimulus with a lower intensity [53]. Boenke, Deliano, and Ohl [54] confirmed that intensity plays a role in the temporal perception of auditory and visual stimuli. They further defined the temporal dynamics of auditory and visual stimuli by showing that the duration of a stimulus also impacts the perception of time, noting that asynchronies in the perception of multiple stimuli appear to be stabilized when the duration of the stimuli is increased [54].

Finally, Freides [36] noted that with complex spatial or temporal pattern recognition, the sensory modality used to represent the data is more critical than the contextual and parametric variables themselves because each modality processes information in a different way, and we automatically use the modality best suited to process variables that represent spatial, temporal, tactile, or kinesthetic relationships.

Research in cross-modal perception plays an important role in the design of multisensory data representations. By using multiple sensory modalities, it is possible to expand the number of data variables that can be represented simultaneously and increase the potential for discovering patterns, trends, anomalies, and outliers. Cross-modal stimuli can enhance the perception of visual and audio information, and it can impact the perception of spatial and temporal relationships. However, when different sensory modalities are used to represent multiple variables in a complex information space, the choice of media is not the only factor to consider. As indicated in the research, other important factors that impact perception include how and when the stimuli are introduced and the location, intensity, speed, and duration of the stimuli. Research has shown that random sounds can enhance the perception of visual information. However, in multisensory data design, the use of auditory stimuli to represent data may result in repetitive or recursive audio patterns, and it is not clear from the current research in cross-modal perception, how repetitive or recursive patterns impact the perception of visual stimuli and the perception of temporal and spatial relationships in data sets.

5   Aesthetics of Data Representation

Aesthetics is another design element that impacts the interpretation of data representations [55, 56]. Information aesthetics refers to the way design is used to organize data and define relationships. Researchers have broadened the definition to refer to the user experience, engagement, and interaction with the data representations, as opposed to merely defining patterns and trends. This definition also highlights the narratives and underlying processes and principles represented by the data [4]. Information aesthetics is also defined by the database design and the way information is organized, filtered, and retrieved to form different associations [57].

Visual and audio designs create relationships that we perceive as "aesthetically pleasing" because they adhere to principles of design, defined by artists, designers, and musicians, that we have learned over time. Aesthetically pleasing designs define "good Gestalt" and use Gestalt principles of perception to help us simplify and organize information intuitively.

Information aesthetics, based on these design concepts, has been applied to graph theory and design [58] to improve the user's ability to locate information, compare relationships, and complete tasks. With interactive systems, research has shown that the aesthetics of an interface design can impact user engagement, completion time, and error rate [59–61]. In these research experiments, the aesthetics of each design was defined by Gestalt laws of perception and grouping (similarity, proximity, continuation, closure, figure/ground), as well as established concepts in visual design theory that define how to use "harmonious" color palettes, contrast, focal points, balance, symmetry, and asymmetry. In some cases, an aesthetically pleasing information design or interface design did not yield the fastest time in task completion, but the visual appeal of the design encouraged the users to stay engaged and ultimately, complete the tasks [62].

However, multisensory data representation can result in unfamiliar audiovisual patterns that do not conform to established principles of design. Multisensory data representation and cross-modal perception are defining new dimensions in information aesthetics that impact the interpretation of data relationships. We have considerable experience reading linear and hierarchical charts, but as we explore new forms of data representation that combine different sensory modalities, physical and virtual spaces, ambient displays, haptic interfaces, and interaction design, we are defining new ways of using perception and cognition to analyze and interpret complex relationships. For example, with the Campfire example previously discussed, participants are presented with an open space in the center of the device that does not contain specific information. However, the space signifies connections between the data on the sides and bottom of the display. The participants can use this space to create cognitive connections between the physical and virtual representations of the data—connections that define additional dimensions that expand beyond two-dimensional data charts and the three dimensional properties of the display itself.

Kinesthetic design in data representation is also defining new dimensions in the aesthetics of information design. In interactive sports simulators, where the participant performs specific physical motions (e.g., swinging a golf club, throwing/kicking a ball) to produce actions and events in the virtual game, the participant's physical interaction promotes engagement and creates mental and physical connections with the information in the virtual space. We can apply these concepts from game design to interactive data representation and use embodiment, spatial movement/distance, rhythm, and time to define data relationships. Kinesthetic design adds sensory information to the user experience that augments the virtual representations of the data and creates a holistic approach to data analysis and interpretation.

In my research, I am designing interactive, multimedia art installations to explore new concepts in kinesthetic design and information aesthetics [1]. In the installations, participants interact simultaneously with two different computer programs and create dynamic visual patterns and sounds in the surrounding environment. The gestures and physical movements the participants make, as they move the interactive hardware to control the computer programs, create layers of visual patterns called "hyperplanes" that are at right angles to the virtual patterns displayed in the space (Fig. 2). Audio stimuli define additional hyperplanes as sounds penetrate the environment and immerse the viewer with sensory stimuli from different angles and directions. The hyperplanes create a counterpoint of audio, visual, and rhythmic patterns that define geometric grids of intersecting spatiotemporal planes that change as the user alters the variables in the data representations [1].

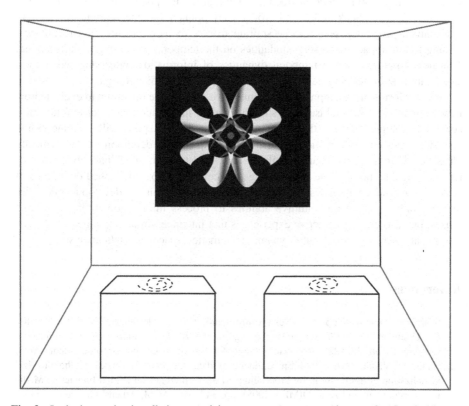

Fig. 2. In the interactive installations, participants move a mouse on the top of pedestals (shown in the front of this illustration) to animate visual patterns projected onto the wall. The dashed lines on the pedestals represent the kinesthetic patterns the participants create as they move the hardware. These patterns define hyperplanes that augment the sensory experience for the participant. Copyright 2014 Patricia Search. All rights reserved.

6 Future Directions

In three-dimensional, multisensory data representations, arrays of sensory stimuli and discursive patterns represent simultaneous and sequential relationships and events. Physical and virtual spaces, interactivity, and individual sensory modalities create a system of perceptual and semantic relational codes that define the data relationships.

Cross-modal perception can enhance and alter the way we interpret information that is represented with different sensory stimuli. It also impacts how we interpret spatial and temporal relationships. Research in cross-modal perception needs to expand into the field of multisensory data design and evaluate how different sensory stimuli, blended spaces, and kinesthetic design impact the interpretation of complex data relationships, including how we perceive the transformation of data relationships over time. The research needs to include studies in the perception of rhythm which is an important element in data representation. In multisensory data design, layers of rhythms, created by the audio and visual stimuli and kinesthetic interaction, highlight the temporal dynamics in data relationships. Spence, Senkowski, and Röder [63] pointed out that current research in cross-modal perception seems to be shifting from a focus on spatial information processing to the impact of sensory modalities on the temporal processing of information. This new emphasis on the temporal dynamics of information processing will play a significant role in defining new directions for multisensory data design.

As new forms of data representation emerge, it will also be important to evaluate how new technologies and multisensory stimuli redefine information aesthetics. With interactive technologies, kinesthetic design and cross-modal perception will continue to add new dimensions to information aesthetics and expand the definition of "aesthetically pleasing" designs. These changes will, in turn, lead to even more innovative ways of representing data because we will no longer be constrained by established definitions of aesthetics and information design. We will be able to envision and develop technologies that not only leverage our intuitive abilities to process information through multiple senses, but also create interactive experiences that integrate virtual and physical objects, actions, and sensory stimuli into dynamic information spaces for data analysis.

References

1. Search, P.: New media perspectives for information and data design. In: Fabel, L., Spinillo, C., Tiradentes Souto, V. (eds.) Proceedings of the 7th Information Design International Conference, pp. 222–229. Brazilian Society of Information Design, Brasilia, Brazil (2015)
2. Zhao, J., Vande Moere, A.: Embodiment in data sculpture: a model of the physical visualization of information. In: Proceedings of the Conference on Digital Interactive Media in Entertainment and Arts (DIMEA 2008), pp. 343–350. ACM, Athens, Greece (2008)
3. Zhang, J., Wang, H.: The effect of external representations on numeric tasks. Q. J. Exp. Psychol. **58A**(5), 817–838 (2005)
4. Vande Moere, A., Patel, S.: The physical visualization of information: designing data sculptures in an educational context. In: Huang, M., Nguyen, Q., Zhang, K. (eds.) Visual Information Communication (VINCI 2009), pp. 1–23. Springer, Sydney (2009)
5. Klemmer, S.R., Hartmann, B., Takayama, L.: How bodies matter: five themes for interaction design. In: Proceedings of Designing Interactive Systems (DIS 2006), pp. 140–148 (2006)
6. Dourish, P.: Where the Action Is: The Foundations of Embodied Interaction. MIT Press, Cambridge (2001)
7. Palmerius, K.L., Forsell, C.: The impact of feedback design in haptic volume visualization. In: Third Joint EuroHaptics Conference 2009 and Symposium on Haptic Interfaces for Virtual Environment and Teleoperator Systems, World Haptics 2009, pp. 154–159. IEEE Press, New York (2009)

8. Wisneski, C., Ishii, H., Dahley, A., Gorbet, M., Brave, S., Ullmer, B., Yarin, P.: Ambient displays: turning architectural space into an interface between people and digital information. In: Yuan, F., Konomi, S., Burkhardt, H.-J. (eds.) CoBuild 1998. LNCS, vol. 1370, pp. 22–32. Springer, Heidelberg (1998)

9. Martialay, M.: Immersive experience: The Campfire. The Approach: Discovery, Innovation, and Imagination at Rensselaer Polytechnic Institute (November 18) (2015). http://approach.rpi.edu/2015/11/18/immersive-experience-the-campfire/

10. Search, P.: The metastructural dynamics of interactive electronic design. Visible Lang. Cult. Dimensions Vis. Commun. 37(2), 146–165 (2003)

11. Berkeley, G.: A New Theory of Vision and Other Writings. E. P. Dutton, New York (1922)

12. Kirsh, D., Maglio, P.: On distinguishing epistemic from pragmatic actions. Cogn. Sci. 18(4), 513–549 (1994)

13. Hollan, J., Hutchins, E., Kirsh, D.: Distributed cognition: toward a new foundation for human-computer interaction research. ACM Trans. Comput. Hum. Interact. 7(2), 174–196 (2000)

14. Fish, J., Scrivener, S.: Amplifying the mind's eye: sketching and visual cognition. Leonardo 23(1), 117–126 (1990)

15. Fish, J.: The Cognitive Functions of the Sketch. Cheltenham & Gloucester College of Higher Education, CAD Centre internal Report, Cheltenham (1993)

16. Klatzky, R.L.: Allocentric and egocentric spatial representations: definitions, distinctions, and inter-connections. In: Freksa, C., Habel, C., Wender, K.F. (eds.) Spatial Cognition: An Interdisciplinary Approach to Representation and Processing of Spatial Knowledge. LNAI, vol. 1404, pp. 1–17. Springer, Berlin (1998)

17. Piaget, J.: The Origins of Intelligence in Children. International University Press, New York (1952)

18. Lakoff, G., Johnson, M.L.: Metaphors We Live By. The University of Chicago Press, Chicago (1980)

19. Abrahamson, D., Lindgren, R.: Embodiment and embodied design. In: Sawyer, R.K. (ed.) The Cambridge Handbook of the Learning Sciences, 2nd edn, pp. 357–376. Cambridge University Press, Cambridge (2014)

20. LeBaron, C., Streeck, J.: Gestures, knowledge, and the world. In: McNeill, D. (ed.) Language and Gesture, pp. 118–138. Cambridge University Press, Cambridge (2000)

21. Condillac, E.: An Essay on the Origin of Human Knowledge, Being a Supplement to Mr. Locke's Essay on the Human Understanding. J. Noursse, London (1746)

22. Wang, Q., Nass, C.: Less visible and wireless: two experiments on the effects of microphone type on users' performance and perception. In: Proceedings of the 23rd ACM SIGCHI Human Factors in Computing Systems, Portland, Oregon, pp. 809–818 (2005)

23. Goldin-Meadow, S., Nusbaum, H., Delly, S.D., Wagner, S.: Explaining math: gesturing lightens the load. Psychol. Sci. 12(6), 516–522 (1991)

24. Goldin-Meadow, S., Beilock, S.L.: Action's influence on thought: the case of gesture. Perspect. Psychol. Sci. 5(6), 664–674 (2010)

25. Kirsch, D.: Embodied cognition and the magical future of interaction design. In: Marshall, P., Antle, A.N., Hoven, E.V.D., Rogers, Y. (eds.) The Theory and Practice of Embodied Interaction HCI and Interaction Design (special issue). ACM Trans. Hum. Comput. Interact. 20(1), pp. 1–30 (2013)

26. Sams, M., Imada, T.: Integration of auditory and visual information in the human brain: neuromagnetic evidence. Soc. Neurosci. Abs. 23, 1305 (1997)

27. Driver, J., Noesselt, T.: Multisensory interplay reveals crossmodal influences on 'sensory-specific' brain regions, neural responses, and judgments. Neuron 57(1), 11–23 (2008)

28. Beer, A., Watanabe, T.: Specificity of auditory-guided visual perceptual learning suggests crossmodal plasticity in early visual cortex. Exp. Brain Res. **198**(2), 353–361 (2009)
29. Röder, B., Stock, O., Bien, S., Neville, H., Rösler, F.: Speech processing activates visual cortex in congenitally blind humans. Eur. J. Neurosci. **16**(5), 930–936 (2002)
30. Poirier, C., Collignon, O., Scheiber, C., Renier, L., Vanlierde, A., Tranduy, D., Veraart, C., De Volder, A.G.: Auditory motion perception activates visual motion areas in early blind subjects. Neuroimage **31**(1), 279–285 (2006)
31. Weeks, R., Horwitz, B., Aziz-Sultan, A., Tian, B., Wessinger, C.M., Cohen, L.G., Hallett, M., Rauschecker, J.P.: A positron emission tomographic study of auditory localization in the congenitally blind. J. Neurosci. **20**(4), 2664–2672 (2000)
32. Hershenson, M.: Reaction time as a measure of intersensory facilitation. J. Exp. Psychol. **63**(3), 289–293 (1962)
33. Nickerson, R.S.: Intersensory facilitation of reaction time: energy summation or preparation enhancement? Psychol. Rev. **80**(6), 168–173 (1973)
34. Posner, M.I., Nissen, M., Klein, R.M.: Visual dominance: an information-processing account of its origins and significance. Psychol. Rev. **83**(2), 157–171 (1976)
35. Simon, J.R., Craft, J.L.: Effects of an irrelevant auditory stimulus on visual choice reaction time. J. Exp. Psychol. **86**(2), 272–274 (1970)
36. Freides, D.: Human information processing and sensory modality: cross-modal functions, information complexity, memory, and deficit. Psychol. Bull. **81**(5), 284–310 (1974)
37. Vroomen, J., de Gelder, B.: Sound enhances visual perception: cross-modal effects of auditory organization on vision. Hum. Percept. Perform. **26**(5), 1583–1590 (2000)
38. Mazza, V., Turatto, M., Rossi, M., Umiltà, C.: How automatic are audiovisual links in exogenous spatial attention? Neuropsychologia **45**(3), 514–522 (2007)
39. McDonald, J.J., Teder-Sälejärvi, W.A., Hillyard, S.A.: Involuntary orienting to sound improves visual per-ception. Nature **407**(6806), 906–908 (2000)
40. Spence, C., Driver, J.: Audiovisual links in endogenous covert spatial orienting. Percept. Psychophysics **59**(1), 1–22 (1997)
41. Chen, Y., Yeh, S.: Catch the moment: multisensory enhancement of rapid visual events by sound. Exp. Brain Res. **198**(2), 209–219 (2009)
42. Bertelson, P., Radeau, M.: Cross-modal bias and perceptual fusion with auditory-visual spatial discordance. Percept. Psychophysics **29**(6), 578–584 (1981)
43. Vroomen, J., Bertelson, P., de Gelder, B.: A visual influence in the discrimination of auditory location. In: Proceedings of the International Conference on Auditory-Visual Speech Processing (AVSP 1998), pp. 131–135. Causal Productions, Sydney, Australia (1998)
44. Vroomen, J.: Ventriloquism and the nature of the unity assumption. In: Aschersleben, G., Bachmann, T., Müsseler, J. (eds.) Cognitive Contributions to the Perception of Spatial and Temporal Events, pp. 388–394. Elsevier Science, New York (1999)
45. Vroomen, J., Bertelson, P., de Gelder, B.: The ventriloquist effect does not depend on the direction of deliberate visual attention. Percept. Psychophysics **63**(4), 651–659 (2001)
46. Lewald, J., EhrenBee, W.H., Guski, R.: Spatio-temporal constraints for auditory-visual integration. Behav. Brain Res. **121**(1–2), 69–79 (2001)
47. Leward, J., Guski, R.: Cross-modal perceptual integration of spatially and temporary disparate auditory and visual stimuli. Cogn. Brain. Res. **16**(3), 468–478 (2003)
48. Talsma, D., Senkowski, D., Woldorff, M.: Intermodal attention affects the processing of the temporal alignment of audiovisual stimuli. Exp. Brain Res. **198**(2–3), 313–328 (2009)
49. Neumann, O., Niepel, M.: Timing of "perception" and perception of "time". In: Kärnbach, C., Schröger, E., Müller, H. (eds.) Psychophysics Beyond Sensation: Laws and Invariants of Human Cognition, pp. 245–269. Erlbaum, Mahwah (2004)

50. Jaśkowski, P.: Simple reaction time and perception of temporal order: dissociations and hypotheses. Percept. Mot. Skills **82**(3, Pt 1), 707–730 (1996)
51. Zampini, M., Shore, D.I., Spence, C.: Audiovisual temporal-order judgments. Exp. Brain Res. **152**(2), 198–210 (2003)
52. Zampini, M., Shore, D.I., Spence, C.: Multisensory temporal-order judgments: the role of hemispheric redundancy. Int. J. Psychophysiol. **50**(1), 165–180 (2003)
53. Neumann, O., Koch, R., Niepel, M., Tappe, T.: Reaction time and temporal-order judgment: correspondence or dissociation. Zeitschrift fur Experimentelle und Angewandte Psychologie **39**(4), 621–645 (1992)
54. Boenke, L.T., Deliano, M., Ohl, F.W.: Stimulus duration influences perceived simultaneity in audiovisual temporal-order judgment. Exp. Brain Res. **198**(2–3), 233–244 (2009)
55. Lau, A., Vande Moere, A.: Towards a model of information aesthetic visualization. In: Proceedings of the IEEE International Conference on Information Visualisation (IV 2007), Zurich, Switzerland, pp. 87–92 (2007)
56. Sack, W.: Aesthetics of information visualization. In: Lovejoy, M., Paul, C., Vesna, V. (eds.) Context Providers, pp. 123–150. Intellect, Bristol (2007)
57. Vesna, V.: Database Aesthetics: Art in the Age of Information Overflow. University of Minnesota Press, Minneapolis (2007)
58. Purchase, H., Allder, J.A., Carrington, D.: Metrics for graph drawing aesthetics. J. Vis. Lang. Comput. **13**(5), 501–516 (2002)
59. Kurosu, M., Kashimura, K.: Apparent usability vs. inherent usability: experimental analysis on the determinants of the apparent usability. In: Conference Companion on Human Factors in Computing Systems, CHI 1995, Denver, Colorado, USA, pp. 292–293 (1995)
60. Ngo, D., Byrne, J.G.: Another look at a model for evaluating interface aesthetics. Int. J. Appl. Math. Comput. Sci. **11**(2), 515–535 (2001)
61. Stasko, J., Catrambone, R., Guzdial, M., McDonald, K.: An evaluation of space-filling information visualizations for depicting hierarchical structures. Int. J. Hum Comput Stud. **53**(5), 663–694 (2000)
62. Cawthon, N., Vande Moere, A.: The effect of aesthetic on the usability of data visualization. In: Proceedings of the IEEE International Conference Information Visualization (IV 2007), Zurich, Switzerland, pp. 637–648 (2007)
63. Spence, C., Senkowski, D., Röder, B.: Crossmodal processing. Exp. Brain Res. **198**(2), 107–111 (2009)

Creative Interaction for Plasma Physics

Han Sol Shin[1], Jee Ho Song[1], Tae Jun Yu[2], and Kun Lee[3(⊠)]

[1] Department of Information and Communication,
Handong Global University, Pohang, Republic of Korea
hansol@handong.edu, vanadate.kr@gmail.com
[2] Department of Advanced Green Energy and Environment,
Handong Global University, Pohang, Republic of Korea
taejun.yu@gmail.com
[3] School of Computer Science and Electronic Engineering,
Handong Global University, Pohang, Republic of Korea
kunlee@handong.edu

Abstract. Particle accelerator has mainly used in nuclear field only because of the large scale of facility. However, since laser-plasma particle accelerator, which has smaller size and spends less cost, developed, the availability of this accelerator is expended to various research fields such as industrial and medical. In these, real-time and interactive applications, accelerating the compute time is a critical problem. We conduct a simulation discussed the method of visualization of multivariate data in three dimensional space by using colored volume rendering and surface rendering. This system offers real-time 3D images via convert various file format comes from PIC simulation into OpenGL texture type to analyze and modify plasma data. We also suggest new method to visualize plasma data by using alpha shape to achieve a different level of detail for the given plasma based particle acceleration data. Many scientists are not familiar with the concepts of programming languages. Therefore, we employ the visual- scripting engine to define the rendering context of plasma physics.

Keywords: Plasma · Data visualization · Visualization toolkit

1 Introduction

Plasma is one of the states of matter, which is consist of ionized electrons and protons. Plasma is electrically conductive, so unlike gas, it responds strongly to electric and magnetic fields or its own nearby particles. Scientists mainly use computer simulation to predict the movement of charged particles of plasma on the influence of electromagnetic fields. For the precise results, most of simulation data is very large. It is impossible to catch the meaning of scientific simulation data, especially high resolution and multi-dimensional data, without visualization. Visualization gives insight to scientists.

Our suggestion includes the method of visualization multi-dimensional data with real-time performance. Real-time performance is important feature because interactive view of visualized data makes it easy for scientists to get some insights. The other feature of our work is the visual-scripting. Visual-scripting helps the scientists who are

© Springer International Publishing Switzerland 2016
A. Marcus (Ed.): DUXU 2016, Part III, LNCS 9748, pp. 214–222, 2016.
DOI: 10.1007/978-3-319-40406-6_20

not familiar with professional programming language to pre-process their data and decide to what to render.

2   Problem Description

Existing visualization toolkits, such as VisIt and ParaView, were developed for general purpose. These toolkits deal with various data format and type. They also rapidly release new version by open source community. However, there are some problems in visualizing plasma-based particle acceleration data. First of all, they require a long configuration time in order to produce desired images due to unnecessary processes incurred by their versatility. Also, they face difficulties in visualizing electric fields and reconstructing surface because of the restricted data pre-processing. Furthermore, their unintuitive interfaces make it harder for unexperienced users to learn them. To solve these problems, we developed a plasma specialized visualization toolkit (Fig. 1).

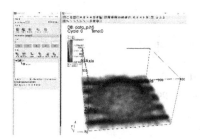 

Fig. 1.   (a) VisIt and (b) ParaView

3   Simplify the Process of Configuration

3.1   Existing Method

We benchmark previous visualization toolkits. We researched the processes from the beginning until getting the rendered image of plasma, using texture-based volume rendering method, in each toolkit while using identical data of charge density in the plasma. Our plasma data is HDF5 three dimensional 32-bit floating point grid data. They have $241 \times 401 \times 401$ resolution. HDF5 is the data model, library, and file format used by scientific data simulations. It has been designed flexibly so it is suitable for various datatypes. Figure 2 is electric charge density data represented by three dimensional array (Table 1).

When operated, VisIt and ParaView show the following process (Table 2).

3.2   Proposed Method

In order to simplify the configuration process, we found the need for a reduction in the setting stage and shortening the time to adjust the setting values, and decided to provide default values and real-time feedback.

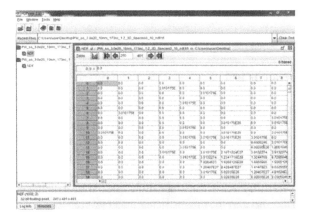

Fig. 2. Three dimensional grid data of electric charge density

Table 1. Data properties

Type	HDF5 Scalar Dataset
No. of Dimensions	3
Resolution	241 × 401 × 401
Data type	32-bit floating point

Table 2. Process of VisIt and ParaView

Step	VisIt	ParaView
1	Open a "HDF5" file	Write a "XMDF" file to recognize "HDF5" file
2	Add a plot "Volume" with "NDF"	Open the "XMDF" file
3	Draw plots	Select "XMDF Reader"
4	Edit "Volume plot attributes"	Apply
5	Select "3D Texturing" in "Render Options"	Select "Volume" in "Representation"
6	Adjust "Color Data" in "1D transfer function" (*appropriately)	Edit "Color Mapping Data" (*appropriately)
7	Apply	

Default Values. We make these common processes concise through offering default values in the basic setup: data type, cell size, color, rendering options, etc. Moreover, we recommend and provide the interpolation of variation by referring to the distribution of data.

Real-Time Feedback. We chose the texture-based rendering amongst many volume rendering method. In real-time application, volume rendering methods which contain numerous computation, including ray casting method, is not appropriate.

Through the process above, the previous setup process was simplified into only two steps to get the result: open files and click the "volume" button.

4   Methods of Visualization

4.1   Texture-Based Volumetric Rendering

For the realistic rendering, volume ray-casting technique is commonly used. But visualization of scientific data, specifically plasma data, is not required serious physical lighting model because seeing plasma is not natural phenomenon. What we need is conceptual image of it. We use OpenGL's 3D texture and alpha blending technique for the real-time performance.

We calculated the linear interpolation between two colors representing minimum and maximum value respectively on data set. We set the alpha value to size of the value of the three dimensional array's component. Figure 3 is gray-scaled image of alpha values. We stack these images up on three dimensional space, and set blend mode to get final color of volumetric image. In Fig. 4, charge density of plasma is represented by color and transparency.

Fig. 3. Slice of generated 3D texture

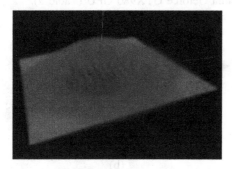

Fig. 4. Visualized image of electric charge density of plasma using OpenGL texture and alpha blending

4.2   Electric Field Computation

It costs high in both memory usage and time consuming to sample the space to compute charge density and calculate electric field on that with large size of plasma data. However, by using convolution theorem, we make O(n^2) problem into O(nlogn) problem. Here are equations we used.

$$V_{net} = \int \rho(\vec{r}) \frac{k}{\left| \vec{R} - \vec{r} \right|} d\,Vol \tag{1}$$

$$h(R') = f(r') * g(R' - r') \tag{2}$$

$$h(R') = F^{-1}(F(f(r')) \times F(g(r'))) \tag{3}$$

Equation (1) is ordinary equation for the electric potential. Equation (2) is the convolution form of Eq. (1). Equation (3) is application of convolution theorem on Eq. (2). We accelerate the FFT (Fast Fourier Transformation) algorithm by using GPGPU (General Purpose Graphic Processor Unit). Using convolution theorem, it can be unwanted result on margin because of periodicity of discrete Fourier transformation. To prevent this, we need to pad the date with zeros as much as size of kernel. In addition, the size of kernel must be same with of image for the point-wise multiplication. So we need additional memory space, and following is required data size of image.

$$N = \left(N^{fw} + N^{gw} - 1\right) \times \left(N^{fh} + N^{gh} - 1\right) \times \left(N^{fd} + N^{gd} - 1\right)$$

when $N^{fw}, N^{fh}, N^{fd}, N^{gw}, N^{gh}, N^{gd}$ are width, height and depth of image and kernel, respectively.

Figure 5 is visualization of intermediate data while calculate electric field, and Fig. 6 is the vector field of electric field in plasma, final result of calculation.

We compared the compute time between convolution on CPU without FFT and convolution on GPU with FFT. We considered the time to transfer the data form CPU memory to GPU memory. Environment of used system are Intel i7 920 CPU, 8 GB DDR3 RAM, and Nvidia Geforce GTX980 GPU (Table 3).

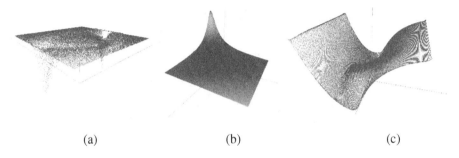

| (a) | (b) | (c) |

Fig. 5. (a) is electric charge density of plasma, (b) is convolution kernel and (c) is calculated electric potential of plasma.

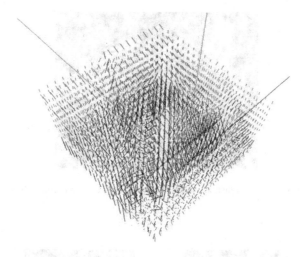

Fig. 6. Line representation of electric field

Table 3. Comparison of the performance for FFT algorithm and conventional convolution algorithm

N	Compute time of convolution on CPU (ms)	Compute time of FFT algorithm on GPU (ms)	Compute time of FFT algorithm on GPU + Time to copy data from main memory to GPU memory (ms)
8k	290	815	815
64k	18.5k	801	803
125k	70k	796	801
5000k	–	1693	1852

4.3   Surface Reconstruction

We offer two method of surface construction. One is iso-surface, the other is alpha shape. We calculated iso-surface using marching cubes algorithm. This algorithm is method to extract triangles that is lying on same value, iso-surface, from a three dimensional grid data. This is mainly used for medical visualization. Figure 8 is rendered image of surface where iso-value is 0, which is generated by the algorithm. Three dimensional charge density data is discrete, therefore this algorithm does not guarantee connectivity of generated surface. That is the reason why we considered alpha shape.

In case of alpha shape, we use the package CGAL (Computational Geometry Algorithm Library). In CGAL, the α-complex of S is a subcomplex of this triangulation of S, containing the a-exposed k-simplices, $0 \leq k \leq d$. A simplex is a -exposed, if there is an open disk (resp. ball) of radius squre root of α through the vertices of the simplex that does not contain any other point of S, for the metric used in the computation of the underlying triangulation. That makes convex hall where α is infinite value (Fig. 7).

Fig. 7. The plasma's surface constructed by marching cubes

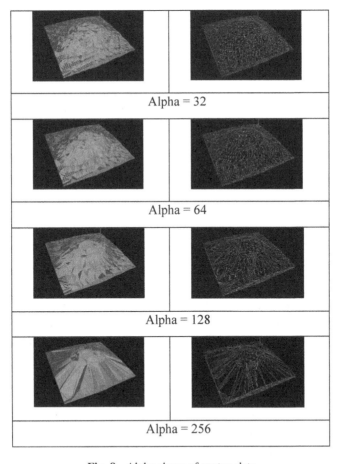

Fig. 8. Alpha shape of proton data

5 Visual Scripting

We used Visual scripting to complement the unintuitive interfaces. Visual scripting is based on node-based interface to writing the logic. Each of nodes represents data, branching control, and operation. Visual scripting is suitable for the data-driven paradigm because it is flow of data. In addition, it easily converted to parallelized computation. Script engine is necessary feature of visualization toolkit for the flexible environment to compose the rendering plot and the data preprocessing. However, many scientists are not familiar with programming language. For example, scientists have to remember a lot of command to use Matlab. It is not only hard to learn, but also easy to make mistakes. With the visual-scripting engine, scientists easily make a render context, the plot of rendered scene. Following script is example of the Matlab commands, and Fig. 9 is example of the rendering context built by visual scripting.

```
load mri D                                  % load da-
ta
D = squeeze(D);                             % remove
singleton dimension
limits = [NaN NaN NaN NaN NaN 10];
[x, y, z, D] = subvolume(D, limits);        % extract
a subset of the volume data

[fo,vo] = isosurface(x,y,z,D,5);            %
isosurface for the outside of the volume
[fe,ve,ce] = isocaps(x,y,z,D,5);            % isocaps
for the end caps of the volume

----------- omit -------------

view(-40,24)
daspect([1 1 0.3])                          % set the
axes aspect ratio
colormap(gray(100))
box on
```

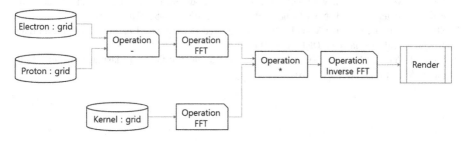

Fig. 9. The rendering context built by visual scripting

6 Conclusions

In this paper, we discuss how to visualize volumetric scattered data. In industrial and medical fields, real-time and interactive applications, accelerating the compute time is a critical problem. We designed our visualization toolkit for interactive and real-time observation of multi-dimensional plasma data. Using texture based volumetric rendering, we achieve both quality and performance. We use GPGPU and convolution theorem to accelerate computing time to calculate electric fields.

To achieve a different level of detail alpha shapes method is applied. Level of detail increases the efficiency of rendering by decreasing the workload. The alpha complex is a sub-complex of the Delaunay triangulation. For a given value of the alpha complex includes all the simplices in the Delaunay triangulation which have an empty circumsphere with squared radius equal or smaller than $\square$. For further research, we are trying to apply this proposed method to the various tri-variate scattered data.

We also suggested visual scripting which have various advantage of representing a rendering plot or context. It is easy to learn even for scientists who have not experience of programming languages.

Acknowledgments. This work was supported by the Industrial Strategic technology development program, 10048964, Development of 125 J•Hz laser system for laser peering funded by Ministry of Trade, Industry & Energy (MI, republic of Korea).

References

1. Rubel, O., Geddes, C.G.R., Chen, M., Cormier-Michel, E., Wes Bethel, E.: Feature-based analysis of plasma-based particle acceleration data. IEEE Trans. Vis. Comput. Graph. **20**(2), 196–210 (2014)
2. Nielson, G.M., Hagen, H., Muller, H.: Scientific Visualization, pp. 477–525. IEEE Computer Society, Washington (1997)
3. Pavel, K., David, S.: Algorithms for Efficient Computation of Convolution, Design and Architectures for Digital Signal Processing. InTech, Rijeka (2013)
4. NVIDIA CUDA Toolkit Documentation v7.0. http://docs.nvidia.com/cuda/index.html. Accessed April 2015
5. Lorensen, W.E., Cline, H.E.: Marching cubes: a high resolution 3D surface construction algorithm. Comput. Graph. **21**(4), 163–169 (1987)
6. Lee, K.: Multiresolution volumetric medical data modeling based on gaussian curvature by using weighted alpha. J. Next Gener. Inf. Technol. **3**(3), 41–51 (2012)
7. Shin, H., Yu, T., Lee, K.: Visualization of scattered plasma-based particle acceleration data. J. Korea Multimedia Soc. **18**(1), 65–70 (2015)
8. Shin, H., Yu, T., Lee, K.: Visualization of internal electric field on plasma. J. Korea Multimedia Soc. **19**(1), 80–85 (2016)

Mining and Construction of User Experience Content: An Approach of Feature Analysis Based on Image

Di Wang[✉], Nan Liang, Jiaming Zhong, and Liqun Zhang

Design Management Institute, Shanghai Jiao Tong University, Shanghai, China
cheirsh_9@163.com, zhanglliqun@gmail.com

Abstract. This research is a preliminary study for a professional museum of print ads during the period of Republic of China. We selected 571 pieces of print ads of the Republic of China as sample to analysis the feature of them to make the visitors of museum could more immersive feel the print ads of the Republic of China and experience the unique charm of imagery modeling and visual language. The main methods used in the research are image feature analysis and image feature quantization calculation, we extract and summarize the common elements and culture style feature based on the analysis of multidimensional design elements. The research results could provide effective guidance for the design of the professional museum, including the overall atmosphere of the museum, thematic construction and situation creation.

Keywords: Image analysis · Feature quantification · Multidimensional scaling analysis · Correspondence analysis

1 Introduction

The period of the Republic of China was important for the transformation of Chinese advertising from tradition to modern. It was not only the beginning of our modern advertising, but also the first development peak of our advertising. Advertising can be seen as the living fossil of the history. Through the study of advertising during the period of the Republic of China, our historical and cultural heritage, from different dimensions, we can understand the width and height the design practice can reach and feel the economic development status of the society in that period which is also called as the early stage of modern design in China.

Culture heritage is the essence extracted from the people's work and living after a long time, and the fusion of a variety of traditional life inherited by generations and closely related to the life of people. With society gradually paying attention to the protection of historical and cultural heritage, more and more libraries and museums concerning the intangible cultural heritage are built. The expression of culture heritage should combine the carrier itself with experience and feelings of people during visiting to make visitors not only have certain knowledge of the carrier but also get a quiet different interactive experience including emotional and cultural awareness and aesthetic, etc. through the interactive relationship between visitors and museum.

© Springer International Publishing Switzerland 2016
A. Marcus (Ed.): DUXU 2016, Part III, LNCS 9748, pp. 223–234, 2016.
DOI: 10.1007/978-3-319-40406-6_21

In order to abstract design elements which meet the demands of contemporary aesthetic and are in accord with the experience of modern aesthetic, we choose 571 pieces of print ads during the period of the Republic of China as samples to analyze their style and characteristics based on the requirement for culture heritage protection.

2 Design the Research

This paper will do research from the following aspects:

- Using a custom-developed software to identify the image feature, abstract the information of image feature significantly related to advertising sample and form the variables indicators.
- Basing on the technology of feature analysis, study the specific attributes in information architecture, visual representation for information, the aesthetic characteristics and construction method, technology and cultural elements, etc. and form the research variable indicators in the process of advertising samples labeling.
- Explore the image significant correlation between the objective elements and subjective cognitive elements and find the main features by analyzing the research variable indicators with statistical calculation method and technologies, such as cluster analysis, factor analysis, correspondence analysis, multidimensional scaling analysis, etc.
- Provide professional and effective guidance for the design of museum basing on the research result, including the overall atmosphere, thematic construction, situation creation, etc.

The samples used in this paper were popular with the economic zone taking Shanghai as the focus during the period of 1910-1940. Figure 1 shows that it contains pieces of print ads, such as posters, paper wrappings, cards, etc. In order to do research, the following pictures are all coded.

Fig. 1. 571 pieces of print ads (partial)

3   Research

3.1   Procedures

- Research on recognizing the image feature of advertising samples basing on calculation: Through chromatographic, color tune and singularity analysis, find the image feature with which sample variable indicators have a tight correlation, extract and label it.
- Image analysis, variable definition and labeling basing on feature analysis (do parallel with step 1): do feature analysis for all the visual advertising samples, make a label list and form nominal level, ordinal level and scale variables for the subsequent statistical analysis.
- Data mining basing on multidimensional indexes: basing on the data achieved from step 1 and 2, excavate the dominant or potential significant correlation in multiple dimensions and multi-facts, build the framework of influencing factors and extract the common and individual feature of samples.

3.2   Research on Recognizing the Image Feature of Advertising Samples Basing on Calculation

The image feature of advertising samples contains several different dimensions. In this paper, image feature refers to image color feature which includes theme tune and representative color.

In this paper, all samples are JPG format data files and their color models are RGB. In the past, some color reduction research for the monuments establishing color reduction algorithm with the help of implements' real color. It made the precedent in color reduction for the monuments. But in this paper, the real objects can't be found to apply the reduction algorithm because the real objects in the picture of samples are abundant, and the samples span 30 years. Because of the limit and in order to protect the initial data, this paper will analyze directly the samples by RGB color model.

The research tools for recognizing the image feature in this paper are developed by our research team with JAVA language, including color spatial distribution analysis tool, theme tune extraction tool and theme tune similarity analysis tool.

Color spatial distribution analysis tool. Color spatial distribution analysis tool generates color points according to pixels in samples (Fig. 2), forming a color space, clusters the points and reduces their dimension by vector computation and principal component analysis to help researchers analyze the color feature of samples.

Theme tune extraction tool. Theme tune extraction tool does color feature calculation of pixel, obtains the constituent of global color tune separately (Fig. 3), then extracts component of the theme tune which can describe 80 % tune in samples (Fig. 4), does batch processing and analysis and generates a theme tune table of every sample for the following multidimensional scaling analysis among samples.

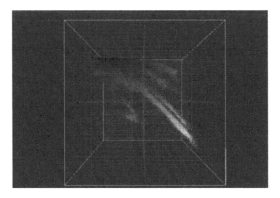

Fig. 2. Color spatial distribution analysis tool colorSpace_3D_v1

Fig. 3. ImageColor_Abstraction_and_Sorting_v2

Fig. 4. ImageColor_Abstraction_and_Sorting_v3

Theme tune similarity analysis tool. Theme tune similarity analysis tool (Fig. 5) calculates the similarity of the theme tune between any two and generates a table with. csv format. The table will be used for the following multidimensional scaling analysis and statistical calculation of MDS.

	SampleCode0	SampleCode1	SampleCode2	SampleCode3	SampleCode4	SampleCode5	SampleCode6	SampleCode7	SampleCode8	SampleCode9	SampleCode10
2	0	29.223278	66.70082	123.85879	175.84084	26.627054	85.90111	155.18376	87.36704	66.71581	131.1259
3	29.223278	0	73.02739	124.34227	175.6303	53.99074	93.27915	150.43936	81.89628	82.78283	132.23463
4	66.70082	73.02739	0	58.034473	109.676796	59.04236	20.639767	92.52567	35.91657	30.757113	64.96922
5	123.85879	124.34227	58.034473	0	52.009613	116.64476	43.52011	38.06573	46.58326	76.66811	8.5440035
6	175.84084	175.6303	109.676796	52.009913	0	167.53806	93.13908	34.43835	95.3782	124.52711	44.877613
7	26.627054	53.99074	59.04236	116.64476	167.53806	0	74.60563	151.50908	88.588936	48.270073	123.146255
8	85.90111	93.27915	20.639767	43.52011	93.13908	74.60563	0	80.70316	41.689327	33.526108	49.487373
9	155.18376	150.43936	92.52567	38.06573	34.43835	151.50908	80.70316	0	69.70653	113.77609	35.52464
10	87.36704	81.89628	35.91657	46.58326	95.3782	88.588936	41.689327	69.70653	0	66.19668	54.08327
11	66.71581	82.78285	30.757113	76.66811	124.52711	48.270073	33.526108	113.77609	66.19668	0	82.29824
12	131.1259	132.23463	64.96922	8.5440035	44.877613	123.146255	49.487373	35.52464	54.08327	82.29824	0
13	62.76556	67.65353	6	62	113.84639	56.124883	25.65151	95.524864	36.249138	31.780497	69.260376
14	74.094536	77.92304	9.433981	49.90999	101.8332	67.96323	18.788294	83.7138	27.910572	38.79433	57.043842
15	95.32051	98.81296	28.86174	29.546574	80.88263	87.19518	16.27882	65.81793	32.04684	49.487373	36.138622
16	27.147743	27	84.0119	138.61456	190.23407	48.02083	102.81051	167.3828	100.6479	84.20214	146.5162
17	45.188496	43.312817	31.38471	81.981705	133.69368	50.783855	51.662363	110.79711	42.272923	51.351727	89.61027
18	46.67976	50.48762	26.1916	79.20859	130.916	47.644516	46.561787	110.059074	42.73172	45.738388	86.28442
19	95.885345	91.10434	39.153545	36.619667	85.24084	95.262794	39.255573	59.766212	12.124355	67.32756	44.56456
20	62.072536	68.03676	8.485281	63.118935	114.75626	55.118053	25.573423	96.87621	39.217342	29.086079	70.434364
21	89.721794	96.68506	23.853722	39.610603	89.050545	78.60661	4.582576	77.071396	41.12177	37.589993	45.321075
22	83.86298	80.454956	28.248894	44.474712	95.189285	83.03011	33.196384	71.44928	11.224972	57.253822	52.564247
23	101.0396	95.921844	44.11349	34.283683	81.27115	100.5296	43.011627	55.072678	14.764823	72.34639	41.70132
24	106.00943	100.86625	53.094257	42.461746	83.96428	106.47535	53.600372	58.532043	23.43075	82.29824	47.307507
25	28.809721	50.675438	44.83187	102.610916	153.85057	16.093477	61.81424	136.96715	73.28711	40.657104	109.15127

Fig. 5. The output result of Themetune similarity analysis tool

3.3 Image Analysis, Variable Definition and Labeling Basing on Feature Analysis

The main task of this paper is to form a structural system of variables to describe samples. After labeling the system, form a normal and ordinal description for variables to support the following descriptive statistics and correspondence analysis and excavate the common and different feature among samples.

This paper raises several variables for description basing on the overall analysis of the 571 pairs of advertising and labels the variables. The variables are classified into 6 categories.

- Content label (theme, product, product type, place of production, consumer orientation, brand, etc.);
- Composition label (diagonal, hub-and-spoke, zigzag, revolving shape, etc.);
- Expression label(direct display, emphasize on feature, contrast and foil, reasonably exaggerate, see big things through small, associative thinking, rich in humor, metaphorical transfer, use wonderful feeling to foil the product, suspense, idol, imitation, mystical method, multi pictures, etc.);
- Visual expression label (oil painting style, printing style, watercolor style, photo style, line drawing style, ink style, meticulous style, etc.);
- Image theme label (person, animal, objects, scene, etc.);
- cultural label (the traditional oriental, the west);

3.4 Measure Data Matrix

The data matrix is a contingence table used for management of samples, the corresponding labels and value. All the value is combined by image feature and artificial label. After the necessary standardization, all the data will be Imported into the SPSS software to do the following descriptive statistics and advanced statistical calculation (Table 1).

Table 1. Sample measure data matrix sheet

Sample No	Smaple	content tags	Composition tag	Expression tag	Vision tag	Theme tag	Feature tag
label	Image						
001							
002							
003							
...							
571							

3.5 The Statistical Calculation and Analysis Basing on Multidimensional Indexes

In this paper, qualitative research and quantitative research are the main method to analyze the information and data. The data required from the process of feature analysis are mainly nominal data, for example, the expression methods used in the sample. It offers data for analyzing the variable distribution in all samples.

Owing to the large number of variables and there are more specific variables and value in six categories, this paper adapts correspondence analysis and multidimensional scaling analysis to dig the feature of samples basing on basic descriptive statistics.

4 Analysis

4.1 Result Analysis of Recognizing the Image Feature

The following are the results basing on the similar color space positioning analysis and calculation of samples (Figs. 6, 7 and 8).

Figure 8 shows that it is clearly seen that the position of all samples in two dimensional spaces are in accordance with the rule of two dimensions:

- In the horizontal dimension, the theme tune shows the transition from black and white color (left) to high saturation color (right).
- In the vertical dimension, samples show the transition from cool tone (down) to warm tone (up).

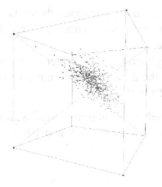

Fig. 6. Position of the themetune of all samples

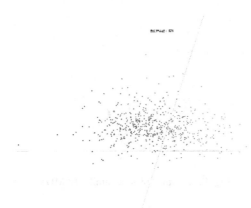

Fig. 7. Position of the themetune rotated of all samples

Fig. 8. Position of the themetune of all samples whose dimension is reduced

- The distribution of samples in the horizontal direction is wider than in the vertical direction, i.e. saturation is more representative than color temperature for the difference of the theme tune.
- The number of samples gathering in the center of the picture is bigger than that in the surrounding area, i.e. the theme tune of the most samples are similar. It reflects the relative uniformity of the theme tune.

The following is the result of multidimensional scaling analysis of MDS using similarity analysis tool of theme tune (Figs. 9 and 10).

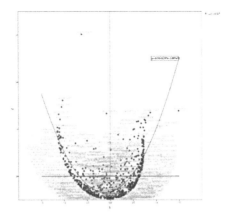

Fig. 9. Position of tune similarity MDS

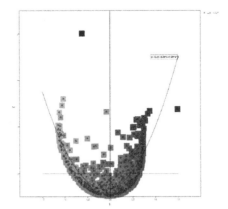

Fig. 10. Position of tune similarity MDS (including color tags) (Color figure online)

Figure 9 shows that it can be easily seen that similarity distribution of the theme tune of all samples shows significant rule. We can achieve the binary regression equation by using twice curve-fitting method.

$$Y = 0.33 + 0.25 * X + 1.09 * X2, \ R2 = 0.527$$

In order to make the analysis result easier to find the distribution rule, researchers give more information to Fig. 9, add color code of theme tune to every sample (Fig. 10).

As can be seen in the picture, although the attribute and content of all samples are different, the feature of theme tune shows obvious rule. Color brightness changes gradually from bright to dark from left to right, but in the vertical dimension, no clear rule can be found. In addition, saturation in center section enveloped by U-shaped curve is higher than that around.

4.2   Result Analysis of Separate Identification of Label Attributes

The following are analysis result of position picture from different variable dimension.

Analysis about tone richness and analysis from other variable dimensions

Analysis about composition way and tone richness. Figure 11 shows that there is no clear relationship between composition way and tone richness in all samples and there is no clear rule that can explain the distribution of composition way in all samples. In addition, it is rare that repeatedly arranged patterning method, diagonal composition method and symmetrical composition method are widely used in the samples.

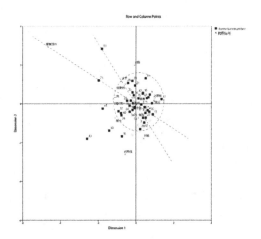

Fig. 11. Analysis about composition way and tone richness

Analysis about expression way and tone richness (Fig. 12). From the result, most of the expression ways can be easily seen in the 571 samples, but several ways, including text announcement method, suspense arrangement act, humorous imitation method, see big things through small ones, etc., are less used than other ways.

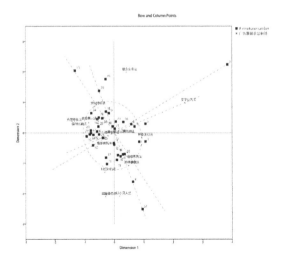

Fig. 12. Analysis about expression way and tone richness

Analysis about visual expression way and tone richness (Fig. 13). From the result, calligraphic style is relatively rare, so are photographic style and painting style, but the latter are used more than the former, the expression of the most samples are similar.

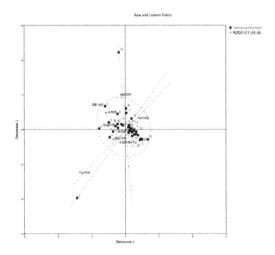

Fig. 13. Analysis about visual expression way and tone richness

Analysis about culture label and tone richness (Fig. 14). In this picture, there is no clear relationship between culture label and tone richness in all samples. In this dimension, it is unique that historical figures and folk customs are used. A lower proportion of appearance may be the reason.

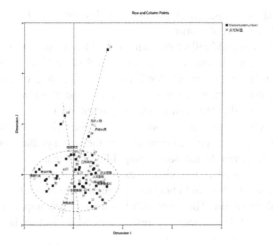

Fig. 14. Analysis about culture label and tone richness

Analysis from other dimensions

Overall, 571 samples show the following common characteristics:

- Textile products are rich in the expression way and 'scenario contrast' and 'imaginations' are most used. Cigarettes, drugs and cosmetic products prefer 'idols' followed by use 'wonderful feeling to foil the product', 'suspense arrangement', 'humorous imitation'. Festive supplies use 'direct display' more. Daily utensils use 'contrast' more.
- Textile products are also rich in culture label and it use 'love', 'nature', 'story', etc. Stationery commodity prefers 'history'. Apparel fabrics use 'idols' more. Daily utensils usually use 'the west'. Tobacco and festival activities use 'a combination of Chinese and Western elements' widely.
- In consumer orientation and choice for culture label, cultural groups prefer 'history' label. 'A combination of Chinese and Western elements' and 'Stylish in business' labels are more used in the female consumer group. Smokers use 'idols' more. Professionals use 'story' more.

5 Conclusion

The research results can offer an effective guidance to the design of Professional museum for print ads mentioned above during the period of the republic of China, including the overall atmosphere, thematic construction, and situation construction of the museum.

The samples dominant tone presents obvious regularity in visual cognition. On the scatter diagrams, the tone of the horizontal dimension is clear changed gradually from light to dark. There is no striking rule on the vertical dimensions. The overall museum atmosphere should be consistent with the samples tone, and keeping responding relation in light-shade & cold-warm.

The sample theme should reflect its own cultural label, such as by telling historical stories, reappearing tales of legendia. The characteristics of the time should be fully embodied by the help of the special idols from the Republic of China, fashionable product and arisen combination elements of Chinese and Western.

The construction of the Museum should pay attention to create story atmosphere, such as stories based on story background, story connection, suspense, and passion things, which makes the viewers be personally on the scene of the stories of the ads. It reflects a unique expression to the ads of Republic of China.

Further more, we can adapt this visual-based approach to design elements research in cultural heritage study, that could help us to evaluate visual products, and to evaluate the effect of visual cognition. This approach has a very high important significance in cultural archeology and design industry research as well as other fields.

References

1. Xie, H., Li, Q., Mao, X., et al.: Mining latent user community for tag-based and content-based search in social media. Comput. J. **57**(9), 1415–1430 (2014)
2. He, W.: Improving user experience with case-based reasoning systems using text mining and Web 2.0. Exp. Syst. Appl. **40**(2), 500–507 (2013)
3. Moscato, V., Picariello, A., Rinaldi, A.M.: Towards a user based recommendation strategy for digital ecosystems. Knowl. Based Syst. **37**, 165–175 (2013)
4. Qi, G.J., Aggarwal, C., Tian, Q., et al.: Exploring context and content links in social media: a latent space method. IEEE Trans. Pattern Anal. Mach. Intell. **34**(5), 850–862 (2012)
5. Shim, H., Lee, S.: Multi-channel electromyography pattern classification using deep belief networks for enhanced user experience. J. Cent. S. Univ. **22**(5), 1801–1808 (2015)
6. Martins, D.S., Oliveira, L.S., Pimentel, M.G.C.: Designing the user experience in iTV-based interactive learning objects. In: Proceedings of the 28th ACM International Conference on Design of Communication, pp. 243–250. ACM (2010)
7. Lei, T., Liu, X., Wu, L., Chen, T., Wang, Y., Xiong, L., Wei, S.: The impact of natural utilization of traditional Chinese cultural elements on the user experience in mobile interaction design. In: Rau, P. (ed.) CCD 2015. LNCS, vol. 9181, pp. 46–56. Springer, Heidelberg (2015)

DUXU in Virtual
and Augmented Reality

Authoring Tools for Augmented Reality: An Analysis and Classification of Content Design Tools

Rafael Alves Roberto[1]([✉]), João Paulo Lima[1,2], Roberta Cabral Mota[3], and Veronica Teichrieb[1]

[1] Voxar Labs, CIn, Universidade Federal de Pernambuco, Recife, Brazil
{rar3,vt}@cin.ufpe.br
[2] DEINFO, Universidade Federal Rural de Pernambuco, Recife, Brazil
jpsml@deinfo.ufrpe.br
[3] University of Calgary, Calgary, Canada
roberta.cabralmota@ucalgary.ca

Abstract. Augmented Reality Authoring Tools are important instruments that can help a widespread use of Augmented Reality. They can be classified as programming or content design tools in which the latter completely removes the necessity of programming skills to develop an Augmented Reality solution. Several solutions have been developed in the past years, however there are few works aiming to identify patterns and general models for such tools. This work aims to perform a trend analysis on content design tools in order to identify their functionalities regarding Augmented Reality, authoring paradigms, deployment strategies and general dataflow models. This work is aimed to assist developers willing to create authoring tools, therefore, it focuses on the last three aspects. Thus, 24 tools were analyzed and through this evaluation it were identified two authoring paradigms and two deployment strategies. Moreover, from their combination it was possible to elaborate four generic dataflow models in which every tool could be fit into.

Keywords: Augmented reality · Authoring tools · Content design tools

1 Introduction

Recently, Augmented Reality (AR) technology started to be widely used in various application domains, such as advertising, medicine, education, and others. However, the time and technical expertise needed to create AR applications is one of the reasons that has prevented widespread use. In this sense, authoring tools have become a largely used solution to boost mainstream use of AR since they facilitate the development of AR experiences [25].

AR authoring tools can be broadly organized into two different approaches: AR authoring for programmers and non-programmers [11]. In the former case, tools are typically code libraries that require programming knowledge to author

© Springer International Publishing Switzerland 2016
A. Marcus (Ed.): DUXU 2016, Part III, LNCS 9748, pp. 237–248, 2016.
DOI: 10.1007/978-3-319-40406-6_22

the application. In this work, these approaches are called programming tools. In the latter case, abstraction is added and low level programming capability is removed or hidden. Thus, tools for non-programmers are content driven and commonly include graphical user interfaces for building applications without writing any lines of code. Here, it is addressed as content design tools.

These two generic categories can be further organized into low-level and high-level, as seen in Fig. 1. Low-level programming tools require low-level coding while high-level ones use high-level libraries. Furthermore, low-level content design tools demand scripting skills and high-level tools use visual authoring techniques. All of these authoring approaches are built upon each other. Abstraction is gradually added and low-level functionalities and concepts are removed or hidden. Also, different abstraction levels address different target audiences with different technical expertise.

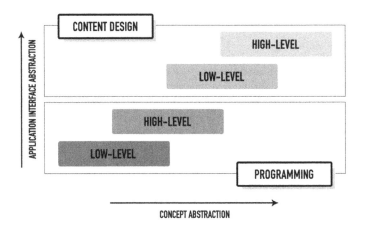

Fig. 1. Schematic view of AR authoring tools [11].

Among the approaches of AR authoring tools, it is important to note the relevance of the content design tools. They are particularly important because they leverage the widespread adoption of AR, since they highly simplify the authoring process and allow the development of applications and content by ordinary users, which do not need to have programming knowledge. Therefore, content design tools in AR have greater relevance when we take into account the potential amount of users that can use AR solutions in the future.

From the first solutions [12] to the most recent ones [27], it is possible to see that several content design tools have been developed. However, there are a few works aiming to provide a classification or to identify tendencies and patterns for such tools. To the best of the authors knowledge, there is only one work that proposes a taxonomy for AR authoring tools. In turn, this classification is according to the application interface and concept abstraction [11], in which the most abstract application interfaces are named content design frameworks and the least abstract are called programming frameworks.

Due to the relevance of content design tools, this paper aims at conducting a trend analysis in order to understand the current tendencies of such tools. This investigation attempts to identify the current tendencies regarding the authoring paradigms and deployment strategies of AR experiences that have been used in both commercial and academic realms. Furthermore, these strategies were combined to elaborate generic dataflow models in which all of the content design tools could fit into. Finally, based on these findings, it was introduced a taxonomy representing the different authoring and deployment trends, as well as each of the general models. This classification may guide researchers and companies to develop solutions aiming at their needs.

This work is organized as follows: Sect. 2 describes the methodology used to perform the trend analysis. Section 3 presents the results obtained from the analysis while Sect. 4 discusses them. Finally, the conclusions of this work are drawn in Sect. 5.

2   Methodology

Three steps were taken to explore the trends regarding AR authoring tools. The first one was the selection of content design tools available in the marketplace and the literature. Then, as a second step, the analysis relied on observing the dataflow of development and access to the AR content of each one of the selected tools. Finally, the third step consisted in discovering the authoring paradigms and deployment strategies used in the content design tools. Their combination was used to elaborate general dataflow models.

2.1   Selection

Initially, the keywords and expressions *("authoring tool" AND "augmented reality")* were searched in IEEE Xplore Digital Library and ACM Digital Library in order to find relevant papers concerning authoring tools in AR. That allowed for an investigation over important publications from 2001 to 2015. During this examination, only authoring tools classified as content design tools were selected for analysis.

2.2   Analysis

Following this, a deeper analysis was performed of each one of the selected authoring tools in order to understand the dataflow for development and access to the AR content. On a high level, this dataflow describes the end-to-end scenario that outlines the authoring and deployment of AR experiences, from the creation of AR semantic through authoring tools to its visualization by end-users.

2.3 Categorization

The deeper analysis performed on each of the selected content design tools made possible the observation of trends regarding authoring and distribution strategies of AR experiences that have been used. Furthermore, this observation also tried to understand (a) how the different authoring paradigms may support AR content development, and (b) how the deployment strategies seek to reach a larger number of end-users. Finally, the identification of AR authoring and deployment trends allowed the translation of the project-specific dataflow, observed in the selected content design tools, into the creation of general dataflow models. In this sense, a minimum number of combinations of trends was performed in order to elaborate generic models, in which all of the content design tools could fit into.

3 Results

The search on the scientific libraries returned 147 papers and 14 works about content design tools were selected for analysis. Moreover, 10 commercial tools that are well consolidated or relevant in the market were chosen. Thus, taking into account both academic and commercial realms, there were 24 content design tools. Thereafter, a dataflow analysis was performed in each of the selected tools.

3.1 AR Authoring Paradigms

Once individual analyses were performed in each of the previous selected content design tools, it was observed that two authoring paradigms have been used to create AR solutions: stand-alone and AR plug-in approaches.

Stand-Alone. AR authoring tools that use the stand-alone paradigm are software with all the necessary components for the development of complete AR experiences, as can be seen in Fig. 2(a). In turn, these components may include a graphical user interface, a series of importers, sensor interfaces, tracking and rendering engines, among others. In this sense, each stand-alone content design tool is a new software that allows designers to create their custom AR projects with more or less ease.

As an example, the Layar Creator [17] provides a complete set of features along the entire creation workflow, such as graphical user interface including drag and drop to ease the scenario creation.

AR Plug-in. Similar to conventional digital plug-ins, AR plug-ins are third-party software components installed on host applications in order to enable additional features, as illustrated in Fig. 2(b). In this sense, these authoring tools provide AR capabilities to software that natively does not support it, such as tracking techniques, access to physical sensors, three-dimensional rendering engine, among others.

It is relevant to note that, from the practical point of view, an AR plug-in instance will appear in the target software as a set of GUI elements, such as one or more menu items and toolbar buttons. Therefore, the whole AR authoring process occurs within the hosting environment, as the designer completely configures the desired AR experience by means of those elements along with the ones already provided by the target software.

As an example, the DART [7] system is built as a collection of extensions to the Adobe Director [2], a widely used environment for multimedia content creation, to support the development of a variety of AR applications.

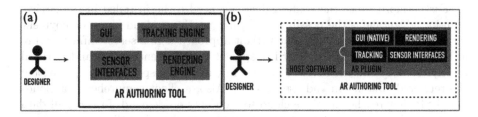

Fig. 2. (a) Stand-alone AR authoring tools enable building entire AR experiences. In order to provide AR capabilities, these tools integrate components such as sensor interfaces, tracking and rendering engines; (b) AR plug-ins provide AR functionalities for non-AR authoring environments. The designer interacts directly with the hosting software in order to create AR experiences.

3.2   AR Deployment Strategies

It was noticed that two deployment strategies have been applied to make these AR experiences available for end-users: platform-specific (PS) and platform independent (PI) methods.

Platform-Specific. In the PS approach, AR projects built using authoring tools are exported to archive files to be independently distributed. Some common archive file formats include .exe in Windows, .dmg or .app in Mac OS, .apk in Android, and .ipa for iOS operating systems. Note that these archive files are software packages used to distribute and install native application software. A native app, in turn, is considered a stand-alone program itself since it is a self-contained program that does not require any auxiliary software to be executed, as can be observed in Fig. 3(a). Native apps are usually available through application distribution platforms, such as App Store, Google Play, and Windows Phone Store. However, they must be downloaded from the platform to the end-user devices, such as iPhone, Android, Windows phones, or even laptops or desktop computers.

As an example, the Wikitude Studio [28] supports deployment options to mobile applications for iOS/Android platforms, and to executable programs for Windows/Mac OS computers.

Platform-Independent. The PI approach delivers the AR solutions as data files read and executed on a software platform (SP) running on the end-user device. Also, it is worth pointing out that, after the authoring process, the generated content requires a platform on which it must be executed. Therefore, the content cannot be considered a stand-alone program. Rather, it comprehends data files (commonly structured in XML-based formats) that are interpreted by the SP, as illustrated in Fig. 3(b).

As an example, k-MART [6] allows designers to export AR solutions as X3D-based data files. In turn, these files are later executed on a separate content browser.

Furthermore, since the content does not need to be installed in the device, a major advantage is the possibility of implementing a cloud-based deployment service. This increasingly popular variant approach uses a server infrastructure as a backbone. The remote server is responsible for content storage and retrieval as requested by the clients. The clients, in turn, are responsible for presenting the retrieved content on end-user devices. Also, a client comprehends a cloud-based SP that reaches into the cloud for contents on demand. In turn, all data files remotely accessed are here referenced as cloud-based applications.

As an example, AR companies like Layar and Wikitude developed Layar App and Wikitude World AR browsers, respectively. To the end-user, an AR browser looks very similar to a typical native app: it is downloaded from an app store, stored on the mobile device, and launched just like a native app. However, the most prominent advantage of AR browsers is that end-users need only one app for multiple contents. Once installed, they pull new cloud-based apps on demand.

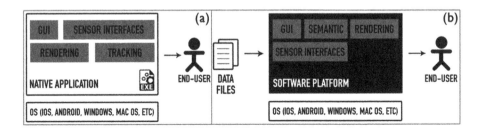

Fig. 3. (a) A native app includes all required elements to execute AR experiences, thus can be considered a stand-alone software itself. Also, the term native comprises applications compiled at runtime, such as an Android app, or precompiled executable programs; (b) Data files are interpreted by a native shell, which provides the required infrastructure to present AR experiences.

3.3   General Models

Given the authoring and deployment trends explored in the previous subsections, it was possible to elaborate four general dataflow models that represent the content design tools' dataflow analysed in this work.

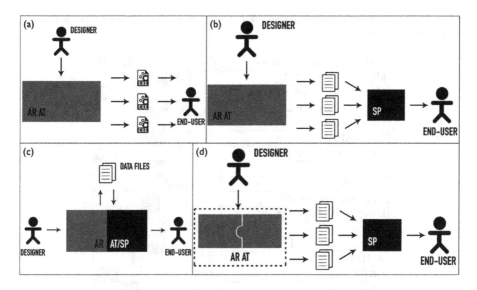

Fig. 4. (a) Model 1 combines a stand-alone authoring with a PS distribution. Therefore, each generated native application is individually installed and accessed by end-users; (b) Model 2 unites a stand-alone authoring paradigm with a PI distribution; (c) Model 3 combines a stand-alone authoring with a PI distribution. Yet, both designers and end-users utilize the same ambient to create and visualize AR solutions; (d) Model 4 merges an AR plug-in authoring with a PI distribution.

Model 1: Stand-Alone PS Model. As can be observed in Fig. 4(a), this dataflow model embodies a stand-alone authoring approach combined with a native distribution strategy. In this sense, the designer first creates AR experiences through stand-alone content design tools. Then he exports the project as PS files, which are used to deliver stand-alone, native applications for Android, iOS, Windows or other operating system.

Model 2: Stand-Alone PI Model. Similarly to the previous model, the designer first builds AR experiences using stand-alone content design tools. However, this model applies a PI strategy for reaching interoperability and maintainability. In this sense, the designer exports the authored AR solutions as data files that run on a separate SP. Note that, a content design tool can generate one or more data files which can be interpreted in a single SP and in different periods of time, as seen in Fig. 4(b). Yet, since each stand-alone content design tool is a brand new software, the data files created by distinct tools generally differ in their structures, logics, and formats.

Model 3: All-in-One Model. As illustrated in Fig. 4(c), in this model, both designers and end-users utilize the same environment to build and access AR solutions. In the sense, the designer creates and saves AR solutions as data files.

Table 1. Classification of each commercial (without year) and academic tool according to the general dataflow models.

Content Design Tools	Year	M1	M2	M3	M4
Metaio Creator [22]	-	■	■		
Metaio AR Creator Plugin [21]	-				■
Wikitude Studio [28]	-	■	■		
Layar Creator [17]	-			■	
Build AR [14]	-			■	
AR-media Plugin [15]	-				■
Playme [23]	-			■	
CraftAR [4]	-	■	■		
Aurasma Studio [13]	-			■	
DAQRI 4D Studio [8]	-			■	
Powerspace [12]	2002			■	
Authoring Wizard [29]	2003			■	
AMIRE [1]	2004			■	
DART [19]	2004				■
CDT1 [18]	2004			■	
ComposAR [26]	2008			■	
VREditor [20]	2009		■		
ARBookCreator [9]	2009			■	
AR Scratch [24]	2009			■	
k-MART [6]	2010	■			
CDT2 [16]	2012		■		
AVATAR [10]	2012				■
CDT3 [3]	2013		■		
CDT4 [27]	2014			■	

Eventually, these files are read and executed within the same environment in order to present the AR experience to end-users. Hence, similarly to the previous model, the all-in-one comprehends a stand-alone authoring approach combined with a PI distribution. However, the major difference resides in the fact that production and delivery services are merged within a single system.

Model 4: AR Plug-in PI Model. In this dataflow model, the designer first builds AR projects using hosting software integrated with AR plug-ins. Then, these projects are saved as data files that are later retrieved and executed on a separate application. In other words, this model includes a plug-in approach combined with a PI deployment strategy, as can be observed in Fig. 4(d).

All the content design tools that were selected and analyzed in this work are listed in Table 1. The table divides the commercial and academic tools and indicates to which of the four general dataflow models each tool belongs. It is important to keep in mind that it is not mandatory for a tool to be categorized into only one general model since a content design tool can provide different distribution approaches and, consequently, different dataflow models.

4 Discussion

The major findings permitted a discussion in regards to (a) the benefits and shortcomings of each of the AR authoring paradigms and deployment strategies and (b) the results obtained from the classification of the analyzed content design tools according to the four generic dataflow models. Each one of these discussions are approached in the following subsections.

4.1 Stand-Alone vs. AR Plug-in

Reusability. Stand-alone authoring tools generally offer a smaller set of features when they are compared to full-fledged hosting software. In the plug-in approach, the designer may create the AR experience by using not only the extra functionalities provided by the plug-in, but also the mature existing features in the target software. On the other hand, it would require strong effort and time to implement these features in a stand-alone authoring tool.

Domain specificity. Another benefit of the AR plug-in over the stand-alone approach is that each created plug-in can be specialized for a specific application domain. By using the plug-in approach, one can propose a set of functionalities tailored to one specific application domain. Thus, only the required features are implemented and not every possible one that usually a stand-alone tool must provide.

Learning curve. Given a situation in which stand-alone tools are focused on specific tasks or application areas, the learning curve and the time employed to learn how to use each new tool, with different interfaces, is longer if compared to integrated tools. Since the plug-ins are usually implemented on the same environment, each focusing on a specific task or application domain, the designer would not need to interact with a new interface.

However, the time spent to learn how to create an AR application using a plug-in can be bigger when compared with a stand-alone solution in case the user does not have experience with the host tool. It is due to the fact that they commonly have a complex interface. Thus, the learning curve for simple and focused tools is usually shorter.

Integration restraints. Bringing AR capabilities inside non-AR authoring tools is neither straightforward nor trivial. First, it must be considered the availability of an SDK for the target software. It is extremely hard to manage the integration when dealing with a closed system. Another factor is the GUI. When designing an integrated AR plug-in for a host software, it is mandatory to create GUI elements with the same look-and-feel as the target software. Moreover, the authoring metaphor must be used in a coherent way with it. In this sense, obstacles may arise during the development of functionalities that follow the traditional authoring style and, at the same time, enable AR content creation with ease.

4.2   Platform-Specific vs. Platform-Independent

Portability. Since native apps are built using the device's native programming language, they only run on their designated platform. This means that the same app cannot be re-used between platforms. Thus, deploying a native app to Android, iOS and Windows Phone would require creating three different applications to run on each platform. Contrastingly, one major promise about platform independence is that designers only have to write the application once and then it will be able to run anywhere, without having to be recreated by the designer for each separate platform.

Maintenance cost. Maintaining native applications is also expensive for the designer. As a native app is built for a particular device and its operating system, whenever new OS versions are rolled out, native apps may require considerable updates to work on these newer versions. Moreover, data files run independent on a PS shell that operates as an abstraction layer that encapsulates the underlying hardware and software updates. Hence, the designer does not have to worry about updating and resubmitting apps.

Offline functionality and speed. An advantage for native apps is the off-line functionality and speed. Since the application remains installed on the device from the original download, depending on the nature of the app, no internet connection may be required. Another area where native apps have a clear advantage is speed. These apps, by definition, run at native speed. PI apps run on top of additional layers, which consume computing resources and can therefore decrease the execution speed.

4.3   General Models

As can be seen in Table 1 the stand-alone PI model is the most used approach in both commercial and academic realms. It can also be noticed that the stand-alone PS model is the less used approach. In turn, these results might indicate that there is a strong trend towards PI strategies, which provide two key determinants for delivering widely deployable AR experiences.

First, it permits cross-platform usage of the created AR experiences and the more platforms are covered, the more people are reached. In this sense, leading AR companies have commercial content design tools that suit into the stand-alone PI model. In these scenarios, AR solutions are executed on their respective AR browsers. In turn, these browsers are cross-platform applications that run across different operating systems.

Second, the PI strategy also allows content aggregation for leveraging distribution and discovering of AR solutions. In this sense, it can provide an unified AR platform to access multiple content, thus avoiding the cumbersome task of downloading and installing each one of the AR solutions.

Table 1 shows that seven out of the eight generic dataflow models target data files for specifying the AR solutions. Therefore, based on these results, it is possible to observe that there is a consensus in academia and industry for adopting descriptive data formats, which includes JSON and, most often, XML-based formats such as ARML, KARML, and XML.

5   Conclusion

AR authoring tools can provide several levels of abstraction, thus targeting audiences within a range of different technical expertise. Particularly, those categorized as content design tools allow non-technologists to explore the AR creation medium and, therefore, these tools are an essential component for helping AR to gain popularity in different application domains. Due to their relevance, several content design tools have been developed recently. However, no work was found that presents an analysis and classification of those tools.

In this sense, this work analyzed 24 commercial and academic content design tools in order to identify tendencies of such tools. The investigation revealed that there are two authoring paradigms and two distribution strategies that have been widely used for such tools. Furthermore, these authoring and deployment trends were combined to elaborate four generic dataflow models.

Furthermore, this paper discussed the authors' findings on the authoring and deployments tendencies by comparing one trend against its alternatives in order to discuss their advantages and limitations. Thereafter, it discussed the results obtained from the classification of the content design tools according to the four general dataflow models.

The authors believe that the proposed taxonomy along with the discussion regarding the major findings can help users to find the best tools for them or guide researchers and companies to develop solutions aiming their needs.

References

1. Abawi, D.F., Dörner, R., Grimm, P.: A component-based authoring environment for creating multimedia-rich mixed reality. In: EGMM 2004 (2004)
2. Adobe Systems Incorporated: Adobe Director, January 2015. http://goo.gl/QnkQni
3. Barbadillo, J., Sánchez, J.R.: A web3d authoring tool for augmented reality mobile applications. In: Web3D 2013 (2013)
4. Catchroom: CraftAR: Augmented Reality and Image Recognition toolbox, January 2015. http://goo.gl/ThRVv7
5. Cho, H., Gray, J., Sun, Y.: Quality-aware academic research tool development. In: APSEC 2012, vol. 2, pp. 66–72, December 2012
6. Choi, J., Kim, Y., Lee, M., Kim, G., Nam, Y., Kwon, Y.: k-MART: Authoring tool for mixed reality contents. In: ISMAR 2010, pp. 219–220, October 2010
7. Coleman, M.G.: Creating augmented reality authoring tools informed by designer workflow and goals. Ph.D. thesis, Georgia Institute of Technology (2012)
8. DAQRI: 4D Studio DAQRI, January 2015. http://goo.gl/y8kLvr
9. Do, T.V., Lee, J.W.: Creating 3d e-books with ARBookCreator. In: ACE 2009 (2009)
10. Fei, G., Li, X., Fei, R.: AVATAR: Autonomous visual authoring of tangible augmented reality. In: VRCAI 2012 (2012)
11. Hampshire, A., Seichter, H., Grasset, R., Billinghurst, M.: Augmented reality authoring: Generic context from programmer to designer. In: OZCHI 2006 (2006)
12. Haringer, M., Regenbrecht, H.: A pragmatic approach to augmented reality authoring. In: ISMAR 2002, pp. 237–245 (2002)

13. Hewlett-Packard Development Company: Aurasma Studio. https://goo.gl/Ix8vgr
14. HIT Lab NZ: BuildAR Pro, January 2015. http://goo.gl/1LtXvt
15. Inglobe Technologies S.r.l.: AR-media - AR-media Products, January 2015. http://goo.gl/TbLeM8
16. Langlotz, T., Mooslechner, S., Zollmann, S., Degendorfer, C., Reitmayr, G., Schmalstieg, D.: Sketching up the world: In situ authoring for mobile augmented reality. Personal Ubiquitous Comput. **16**(6), 623–630 (2012). http://dx.doi.org/10.1007/s00779-011-0430-0
17. Layar: Layar creator, January 2015. http://goo.gl/rQ0PlP
18. Lee, G., Nelles, C., Billinghurst, M., Kim, J.: Immersive authoring of tangible augmented reality applications. In: ISMAR 2004, pp. 172–181 (2004)
19. MacIntyre, B., Gandy, M., Dow, S., Bolter, J.D.: DART: a toolkit for rapid design exploration of augmented reality experiences. In: UIST 2004 (2004)
20. Mavrogeorgi, N., Koutsoutos, S., Yannopoulos, A., Varvarigou, T., Kambourakis, G.: Cultural heritage experience with virtual reality according to user preferences. In: CENTRIC 2009, pp. 13–18, September 2009
21. Metaio GmbH: metaio — AR Creator Plugin — Products, January 2015. http://goo.gl/Z5E9ym
22. Metaio GmbH: metaio — Creator Overview, January 2015. http://goo.gl/6xwgyF
23. Playme AR: Playme AR Creator Features — Playme AR - Simple Augmented Reality Software, January 2015. http://goo.gl/nGAf9t
24. Radu, I., MacIntyre, B.: Augmented-reality scratch: A children's authoring environment for augmented-reality experiences. In: IDC 2009 (2009)
25. Ramireza, H., Mendivila, E.G., Floresa, P.R., Gonzalez, M.C.: Authoring software for augmented reality applications for the use of maintenance and training process. In: International Conference on Virtual and Augmented Reality in Education. pp. 189–193, October 2013
26. Seichter, H., Looser, J., Billinghurst, M.: ComposAR: An intuitive tool for authoring ar applications. In: ISMAR 2008, pp. 177–178, September 2008
27. Shim, J., Kong, M., Yang, Y., Seo, J., Han, T.D.: Interactive features based augmented reality authoring tool. In: 2014 IEEE International Conference on Consumer Electronics (ICCE), pp. 47–50, January 2014
28. Wikitude GmbH: Wikitude Studio - the world's easiest augmented reality creation tool, January 2015. http://goo.gl/Lr0uOK
29. Zauner, J., Haller, M., Brandl, A., Hartman, W.: Authoring of a mixed reality assembly instructor for hierarchical structures. In: ISMAR 2003, pp. 237–246, October 2003

Remote HRI and Mixed Reality, an Ontology

Carolina Cani D.L.[✉], Felipe B. Breyer, and Judith Kelner

Virtual Reality and Multimedia Research Group,
Universidade Federal de Pernambuco, Recife, Brazil
{ccdl, fbb3, jk}@cin.ufpe.br

Abstract. This work builds a panorama of resources in Remote HRI identified
in a systematic literature review with focus on Mixed reality solutions. This
study builds a panorama of HRI with mixed reality through the definition of the
terms presented in this ontology which serves as a reference to facilitate to
create new robotic solutions relying on this resource.

Keywords: HRI · Human robot interaction · Remote control · Teleoperation ·
Augmented reality · Virtual reality · Mixed reality · Augmented virtuality

1 Introduction

Robotics is an area in great expansion, the improvement of remote human robot
interaction (HRI) side by side with lower costs of the robotic systems, has made robots
accessible to the masses the same way personal computers have become part of customary life, such as irobot roomba and other home solutions. Many studies [1] focus
on the study of human robot interaction design, but there is still a lot of work to do to
improve interaction with the users.

Robots have evolved throughout the years focusing on more complex tasks,
however, completely autonomous robots are usually specialized for a few specific
tasks. When the task requires a higher level of comprehension of the surroundings, the
robot may need help from a human operator to execute the adequate action.

Remotely operated robots have been developed to perform complex activities in
inaccessible places or places that present high risks to humans. For example, the
maintenance of nuclear plants where there are high levels of radiation [2] as well as the
use of robots in space exploration missions [3]. Robots are also used for search and
rescue after urban disasters such as WTC attack [4] and earthquakes. The enhancement
of robots for urban search and rescue has been constantly improved in international
competitions [5].

The objective of this paper is to produce an ontology that maps the current possibilities of HRI and the use of Mixed reality as a facilitator for remote operations. In
order to achieve this goal, a systematic review was conducted including articles published up to July 2015. The contents of this paper are organized in 6 sections. In
subsequent sections of this work will be presented Related Works in Sect. 2, followed
by methodology design in Sect. 3. The resulting Ontology is presented in Sect. 4,
followed by Conclusion and Future Works in Sect. 5.

© Springer International Publishing Switzerland 2016
A. Marcus (Ed.): DUXU 2016, Part III, LNCS 9748, pp. 249–257, 2016.
DOI: 10.1007/978-3-319-40406-6_23

2 Related Works

The field of HRI was the subject of a survey [1] that mapped key topics of matter. After presenting a brief history of robotics and interaction, the study presented HRI problems regarding robots design, information exchange, application areas, and possible solutions. Goodrich and Schultz also pointed information fusion as a possible solution to provide operational presence to the robot in remote interaction. They also claim that new ways to integrate those information have to be found. In this ontology we present characteristics of Mixed Reality Displays for HRI and resources to create interfaces with integrated information. Based on this study, we identified the four first classes of our ontology and named the topics robots, interaction, human factors and scenarios.

In turn, Green et al. [6] conducted a literature review about human robot collaboration with emphasis on AR solutions to aid interactions. Our ontology expands this approach in its Mixed Realities branch by including solutions not only with AR, but also Virtual Reality, Augmented Virtuality and Videocentric displays.

Sheridan defined the concept of Levels of Automation (LOA) in [7] on a scale that includes ten levels of automation in a teleoperated system. He subsequently compiled in [8] frameworks that resulted in the flexibilization of this scale under the concept of adaptive autonomy. This concept of autonomy was added as a subclass of the branch robots in this study since the variation range of the robot directly impacts the design of HRI.

Milgram [9] defined a taxonomy of mixed reality visual displays and a virtuality continuum to classify the level of reality or virtuality in a visual display. In our work we adapt the continuum to the field of HRI and presented display possibilities as branches in interaction output, next to the resources that arise from this mixed reality interfaces. The far end of Milgram continuum are Virtual Environment and Real Environment. In the context of remote operation, the operator is never in the same environment with the robot, therefore, the most realistic interface that we identified in our field of interest was videocentric display. In this ontology we believe that by means of vast literature review it is possible to organize the knowledge field of Remote HRI and Mixed Reality Displays.

3 Methodology

The search for articles began in 5 search engines: ACM Digital Library, IEEE Xplore, Science Direct, Springer Link and Scopus covering from 2005 to 2015, accessed in June, 2015. Search terms included the words and variations for Robot, Teleoperation, interaction, HRI, "augmented reality", "Virtual reality", "augmented virtuality" and "mixed reality". The result was 893 articles, 46 of which were found to be duplicated, leaving a total of 847 for the initial analysis. Articles within the scope of the review were identified by the analysis of title, abstract and keywords, therefore 316 articles passed on to the next phase. In addition to, 12 articles were manually included through related studies and manual search in conferences HRI and IFAC, totaling 328.

Inclusion and exclusion criteria were then applied to the 328 remaining articles to ensure the scope of the articles relates to the field of interest of this study. The inclusion criteria were presence of remote interaction and mixed reality display. Studies without human factors, and robots were excluded from the review. Therefore 222 articles were eliminated, resulting in 106 articles for reading and quality evaluation.

To ensure that the articles were complete and adequate to empirical methods, according to the proposed solutions, the articles were meticulously evaluated to what regards to completeness and quality of the studies. The articles were evaluated in 16 parameters, with attributed grades from 0 to 1. The final score of the article was the product of the weighted average of these factors, 13 with weight 1 and 3 with weight 2, resulting in a grade from zero to 100 %.The three parameters with greater weight refer to: presence or absence of a detailed description of user testing; if the paper proposes an interface or interaction tool; and if the interface proposed was clearly described in the study. These parameters were defined with greater weight due to its importance for this review since they aim to certify presence of relevant information to this review. At the end of the process, 32 articles were selected to the data extraction phase, and elements of proposed solutions in HRI with mixed reality were selected based on the occurrence on them to build the ontology.

According to Noy and McGuinness [10], ontology is a method to share and annotate information and common vocabulary of a field of study. This study aims to group relevant terms of HRI remote interaction and mixed realities. After selecting the articles, the relevant information about the four initial classes of the ontology, Robots, Interaction, Human Factors and Scenarios, and Mixed Reality Display subclass were extracted and organized to compose the subsequent branches of the ontology.

The identified factors were cataloged hierarchically, building a structure of classes and subclasses. Classes and subclasses were graphically organized in form of branches to represent the relation between them. Due to this representation classes and sub-classes are often referred as branches in this study. Interaction was the class with more branches since the scope of the ontology covers the factors that influence the interface design using mixed reality displays for HRI.

4 Mixed Reality in HRI Ontology

The ontology was organized with four initial branches (Fig. 1), Humans Factors, Robots, Interaction and Scenarios, which subdivide into subsequent branches, detailing the universe of remote HRI and mixed reality displays. The resulting terms were defined according to the adequate meaning for the field of mixed reality in remote HRI.

4.1 Scenarios

Scenarios are the ambient robot solutions are designed to operate. Each environment presents different challenges that applications of remotely controlled robot have to overcome to execute the task. [11] developed an interface to control robot in a military scenario in target recognition tasks, they simulated situation of a multitask environment to evaluate the interfaces proposed in the experiments.

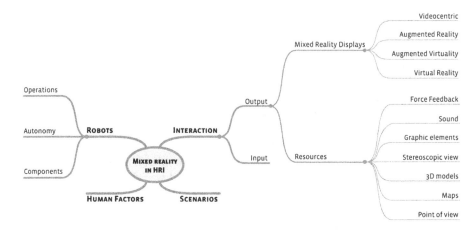

Fig. 1. Ontology ramification including Mixed Reality Displays branch

To enhance the performance of an Urban Search and Rescue (USAR) robotic system [12] developed an interface to aid navigation tasks, once the scenario of USAR involves challenging navigation terrain. It is important to identify and understand peculiar characteristics in each environment, and the specific tasks to each scenario in order design HRI systems.

4.2   Robots

Remotely controlled Robots receive the instructions from the remote user and operate the action in the surroundings. Robots also send relevant information and feedbacks to the operator. With several building possibilities and different levels of automation, robot design should suit the nature of the operations that it will execute, with proper components.

Operations. According to Steinfeld et al. [13] robot operations may be classified in five categories: navigation, manipulation, social, perception and monitoring. The remote interface design must take into consideration the specific needs from the task to be performed in order to provide the necessary information in an objective way.

Automation. Robots have different levels of automation (LOA), Sheridan [8] presents frameworks and automation classification models that evolved throughout the years covers the concept of adaptive autonomy, where the level of automation varies according to the necessity. In Adaptive autonomy exists the presence of an Authority Allocation Agent, the role can be executed by a computer or human. In the model defined by Parassuraman et al. [14] Adaptative Automation is partitioned in four information processing stages: information acquisition, analysis, decision and action implementation. Which steps should be automated and which should be controlled by an operator should be taken into consideration when designing a remotely operated system.

Components. When building a robot the components that will be needed to attach to execute the desired task must be taken under consideration. Sensors are the equipment responsible for detection of environmental signals, as for instance cameras, laser radars and GPS. Actuators are the mechanisms by which the robot will interact with the environment. Robotic arms, wheels and claws are common examples of robot actuators. The components that compose the robot may cause impact on the way that the remote control interfaces are designed.

4.3 Interaction

Interaction covers the means by which robot and user exchange information. The operator sends controlling commands, and the information is sent by the robot and presented to the operator. This branch covers controls techniques and information design resources to create HRI interfaces. Mixed Reality Displays modalities and interactive resources are described in Output branches. In Input branch, some possibilities that enable the user to send commands to the robot are exemplified.

Output. Is the information reaching the user through the system. Define how and which information is part of the interface design process. It should also be noted how the information will be arranged for the operator. Subsequent branches refer to mixed reality displays and resources that can be used to build them.

Mixed Reality Display. This branch relates to which information is displayed to the user and how it will be organized, each modality has characteristics that will benefit usability in distinct ways. Milgram and Kishino [9] defines a taxonomy concerning mixed reality displays and represented the variation of display environments in a virtuality continuum. In this study from the point of view of remote HRI, we considered videocentric display as the reality extreme of the continuum. In order to design the remote operation interface, a display must be chosen to suit the system's purpose.

- Video Centric. A teleoperation interface that displays streaming video sent by the robot as the center of attention of the user, may or may not be composed of more adjacent information, but independently, separate from the video image. This type of interface can be used as comparison to other interfaces in the mixed reality continuum because it does not use overlapping virtual elements. [15] developed an interface denominated videocentric with the objective to compare with other interface with augmented reality. [16] compared multiple displays with mixed reality elements to a videocentric interface.
- Augmented Reality. According to Azuma et al. [17] AR interface is defined by the coexistence of real and virtual objects in a real environment aligned with each other and running interactively in real time. In HRI remote interaction AR is a powerful resource to help the operator to perform teleoperated robot tasks. Often used to enhance depth by introducing distance information, AR interfaces may help reduce collision rate. In [18] AR interfaces were developed to aid robot navigation tasks to enhance accuracy by reducing collision and close calls.
- Augmented Virtuality. Real images or real objects are added to the virtual environment. Interfaces with these features were positive for assisting robot navigation tasks in [15] and in [12] streaming video was sent from the environment and combined with virtual maps.

- Virtual Reality. Composed only by virtual objects without images of the real environment displayed [9]. [19] developed a laser based teleoperation interface for navigation tasks that renders a Virtual Reality environment to the operator. The laser-based data transferred faster than video streaming, reducing delay between operator and robot.

Resources. In this branch are presented recurrent resources used in reviewed studies. Other resources may be added to this topic as other solutions are developed.

- Force feedback. It can be stated to the user both by haptic devices and by vibration. Barros et al. [20] developed an interface that informs the user through a vibration feedback about objects proximity when teleoperating a robot. The distance is informed through the intensity of the vibration and the position of objects advised by a belt attached to the operator's waist with vibrotactiles distributed accordingly to the relative position of the robot. In [21], haptic feedback was applied to indicate object proximity in a navigational task resulting in better performance and presence than other interaction variables in the conducted experiment.
- Sound. Audible feedback can be used as a form of verbal warning or also abstractly, with specific meanings to the sound in the system. [22] used spatial audio as one of the elements of the robot control interface to perform a search task in order to reduce the operator's workload.
- Graphic elements. Points, lines, planes and icons are recurrent elements in interface design. In mixed reality displays for remote HRI these elements can be used in an integrated way to robot environment. [18] developed a interface which allows the user to plan robot trajectory with previous line drawing of the path that the robot will navigate.
- Stereoscopic view. Resource that enhances depth visualization by displaying stereo images to the user. [21] used stereoscopic view in navigation tasks and noted enhanced performance and sense of presence when the user received only stereoscopic feedback.
- 3D models. Objects can be represented in mixed reality display with 3D models, studies represented the robot with virtual 3D models with the aim to enhance situational awareness in manipulation [23] and navigational tasks [20]. The objects can be represented with realism or simplified elements.
- Map. Especially useful in navigation tasks, maps can be displayed in the mixed reality display aside the video streaming or virtual environment or integrated. Maps can be static or animated to match the robot's position; can be represented in 2D or 3D. [24] studied the impact of different map representations to teleoperate a robot in a home environment.
- Point of view. The position of the virtual or real camera can change the remote interface. In remote HRI, two possibilities are: Exocentric view that shows the robot on the interface; and Egocentric view that shows the scenario from the point of view of the robot, the camera can also be mobile, controlled by the operator. [3] studied the impact of the camera position on the task performance in space telerobotic manipulation by comparing exocentric, egocentric frames of reference, results indicated that egocentric view may promote potential improvement of the performance.

Input. Regards to the means by which the user sends commands to the robot, controllers and sensors focused on the operator. Gestures recognition by image [18] or haptics devices [21], joypads, joysticks [16], and the more common mouse and keyboard are identified devices in the literature review. User input has to merge with the mixed reality device to afford appropriate user experience.

4.4 Human Factors

Human Factors is the collection of variables deriving from the user that should be taken under consideration when the interaction is being designed or evaluated. To evaluate user human factors the studies reviewed used both qualitative and quantitative approaches. Validated questionnaires were used to gather information about qualitative information. [15] measured subjective operational workload based on NASA task load index (NASA-TLX) [25].

Variables such as time to completion, number of collisions, and robot idle time without instructions were quantified to estimate and compare performance. To evaluate performance, [20] analyzed quantitative data of time taken to complete the search task, average robot speed, the number of collisions and other quantitative variables combined.

5 Conclusion and Future Works

A literature review was conducted in order to identify resources and mixed reality display solutions for remote HRI. Starting from 893 reviewed articles, 32 were selected after adequacy assessment of the scope and completeness and quality of the studies. After articles selection, identified factors were organized in an ontology with four initial classes and 18 subclasses.

The categories were described to organize a specific vocabulary of remote HRI and mixed reality displays solutions highlighting particular potential and challenges of each branch. Through the definition of the terms present in this ontology, this study builds a panorama of HRI with Mixed Reality Displays, which serves as a reference to facilitate the creation of new robotic solutions with integrated information. With 27 branches, this study also aims the identification of subjects to be studied as well as aiding the design of experiments with users, based on the proposed field mapping.

The scope of this work focused on interaction techniques, in future works we aim to expand this ontology in what regards to scenarios, human factors and robots construction and development. This ontology will also expand throughout technology development to embody the progress.

References

1. Goodrich, M.A., Schultz, A.C.: Human-robot interaction: a survey. Trends Hum. Comput. Interact. **1**(3), 203–275 (2007)

2. Heemskerk, C., Eendebak, P., Schropp, G., Hermes, H., Elzendoorn, B., Magielsen, A.: Introducing artificial depth cues to improve task performance in ITER maintenance actions. Fus. Eng. Des. **88**(9–10), 1969–1972 (2013). Proceedings of the 27th Symposium on Fusion Technology, Belgium, pp. 24–28 (2012)

3. Lamb, P., Owen, D.: human performance in space telerobotic manipulation. In: ACM Symposium on Virtual Reality Software and Technology, VRST 2005, pp. 31–37. ACM, New York (2005)

4. Casper, J., Murphy, R.R.: Human-robot interactions during the robot-assisted urban search and rescue response at the World Trade Center. IEEE Trans. Syst. Man Cybern. Part B Cybern. **33**(3), 367–385 (2003)

5. Liu, Y., Nejat, G.: Robotic urban search and rescue: a survey from the control perspective. J. Intell. Robot. Syst. **72**(2), 147–165 (2013)

6. Green, S., Billinghurst, M., Chen, X., Chase, G.: Human-robot collaboration: a literature review and augmented reality approach in design. J. ARS, 1–18 (2007)

7. Sheridan, T.B., Verplanck, W.L.: Human and computer control of undersea teleoperators. Technical report, MIT Man-Machine Laboratory, Cambridge, MA (1978)

8. Sheridan, T.B.: Adaptive automation, level of automation, allocation authority, supervisory control, and adaptive control: distinctions and modes of adaptation. IEEE Trans. Syst. Man Cybern. Part A Syst. Hum. **41**(4), 662–667 (2011)

9. Milgram, P., Kishino, F.: A taxonomy of mixed reality visual displays. IEICE Trans. Inf. Syst. **77**(12), 1321–1329 (1994)

10. Noy, N.F., McGuinness, D.L., et al.: Ontology development 101: a guide to creating your first ontology. Volume 15, Stanford knowledge systems laboratory technical report KSL-01-05 and Stanford medical informatics technical report SMI-2001-0880, Stanford, CA (2001)

11. Chen, J.Y., Barnes, M.J.: Robotics operator performance in a military multi-tasking environment. In: 3rd ACM/IEEE International Conference on Human Robot Interaction, HRI 2008, pp. 279–286. ACM, New York (2008)

12. Nielsen, C.W., Goodrich, M.A., Ricks, R.W.: Ecological interfaces for improving mobile robot teleoperation. IEEE Trans. Robot. **23**(5), 927–941 (2007)

13. Steinfeld, A., Fong, T., Kaber, D., Lewis, M., Scholtz, J., Schultz, A., Goodrich, M.: Common metrics for human-robot interaction. In: 1st ACM SIGCHI/SIGART Conference on Human-Robot Interaction, HRI 2006, pp. 33–40. ACM, New York (2006)

14. Sanguino, J.T.M., Márquez, M.J.A., Carlson, T., Millán, J.: Improving skills and perception in robot navigation by an augmented virtuality assistance system. J. Intell. Robot. Syst. **76**(2), 255–266 (2014)

15. Parasuraman, R., Sheridan, T.B., Wickens, C.D.: A model for types and levels of human interaction with automation. IEEE Trans. Syst. Man Cybern. Part A Syst. Hum. **30**(3), 286–297 (2000)

16. Michaud, F., Boissy, P., Labonté, D., Brière, S., Perreault, K., Corriveau, H., Grant, A., Lauria, M., Cloutier, R., Roux, M.-A., Iannuzzi, D., Royer, M.-P., Ferland, F., Pomerleau, F., Létourneau, D.: Exploratory design and evaluation of a homecare teleassistive mobile robotic system. Mechatronics **20**(7), 751–766 (2010). Special Issue on Design and Control Methodologies in Telerobotics (2010)

17. Azuma, R.T.: A survey of augmented reality. Presence Teleoper. Virtual Environ. **6**(4), 355–385 (1997)

18. Green, S.A., Chase, J.G., Chen, V., Billinghurst, M.: Evaluating the augmented reality human-robot collaboration system. In: 2008 15th International Conference on Mechatronics and Machine Vision in Practice, M2VIP 2008, pp. 521–526 (2008)

19. Livatino, S., Muscato, G., Sessa, S., Neri, V.: Depth-enhanced mobile robot teleguide based on laser images. Mechatronics **20**(7), 739–750 (2010). Special Issue on Design and Control Methodologies in Telerobotics (2010)
20. de Barros, P.G., Lindeman, R.W.: Performance effects of multi-sensory displays in virtual teleoperation environments. In: 1st Symposium on Spatial User Interaction, SUI 2013, pp. 41–48. ACM, New York (2013)
21. Lee, S., Kim, G.J.: Effects of haptic feedback, stereoscopy, and image resolution on performance and presence in remote navigation. Int. J. Hum Comput Stud. **66**(10), 701–717 (2008)
22. Haas, E., Stachowiak, C.: Multimodal displays to enhance human robot interaction on-the-move. In: 2007 Workshop on Performance Metrics for Intelligent Systems, PerMIS 2007, pp. 135–140. ACM, New York (2007)
23. Sauer, M., Leutert, F., Schilling, K.: An augmented reality supported control system for remote operation and monitoring of an industrial work cell. In: 2nd IFAC Symposium on Telematics Applications, pp. 83–88 (2010)
24. Ryu, H., Lee, W.: Where you point is where the robot is. In: 7th ACM SIGCHI New Zealand Chapter's International Conference on Computer-Human Interaction: Design Centered HCI, CHINZ 2006, pp. 33–42. ACM, New York (2006)
25. Hart, S.G.: NASA-task load index (NASA-TLX); 20 years later. Hum. Factors Ergonomics Soc. Annu. Meet. **50**(9), 904–908 (2006)

Virtual Display of 3D Computational Human Brain Using Oculus Rift

Seung-Wook Kim and Joon-Kyung Seong[✉]

Department of Biomedical Engineering, Korea University,
Seoul, Republic of Korea
sakimos@naver.com, joon.swallow@gmail.com

Abstract. Creating a 3D environment by Game Engine is a useful way to integrate various types of information into one platform. As a result, it becomes more convenient and rapid to share massive information to the others. Also, using Virtual Reality technology makes visual information to be more detailed and intuitive. In this study, by combining these advantages of Game Engine and VR technology to present brain imaging technologies, we tried to provide more detail and more convenient information about cephalic anatomy or brain disease.

We used the brain images of a patient with subcortical vascular cognitive impairment (SVCI), which is randomly selected from formal studies. Two types of brain image were loaded on Unity3D game engine by different method each, and then we observed the final data with a VR device named Oculus Rift.

There were some limitations and there are few things that should be complemented through future studies, but we obtained virtual image which is controllable enough in three-dimensional environment (Unity3D game engine), and was able to observe it via virtual reality device (Oculus Rift DK2).

Keywords: Brain imaging · Diffusion tensor imaging · Unity3D · Oculus rift · Virtual reality

1 Introduction

Brain MRI, in the clinical practice, is a powerful imaging tool for diagnosing brain diseases. Unlike the past traditional measures such as history taking and physical examinations, MRI scan shows the lesion's location, size, nature, and response after treatments accurately and quickly. Such diagnostic feature, if combined with anatomical knowledge and functional role of the structure, may greatly improve the accuracy and details of the diagnosis.

Brain can be classified into two parts – neural tissues (Nerve cell bodies and axons) and subsidiary part (vessels, stroma, matrix and other organizations) – and nerve cell part can be simplified as streams (pathways/tracts) of neuron bundles. Scanning techniques of MRI have been improved recently up to capture these streams of bundles, and Diffusion Tensor Imaging (DTI) is representative among those techniques. DTI techniques to reconstruct tractography is already being used in clinical researches such as epilepsy, and its inter-observer or intra-observer reliability is verified to be acceptable.

© Springer International Publishing Switzerland 2016
A. Marcus (Ed.): DUXU 2016, Part III, LNCS 9748, pp. 258–265, 2016.
DOI: 10.1007/978-3-319-40406-6_24

Space occupying lesions inside the brain or destructive brain lesions such as infection tend to deform the brain structures. In these cases, direct application of normal anatomical knowledge to conventional brain MRI might has limitations to locate the exact anatomic structures or even more limitations to predict the physiological deficits caused by the lesions due to deformed brain structures. But if it is possible to obtain tractography via DTI and locate the lesions onto the specific tracts, we may have got more accurate diagnosis of the lesions by tracking the lesion's tract or bundle, regardless of anatomical deformations.

Nerve bundles in the brain do not simply link one part of the brain to one part of the body with a tract. The bundles exchange information with other surrounding tracts, nuclei and grey matters (crossing or kissing fibers). These compound interconnections make the interpretation of tractography expressed in 2D monitor quite difficult and complex. The purpose of this study was to reconstruct brain tractography in 3D virtual reality (VR) space, so as to make it easy to handle and to trace up and down, using Unity3D and Oculus Rift. These trials may contribute to understand exactly and conveniently the complex relations of these neural bundles.

2 Material

2.1 Study Design

We have reported previously the functional research of white matter tract, by observing 114 subcortical vascular cognitive impairment (SVCI) patients [1]. From this study, we obtained following three facts. FA (fractional anisotropy) values in the middle portion of CG (cingulum) were associated with scores in language, visuospatial, memory and frontal functions. FA values in the anterior portion of ATR (anterior thalamic radiation) were associated with scores in attention, memory and frontal executive functions, while FA values in its middle portion were associated with language function score. In SLF (superior-longitudinal fasciculus), FA values in the posterior portion were associated with visuospatial dysfunction while FA values in the middle portion were associated with memory impairment.

The study shows disconnection of specific white matter tracts, especially those neighboring and providing connections between gray matter regions important to certain cognitive functions, may contribute to specific cognitive impairments in patients with SVCI.

In this study, we get the T1 image and DTI-Tractography of the selected patient with SVCI involved in previous research, and we reconstruct these images into 3D objects able to be observed and handled using VR (virtual reality) device.

2.2 Image Acquisition

T1 and diffusion weighted images (DWI) were acquired from a subject at Samsung Medical Center using the same 3.0 T MRI scanner (Philips 3.0T Achieva). T1 weighted MRI data was recorded using the following imaging parameters: 1 mm sagittal slice thickness, over-contiguous slices with 50 % overlap; no gap; repetition time (TR) of

9.9 ms; echo time (TE) of 4.6 ms; flip angle of 8°; and matrix size of 240 × 240 pixels, reconstructed to 480 × 480 over a 240 mm field of view. In the whole-brain diffusion weighted MRI examination, sets of axial diffusion-weighted single-shot echo-planar images were collected with the following parameters: 128 × 128 acquisition matrix, 1.72 × 1.72 × 2 mm^3 voxels; reconstructed to1.72 × 1.72 × 2 mm^3; 70 axial slices; 220 × 220mm^2 field of view; TE 60 ms, TR 7383 ms; flip angle 90°; slice gap 0 mm; b-factor of 600 s/mm^2. With the baseline image without diffusion weighting (the reference volume), diffusion-weighted images were acquired from 45 different directions. All axial sections were acquired parallel to the anterior commissure-posterior commissure line.

3 Method

3.1 Image Preprocessing

DTI images and structural MR images of each subject were acquired to be used in this study. All processes took the following steps: First, DTI images were corrected for Eddy current distortions, using FSL program. Second, HARDI-based deterministic tracking was executed, generating track file. Third, non-brain tissue from DTI images and structural MR images (T1) of the whole head was deleted using BET (Brain Ex-traction Tool). Forth, images were spatially adjusted to standard brain image. Registering a set of T1 images to a standard template was executed by FNIRT (FMRIB's Linear Image Registration Tool), and registering DTI images to T1 images was executed by FLIRT (FMRIB's Linear Image Registration Tool). Registered images were inversely adjusted to previous images again, getting spatially normalized images.

We obtained streamlines resulting from whole-brain tractography. The streamlines are grouped into following seven major fiber tracts, such as anterior thalamic radiation (ATR), cingulum (CG), corticospinal tract (CST), inferior fronto-occipital fasciculus (IFO), inferior-longitudinal fasciculus (ILF), superior-longitudinal fasciculus (SLF), and uncinate fasciculus (UNC), based on their shapes and positions [2].

Then, we computed cortical surface meshes using FreeSurfer v 5.1.0 (http://surfer. nmr.mgh.harvard.edu). FreeSurfer uses following algorithm: Outer and inner cortical surface meshes were first constructed from T1-weighted MR data. The inner surface represented the boundary between white matter and cortical gray matter, and the outer surface was defined as the exterior of the cortical gray matter. As the outer surface was constructed by deforming the inner surface, the two surface meshes are isomorphic, with the same number of vertices and edge connectivity.

Through FreeSurfer, we parcellated the cerebral cortex into 68 cortical ROIs based on the Desikan-Killiany Atlas [3] and obtained the cortical thickness of each cortical ROIs for each subject. We reconstructed T1-weighted MR images and ROI atlas volumes from FreeSurfer data of each patient for using coregistration with DWI images.

3.2 Platform

Unity Game Engine. Unity3D (© Unity Technologies, San Francisco, California, USA. Unity3D ver. 5.3.2) is a tool which is mainly used when producing games of three-dimensional environments. It is comfortable to load and handle 3D objects from both inside and outside the program. We load T1 data and DTI data on Unity tools, each using somewhat different ways.

Developing environments in Unity3D has several steps. First we make New Project. Then Scene, Game, and Console window will show up. Most of the project making will take time in 'Scene' tab. The default scene contains one default camera and a directional light, which you can check out from the hierarchy tab. You may create some template 3D figures (cube, sphere, cylinder, etc.) from hierarchy tab, and if necessary, we can load other 3D objects from outside the Unity3D program by simply dragging the objects into project-assets tab, and then loading them on the scene or hierarchy tab.

T1 images which we obtained exist in form of 'obj' files. Since 'fbx' files are more suitable at processes like Motion Tracking or Animated movements [4], we recommend converting 'obj' files into 'fbx' files via programs such as 'Autodesk FBX Converter (© 2016 Autodesk, FBX® 2013.3 Converter)' before uploading the data on Unity scene. Such programs are freely provided from 'autodesk.com'.

DTI data, unlike T1 data, exists in a form of text file which contains three-dimensional coordinate values of each fiber. To load these data on Unity3D scene, we coded a script which saves the number of bundles, names of each bundles, the number of fibers in each bundles, number of coordinates which constitute each fibers, and the coordinate values itself. Then connect every two coordinates with a thin cylinder for every fiber to implement the form of streamlines. This step was done by a code which instantiates a cylinder prefab (sample) between selected two vectors (3D coordinates). You may select the number of fibers or skip some coordinates depending on your computer's specifications (at the given figure, half of the number of fibers, and one-fifth of the coordinate values were selected).

To differentiate one bundle from others, we colored each bundles in color red, blue, green, yellow, magenta, cyan, and black. This was done when instantiating the cylinders between coordinates, by reading the name of the bundle which the coordinate belongs to.

3.3   Device

Oculus Rift Development Kit 2. Oculus Rift is a virtual reality (VR) device (© 2016 Oculus VR, LLC, Menlo Park, California, USA. Oculus Rift Development Kit 2). VR is a technology which is a simulated version of the real environment and can be experienced in three dimensions (3D). The device displays two adjacent images, one image for left eye and one for right eye. The alignment of the two lenses enables the zoom in-out and re-shaping the pictures for both eyes, which makes the picture a stereoscopic 3D image [5].

To link the Unity scene with Oculus device is simply done by downloading 'Oculus Utilities for Unity 5 V0.1.3.0-beta' from 'developer.oculus.com', then load the utilities on Unity3D project, and exchanging the default camera with camera and cardboard for

Oculus Rift. The following figure shows the in-game view (the view we may see when we run the program) between default camera and oculus camera each (Fig. 1).

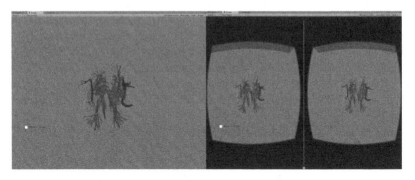

Fig. 1. View Comparison between Unity3D Default Camera (left) and Oculus-Provided Camera (right)

The screenshots are taken from two cameras at the same position of the Unity3D scene. Since Oculus rift have to send one screen to two eyes, the screen itself must be divided into two parts, which are already prepared to make stereoscopic 3D image (Fig. 2).

Fig. 2. Scene view of DTI Tractography

4   Results

The colors corresponding to the bundles are red (ATR), blue (CST), green (CG), yellow (IFO), magenta (ILF), cyan (UNC), and black (SLF).

Abbreviations: ATR, anterior thalamic radiation; CST, corticospinal tract; CG, cingulum; IFO, inferior fronto-occipital fasciculus; ILF, inferior-longitudinal fasciculus; UNC, uncinate fasciculus; SLF, superior-longitudinal fasciculus.

The brighter part of the brain represents white matter, and the darker part represents gray matter. The observer may select the information he/she wants to see by clicking

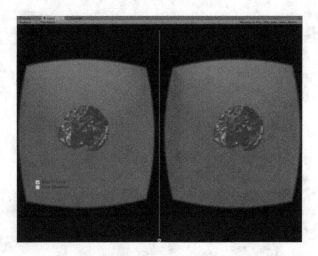

Fig. 3. Oculus view of T1 image

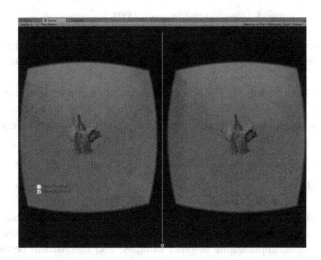

Fig. 4. Oculus view of DTI Tractography

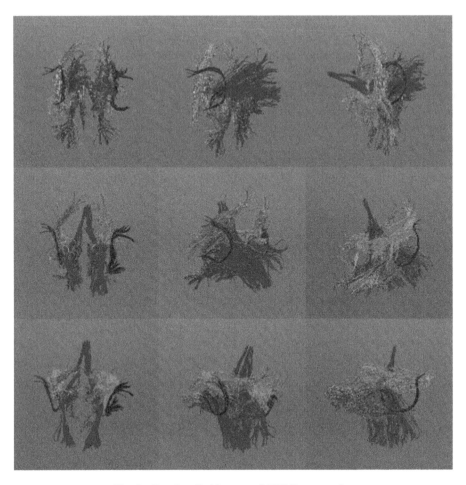

Fig. 5. Free-handled images of DTI Tractography

the toggle button at the left-bottom side. The object rotates in horizontal/vertical direction as direction key input value. The screenshot was taken after such operations in Unity3D.

Details are same as Fig. 3. The screenshot was taken at the same angle as Fig. 3, and the Toggle button 'Show Streamlines' was selected. Both the screen from Figs. 3 and 4 seems stereoscopic and three-dimensional when the observer is equipped with Oculus Rift.

5   Conclusions

From this study, we obtained virtual image which was manipulable enough in three-dimensional environment. But several things are seem to be necessary – objectivity of the sample, applications of other samples, and comparison between normal brain and patient's brain. We are expecting to complement these points, including the following 'limitation of this study', through future studies (Fig. 5).

5.1 Limitation of this Study

Exquisiteness of the DTI data. Since we controlled the number of fibers and coordinates, we cannot tell whether the image is the exact form of the Streamlines obtained through DTI data. This problem can be complemented by upgrading the specification of the computer.

Controllability of the Image. Options like zooming in-out through mouse wheel scroll, and rotating images through dragging instead of direction keys could be helpful to make the handling easier and more comfortable. If it is possible to use Motion tracking function of the Oculus Device, then the observer may feel more vivid VR experience. We may complement these problems by studying more about how to treat the input-outputs of information and user-interface (UI).

Non-Automatic Functions. While T1 image is automatically laid at the center of the screen when loaded, the coordinate of DTI data is fixed somewhat differently when the data is obtained. Since the coordinate systems of the two data are different, we need to set the position information of one data to fit into the other manually. If we can refer to what coordinate system it is set to when the DTI data is obtained, then we may load the DTI data at the same position with the T1 data by automatically adjusting it.

References

1. Jung, N.-Y., Han, C.E., Kim, H.J., Yoo, S.W., Kim, H.-J., Kim, E.-J., Na, D.L., Lockhart, S. N., Jagust, W.J., Seong, J.-K., Seo, S.W.: Tract-specific correlates of neuropsychological deficits in patients with subcortical vascular cognitive impairment
2. Yoo, S.W., Guevara, P., Jeong, Y., Yoo, K., Shin, J.S., Mangin, J.-F., Seong, J.-K.: An example-based multi-atlas approach to automatic labeling of white matter fibers (2015)
3. Desikan, R.S., Segonne, F., Fischl, B., Quinn, B.T., Dickerson, B.C., Blacker, D, Buckner, R.L, Dale, A.M, Maguire, R.P, Hyman, B.T: An automated labeling system for subdividing the human cerebral cortex on MRI scans into gyral based regions of interest
4. http://blog.digitaltutors.com/cg-file-formats-you-need-to-know-understanding-obj-fbx-alembic-and-more/
5. Goradia, I., Doshi, J., Kurup, L.: A Review Paper on Oculus Rift & Project Morpheus

Designing Affordances for Virtual Reality-Based Services with Natural User Interaction

Takayuki Miura, Akihito Yoshii, and Tatsuo Nakajima[✉]

Department of Computer Science and Engineering, Waseda University,
Tokyo, Japan
{t.miura,a_yoshii,tatsuo}@dcl.cs.waseda.ac.jp

Abstract. The progress of new technologies makes virtual reality (VR) easier, and inexpensive head-mounted displays (HMDs) accelerate the development of advanced VR services. The advantage of the technologies is to offer the better immersion of a VR world, to use natural user interface (NUI) devices and to operate them with a user's gesture. The problem to use NUI devices for VR-based services is to take into account various types of NUI devices. We need to consider how a user to use NUI devices in a proper way, in particular, when an HMD limits his/her view of the real world. Our approach to solve the problem is to use an affordance that offers implicit information how to navigate VR-based services. However, there are a little researches to investigate the relationship between different types of NUI devices and the design of proper affordances to navigate VR-based services. The paper provides some insights how respective types of NUI devices influence affordance design to navigate VR-based services. For extracting effective insights, we have developed two VR-based services, where we discuss two types of operating methods and three types of affordances for respective operating methods are examined. Also, we chose two types of NUI devices for navigating the VR-based services. Then, we conducted some experiments to extract some insights as a guideline to develop future VR-based services. The result shows that the differences among respective NUI devices may not significantly influence affordance design, however have strong effects on understanding how to navigate VR-based services. The understanding also affects how each user prefers which NUI devices, because NUI devices require us to use gesture to navigate the services, but the intuition that differs in each individual is important.

Keywords: Natural user interface · Virtual reality · Affordance

1 Introduction

Recently, as shown in [2, 6], virtual reality (VR) technologies have revived due to the progress of new technologies that make it easy to develop advanced VR-based services like programming platforms: *Unity*[1] and inexpensive and practical commercial head-mounted displays (HMD): *Oculus Rift*[2]. These technologies make it easy to

---

[1] Unity - Game Engine: http://japan.unity3d.com/, accessed 2015/12/22.
[2] Oculus Rift | Oculus: https://www.oculus.com/en-us/rift/.

© Springer International Publishing Switzerland 2016
A. Marcus (Ed.): DUXU 2016, Part III, LNCS 9748, pp. 266–277, 2016.
DOI: 10.1007/978-3-319-40406-6_25

develop various types of the VR-based service, and make it possible to use VR-based technologies in commercial purposes.

When offering desirable interactive user experiences, natural user interaction (NUI) devices like *Microsoft Kinect (MS Kinect)*[3] or *Leap Motion*[4] are widely used. Many VR-based games are already developed, and they assume to use these devices, because these devices offer an immersive user experience through the natural interaction [3] with the virtual world without prior knowledge. However, the assumption to use the current NUI devices causes a gap between the ideal expectation and the reality. In particular, using NUI devices with an HMD may cause a new problem. For example, Yang and Pan reported that *MS Kinect* fails to track a user's body when the user does not have sufficient experiences with an HMD [11].

When using NUI devices, it is usually assumed that a user can easily find where the devices are and how to navigate them, but the devices cannot be seen when the user wears an HMD. In computing environments, various commodity NUI devices will be used to develop new VR-based services; thus the described issues will become a more serious problem soon. One approach for overcoming the problem is using affordance [1], which is the information for ensuring the proper operation and can be used to navigate human behavior [7]. We also need to investigate what types of affordance is appropriate for respective NUI devices. We actually discuss three types of affordance — *inherent, image* and *sentence affordances* by referring to [10]. Furthermore, we like to research whether different features of NUI devices influence the appropriateness of the types of affordance. Thus, the research question in this paper is that a different NUI device needs a different affordance.

In this paper, we demonstrate how we can design proper affordances for respective NUI devices. The insights extracted from our experiment are useful for designing future NUI devices and VR-based services. We have developed a VR-based photo viewer service and a shooting game application for demonstrating the proposed ideas as case studies. The current case studies assume to use either *MS Kinect* or *Leap Motion* as NUI devices. We have designed three affordances for the respective NUI devices. *MS Kinect* tracks the positions of a user's body. In this case study, the position of a user's arms is captured for moving the cursors. Conversely, *Leap Motion* tracks the position of the joints of a user's hands. In this case study, the position of a user' hands is detected to move the cursors.[5]

2 Related Work

Terrenghi et al. claimed that the difference of user interfaces requires different affordances [9]. In their research, the participants were imposed to perform a puzzle task and a photo sorting task with physical and digital pieces and photos. Figures 1 and 2 are the scenes to perform the tasks. The result showed that even in the same task, the difference

[3] Xbox 360 – Kinect: http://www.xbox.com/ja-JP/kinect, accessed 2015/12/26.

[4] Leap Motion: https://www.leapmotion.com/?lang=jp, accessed 2015/12/22.

[5] A preliminary result was reported in [4], and the paper enhances insights discussed in the paper.

Fig. 1. Photo sorting tasks [9]

Fig. 2. Puzzle tasks [9]

in physical and digital makes participants' action different. This means that the differences in interfaces require different affordances.

Shin et al. showed the difference in devices needs different affordances [8]. In this research, they asked participants to play a VR-based application while a user wears an HMD, using *Hydra Controller*[6] and *MS Kinect* for operating the application. Figure 3

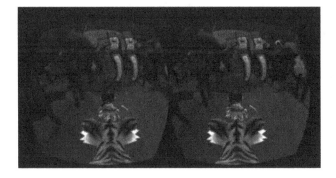

Fig. 3. The VR-based application with HMD [8]

---

[6] Razer Hydra Portal 2 Bundle Gaming Controller - PC Motion Sensor - Razer United States: http://www.razerzone.com/gaming-controllers/razer-hydra-portal-2-bundle, accessed 2015/12/25.

shows the scene of the application. The results showed that different devices cause different problems even in the same VR-based application when a user wears an HMD. This means that in a VR-based application that uses an HMD, different devices may need different affordances.

3   A VR-Based Service and its Affordance Design

3.1   VR Frameworks, HMD, NUI Devices and Operating Objects in VR-Based Services

For developing a VR-based service, we adopted *Unity4.6.5*[7], that is a platform for easily creating a VR-based service. We also adopted *Oculus Rift*[8] as an HMD.

In our research, we selected two NUI devices: *MS Kinect* and *Leap Motion*. *MS Kinect* can track the entire whole body of a user, but the detection error is bigger than *Leap Motion*. Although *Leap Motion* makes accurate tracking possible rather than *MS Kinect*, it is only able to track a user's hands or small objects. By tracking a user's arm by *MS Kinect* or hands by *Leap Motion,* we arrange some objects in a VR world that performs the same movement as the user's arms or hands: we call them arm objects or hand objects. These arm/hand objects are used to operate the objects in the VR-based services.

3.2   An Overview of a VR-Based Service

When we considered VR-based services, we decided to create two types of services for extracting more insights from the experiment for them. For investigating extreme different cases, we have developed a VR-based service that is easy to understand named *Image Planet*, and the one is difficult to understand named *Shooting Game*. Also, for extracting more useful insights from the experiment, we created two types of operating method that are specialized and the general-purpose to the service: the former is called the *specialized operation* and the latter the *general-purpose operation*.

Image Planet as shown in Fig. 4 is a VR-based service developed as an example to offer simple operations. In this service, many images are floating over and rotating around a user. The background of the service is like the universe, so respective images look like stars. A user can select and expand the images by his/her operation on them, and also control the movement of the images through the panels for controlling them. As the *specialized operation*, a user uses a red line like a laser pointer attached to an arm object or a hand object to point the images or panels, and as the *general-purpose operation*, a user needs to move his/her arm/hand object over the images or panels. In this service, a user can use only his/her right arm or hand, and choose the proper pace to operate the objects that a user likes. This makes it possible to understand how to operate objects easily.

---

[7] Unity - Game Engine: http://japan.unity3d.com/, accessed 2015/12/22.

[8] Oculus Rift | Oculus: https://www.oculus.com/en-us/rift/, accessed 2015/12/26.

Fig. 4. Image planet (Color figure online)

Shooting Game as shown in Fig. 5 is the service developed as an example to offer complex operations. In this service, a user attacks and destroys enemies in the VR world, while guarding from the enemies' attack. In the *specialized operation*, a user operates a gun by his/her right arm object or right hand object, and attacks enemies. Also he/she operates a translucent wall for guarding from enemies' attack through their left arm/hand object. In the *general-purpose operation*, a user needs to move his/her arm/hand objects over enemies to attack them or over a panel that controls the wall to guard. This service needs to use both arms or both hands to attack enemies and guarding from them. It is also an important design intention to make a user hasty through the enemies' attack. The aim of the service is to investigate insights how complex operations influence affordance design.

Fig. 5. Shooting game

3.3   Affordance Design

For affordance design, we define three types of affordances, *inherent affordance*, *image affordance*, and *sentence affordance* based on the discussions described in [10].

Inherent affordance is an affordance that uses an object's shape, color, positions and so on, without directly offering images or sentences as the information for supporting the proper operation in a VR-based service, and this means that the intuition of a user is important for understanding how to navigate the service. This affordance is similar to the *perceived affordance* that Norman explained in [5], and is widely used in daily objects' design. In this case study, we implemented the affordance as follows; we designed an arm/hand object as the 3D models of an arm or hand, for making a user to understand that they can operate the arm/hand object by his/her own arm or hand. In particular, in *Leap Motion*, we arrange the object that represents the detectable spatially limited region for the interaction by the NUI device because the detectable region for the interaction of *Leap Motion* is very small. We also try to separate *inherent affordance* with the operating methods for the objects representing the affordances. *Inherent affordance* used for the *specialized operation* is called *high-inherent affordance,* and one used for the *general-purpose operation* is called *low-inherent affordance.* Figure 6 shows one example of *inherent affordance*.

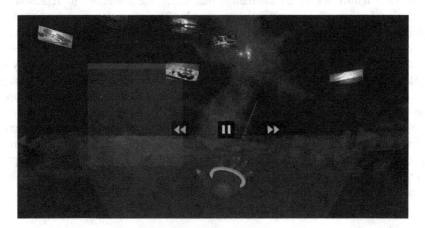

Fig. 6. Inherent affordance

Image affordance is an affordance that uses images to offer the information for operating objects representing the affordance properly. An example used in the real world is a pictogram, like a sign used for the emergence exit. In our approach, we use this kind of image that explains how to use a user's arms or hands to operate the arm/hand objects in a VR-based service, and how to navigate the service. Different from *inherent affordance*, the arm/hand objects in a VR-based service are not the 3D models of arms or hands, but a white sphere. On the other hand, similar to *inherent affordance*, we classify *image affordance* into two types by operating method. The affordance with the *specialized operation* is *high-image affordance*, and one with the *general-purpose operation* is *low-image affordance.* Figure 7 presents an example of *image affordance*.

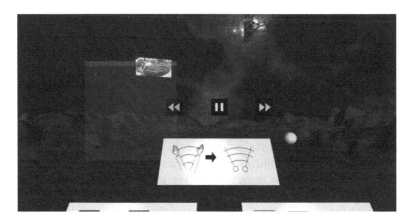

Fig. 7. Image affordance

Sentence affordance is an affordance that offers the sentences to represent the information for operating an affordance properly. The sentences are often used for explaining how to operate the affordance. In our approach, we offer the sentences to explain how to operate the affordance properly as *sentence affordance*. Similar to *image affordance*, arm/hand objects are represented as white spheres, and also we classify the affordance into two types of operating method. The affordance with the *specialized operation* is named *high-sentence affordance*, and one with the *general-purpose operation* is *low-sentence affordance*. Figure 8 shows an example of *sentence affordance*.

We have developed two VR-based services to offer two types of the operating method, and three types of affordances that support two operating methods. Also, in respective affordances, two NUI devices: *MS Kinect* and *Leap Motion* are adopted. Therefore, we totally conducted 24 patterns in the experiment of our approach as described in the next section.

Fig. 8. Sentence affordance

4 Experiments

In our experiment, we asked participants to perform tasks for respective VR-based services. Thus, there are 12 patterns for each, then we asked them to answer the questionnaires about whether they feel that these affordances are easy to understand to operate objects representing them. The tasks conducted in the experiment are as follows; in *Image Planet*, a participant selects and expands three photos that they like. In *Shooting Game*, a participant attacks and destroys three enemies while guarding from the enemies' attack. In our experiment, 17 participants whose ages are between 22 and 29 participated. The experiment for each person took about 2 h. We conducted the semi-structured interview for each participant after the experiment. Figure 9 shows one scene in the experiment.

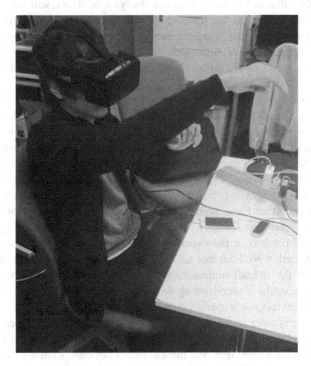

Fig. 9. A scene in our experiment

In the questionnaire, we asked the participants "*Did you think this affordance is easy to understand the meaning of an affordance in the service?*", and also "*Did you think this affordance is appropriate to express the meaning of an affordance in the service?*". The first question is the main question to extract participants' opinions explicitly for our research questions in this research, but we consider the question is not sufficient, because the question does not consider the whole cognitive load of a user. The cognitive load, that prevents a user from understanding the meaning of an affordance, indicates not only the easiness to the understanding, but also the trouble-someness for the understanding, for example the troublesomeness of reading the sentences in an affordance. Therefore, we need to ask the second question that is the question for investigating a user's whole cognitive load.

Before conducting the experiment, we had a hypothesis that *image* and *sentence affordances* have no significant differences for respective NUI devices, and for *inherent affordance*, *Leap Motion* is preferred than *MS Kinect*. This is because that we thought images and sentences are very easy to understand, and there are no rooms to specialize the influence of the differences in NUI device, but *inherent affordance* needs a user's intuition for understanding the meaning of an affordance, thus *Leap Motion*, which offers a very accurate and good feedback is preferred. Also, we thought that the differences in NUI devices more influence on affordance design as operating the object that represents an affordance becomes more difficult. However, actually the result of the experiment shows that our hypothesis is not always true. The result shows that *image* and *sentence affordances* do not have much differences according to the differences appeared in NUI devices, and also *inherent affordance* is not significantly affected by the differences appeared in NUI devices. Moreover, the different types of VR-based services does not significantly influence the affordance design that needs to reflect the differences in NUI devices.

In the interview in the experiment, many participants said that *MS Kinect* is not good in terms of the precision, and *Leap Motion* is very good rather than *MS Kinect*, but also, some participants said "*I prefer MS Kinect because moving my arm is very intuitive for me, and it helped me to understand how to operate objects representing an affordance*", and "*I dislike Leap Motion because the detectable region for the inter-action is too narrow for me.*" This opinion expresses that some participants think that the precision is not important, but the detectable region for the interaction is more significant. On the other hand, some participants said "*I like Leap Motion because I need not to move my hand widely, and it is very intuitive.*" Similar opinions were appeared in most patterns in the experiment. For these reasons, we consider that the differences appeared in NUI devices are not a big factor to influence affordance design, but to influence the overall understanding how to operate objects representing an affordance, and also the understanding the meaning of an affordance differs in each individual. NUI devices use a user's gesture for the interaction, and this means that the intuition of a user is more important, where the intuition is differed for each individual largely. This insight can be used for the decision of what NUI devices should be used for respective VR-based services. We must consider not only what are the efficient and easy to use functions of NUI devices for operating an object representing an affordance, but also what functions each user prefers. Therefore, the usability and the comforta-bility need to be taken into account independently when designing good affordances. In the future, many types of inexperience NUI devices will be appeared, so we may be able to select NUI devices in terms of both usability and comfortability.

We also had a hypothesis about the easiness and the appropriateness for under-standing the meaning of an affordance. We thought that *sentence affordance* is prob-ably the most preferable in terms of the easiness for understanding the meaning how to operate objects representing affordances, and the next is *image affordance*, then *high-inherent affordance*, and the worst is *low-inherent affordance*. In terms of the easiness of understanding the meaning of an affordance, a sentence has a significant advantage because it can explain how to operate an object representing an affordance concretely, and the next is an image. Comparing *high-inherent* and *low-inherent affordance*, the *specialized operation* is more understandable than the *general-purpose operation*, so *low-inherent affordance* was thought as the worst. As an early hypothesis, we thought that VR-based services with more complex operations have more significant influences on affordance design. However, the result showed that only some parts of the hypothesis are corrected. Similarly, as we expected, *sentence affordance* is the best, and *low-inherent affordance* was the worst. But, when actually comparing *image affordance* with *high-inherent affordance*, there is not so big difference between them. We consider that this is because the preference for *high-inherent affordance* can be changed in each individual. The understandability of *inherent affordance* depends on the intuition of a user, and it means that the individual difference influences the understandability of an affordance largely. We consider the reason of the result that most participants prefer *high-inherent affordance* used in the experiment in many cases.

In terms of the appropriateness of an affordance, our hypothesis is that *high-inherent affordance* may be the most preferable, and the next is *image affordance*, and *sentence affordance* is the worst. This is because we thought that a sentence that may cause serious troublesomeness in reading requires the heaviest cognitive load, and the cognitive load to understand an image is lighter than a sentence. Also, we assumed that *high-inherent affordance* is the lightest in terms of a user's cognitive load. However, the result is actually as follows; *sentence affordance* is the best when considering the gap between the easiness and appropriateness, but comparing the appropriateness in respective affordances, in all patterns, the effect of *sentence affordance* is almost the same as the effect of other affordances. We consider that there are two reasons for the result. The first is that the easiness is just one element to increase a user's cognitive load. Some participants said *"Sentence affordance allows me accurate understanding the meaning of an affordance rather than inherent and image affordances."* The easiness for understanding the meaning of the *sentence affordance* avoids the decrease of its appropriateness. The second causes due to an individual's difference. For some participants, a difference between the easiness and appropriateness is not so important, but other participants said that they differ very much. Before the experiment, we considered that for every participant, the difference between the easiness and appropriateness is significant, so the aspect decreases the appropriateness of *sentence affordance*.

From the results in terms of the easiness and appropriateness, we are able to investigate the combination of affordances. It means that if easy to understand is more important, *inherent* or *image affordance* should be used to reduce the cognitive load, but when a developer expects that a user needs to understands precisely how to operate objects representing affordances in VR-based services, *sentence affordance* should be used, even when a user's cognitive load will be increased. Another way is to use these affordances together. As the result showed, how a user feels the difference between the easiness and appropriateness differs in each user. So offering multiple affordances at the same time and making a user to select his/her preferable affordance can be a promising way to design better affordances.

5 Conclusion

Recent development of a VR-based service that is based on common VR developing platforms and HMDs, which significantly increases the immersion of a VR world, requires NUI devices for enhancing the immersion. When using NUI devices, however, the proper operation of the devices should be offered, in particular, with HMDs. One approach to support the proper navigation is to offer an affordance, but there is also a new problem because there are a little researches to investigate the relationship between the differences in NUI devices and affordance design. Considering the future progress of NUI devices and the increase of their usages in many commercial VR-based services, more researches are necessary to extract sufficient insights for developing better VR-based services.

This paper is willing to offer a guidance how the differences in NUI devices influence affordance design. In this research, we have developed two VR-based services, two types of the operating method and three types of affordance for each ways of operations, and also we used two NUI devices: *MS Kinect* and *Leap Motion*. The result of the experiment to explore our approach showed that the differences in NUI devices may not significantly influence affordance design, but have significant effects on the overall understanding how to operate objects representing affordances in VR-based services. In particular, the understanding the meaning of an affordance differs in each individual. In an aspect of what affordance should be used for operating the objects representing affordances, when easy to understand is important, *inherent* or *image affordance* should be chosen to reduce a user's cognitive load, but when a developer wants a user to precisely understand the meaning how to operate objects representing affordances, *sentence affordance* should be adopted.

The conclusion in this research is that affordance design may not be influenced by the differences in NUI devices, but the difficulty of the operation for objects representing affordances in VR-based services, and the differences in NUI devices significantly influence the overall understanding of the meaning of an affordance.

In the next step, we need to investigate other types of NUI devices. More experiments may make us extracting more useful insights. Also, we need to investigate the reasons why people do not like some images and sentences or how the images and sentences are difficult to understand.

References

1. Corte, T.R., Marchal, M., Cirio, G., Lecuyer, A.: Perceiving affordances in virtual reality: influence of person and environmental properties in perception of standing on virtual grounds. Virtual Reality 17(1), 17–28 (2013)
2. Linowes, J.: Unity Virtual Reality Projects. Packt Publishing, Birmingham (2015)
3. Macaranas, A., Antle, A., Riecke, E.B.: Three strategies for designing intuitive natural user interfaces. In: Proceedings of Extended Abstracts of the Designing Interactive Systems (ACM DIS) Conference (2012)
4. Miura, T., Urakawa, S., Isojima, M., Yu, J., Yoshii, A., Nakajima, T.: Natural user interaction requires good affordance when using with a head-mounted display. In: Proceedings of the Eighth International Conferences on Advances in Multimedia (2016)

5. Norman, D.: The Design of Everyday Things. MIT Press, Cambridge (2014). revised and expanded
6. Parisi, T.: Learning Virtual Reality: Developing Immersive Experiences and Applications for Desktop, Web, and Mobile. O'Reilly Media, Sebastopol (2015)
7. Sakamoto, M., Nakajima, T.: In search of the right abstraction for designing persuasive affordance towards a flourished society. In: Proceedings of the 9th International Conference on Design and Semantics of Form and Movement, pp. 251–260 (2015)
8. Shin, S., Kim, S., Chang, J.: An implementation of the HMD-Enabled interface and system userbility test. In: ISSSG 2014, pp. 183–193 (2014)
9. Terrenghi, L., Kirk, D., Sellen, A., Izadi, S.: Affordances for manipulation of physical versus digital media on interactive surface. In: HCI 2007 Proceedings, Novel Navigation, pp. 1157–1166 (2007)
10. Wesveen, S.A.G., Djajadiningrat, J.P., Overbeeke, C.J.: Interaction frogger: a design framework to couple action and function through feedback and feedforward. In: Proceedings of the 5th Conference on Designing Interactive Systems, pp. 177–184 (2004)
11. Yang, X., Pan, L.: Navigating the virtual environment using microsoft kinect. In: Proceedings of the 12th International Conference on Construction Application of Virtual Reality (2013)

Metaphors and Embodiment in Virtual Reality Systems

Ana Carol Pontes de França$^{(\boxtimes)}$ and Marcelo Márcio Soares

Federal University of Pernambuco, Recife, Brazil
acpsicologa@gmail.com, soaresmm@gmail.com

Abstract. The dissemination and development of digital technology over the years allowed people to integrate products and computer systems to everyday life. These technologies, in turn, enables communication and human interaction and can be employed for many purposes, such as education, entertainment and entrepreneurial. In this scenario, the interface occupies a prominent place, allowing the user to be related with the system itself and interact with others in cyberspace. In such situations, there is an expansion of the user's consciousness that manifests expectations, desires, likes and interests through avatars. Although presented as a sign, the user takes the physical body as a reference with which he/she coordinate his/her actions in the virtual environment. In this sense, this paper aims to discuss the representation of the body in Virtual Reality (VR) systems considering the relationship between information, communication, culture and technology by the theorical and conceptual framework of Ergonomics and Human Factors Psychology, Informational Design, Cultural Psychology and Semiotics.

Keywords: Virtual reality · Semiotics · Metaphor · Interface

1 Introduction

The early years of the computers' history were characterized by its use by experts, like programmers, engineers, mathematicians and physicists, and by the design focused on technology. However, over time, computers have been incorporated into many products, becoming more accessible to a wide range of users, transforming both: work and social relations.

Due the increased demand for cognitive effort while performing a task with computacional devices, it became increasingly necessary to understand the characteristics, skills and human limitations of perception, learning, memory and problem solving in computational systems.

Consequently, the cognitive approach of the users characteristics and performance in these systems has become a key to the design and analysis of interfaces, which shifted the focus of technology-centered design for user-centered design[1].

---

[1] https://www.nngroup.com/articles-want-human-centered-development-reorganize/.

© Springer International Publishing Switzerland 2016
A. Marcus (Ed.): DUXU 2016, Part III, LNCS 9748, pp. 278–286, 2016.
DOI: 10.1007/978-3-319-40406-6_26

Based on this principle, to be designed for human use, an object, system or environment must be adapted to the physical and mental characteristics of the' user, so that the product be better integrated into the task context [1].

Adopting such considerations as a starting point, this study invites the reader to think how the cyberculture, with its technological artifacts and languages, mediates the communication and human interaction so that fiction and non-fiction become intertwined and take shape in images, virtual beings and parallel worlds in Virtual Reality systems.

2 Ergonomics and Informational Design

Considered a scientific discipline, Ergonomics takes a systemic approach to matters related to human activity. To do this, it employs scientific methods and techniques seeking to adapt the work to the physical and psychological characteristics of the human component in order to adapt the work to the worker, as well as the product to the user [1].

In this sense, it seeks to investigate, evaluate, weaving recommendations and ergonomic interventions in order to design environments, products and systems more compatible to support the users' needs, limitations and abilities.

According to Moraes and Mont'Alvão [1], based on the systemic and informational approaches, ergonomics, as an operative technology, sets to projects and products, workstations, control systems, information systems, computerized dialogue, labor organizations, task implementation and instructional programs, the following parameters: interfacial, instrumental, informational, actional, communication, cognitive, movimentation, spatial/architectural, physical-environmental, chemical-environmental, security, operational, organizational, instructional, urban and psychosocial.

That is, through methods, techniques and procedures, Ergonomics proposes tailor the presentation of the information to the users' mental model in order to understand how users search and organize information and solve problems while performing tasks in computational systems.

In addition, the ergonomics also seeks to understand how the objective and subjective experiences interfere with the users' strategies and how these strategies change with practice and with context changes.

According to Quintão and Triska [2], the Brazilian Society of Informational Design defines informational design as a graphical design area that aims to equate the syntactic, semantic and pragmatic aspects involving information systems through contextualization, planning, production and graphical user interface information along to your target audience. Its basic principle is to optimize the information acquisition process performed in analogic and digital communication systems.

In this sense, meet the ergonomic requirements enables maximize comfort, satisfaction and well-being, ensure safety, minimize constraints, human costs and cognitive load, optimize task performance, labor income and productivity of the human-machine system [1].

Thus, Ergonomics and Informational Design, focusing on the interface design optimization, are related to the users' mental models and to the reduction of the psychic and cognitive load which arise from the user experience.

3 Paralel Worlds and Virtual Beings in VR Systems

The Encyclopedia Britannica defines Virtual Reality as the use of computer modeling and simulation so that the person is able to interact with an artificial three-dimensional environment or any other sensory environment. In virtual reality applications the user is immersed in an environment generated by computer that simulates reality through the use of interactive devices that send and receive information and are used as goggles, gloves, headphones or clothing. Typically, a virtual reality user wearing a helmet with a stereoscopic screen see animated images of a simulated environment [3].

Consequently, Virtual Reality could be understood as part of a continuum: at one extreme we would have a picture or painting, which transports the reader or the viewer to the context of the story or image. At the other extreme we would have the ultimate display that according to Sutherland, its creator, would be a room in which the computer would control the existence of matter, so that in such room, a chair would be good enough to sit, handcuffs displayed in this room could arrest us and a bullet triggered in this room would be fatal [3].

As França and Soares [4] suggest, Virtual Reality (VR) is an advanced human-computer interface technology, which aims to recreate, with the highest degree of reliability as possible, the sense of reality, so that a person adopts this environment and the interactions occurring in it as one reality circumstantially plausible.

It's a synthetic environment with graphic simulation of fictitious and non-fictitious situations, computer generated, which can be constructed with a higher degree of accuracy by comparing with other grafic interfaces, such as multimedia, for example.

In this context, the (re)construction of daily life by technology allows us to think about the human condition in VR systems, so that, environments and devices, by principle considered products, be adopted as ludic elements and symbolic representation.

Think about the symbolic representation of the human in the virtual environment requires thinking about the physical body and how we consciously and unconsciously use it in our everyday life of screens: when we are in virtual environments we can enter, leave, perceive the environment, be located, interact, look, focus attention, gesturing, set the mood, to communicate, to talk about a point of view, shape the environment and create whatever it is from everything we know about the physical world, from everything that is familiar for us [5].

These representations of the self incorporate customized and anthropomorphic virtual bodies, the avatars, which are semiotic structures that visually communicate and replicate aspects of our identity and how we would like the others to realize us.

In this perspective, the avatars in virtual environments not only allow the representation of the subject in the virtual environment as well as enable human interaction through body movements and nonverbal communication (semiotic interactions) between the users.

In other words, while transiting the parallel worlds, the user adapts him/herself to the context changes assuming new perspectives and positions ("I" positionings in the digital world) which in turn is not independent of the "I" positionings manifested in the physical world [6].

In such situations, identities and digital lifestyles express how the users manifest their corporeality through digital culture. The virtual experience, subjective, multiple, fluid and complex, expands the user's notion about his own body (sense of presence) in ways that he/she can feel the simulated sensations by VR as his/her own sensations.

For Johnson [7], "an easy way to build a consistent interface is to follow the codes and conventions of the real world." In this sense, the characters created by the users present themselves looking like humans (anthropomorphism) in ways that they communicate, look, move, dress and gesture, not only to be more convincing and credible, favoring a greater appreciation and enjoyment of users [8], but also enabling the orchestration of the visual-motor aspects (physical body) and the semiotic mediation (metaphors on the screen), which helps the user to build a sense of self and of the environment that allows to act in and update the synthetic world [5].

Thus, the customization of the virtual environment, the avatar's creation, the playfulness and the narrative power of the digital world not only awaken the subject to an aesthetic experience (manipulating and creating virtual elements) but also invites him/her to inhabit the virtual environment, experiencing the sensations simulated by technology.

4 Interface and Interaction in Virtual Environments

Virtual reality allows the user to view three-dimensional environments, move in them and manipulate virtual objects which, in turn, can be animated, with autonomous behaviors or triggered by events [9].

In Virtual Reality, interaction is a fundamental concept and at the interface it is related to the computer's ability to detect and react to user actions. When interacting with a realistic three-dimensional virtual environment, the user can change the cenary, making a richest and most natural interaction, which leads to more engagement and efficiency while performing the task [9] (Fig. 1).

Fig. 1. A 3D realistic VR environment (source: https://www.youtube.com/watch?v=cML814JD 09g&feature=youtu.be)

By engaging him/herself in a process of interaction in a virtual reality system, the user seeks to achieve a goal in a given context of use. For Barbosa and Silva [10], the context of use is characterized by all relevant situation for the user interaction with the system, which includes both the moment of use as well as the physical, social and cultural environment in which the interaction occurs.

In this scenario, the cognitive research began to emphasize the interaction, communication and machine-mediated dialogue [6, 11], instead of the traditional operation of machines, as shown, for example, since the beginning of Ergonomics [10, 12].

From a conceptual point of view, it is necessary to distinguish both the simplest and the complex VR interactions. In the simplest interactions, the user navigates jogging in 2D space, making use of devices such as mouse, keyboard and microphone, seeing the others users' point of view about the scenery, also marking the scene with his/her own point of view. An example of this type of navigation would be the *facebook*[2], in which the user can not only view and explore, but can also manipulate and transform the environment.

However, the more complex interactions will require from the user a higher level of immersion provided by the multimodal[3] devices and by the stereoscopic[4] effects available in virtual reality systems.

Through these devices and the system itself, the senses and abilities of people are magnified in intensity in time and space [13] so that people not only dip into an illusion but to perceive contextually the experience by even the sensation of physical involvement [4, 5, 14, 15].

That is, while interact, the users manipulate and transform the virtual environment, activating or changing the virtual objects, as well as he/she actively uses the imagination and the senses, activating the motor areas of the brain responsible for the body movement, in ways that allows the user to react in a virtual environment similarly what he/she would do in the physical world.

Developed to support interaction, the interface connects the virtual world to our bodies, immersed, that while act and interact, update the environment [5].

This allows the user to command and coordinate his/her actions in the virtual environment in order to be able to develop skills and knowledge from the semiotic interactions experienced in the synthetic environment.

For this reason we should conceive the interface ultimately as a synthetic way, in both senses of the word. It is a kind of hoax, a "false" landscape passing by the "real" thing, and - perhaps most important - is a form that works in the service of synthesis, bringing together disparate elements into a cohesive whole [7].

As Johnson suggests, our interfaces are histories we tell ourselves to ward off the meaninglessness: memory palaces built of silicon and light. They will continue to

---

[2] https://www.facebook.com.

[3] Visual, audible, tactile and kinesthetic that provides users with multiple informational inputs and outputs and hence a greater degree of immersion, presence, involvement and interaction in the system.

[4] The process by which two pictures of the same object taken at slightly different angles, are viewed together, creating a sense of depth and solidity. Available in: www.soundidea.co.za/home/Sound_Idea_3D-755.html.

transform the way we imagine the information, and in doing so will transform us too. - for better and for worse" [7].

Thus, this study considers the interface as the means of contact between a computer system and the human component of the system, whereby a person comes in physical, perceptual and conceptual contact, in order to explore, manipulate and change the environment virtual and him/herself.

5 The Tension Between Metaphor and Simulation

One aspect that calls Virtual Reality users' attention is that the higher level of immersion guaranteed by technology, provides people with a degree of involvement to the point of them feel present in the virtual environment, acting and interacting integrated to the context.

In this sense, the concepts of immersion, presence, interaction and involvement are fundamental to the study of virtual reality and are relevant to the physical and psychological understanding of users in these systems [3–5].

Although the 'presence' occurs when the brain processes, interpretes and understands multimodal stimulations (images, sound, etc.) as consistent environments, where is possible to the user to act and interact, the sense of presence is subjective [3–5].

This subjective aspect, however, is related to our experiences in the physical world, about the way our body feels and measures the world. In this sense Domingues [16] states that although we measure objectively the space in inches, feet, meters, our presence in the world is more subjective. It depends on the body as a measurement base for everything and sets our standards of scale and suitability. Just waiting so some feelings that they become transparent to us: the pressure on our feet when we walk, the sun on our heads, the horizon uniting earth and sky. Deviations from these expectations cause us discomfort and anxiety. Naturally we accept these standards, which are our guarantee that the world is in order.

Thus, the user perceives the virtual environment instead of his/her physical location and the necessary conditions to experience this presence are the involvement and immersion [3, 4].

However, our relationship with the physical world is not restricted to objects and environments. It also involves our relationship to each other. Similarly, while presents him/herself in the virtual environment, the user adopts as a reference the forms of life that he/she knows about the physical world, so that he/she can integrate the physical world to the imagination and fiction. In this sense, this study assumes that in the virtual environment, body and message are intertwined and constitute an event in which the subject is presented as a sign [11, 15].

Accordingly, on the cognitive point of view, the metaphor would be the link between the physical and mental worlds. Given that the virtual environment is symbolic, its contents use the physicality to acquire substance, since they have no own content effectively [16]. Thus, the user is able to establish connections, similarity relations and association of concepts in order to understand and grasp the new, the novelty [17].

In the book entitled 'Culture of Interface", Johnson [7] already warned us to the fact that our digital age belongs to the graphical interface, and it's time to recognize the work of the imagination that creation requires, and to prepare ourselves for the imagination's revolutions to come.

In this sense, virtual reality, since its inception, is revealed as an exciting and challenging technology that integrates devices, products and situations of the physical world to the users' fiction, imagination and creativity.

However, as a technology that requires edge devices, VR designers need, among other things, be attentive to the concept of affordance, which is considered essential to the analysis and development of interfaces. About that, Barbosa and Silva [10] state that the physical characteristics of a product provide evidence on what to do with it and how to use it. Similarly, the user interface keeps a set of features and operations that are important to guide the user about what the system is able to do and how he/she can handle the interface to do so.

With its origins in Psychology, the term affordance, adopted by Norman and adapted to HCI (Human Computer Interaction) area, corresponds to the set of characteristics of a product or system which are capable of revealing the operations and manipulations that the users can do with this system or product.

In a graphical user interface, for example, the affordances of a command button is the possibility to press it using the mouse or keyboard and thus trigger an operation in the system [10].

According to Preece, Rogers and Sharp [8], one design mistake is to try to design a metaphor interface in ways that it looks like and behave literally as the physical entity that it represents - which ultimately neutralizing the advantages of developing interface metaphors. As noted above, they are used to map the familiar with the unfamiliar knowledge, allowing users to understand and learn the new domain. Design interface's metaphors only like literal models of what is being used in comparison has been criticized, which is perfectly understandable.

According to Johnson [7], in interface design, as in modern art and pulp fiction, realism can sometimes be a vulnerability. In order to avoid restricting the user reasoning, it is necessary that the interface designers develop metaphors that combine the knowledge that people have about the physical world with the new features of the system.

About metaphor, Johnson [7] states that if the user has to relearn the language interface for each new project, the power of this unique metaphor will be seriously compromised. In other words, although what is being represented in the interface be something fictional, the user only understands and recognizes it as a realistic thing based on everything you that he/she knows from the physical world. Thus, while he/she interacts and interprets, the user recognizes the system responses in ways that he/she can plan the next steps of his/her interaction.

Thus, the metaphor fulfill its function since it would transport the meaning from one side to another between the materiality and abstraction [16] both in social and psychological levels.

6 Discussion

Over the years, several factors have contributed to the development of Virtual Reality products and systems. Among them, we can mention the researches' development, languages' development and applications as well as the availability of devices and products at increasingly acessible prices.

The evolution and greater accuracy of technological devices, in turn, provided a higher quality of the visual, facial and motor tracking, greatly improving the user's perception as part of the system. In this sense, the user do not only moves him/herself on the virtual environment, but he/she also grab, move, manipulate and feel virtual objects, that provide to users, in turn, more complex interactions.

Beyond these, other system attributes are also required so that these interactions can occur: the ability to reproduce the natural movements of the user (to point, select and manipulate objects), and the control through metaphors available in the interface or even through the user thoughts, as we have now seen in brain-computer interfaces.

These new possibilities of use focuses on the people in a more dynamic and creative way, making them more able to cope with challenges, solve complex problems and propose solutions.

However, in fictional environments, the novelty facing the unkown can cause discomfort to the user, as well as the need for adaptation and training to technology in some cases.

Whereas the virtual environment is fundamentally symbolic, based on metaphors, it is essential to understand how occur the relationships between the physical and the symbolic, between fiction and non-fiction, between virtual and physical "self", in order to better clarify how virtual reality can actually contribute to a better performance and human improvement.

In addition to its potential it is also necessary to identify the possible limitations of products and systems in order to offer ergonomic recommendations, improvements as well as better and new products and systems.

References

1. Moraes, A., Mont'alvão, C.: Ergonomia: conceitos e aplicações. Teresópolis: 2AB editora (2012)
2. Quintão, F.S., Triska, R.: Design de informação em interfaces digitais: origens, definições e fundamentos. Revista Brasileira de Design da Informação. 10(02), 105–118 (2013). São Paulo
3. Soares, M. et al.: Virtual Reality in consumer product design: methods and applications. In: Human Factors and Ergonomics in Consumer Product Design: Methods and Techniques. CRC Press (2011)
4. França, A.C.P., Soares, M.: Realidade virtual aplicada à educação: a era Matrix do processo de ensino e aprendizagem. In: XIII Congresso Internacional de Tecnologias na Educação (2015a)
5. França, A.C.P., Soares, M.: Digital self on Virtual Reality systems: presence and embodiment in human situated interaction. In: 6th International Conference on Applied Human Factors and Ergonomics (AHFE 2015) and the Affiliated Conferences (2015b)

6. França, A.C.P.: Self digital: explorações acerca da construção do "eu" na internet. Dissertação [Mestrado]. Pós-graduação em Psicologia Cognitiva, Universidade Federal de Pernambuco, Pernambuco, 176 p. (2008)
7. Johnson, S.: Cultura da interface: como o computador transforma nossa maneira de criar e comunicar. Zahar, Rio de Janeiro (2001)
8. Preece, J., Rogers, Y., Sharp, H.: Design de interação: além da interação homem-computador. Bookman, Porto Alegre (2005)
9. Kirner, C., Siscoutto, R.A.: Fundamentos de Realidade Virtual e Aumentada. In: Realidade Virtual e Aumentada: conceitos, projeto e aplicações. Livro do Pré-Simpósio. IX Symposium on Virtual and Augmented Reality. Rio de Janeiro/Brazil. (2007)
10. Barbosa, S.D.J., Silva, B.S.: Interação Humano-Computador. Elsevier, Rio de Janeiro (2010)
11. Peres, F.: Diálogo e autoria: do desenvolvimento ao uso de sistemas de informação. Tese de Doutorado. UFPE, Psicologia Cognitiva, Recife (2007)
12. Iida, I.: Ergonomia: projeto e produção. Blucher, São Paulo (2005)
13. Tori, R., Kirner, C.: Fundamentos de realidade virtual. In: Fundamentos e Tecnologia de Realidade Virtual e Aumentada. Livro do pré-simpósio. In: VIII Simposium on Virtual Reality. Belém-PA (2006)
14. de França, A.C.P., Soares, M.M., de Lemos Meira, L.R.: Is reality real? Thoughts and conjectures about culture, self, intersubjectivity and parallel worlds in digital technologies. In: Marcus, A. (ed.) DUXU 2013, Part I. LNCS, vol. 8012, pp. 68–73. Springer, Heidelberg (2013)
15. França, A.C.P.: Bem-vindos à Matrix: questões sobre cultura, self, subjetividade, realidade e mundos paralelos em tecnologias digitais. XI Congresso Internacional de Tecnologia na Educação, Recife-PE (2013)
16. Domingues, D.: (Org): Arte e vida no século XXI: tecnologia, ciência e criatividade. Editora UNESP, São Paulo (2003)
17. Lima, N.E.A., Nagem, R.L.: A função cognitiva da metáfora na ciência e na tecnologia (2015). http://www.senept.cefetmg.br/galerias/Anais_2014/GT10/GT_10_x8x.PDF

We Are All Cyborgs: Body-Machine and Body-Information in Virtual Reality Systems

Ana Carol Pontes de França[(⊠)],
Joaquim de Vasconcelos Pereira Neto, and Marcelo Márcio Soares

Federal University of Pernambuco, Recife, Brazil
acpsicologa@gmail.com, jvpn.joaquim@gmail.com,
soaresmm@gmail.com

Abstract. This study discusses the relationship of the human body with digital technologies, based on the discursive panorama so called 'post-human', here represented by the 'biological-artificial' continuum. From this perspective, it addresses the Human Body reconfigurations focusing on the information processes of Virtual Reality systems (RV). As a consequence, this study considered: (1) the ergonomic aspects which involves the design, analysis and development of VR interfaces applied to training situations; and (2) the relationship among ergonomics and the User-Centered Design perspective, which puts the user in the core of the design process and also integrates usability to the conception and development of products and systems.

Keywords: Virtual reality · Cyborg · Body-machine · Body-information · User-centered design

1 Introduction

Theme extensively explored by science fiction, especially on the 70 s, 80 s and 90 s, the body reconstruction in the form of mechanical and electronic implants, with emphasis in the fields of robotics, bionics and artificial intelligence, became movie and entered to people's homes through the television media.

At that time, productions such as: *Cyborg – The Six Million Dollar Man*[1] (series, USA, ABC [1974–1978], color, 60 min, 05 seasons, 100 episodes), *The Bionic Woman*[2] (series, USA, ABC [1976–1977] / NBC [1977–1978], color, 48 min, 03 seasons, 58 episodes) and *Robocop*[3] (film, USA, MGM, 1987, color, 102 min), have

---

[1] The work of science fiction written by Martin Caidin, originally published in 1972 under the title *Cyborg*, comes to the big screen with the title *Cyborg: The Six Million Dollar Man*. Starring the actor Lee Majors, the film became a TV series and is now displayed in the US by ABC TV channel from 1974 to 1978. For more information see: https://pt.wikipedia.org/wiki/The_Six_Million_Dollar_Man.

[2] Starring Lindsay Wagner, this TV series was shown by US broadcasters ABC and NBC, in the years from 1976 to 1978. See: https://pt.wikipedia.org/wiki/The_Bionic_Woman.

[3] Written by Edward Neumeier and Michael Miner, the film is originally starred by Peter Weller, who plays Alex Murphy: a policeman brutally murdered by criminals who came back to life as a cyborg called RoboCop. See: https://pt.wikipedia.org/wiki/RoboCop.

© Springer International Publishing Switzerland 2016
A. Marcus (Ed.): DUXU 2016, Part III, LNCS 9748, pp. 287–293, 2016.
DOI: 10.1007/978-3-319-40406-6_27

become popular by suggesting hybrids of men with machines whose mechanical and electronic components, with their sophisticated ways to transpose the obsolescence of the biological body, visually distinguished the organic matter [1].

These boundaries, however, loses more and more clarity when we enter the field of genetic engineering[4] and nanotechnology[5], which makes it increasingly difficult to distinguish the bodies of the artificial intelligence entities of human bodies: as the film *Artificial Intelligence*[6] (film, USA, Warner Bros., 2001, color, 146 min) and the masterpiece *Blade Runner*[7] (film, USA, Warner Bros., 1982, color, 117 min), resulting by this process, new metaphors and body images.

This scenario also includes the molecular biology, psychology, cybernetics and digital technology. This last one, with its body tracking systems[8], infrared termography imaging[9], brain mapping and thoughts command[10] and three-dimensional graphic images increasingly realistic, allows the "scanning and virtualization of the body." [1] These in turn potentializes the biological characteristics, making it possible for the human, not only transit but also live, feel[11] and transform the virtual world.

In this sense, with origins in the field of science fiction, the 'post-humanism' allows us to think about that moment of cinema and American literature and can be a term used to refer to a person or entity resulting from a hybridization process the biological body with cybernetic [1, 2].

Similarly, the Virtual Reality systems (VR) keeps continuity aspects between humans and machines, between the physical and the virtual, transcending the boundaries of a physical body, while incorporates new cultural prosthesis (such as Oculus Rift® and haptic glove) to the biological structure.

Resulting from this process, the user starts to perceive and interpret the world and the things, in a way never seen before in human history, in which the imagination takes

---

[4] Intervention in human genetics structure through manipulation of genes in an organism. It usually occurs in an artificial way and aims to produce genetically enhanced organisms [3].

[5] Development of materials or components in the nanoscale (atomic scale). Applied to various fields such as medicine, the nanotechnology enables less invasive procedures for diagnosis and treatment, and can be used to streamline and enhance organic activities, such as memory and human intelligence.

[6] Starred by Haley Joel Osment in the role of android David, the film deals with the possibility of creating artificial intelligence entities with feelings. For more details see: https://pt.wikipedia.org/wiki/A.I._-_Intelig%C3%AAncia_Artificial.

[7] Considered a masterpiece of cinema, the science fiction film Blade Runner depicts a city of the future: the plot is set in Los Angeles in the year 2019, at which humanity colonizes other planets. In the plot the Tyrell Corporation creates genetically altered creatures called Replicants. Although similar to humans, these beings are stronger and more agile and therefore are employed in heavy, dangerous or degrading tasks in the new colonies. By being aggressive, the Replicants have a life restricted to a period of four years. For more details see: https://pt.wikipedia.org/wiki/Blade_Runner.

[8] As in visual tracking systems (eye tracking).

[9] Very used in diagnostic medicine.

[10] As the brain-computer interfaces controlled by electroencephalographic devices adjusted to the users' scalp.

[11] Atualmente já existem dispositivos hápticos que permitem os usuários de sistemas de RV sentirem e tocarem objetos virtuais.

shape, affects our relationship with the body and actively participates modifying both the virtual world as the physical world.

Paradoxically, it is in this context that the human and technological, natural and artificial, biological and cybernetic, fiction and nonfiction, walk intertwined, which allows us to rethink the concept of 'human' and even speak about a post-human condition. This, in turn, calls into question alleged dichotomies, such as: real vs. virtual, mind vs. body, objective vs. subjective, something vs. no-thing, by adopting an integrated perspective that is opposed above all to univocal trends, essentialist and metaphysical, as common to the anthropocentric-humanistic concepts and to the modern science [1, 2, 4].

2   The Representation of the Post-Human Condition Through the Biological-Artificial Continuum

By the relationships of the body with digital technologies is inaugurated a discursive panorama called 'post-human'. In this, the emergence of the cyborg as a political / scientific project for the XXI Century [5] leads us to a new context marked by the resultant hybridism of man-machine relations, here represented by the 'biological-artificial' continuum: (Fig. 1).

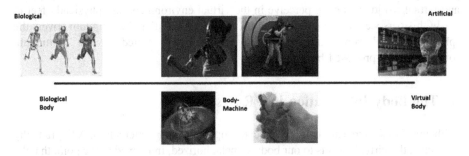

Fig. 1. The 'biological-artificial' continuum (Source: the authors, adapted from google images)

At one extreme we have the biological body which gradually becomes artificial, while incorporates technologies such as: VR devices, prostheses originated by 3D printers which replace damaged organs, bionic limbs and even medical applications involving nanotechnological components.

At the other extreme we have the virtual body, that even though artificial, is closely related to the physical body: the brain-computer interfaces in which the users toughts commands the avatar's[12] actions; In turn, in VR systems, the users command the avatar from devices adjusted to their physical body.

---

[12] Avatar: graphical representation of a user in Virtual Reality. According to the technology, can range from a sophisticated 3D model to a simple scanned image [4].

At the same time, what is happening in the virtual environment with the avatar can be felt by the biological body in the physical environment, such as in situations where the user has tachycardia and sweating while simulates a ride on a roller coaster, or even when the users can touch and feel virtual objects through haptic devices.

That is, in some circumstances the body-machine[13] approaches the physical body by acquiring a prosthesis function. In other situations, the body-machine gradually begins to support the actions and interactions of a virtual body[14], represented by the avatars in the virtual environments.

Whereas these technologies are closely related to the ways we interact with the world, we can say that in VR systems, while we transit from one side to another, between the biological and the artificial, between the physical and virtual worlds, taking on new body configurations. These new forms, however, not only simulate human characteristics: they potentialize the biological body.

In this context, VR systems keep a peculiarity that characterizes and distinguishes it from other technologies: the coexistence of biological and virtual bodies that act coordinately so that the user can perform and interact in the virtual world.

Beyond that, in VR systems, the physical body, metaphorically incorporated to the virtual environment, is presented as information from which the user himself and the others can make a reading of the context to interpret the situation and make decisions.

This human transfiguration would be, in turn, the result of a physical body integration process with the body-machine, allowing the user move between the physical and virtual worlds and even perceive in the virtual environment and physically feel it.

In this perspective, we can say that the 'biological-artificial' continuum covers the 'physical-virtual' continuum which, in turn, closely related to the continuum 'offline-online', proposed by França [4].

3   The Body-Information in VR Systems

With interfaces increasingly developed to support human interaction, VR gradually integrated the virtual worlds to our bodies, metaphorized, immersed to the point that the users can manipulate and even feel the virtual objects.

In this perspective, the dematerialized body, becomes storable and retrievable through network connections, readable through the displays and screens and even printable in certain circumstances[15].

However, despite all these changes, we still inhabiting our human bodies. As a result, while we present ourselves, we act and interact in the virtual environment, we refer everything we know of the physical world, all that is familiar to us, including our own body: to enter, exit, find, perceive the environment, look, focus attention, define a

---

[13] The machine body is used here to refer to the result of the incorporation of mechanical and electronic prostheses to the biological body. Throughout the text, also we refer to these mechanical and electronic prostheses as "cultural prostheses", resulting from digital culture.

[14] In virtual environments body and message are intertwined and constitute an event in which the subject is presented as a sign [6].

[15] As in the case of human organs obtained by 3D printers.

state, set the mood, communicate, share a point of view, model, create, gesture (body language), representing the many ways of being human [4, 7].

In such circumstances, we can see the interdependence between body, information and sign, considering that the body is the first human informational support and it is continuously formed from the exchanges carried out with the environment. From the perspective of contemporary culture, the information, as a sign, has an active role in the body's mediations with any phenomenon in the world and this relationship is becoming more complex with the growing and intensive use of information technologies, which approximate even more men and machines [8].

In other words, VR employs multimedia, computer graphics, image processing and other resources to create synthetic environment in which the body acts both as support for the prosthesis (dressed user with VR devices) or as sign (immersed user, metaphorically, in virtual environment).

4 Ergonomic Aspects of VR Systems Applied to Trainning Situations

Often used for training high risk and complex procedures, VR allows the user to experience problem-situations in detail, in a synthetic computer-generated environment. Although artificial, the generated environment guards features and similarities with the physical world, so that allow the user to contextually undergo the experience that lead to the sensation of physical involvement [9].

In these systems, the simulated environments need to provide a level of realistic representation, which in turn is related to the degree of realism of the interface. Therefore, we seek to take advantage of the knowledge that people have about the physical world in their everyday life [10].

In training, the VR user is prepared to address problem situations, perform procedures and make decisions from simulations with a high degree of realism. To this end, the RV user is immersed in a three-dimensional computer-generated environment, which simulates the physical world through interactive devices that send and receive information.

During the training, the user takes as reference the body itself and everything that he/she knows about the physical world in order to act and interact in simulated virtual environment. In this context, the set of information available in the interface is crucial for the user to interpret and analyze the situation and make decisions.

With regard to the aspects of ergonomic nonconformity, in some cases these interfaces take the user to a greater cognitive effort. In others, hardware and devices, both can overload the user and restrict their actions due to physical constraints.

Attentive to these and other issues, ergonomics has significant contributions to the design, analysis and development of VR interfaces in order to promote a better integration of the product with the user and hence a better performance.

Thus, it is up to the ergonomist be aware about the characteristics, expectations, needs and desires of the users in order to provide them more enjoyable, engaging and challenging experiences.

5 Ergonomics and the User-Centered Design in VR Systems

An important theme in ergonomics is the design for humans which can be summarized as the principle of the user-centered design: if an object, system or environment is designed for human use, then its design should be based on the physical and mental characteristics of the user [11].

In order to consider people's knowledge about the physical world [10] and in order to provide even more immersive and engaging experiences, RV system designers seek to offer interfaces and devices that approximate the users' actions to their physical movements and sensations observed in their everyday lives, in order to provide an even more realistic experience.

In this context, however, many products are still designed with a focus on the technology, without taking into account the users' characteristics and needs. Traditionally, projects focused on the function of the product can bring harm to people considering their efforts, the time taken to perform the task or even damage to the physical and mental health of users.

In such situations, the development of VR systems presents itself as a great challenge. Despite its importance and social impact, the design of these technologies requires multidisciplinary efforts to overcome the technological limitations without compromising the usability of devices and simulated environments.

In this scenario, the User-Centered Design paradigm then puts the user at the center of the design process in order to integrate the usability to the design and development of products and systems.

In turn, the usability study in VR systems allows researchers to understand how people feel when interacting with products and systems in order to explain the user experience in subjective terms [10].

Focusing on a better understanding of the users, it is indispensable to the ergonomist be aware about their characteristics, expectations, needs and desires in order to optimize the user's interactions and to design more effective, efficient and easy-to-learn interfaces which, in turn, provide an even more enjoyable, engaging and challenging experience to them.

6 Discussion

Given the above, we consider that the posthuman condition happens not detached from our biological condition, since from birth, we inescapably inhabit our physical bodies.

Adopting the body as a reference and from their anatomical and physiological components (brain, sense organs, vocal tract, etc.) coordinate our actions, we manage our interactions and we position ourselves in the world. By extension, our presence is not limited to our physical existence, but it involves our positionings as beings in physical or virtual worlds.

Similar to fiction in some extent we would be living in a matrix[16] so that we do not realize ourselves without machines. Consequently, with the digitalization and

---

[16] Matrix, the movie (USA/Australia, 1999, color, 136 min).

virtualization of the bodies, calls into question the idea of finitude linked to the anatomy of the biological body.

In this context, the body goes to be built and modeled, so that the obsolescence of the natural body be considered from overcoming the physiological body limits: connecting our bodies to machines, our minds to technology, we become flesh, blood and pixels beings, immortalizing ourselves while simultaneously we inhabit the virtual world.

References

1. Lima, H.L.A.: Do corpo-máquina ao corpo-informação: o pós-humano como horizonte biotecnológico. XXIX Encontro Anual da ANPOCS, GT: 24 Tecnologias de informação e comunicação: controle e descontrole, 25 a 29 de outubro (2005)
2. Santaella, L.: Pós-humano – por quê? REVISTA USP, São Paulo, n. 74, pp. 126–137, junho/agosto (2007)
3. Cunha, P.G.A.: Do gênio biológico ao ser biônico. Bagaço, Recife (2010)
4. França, A.C.P.: Self digital: explorações acerca da construção do "eu" na internet. Dissertação [Mestrado]. Pós-graduação em Psicologia Cognitiva, Universidade Federal de Pernambuco, Pernambuco, 176 p. (2008)
5. Siqueira, H.S.G., Medeiros, M.F.S.: Somos todos ciborgues: aspectos sociopolíticos do desenvolvimento tecnocientífico. In: Revista de Sociologia Configurações: Cultura, Tecnologia e Identidade, 8 (2011). http://configuracoes.revues.org/570
6. Peres, F.: Diálogo e autoria: do desenvolvimento ao uso de sistemas de informação. UFPE, Psicologia Cognitiva, Tese de Doutorado, Recife (2007)
7. França, A.C.P., Soares, M.: Realidade Virtual aplicada à educação: a era Matrix do processo de ensino e aprendizagem. In: XIII Congresso Internacional de Tecnologias na Educação (2015)
8. Andrade, G.C.: Nós em rede: informação, corpo e tecnologias. Dissertação [Mestrado]. In: Programa de Pós-graduação em Ciência da Informação, UFMG, Minas Gerais, 210 p. (2008)
9. de França, A.C.P., Soares, M.M., de Lemos Meira, L.R.: Is reality real? Thoughts and conjectures about culture, self, intersubjectivity and parallel worlds in digital technologies. In: Marcus, A. (ed.) DUXU 2013, Part I. LNCS, vol. 8012, pp. 68–73. Springer, Heidelberg (2013)
10. Preece, J., Rogers, Y., Sharp, H.: Design de Interação: Além da Interação Homem-Computador. Bookman, Porto Alegre (2005)
11. Moraes, A., Mont'alvão, C.: Ergonomia: conceitos e aplicações. Rio de Janeiro: 2AB (2012)

Use of Virtual Reality and Human-Computer Interface for Diagnostic and Treatment Purposes in Human Sexuality Research

Daniel Říha[1,2(✉)], Klára Bártová[1,2], and Jakub Binter[1,2]

[1] Faculty of Humanities, Charles University in Prague,
Prague, Czech Republic
daniel.riha@fhs.cuni.cz
[2] National Institute of Mental Health, Klecany, Czech Republic

Abstract. Virtual reality technology allows designing of immersive virtual environment that might be used for diagnostics and treatment of persons with minor sexual preference that is ego-dystonic or is perceived as dangerous to society. We do operate with the theoretical framework that is based on sexual motivational system, which we reintroduce. The eye tracking, electroencephalography and galvanic skin response in combination with phalopletysmography – the change of penile tumescence in male users are data to be collected to distinguish between sexual arousal and stress. The bio-cybernetic loop will consist of combination of positive and negative feedback loop to diverge the scenario. The biofeedback training should allow us to shape the preference by employing biofeedback training of suppression of the arousal to previously created scenario. This procedure might allow better diagnostics and treatment. Although we have in mind individualization of scenario creates problems in comparison during diagnostic phase, and is more important in case of future therapy. The resulting adaptable GNU software will be available to partner and other interested research centers.

Keywords: Virtual reality · Bio-cybernetic loop · Biofeedback · Sexual paraphilia · Diagnostics

1 Introduction

For decades, we may trace the growing interest in design of a direct human-computer connection amongst professionals, enthusiasts, and even public. Until constructing first bio-cybernetic loop (also human-computer interface) [1], the human-computer relationship may be best described as monologic – the initiation has always been on the side of human and all input are highly asymmetric. The standard control of the computer is implementing the keyboards, mouse, joysticks or various types of touchpads, and more recently touchscreens. The volume of information that one person would gather on/from computer is much higher than the computer could gather about the person who is in control. A dialogue, two-way information sharing, would be much more advantageous since there is very specific population that is mostly disqualified from using standard ways of controlling electronic devices i.e. users with disabilities.

© Springer International Publishing Switzerland 2016
A. Marcus (Ed.): DUXU 2016, Part III, LNCS 9748, pp. 294–305, 2016.
DOI: 10.1007/978-3-319-40406-6_28

There are several approaches to enable their engagement in computer control. The first and currently easily accessible interface is a voice-control that allows a user to execute the additional activity while using their hands for primary activity simultaneously. So, in this case we can talk about the monologue even literally. Electroencephalograph (EEG) has also been implemented to allow paraplegic users to control their electronic devices.

EEG was originally, in HCI context, applied to diagnose specific brain activity and distinguish between several mindsets such as engagement in the task or extreme workload. That is why NASA has adopted this technique to diagnose pilots' ability to cope with specific situations that can occur during aerospace operations for example [2]. The examples listed in this contribution do relate to the unidirectional information flow from human to computer. These examples can also state control measures during psychological testing to obtain data about the subject's attention where adaptation is not undergoing analysis based on the EEG data [3]. These approaches are characterized by the fact that does not need real time feedback and might be analyzed retrospectively but are generally applicable to non-patient population.

With a priority to focus more on the dialogic options, we might set an extension of the above mentioned examples to change the environment based on the information obtained through psychophysiological measures [4]. Users of such loop are often healthy users and one of the intended implementation is in area of entertainment. We are informed about ongoing research on other applications of bio-cybernetic loop in psychology related research.

While there are unquestionable benefits raising from adoption of such approach, we may trace related risks. The gameplay relation must be executed in a real-time or close-to-real-time mode of analyses and adjustment. The user and gaming-like application need to set up a sort of co-evolution while using such a platform, especially in the initial phases. In other words, the butterfly effect of player-game interaction will occur [5]. That avoids comparative measuring of players' gameplay performance due to differences in gaming environment design as each players' gameplay establishes an individualized environment for each player. The same problem we can spot when using bio-cybernetic loop for scientific use, namely diagnostics. In our research, we attempt to challenge this premise.

Currently, we do proceed with a research on (above-listed options) at the Laboratory of Evolutionary Sexology and Psychopathology associated with National Institute of Mental Health in the Czech Republic.

2 Current Research

Our recent research activity has been including as one of the team priorities a focus on utilization of immersive virtual reality technology and animated avatars design. We may list a number of benefits when implementing virtual reality technology in sexuality research such as: (a) bespoke animated stimuli can be created and customized, that is especially important when researching paraphilia (unusual sexual preference) and sexual preferences; (b) stimulus production is less expensive and easier to produce when compared to real world stimuli; (c) virtual reality allows our researchers to record data such as physiological reasons to stimuli, data that would be normally not available to capture before (without resorting to self-report measures that are especially problematic in this research domain); (d) ethical, legal, and health and safety issues are less complex since neither physical nor psychological harm is being caused to animated characters, which allows for the safe presentation of stimuli involving vulnerable targets [6].

This research intends to combine the various approaches and design a diagnostic tool and training environment for users with various difficulties such as social, developmental and, since it is our primary interest, sexual preference disorders that will allow us to more accurately diagnose, and possibly treat these users.

The final product interface/software with adaptive environment control should be available to wide public since all patents we would produce would be of GNU General Public License and can be adapted for various implementations. Namely, we would like to employ the bio-cybernetic loop for diagnostic purposes of people with unusual (in scientific literature also called minor) sexual preferences such as pedophilia or sexual aggression. For each case, the loop will be applied in a specific way as described further.

2.1 Theoretical Framework of Paraphilia

First, we should explain theoretical approach to paraphilia that is being employed for better understanding of the loop design and paradigm of changes. Currently, the research in its entirety to be primarily focused on men since their sexual reactivity is object and activity specific as opposed to women, who seem to exhibit much less stable sexual preference and reactivity. Also male paraphilics are much more common, therefore scientific literature on female paraphilia is rather scarce, and male offenders are more dangerous to society than female ones. Moreover, there is relatively high concordance between self-report measures of male sexual arousal and measures obtained by using psychophysiological measures. As for preference of object (usually a person, but not necessarily) and activity we feel need to give decryption of terms used further in text. Preference for sexual partner of adult age is called teleiophilia and in the article it will be used as opposite to pedophilia which can be described as predominant preference for sexual partners that are underage, in research usually defined as being between 4 and 12 years of age (even though we are aware that the complete opposite is gerontophilia – predominant preference for partners of elderly age).

Also we will use description of two types of sexual behavior towards partner differing based on consent. The usual preference during which the partner is cooperative and willing will be called consenting. People with this preference do have conventional sexual preference and usually are healthy controls[1]. The second type, coercive, where aggression and pressure is present and the sexual intercourse is initiated even when the sexual partner is non-consenting. This distinguishes such preference from consensual sado-masochistic preference where is also present certain degree

---

[1] Non-patient population used to show contrast between specific participants and "normal" population.

of violence but both partners are consenting, and the interaction can be interrupted at any moment. To be able to diagnose and treat patients with unusual preference we need to understand etiology of such preference.

One of the influential theories having its origin in research conducted in the Czech Republic attempts to explain various unusual sexual preference as an expression of a common "underlying disorder" is the theory of disruption of Sexual Motivation System derived from the model of "courtship disorders" by Freund [7] and the "theory of vandalized lovemaps" by Money [8]. SMS posits premise that sexuality can be seen as hierarchically ordered and an interconnected system of particular sexual motivation levels that refer to a sequence of courting behaviors found in female mammals including humans and corresponding male reactions. According to the SMS approach, pre-intercourse cognitions of a female sexual object and its sexual interest precede the start of male sexual reaction and successful sexual act. Particular parts of male SMS system are:

- Attractivity (attention to a sexual stimulus with specific physical traits, e.g., adult female)
- Proceptivity (appetence for signals of female attraction to a male and attempts to seduce),
- Receptivity (appetence for signs of female readiness to copulate and of cooperating copulative behavior) [9].

Importantly, SMS theory suggests that the hierarchy of behaviors and their specific cognitive patterns occur sequentially. That is, the fulfilment of lower motivation levels must be achieved for the next step in motivation to be employed (e.g., attractivity must be complete before proceptivity is employed). If the motivational levels occur out of sequence, or some are omitted, the system inhibits sexual arousal (e.g. proceptivity of a female without previous attraction to her). The first two phases are key phases to understand unusual sexual preferences. In the first one, attractivity, the object (most likely person of preferred age and sex) plays major role. Male heterosexual teleiophilic would be attracted to adult female, male homosexual teleophilic would be attracted to adult men. Male heterosexual pedophile would be attracted to underage girl and male homosexual pedophile would be attracted to underage boy. In the second, proceptive, phase it would decide whether the courtship would be consenting or coercive (based on positive or negative signals coming from the sexual object chosen in phase of attractivity).

2.2 Environment

The research that includes the bio-cybernetic loop design has an objective to design environment that will enable for testing of sexual preferences, or rather distinguishing between various (above described) pre-defined preferences. This type of testing method is especially helpful when combined with immersive virtual reality environment and implementations of near-photorealistic designed avatars. The implementation of virtual reality environment will offer to design (technically speaking) infinite amount of realistic appearing avatars with a goal to increase the fit of preference of each person tested. This is especially advantageous in case of studying preference of sexual aggressors and pedophiles since in both cases they seem to "have a type". In other words, the person does prefer certain characteristics such as specific age, sex, color of hair and eyes, etc. The first part of the procedure is aimed to determine the preferred type of interacting avatar.

The environment itself will be created in one of the commercially available game engines. We are still in testing phase of the study and based on the outcome, Unity[2] or Unreal[3] game engine will be used to meet criteria such as immersion, photorealism, and loop design functioning. Preferably, there will be no animated objects or other avatars in any of the scenarios. We expect that the environment does not need to be complex since the attention should be focused solely on the interacting avatar itself. In case of out of the door scenario, the city environment will be used with unified color and light conditions will be controlled since eye-tracking and pupilometry used during this phase are light-condition sensitive procedures. Indoor scenario will always take place in same looking room, with low complexity for the above mentioned reasons. All scenarios will be presented from first person perspective.

The avatars will be interacting in the same manner, the same (on scientific literature [10] based, consenting and coercive) behavior – the movement will be the same (except for underage avatars, as described lower in the text). For this purpose, prototypic types of appearance respecting avatars will be pre-made. The expected amount is 10 avatars of each sex and age group to capture the variability of population. In the first set, only Caucasian race will be present since racial diversity of Czech population is very low. There will be four age groups present in the stimuli sets: (a) 4–6, (b) 10–12, (c) 14–16, and (d) 20–25 years of age. The age groups are based on previous scientific literature and Tanners development stages. In total, there will be 10 (appearance) $\times$ 2 (sex) $\times$ 4 (age) = 80 different types of avatars. Each avatar will also be presented in consenting and coercive proceptive behavior (80 $\times$ 2 different types of stimuli). Also sexual activities represented for each avatar type will be presented but in this case, only genital interaction (of neutral age) respecting the sex of the preferred avatar will be presented (2, penile-vaginal or penile-anal intercourse) for ethical reasons. The total amount of stimuli prepared for this study will be then 162.

Four time-loops with same amount of behavioral displays of each type (consenting and coercive) will be created to create illusion of ongoing interaction for case of prolonged exposure in training with a possibility of terminating the loop and starting a new one, with fluent change. In case of biofeedback, we expect that there can be two possible ways of visualization. One is to present the person with bars representing degree of arousal and stress. The other, perhaps more useful in later stages of training, is processing of saddle color changes in the environment, such as color filter engagement, respecting certain amount of stress and arousal. Or only specific object color change can be applied (e.g., vase on a table will change color on a scale from blue to red, clock will change time based on arousal (minute hand) and stress (hour hand) to allow biofeedback training with smaller amount of disruption of the situation, which we find novelty. The whole project is under development and actual outcome may differ.

---

[2] https://www.unrealengine.com/what-is-unreal-engine-4.

[3] https://unity3d.com/.

2.3   Procedure

The participant will be comfortably seated in room with all the equipment ready, researcher will attach all the sensors. Participant will be asked to attach the head-mounted-monitor (if compatible, eye-tracking is available, if not, monitor and eye-tracker will be used). Neutral movie with controlled light environment will be presented to obtain basal levels of psychophysiological measures.

First, the participant will be virtually walking on a street (speed will be adjusted) and on each side of the street there will be an avatar of certain type. Since visual attention and sexual preference are in concordance in men, as was shown in past research, the type of avatar that will be given attention will be automatically further developed in scenario. During this part, EEG data will also be collected to distinguish the preference. We expect that avatars will be presented wearing clothes, but possibly they will be presented naked in case of adult ones and in swimming suit for case of children. The decision logic will be tested but by now we expect that the hierarchy of choice will follow these lines: sex (male vs. female), age (10–12 years old vs. adult avatars) – in case of preference of underage avatar, all three underage categories will be tested against each other. Number of trials will be chosen based on pilot study and specific physiological reaction, expectedly EEG data will be used, accompanying the eye-tracking procedure. Once age and sex are selected, other properties will be tested as well.

As an alternative to this procedure there is one suggested by Patrice Renaud and his colleagues, using magnetic resonance [11]. In this scenario, the age of pre-chosen sex is dynamically changing and based on psychophysiological reactions during certain period of presentation, highlighting the age of avatar can be used as decision-making procedure. Such design is especially helpful in treatment in future phases.

Nevertheless, once the looks are decided, the scenario will shift to interior spaces where the avatar will be presented in the non-interactive manner to fulfill the phase of attractivity. Length of presentation will be also adjusted based on pilot study and individual reactivity. As next, both, coercive and consenting proceptivity will be presented in randomized order directly followed by receptivity (sexual act). During all phases, psychophysiological measures will be collected to distinguish between the above mentioned sexual preferences. As control condition, non-preferred avatar will be presented in the same scenarios and data from both conditions will be compared. The same will follow, but this time the appearance will be kept, but proceptivity will differ. In case of clear negative reaction (change of EEG pattern, change of galvanic skin response are expected variables) towards the stimuli, the scenario will be changed. During the calibration phase, self-report data will be also collected. This will allow us to create profile of preferences that the person has for future testing.

Such scenarios will be, in case of patients, saved for case of bio-feedback training during which the person will learn how to cope with their sexual preference.

Since one of the intended implementation of the loop is treatment and behavior adjustment, the biofeedback training will be employed. Based on previous diagnostic session, the scenarios will be created respecting the appearance and activity that the tested person exhibited. In case of participants with sexual preference that, for legal or personal reasons, needs modification, alternative scenario, respecting target preference, will be constituted. In the next part we will use original scenario – the one based on participant's preference, and target scenario – the one that is respecting legal, or personal (in some cases) boundaries.

In phase of biofeedback training, during scenario presentation, the tested participant will be exposed to visual representation of his mental state, especially sexual arousal and stress (generally negative reaction). The aim of the procedure is to enhance participant's ability to suppress their sexual arousal in inappropriate scenario, but also to maintain control over their negative and stressful reaction during periods of suppression. In ideal world, we would hope to enhance ability to consciously increase arousal in the appropriate scenario.

Since the theory of SMS is based on hierarchical model where each phase is followed by hierarchically higher motivation (attractivity => proceptivity => receptivity), we can let the participant stay in specific phase for all the time needed to achieve the goal and change the scenario based on outcome of the previous phase.

2.4   Sample of Participants

Since we want to use the diagnostic tool to distinguish between males with usual (homosexual teleiophilia is considered usual sexual preference) and unusual sexual preferences based on the age they prefer (child or adult), sex they prefer (male or female) and type of proceptivity (positive and negative). For this reason we decided to ask patients with the matching sexual preferences (pedophilic preference, sexual aggressors, approx. 15 of each preference, 30 in total) and healthy controls (male heterosexuals and homosexuals of matching age, with no history of sexuality related problems, approx. 40) to participate in the study. All participants will go through procedure of sexual diagnostics before participation and rules for ethics of psychological research will be strictly obeyed. Advantage of use of these target groups is also that each target group reacts by positive reaction and sexual arousal to presentation of stimuli that match their preference but has rather negative reaction towards all other categories of stimuli.

2.5   Measurements

In the past research, many potential problems of measurement have been identified. The primary problem is that representation of mental state by changes in psychophysiological measures does not have to be linear. For more, the psychophysiological change can relate to more than one state. And vice versa, one state can be demonstrated in more than one psychophysiological measure change.

In the existing scientific literature, it has been recommended to use more than one measurement to represent the mental state of a person. As suitable for such loop construction several psychophysiological measures were suggested. Among these, eye tracking[4] and pupilometry[5], galvanic skin response[6], electrocardiography[7], data about

---

[4] Area of visual attention related data are collected to estimate area of interest.

[5] Measuring the size of pupil to estimate mental states.

[6] Measured to estimate level and type of excitation.

[7] Data about heart rate change will be collected to distinguish between emotional states.

respiratory rate[8]. Newly, we would like to add penile-pletysmography[9] on the list of measures used to construct bio-cybernetic loop, since it is one of measurements with relatively high accuracy and is well studied in scientific literature [12]. Also electroencephalography is possibility that will be considered since scientific literature shows that specific emotional states can be represented by changes in electrical activity of the brain and specific response is demonstrated when their preference matching type of stimuli is presented. The advantage is that since different part of human body are used to collect data, more measurements can be collected simultaneously resulting in possibility of using variety of combinations to define mental state more accurately. All of the above mentioned measures have also been used in research of human sexuality individually or in combination, and we believe we will create functional loop based on these measurements. Process of testing is described lower in text.

2.6   Equipment

For this study we dispone with dedicated experimental room at National Institute of Mental Health of Czech Republic. The bio-cybernetic loop will consist of: personal computer (HP Envy gaming series 2015 desktop seems to meet the our requirements so far) – head mounted display (e.g., Oculus Rift, FOVE or 4 k phone display) – human – device for psychophysiological data collection – computer. We will employ BioPac MP[10] as the device for psychophysiological data acquisition allowing the collection of more physiological measures simultaneously, when special modules, present in the lab to be added to the device. All of the above mentioned psychophysiological measures can be measured using one single device. The device also can be used for signal amplification and redirection of the data to computer to close the loop.

Specialized software is to be used to collect data about the user, as an interface, and set thresholds on individual variables allowing storing individual profiles of tested participants in memory. The software will also be used for visual representation of mental state, or single variable(s), on the screen for the bio-feedback training in later phases that are not described in this article. Also, we will use a device for self-report data acquisition preferably of a lever construction with possibility of visual representation of choice on the screen to allow employ the head-mounted monitor on. Virtual reality environment is currently developed and tested in Unity 5 game engine, while Unreal 4 having as a possible alternative. All devices and software are being tested with the goal to identify and optimize the virtual environment production pipeline (capacity, compatibility, efficiency, and ease of use).

2.7   Testing Process and Development of the Loop

Testing of the loop will follow 6 phases suggested by Fairclough [13]:

---

[8] Collected since it is related to emotional states and for more is under voluntary control.

[9] Data about penile blood flow are collected to estimate sexual excitement.

[10] Device for psychophysiological measurement data acquisition.

1. Conceptual Model (s) – Model of psychological states during specific situations was put together based on scientific literature to conceptualize specific user behaviors. In our case we made bipolar labels of possible reaction on stimulus. As mentioned above, we expect rather sexual positive reaction on preference matching stimuli and rather sexual negative reaction on all other categories of stimuli.
2. Psychophysiological Interference – At this stage we have elected and chose psychophysiological measures to represent each mental state. Namely, we focused on eye tracking data, EEG, and PPG measures for which scientific literature is very clear and we will test all other variables in combination to find best possible solution. All participants will go through all possible testing scenarios collecting data from psychophysiological measures as well as self-reports. Also there will be phase during which they will have possibility of voluntary decision in times where the future loop would make scenario shift.
3. A Quantified Model of User State – We will develop the way in which the user state or behavior is represented within the bio-cybernetic loop. The minimum requirement of the quantified model will be that the user is represented with sufficient fidelity to enable the process of adaptation within the loop. In other words, the target states that drive the adaptive logic of the loop will be clearly defined during this part.
4. A Real-Time Model of User State – Based on previous generic formulation defining "data space" the model to trigger adaptation in real time. The model will be populated with criteria and classes that define regions of user state representation. Also individual user customization of thresholds possibility will be brought out in this stage.
5. Design of Adaptive Interface – The way that the loop makes adaptations will be tested during this testing phase. Main concern would be whether the change is efficient and noticed or not by the participant, and the change is in concordance with researcher's expectations and matches preference of each tested target group. Testing will also focus on concordance with self-perceived adequacy of the change and states before and after change will be compared to see whether the change does not create confusion or immediate notable change in participant's state showing that the change can be rather disturbing.
6. Evaluation – During this stage all benefits of creation of bio-cybernetic loop will be considered and analyzed, and the result will be compared with possibility of direct testing or use of other method to reach the goal of research.

The loop will be designed as a combination of positive and negative control loop, so called "toggling loop". Negative control loop has been proven to be more stable and seem to be advantageous in cases in which psychological comfort and wellbeing during testing is preferred. In all instances of testing and biofeedback phases there will be "safe" (neutral) scenario for case of procedure induced stress where participant would be redirected if needed. The positive control loop is applied in case of scenario diverting (for each sexual preference based on change of psychophysiological changes during presentation of the stimuli) but will have control in negative control loop to ensure the stability and control for time variable.

2.8   Ethical Aspects of the Proposed Study

There are a number of ethical issues associated with the design and use of physiological computing systems. This technology is designed to tap private psychophysiological events and use these data as the operational fulcrum for a dynamic HCI. The topic is even more tormenting since the primary use of this loop is sexual diagnostics which is very sensitive topic in general, for more it is related to sexual acts that are in conflict with law (pedophilia and sexual aggression).

All personnel directly participating on this research are skilled researchers of human sexuality with years of training, trained psychologist and a medical doctor will be present for case of need of intervention. After the whole session, there will be time for debriefing that will take approx. 20 min and will consist of watching neutral video about traveling (to induce calm emotional state), and short consultation with a skilled psychologist. The debriefing will be prolonged in case of complication. Permission of institutional review board will be obtained before the whole study will be conducted and all participants will be informed about sexual nature of the experiment and will be clearly informed that they can terminate their participation at any time. We also guarantee strict anonymization of the data as well as blindness of researchers to individual sexual preferences during testing phase. Underage avatars will not be present in the erotic pose; the main focus is on child typical nonverbal displays in avatars. Consultations of stimuli content with forensic experts and judge advocates in field of sexology is clear.

3   Conclusion

We would like to emphasize the option to design an environment that is based on user's preference and allows for more accurate diagnostics than currently available methodology due to possibility of authoring the stimuli to fit user's preference in appearance and behavior. This should allow us to distinguish between sexual aggressors, pedophiles and healthy controls. We do consider two mental states, sexual arousal and stress (negative reaction), that will allow us to distinguish between preference for such stimuli or aversion towards it in male users. As a theoretical framework for minor sexual preferences, we have decided to apply a theory of sexual motivational system that can be seen as hierarchically ordered and an interconnected system of particular sexual motivation levels that refer to a sequence of courting behaviors. In phase of attractivity, the looks and appearance will be selected, in second stage, proceptivity, the consent related behavior will be decided. The advantage is that persons with chosen minor preferences are known to be highly reactive towards preferred stimuli and do not react (by arousal) to other types of stimuli, the opposite is valid for healthy controls who are rather repulsed and vice versa. To distinguish between the two mental states, we will collect data about eye gaze, brain activation, and galvanic resistance of skin in combination with the change of penile tumescence. There will be total of 162 stimuli needed to be created to fulfill the criteria of testing. We hope that once the user is correctly diagnosed with sexuality related disorder and the therapy is needed, the biofeedback training will allow them to suppress their arousal in inappropriate situations and hopefully to shape it toward more socially and personally acceptable preferences. We are aware of numerous ethical issues related to such procedure but only skilled and experienced professionals will participate on the whole procedure.

Acknowledgement. This publication was supported by the project "National Institute of Mental Health (NIMH-CZ)", grant number ED2.1.00/03.0078 (and the European Regional Develo-pment Fund), and by the Czech Science Foundation, grant nr. 16-18891S. KB and JB were supported by the Charles University Research Center (UNCE 204004) and Czech Ministry of Education Grant SVV no. 260 239. Also we would like to thank to Kateřina Klapilová, Renata Androvičová for cooperation on the sexological part as well as to 3DSense ltd. for support in testing the multimedia production pipeline. Finally to Kristýna Kubáčová for language corrections.

References

1. Merrill, M., Maes, P.: Augmenting looking, pointing and reaching gestures to enhance the searching and browsing of physical objects. In: LaMarca, A., Langheinrich, M., Truong, K. N. (eds.) Pervasive 2007. LNCS, vol. 4480, pp. 1–18. Springer, Heidelberg (2007)
2. Prinzel, L.J., Parasuraman, R., Freeman, F.G., Scerbo, M.W., Mikulka, P.J., Pope, A.T.: Three Experiments examining the Use of Electroencephalogram, Event-related Potentials, and Heart-rate Variability for Real-time Human-centred Adaptive Automation Design (No. NASA/TP-2003-212442): NASA, pp. 1–62 (2003)
3. Kapoor, A., Burleson, W., Picard, R.W.: Automatic prediction of frustration. Int. J. Hum.-Comput. Stud. **65**, 724–736 (2007)
4. Allison, B., Graimann, B., Graser, A.: Why use a BCI if you are healthy? In: Proceedings of the International Conference on Advances in Computer Entertainment, Salzburg, Austria, pp. 7–11 (2007)
5. Klein, G., Woods, D.D., Bradshaw, J.M., Hoffman, R.R., Feltovich, P.J.: Ten challenges for making automation a "team player" in joint human-agent activity. IEEE Intell. Syst. **19**(6), 91–95 (2004)
6. Binter, J., Klapilová, K., Zikánová, T., Nilsson, T., Bártová, K., Krejčová, L., Androvičová, R., Lindová, J., Průšová, D., Wells, T., Riha, D.: Exploring the Pathways of Adaptation an Avatar 3D Animation Procedures and Virtual Reality Arenas in Research of Human Courtship Behaviour and Sexual Reactivity in Psychological Research. Inter-Disciplinary Press, Oxford (2016). Accepted for publication
7. Freund, K.: Courtship Disorder. In: Marshall, W.L., Laws, D.R., Barbaree, H.E. (eds.) Handbook of Sexual Assault, pp. 195–207. Springer, US. (1990)
8. Money, J.: The Lovemap Guidebook: A Definitive Statement. Continuum, New York (1999)
9. Kolářský, A., Brichcín, S.: Priorities in male erotic activation and paraphilias. Psychiatrie **3**(1), 3–8 (1999)
10. Moore, M.M.: Nonverbal courtship patterns in women: context and consequences. Ethology Sociobiol. **6**(4), 237–247 (1985)
11. Renaud, P., Joyal, C., Stoleru, S., Goyette, M., Weiskopf, N., Birbaumer, N.: Real-time functional magnetic imaging-brain-computer interface and virtual reality. Promising tools for the treatment of pedophilia. Prog. Brain Res. **192**, 263–272 (2011)

12. Chivers, M.L., Seto, M.C., Lalumiere, M.L., Laan, E., Grimbos, T.: Agreement of self-reported and genital measures of sexual arousal in men and women: a meta-analysis. Arch. Sex. Behav. **39**(1), 5–56 (2010)
13. Fairclough, S.H.: Psychophysiological inference and physiological computer games. In: Brainplay, Brain-Computer Interfaces and Games Workshop at ACE (Advances in Computer Entertainment), vol. 7, p. 19 (2007)

DUXU for Smart Objects
and Environments

The Interaction Design of Household Intelligent Breathing Training System

Zhanxun Dong[(⊠)], Lu Liu, and Weiwei Li

School of Media & Design, Shanghai Jiao Tong University,
800 Dong Chuan Road, Min Hang District, Shanghai, China
{dongzx,ibetray,lww0125}@sjtu.edu.cn

Abstract. This paper achieved the acquisition of the breathing signal and identification of different respiratory modes by several attempts. On this basis, we designed an intelligent breathing-exercise system to meet the household needs. The intelligent system consists of three parts: the first part is the user interface of the breathing-exercise system, the second part is the background database and the last part is the internet community platform. The user interface of the breathing-exercise system is used for displaying user's breathing curve and other visual feedback. All the breathing training data will be recorded in the second part: database. Those breathing exercisers can share their results on the internet community platform. The intelligent breathing-exercise system will provide a memorable user experience for users by blending these three parts.

Keywords: Breathing training system · Interaction design

1 Introduction

Nowadays, as the air pollution is getting worse and the incidence of respiratory disease is becoming Soaring, more and more people are concerned about the topic of breathing exercise. From the current point of view, research on the breathing exercise and product development are mostly concentrated in the medical field. These studies focus on two major problems: the first one is the treatment of respiratory diseases and the second one is the rehabilitation of respiratory diseases. American Academy of Family Physicians (AAFP) found that those with COPD (Chronic obstructive pulmonary disease) who use breathing exercises experience greater improvements in exercise capacity than those who do not. So, the fact is breathing exercise is really an effective treatment way for those respiratory diseases like Chronic obstructive pulmonary disease, Chronic pneumonia and other respiratory diseases. According to the survey, we find that the typical products include the breathing training device and the respiratory therapy device. These medical devices are so highly targeted and professional that they are difficult to meet the needs of breathing training in home. In terms of the range of application, these medical breathing trainers are a bit more restrictive. With wearable healthy devices becoming more and more popular, people started to pay more attention to their own health data. It is easy to calculate that people want to get the respiratory data by household intelligent devices. This shows a household intelligent breathing exercise

© Springer International Publishing Switzerland 2016
A. Marcus (Ed.): DUXU 2016, Part III, LNCS 9748, pp. 309–318, 2016.
DOI: 10.1007/978-3-319-40406-6_29

device will be more practical than a medical breathing training device. So, it is not difficult to find that household intelligent breathing trainer has broad research space and market prospects.

As we all know, the daily breathing exercise is an important means of strengthening respiratory muscles, which can improve respiratory function and relieve mental stress and tension. Abnormalities in respiration have been postulated as an important factor in the development or maintenance of anxiety disorders [1]. It can be known that breathing training is an effective way to treating the panic disorder. When we talking about daily breathing training, it is inevitable to introduce an important breathing training way: Lamaze breathing. Lamaze breathing historically is considered the hallmark of Lamaze preparation for childbirth [2]. The breathing method is generally considered as a controlled breathing way to enhance relaxation and decrease perception of pain. Conscious breathing and relaxation, especially in combination with a wide variety of comfort strategies, can help women avoid unnecessary medical intervention and have a safe, healthy birth. In restricted birthing environments, breathing may be the only comfort strategy available to women. The deep-breathing also called abdominal respiration is well known another important breathing method to reduce feelings of stress. We cannot ignore that most of the office workers have to face the computer all day to accomplish their works in stressful working conditions. According to the survey, people who face the computer for a long time will be in a short-winded breathing mode, which will lead to insufficient ventilation even in the normal respiratory rate. Apart from the insufficient ventilation, the carbon dioxide will accumulate gradually in the short-winded breathing status and then lead to Listlessness. All the shortcomings above described will result in adversely affect for people. Conversely, if they take a deep breath training, they will be benefited greatly including the improvement of the lung capacity, the improvement of alveolar utilization rate and so on. In view of this, design and development of a suitable daily breathing exercise interactive system has a high practical value and huge market potential. Figure 1 shows the trend of the key-word "breathing training" in Google search. As can be seen from the figure, since the 2006 "breathing training" peaked a search until the year 2015. So far, the heat of search is still maintained at between 60 and 80.

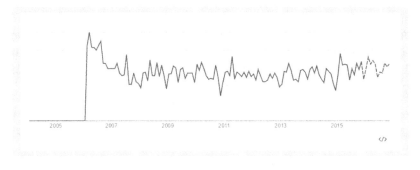

Fig. 1. The trend of "breathing training" in Google search

1.1 Research of the Breathing Training

We designed a questionnaire of the breathing exercises to understand some of the current problems that exist in breathing exercise. We sent 33 questionnaires and all the questionnaires are recovered successfully, of which include 14 white-collar workers and 19 students. According to survey results, 92.9 percent of white-collar workers said deep breathing exercises help relieve stress and fatigue. 89.5 % of the student population believe that the deep breathing exercises contribute to relieve stress as we can see in Fig. 2.

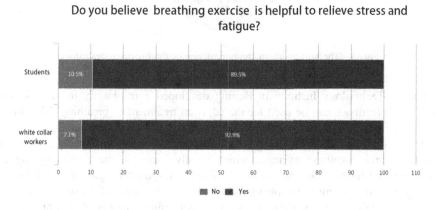

Fig. 2. The survey about the relieving stress by breathing training

At the same time, we made a simple research for other problems existed in breathing exercise, such as the persistence of the breathing training. Results of the research show that 75.76 % of respondents find it difficult to adhere to the breathing exercise shown in Fig. 3.

1.2 Research Status

As we all known, breathing training can strengthen breathing muscles, relieve stress and promote the rehabilitation of lung function, and thus play to enhance physical fitness, disease prevention and promote rehabilitation. A variety of detection devices and instruments abound in the study of aspects of breathing exercise. Which are more representative of the product at home and abroad, as described below.

Gila Benchetrit from French designed a breathing exercise apparatus to collect respiration signal by a sleeveless jacket [3]. The principle of the device is equipped with a sleeveless jacket can be folded in a special material that can be received by a lateral extension of the diaphragm, abdominal volume change. The device can also filter out the biggest natural breathing graphics, and based on the graphical boot subject's breathing lungs rehabilitation training.

Do you find it difficult to adhere to the breathing exercise?

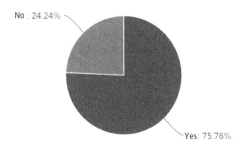

No : 24.24%

Yes: 75.76%

Fig. 3. The survey about the persistence of the breathing training

Bardon Technology Institute in Beijing developed a respiratory therapy device based on biofeedback can be used for the adjuvant treatment of breathing difficulties. The therapy device can measure respiration rate, and gives real-time feedback.

According to the review above, we can see that there are still some deficiencies in current research breathing exercise, which mostly focus on the respiratory signal acquisition and feedback on their own. The form of respiratory signal feedback in the majority of studies seems monotonous and boring. Besides, most of the studies pay less attention to daily breathing exercise. So, it is not difficult to find that a household intelligent breathing training system maybe a more reasonable solution.

2 The Acquisition and Processing of Respiration Signal

Nowadays, respiration signal detected in clinical care has been one of the more important indicators. With the development of society and technology, real-time, dynamic and continuous monitoring of the respiratory signal will become the future trend of family health. Through research and pilot testing, we decide to use a kind of acoustic signal to characterize breathing signals. This method seems safe, simple and non-invasive compared to other methods, and provides a more flexible way to wear. Relying on the microphone with advanced noise reduction and filtering processing, we can get more accurate and clear identification of the respiratory signal.

After determining to characterize the respiratory signal using acoustic signals, we need to collect the original acoustic signal and process the signal by using pre-emphasis method firstly. Given the MATLAB software owns powerful features in signal processing and acquisition, in this study, we use MATLAB to collect and process breathe signal. In MATLAB software, there are two ways to collect acoustic signals, one of which is the acquisition of analog signals, and the other is using of "audiorecorder" function to achieve signal acquisition. This paper uses the second way, which is using "audiorecorder" function to achieve the acquisition of acoustic signal. We can see the original respiratory signal waveform from Fig. 3 clearly.

The high frequency part of the proportion is small in the collected acoustic signal. The aim of the pre-emphasis is to boost the high frequency part of the process, so that the spectrum of the signal become flat. By means of the filter function in MATLAB, we can directly implement the pre-emphasis of the acoustic signal. As we can see, Fig. 4 shows the Pre-emphasis waveform of the breathing signal.

To be able to see the trends and changes of the respiratory signal waveform, we need to make further processing for the waveform diagram. Short-term energy is an important method for time-domain signal analysis, which can clearly show trends and changes in the amplitude of the waveform. As we can see in Fig. 5, short-term energy diagram shows the time-varying characteristics of the respiratory signal.

On the basis of short-term energy chart, we need to judge the critical point between the exhale signal and the inhale signal. After several tests and debugging, the paper found the demarcation point between exhalation and inhalation signals, and according to this cut-off point made a further clipping processing. Finally, we get a clear exhalation and inhalation waveform shown in Fig. 6.

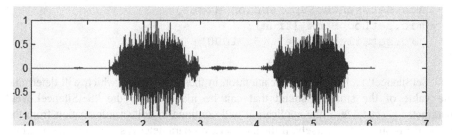

Fig. 4. Original waveform of the breathing signal

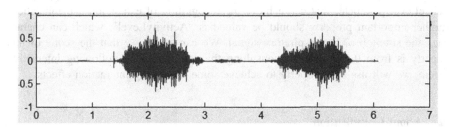

Fig. 5. Pre-emphasis of the breathing signal

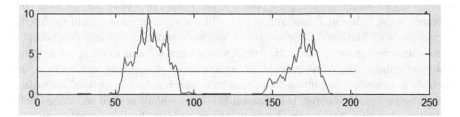

Fig. 6. Short-term energy diagram

3 The Interaction Design of the Breathing Training System

3.1 The Development Principle of the Household Intelligent Breathing Training System

In the above, we have successfully acquired and processed breathing signal by MATLAB software. At the same time, we also verified the feasibility of using acoustic signal to characterize the respiratory signal by MATLAB software. In the following part, we will discuss how to get specific respiratory signal in FLASH actionscript 3.0 Language. Actionscript 3.0 achieved the acquisition of audio signal through a special class called "Microphone". We can get the class of "Microphone" and set up related properties through the following code:

```
Var mic: Microphone = Microphone.getMicrophone ();
mic.gain = 60;
mic.rate = 11;
mic.setUseEchoSuppression (true);
mic.setLoopBack (true);
mic.setSilenceLevel (5, 1000);
```

"SetSilenceLevel" deserves our attention in these properties, which will determine the value of the smallest sound that can be identified. If the "SetSilenceLevel" parameter is set to zero, the application will continue to collect information from the audio microphone. Conversely, if the silenceLevel parameter is set to 100, the program will prevent the microphone's activities. According to the previous method for distinguishing between exhalation and inhalation, we only need to set up an appropriate silenceLevel parameter that can achieve the recognition of exhalation and inhalation. Another important property should be valued is "ActivityLevel", which can characterize the strength of the respiratory signal. We can easily see that the scope of this property is from 0-100 through consulting the manual. In the following interactive system, we will use this property to achieve some interesting interaction effects.

3.2 About Gamification

In order to increase the fun of the interaction system, we introduced the concept of Gamification. Gamification has raised a lot of interest both in industry and also increasingly in academia during the past few years [4]. The word "Gamification" first appeared in the 2010 DICE conference, then with the rapid development of the Internet is gradually well known. A large number of internet companies applying the concept of gamification into practice, made this word become a real solution to the problem from a new vocabulary. The core concept of gamification is applying mechanisms and methods in game to non-gaming areas, thereby enhancing the participants' enthusiasm and participation. Nowadays, gamification has been widely applied to various fields including education, health care, Internet, design, tourism, business management and so on. About the definition of "Gamification", until now, little academic attention has been paid. Sebastian from Hamburg University proposed the following definition: "Gamification" is the use of game design elements in non-game contexts, and then unpacked this definition in his paper [5].

So far, we have a clearer understanding of the concept of the gamification. In the following part, we will introduce some of the commonly used methods in game design, including the rating system, points system, ranking system, and medal system. In addition to the methods of gamification, we should also understand the game mechanics, also known as game elements. The game elements can be classified as self-elements and social-elements. Self-elements consist of points, achievement badges, levels, or simply time restrictions. Social-elements on the other hand are interactive competition or cooperation, like for example leaderboards [6]. In the following inter- active system, we will apply these methods and elements to polish our system.

3.3 System Design

As we talked in the abstract, this system consists of three parts: the first part is the user interface of the breathing-exercise system, the second part is the background database and the last part is the internet community platform. The following sections unpack the system in detail.

User Interface. In this part, what we should consider is how to design appropriate interface and mechanisms to improve the fun and challenge of the system in order to achieve a good training effect. When we design the user interface, we hope to achieve the following three objectives:

1. Interface consistent with user's mental model
2. Breathing training system has instant visual feedback
3. There is a clear distinction between expiratory and inspiratory phase

After several attempts and thinking, we finalized the interactive program shown in Fig. 7. Users can control the target object by the intensity and duration of inhalation and exhalation, enabling interactive process with the respiratory training system.

The system mainly focuses on two parameters which include the breathing depth and the breathing duration. The spacing between the obstacles is used to control a single duration and the height of obstacle will be used to control breathing depth, as we can see in Fig. 8.

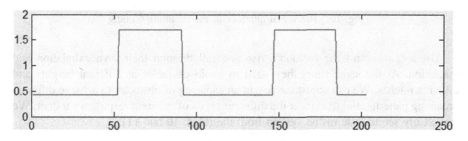

Fig. 7. The waveform after the clipping

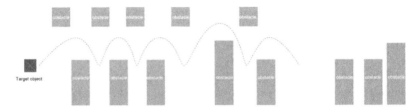

Fig. 8. The layout of the system interface

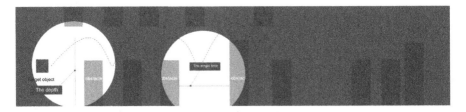

Fig. 9. The breathing depth and breathing duration

On the basis of the interaction design, we established the visual style and interface elements of the respiratory training system. In the terms of overall style, we adopted a flat style, which can reduce people's cognitive load and highlight the core elements. In terms of color, we adopted a light blue background, giving a fresh and invigorating feeling. We made the green balloons become the focus of the whole picture, in order to make the trainers see the feedback of their training results accurately. The specific visual interface is shown in Fig. 9.

Fig. 10. The visual interface of the breathing training

Users can control the balloon's rise and fall through their own exhalation and inhalation. At the same time, they need to avoid obstacles at different heights and different pitches. We can adjust the height and spacing of obstacles to achieve different breathing patterns, and thus meet the different needs of different respiratory trainer. We can clearly see the use of the system from the (Figs. 10 and 11).

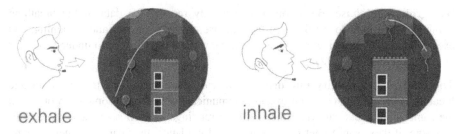

Fig. 11. Using description of the system description

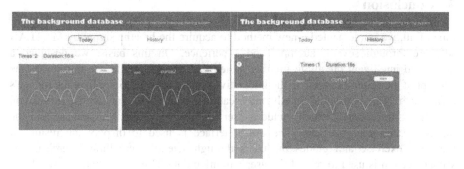

Fig. 12. Background database

Fig. 13. Rankings of the trainer's score in community platform

Background-database. Background data mainly records the data of the breathing training, which include the times of the exercise, the time of continuous training, and exercise duration, etc. In addition, users can view their own history to understand their dynamic exercise (Fig. 12).

The internet community platform. Users can share their own training data and breathing curve in the community and communicate with more people each other. At the same time, users can view the real-time rankings of their score anywhere. Furthermore, if they want to get more professional guidance, they can send their training data to health professionals (Fig. 13).

4 Conclusion

First of all, we implemented a new method to acquire the breathe signal by MATLAB software through several attempts and experience. On this basis, we designed a household intelligent breathing training system. At the same time, we introduced the concept of the "Gamification" in the interactive system in order to improve the trainer's enthusiasm. The household intelligent breathing training system with gamification consists of three parts, which includes user interface, background database and the internet community platform. The user interface is used to display the results of breathing exercise and guides the users through scientific breathing exercise. The second section is used to record the user's training data. Users can share the results of their training to the community platform, or sent to the health professional to get professional guidance through the third part.

Acknowledgments. This work was supported in part by Humanities and Social Sciences Foundation of the Ministry of Education (12YJCZH031).

References

1. Meuret, A.E., Wilhelm, F.H., Ritz, T., et al.: Breathing training for treating panic disorder useful intervention or impediment? Behav. Modif. **27**(5), 731–754 (2003)
2. Lothian, J.A.: Lamaze breathing: what every pregnant woman needs to know. J. Perinat. Educ. **20**(2), 118 (2011)
3. Calabrese, P., Baconnier, P., Laouani, A., et al.: A simple dynamic model of respiratory pump. Acta. Biotheor. **58**(2–3), 265–275 (2010)
4. Huotari, K., Hamari, J.: Defining gamification: a service marketing perspective. In: Proceeding of the 16th International Academic MindTrek Conference, pp. 17–22 (2012)
5. Deterding, S., Dixon, D., Khaled, R., et al.: From game design elements to gamefulness: defining "gamification". In: Proceedings of the 15th International Academic MindTrek Conference: Envisioning Future Media Environments, pp. 9–15 (2011)
6. Soman, D., Huang, W.H.-Y.: A Practitioners Guide to Gamification of Education. Roman School of Management (2013)

Speech Matters – Psychological Aspects of Artificial versus Anthropomorphic System Voices in User-Companion Interaction

Swantje Ferchow[(✉)], Matthias Haase, Julia Krüger, Matthias Vogel,
Mathias Wahl, and Jörg Frommer

Department of Psychosomatic Medicine and Psychotherapy, Medical Faculty,
Otto-von-Guericke University Magdeburg, Magdeburg, Germany
{swantje.ferchow,matthias.haase,julia.krueger,
matthias.vogel,mathias.wahl,
joerg.frommer}@med.ovgu.de

Abstract. The design of this forthcoming study was created to investigate the influences of different system-voices on users while they interact with a simulated Companion-system. By using a Wizard of Oz experiment, we want to find out what kind of voice output (artificial vs. anthropomorphic) is better suited for keeping up users' cooperation with a system while solving a task. The goal of this study is to gain a deeper understanding of influences of the speech-output in User-Companion Interaction. Users' perceived trustworthiness towards the system, their experienced affective states and individual user characteristics as important mediators are the main focus of the present study.

Keywords: Companion-system · Wizard of Oz experiment · System voice · Anthropomorphism · User characteristics

1 Introduction

For speech-based dialog systems without visual representation, the system's voice is the only feature a user can relate to. Therefore, it has to be perceived as trustworthy and empathic. This especially applies to Companion-systems, which are "cognitive technical systems with their functionality completely individually adapted to each user [...which] interact with [him/her] as competent and cooperative service partners" [1]. Companion-systems should be able to support every user in different situations and in all kinds of emotional states – positive as well as negative [1].

In general, anthropomorphic and/or naturally sounding voices are used in most areas of Human-Computer Interaction (HCI), like navigation systems, smart home environments or voice user interfaces (VUIs) in smartphones [2]. There is indeed evidence for the human tendency to use schemes from human-human interaction for the communication with computer systems or virtual agents, regardless of the level of anthropomorphism of their voice [3]. However, empirical findings, which support the hypothesis that human-like, anthropomorphic voices most likely support human-computer cooperation as well as users' perceived trust, are rare in comparison to

© Springer International Publishing Switzerland 2016
A. Marcus (Ed.): DUXU 2016, Part III, LNCS 9748, pp. 319–327, 2016.
DOI: 10.1007/978-3-319-40406-6_30

artificial voices [4]. In order to provide a deeper comprehension of users' individual experiences with different kinds of voices, an established experimental design [5] was adapted with the focus on users' subjective perceptions of two diverse voices in a task-related dialog with a simulated Companion-system.

2 Background

During the past decades, the recognition of the importance of users' emotions increased significantly in the field of HCI, which lead to the emergence of the research area of Affective Computing [6]. Up to now, it hardly seems imaginable to do research without the consideration of users' affective states, especially as far as User-Companion Interaction (UCI) is concerned [7]. Actual user affect influences most factors of users' perception of and experience with systems, e.g. performance, cognition, concentration, or memory [8]. Therefore, systems must be able to avoid negative affective states for creating and perpetuating cooperation as well as trust. For this current research, this shall be realized by the voice solely.

The question arose if the variation of the speech-output at all is able to fulfill this requirement. To answer this, several studies which investigated the impact of systems' voices on users' perception and user behavior were surveyed. Here, important effects were detected regarding system voices and their influences on users. The variation of the voices' gender, speed, volume, manner etc. e.g. [9–11] has different impacts. For example, a female voice helps to communicate emotional content, whereas male voices tend to sound competent and convey task-related information [9]. The manner can help to increase interaction success, e.g. when motivational feedback is provided [10, 11]. In comparison of a human-sounding voice with a computerized one, users significantly prefer the human-sounding voice; even learn faster while solving a task [10]. These findings prove that a system voice indeed is able to affect the interaction. Furthermore, users' personality characteristics strongly influence the perception of speed and volume of system voices. For example, introvert users prefer low speed and volume; extrovert users sympathize with louder and even exaggerated tones [12]. Therefore, user characteristics also have be taken into account when examining the effect of different voices on users.

Before an explanation of the intended research goal, it still needs to be clarified when an interaction between a Companion-system and a user can be labeled as successful. For this purpose, Frommer et al. [13] developed a Wizard of Oz (WOz) experiment where users had to interact with a simulated Companion-system (description follows below) while solving a task. An artificial, computerized voice was chosen for guiding users through this experiment. During the interaction, challenges occurred at specific stages, which demanded the adaption of current task-solving strategies from the users [5].

Quantitative as well as qualitative methods were used to analyze users' perceptions, their interaction behavior as well as user characteristics. This research process established the basis for the forthcoming study introduced here. Individual user characteristics (e.g. personality traits, socio-biographic variables or technical experience) influence actual user behavior directly and have to be taken into account while analyzing data of users of technical devices [14]. User characteristics were shown to influence users' (task-)performance, especially during situations that were perceived as challenging. Participants with greater performance "were younger, more experienced with computers, showed lower amounts of neuroticism and higher amounts of agreeableness (NEO-FFI) on average." [15]. Furthermore, the analysis of semi-structured interview material showed the importance of the subjective experience of users while interacting with the artificial speech-based system. It became obvious that users tended to anthropomorphize the system, even if it's just a voice and a screen [16]. But this is not necessarily linked to comfortable feelings in the interaction. In fact, the artificial voice is associated with feelings like anxiety or scariness and with the tendency to distance from the system by reducing initiative. Hence, wishes for a change of the artificial voice into a more human-like one occurred, maybe as a result of imagining a deeper and more trustworthy relationship including a more comfortable interaction atmosphere with such a system voice [16, 17]. Furthermore, participants used more negative attributes for the description of the voice than neutral or positive attributes [18].

To deal with these findings, the aforementioned experiment was modified and the application of two different voices was chosen: an anthropomorphic voice compared with an artificial one. The psychological research goal is to find out which effects the voice has on users' perception of its support while solving the task. This study shall also evaluate which kind of voice is most likely to evoke positive affect and greater perceived trust in users. Furthermore, we want to survey the influence of user characteristics on the voice preference.

3 Methods

The aforementioned WOz experiment represents a suitable approach for our research. Before we explicate the modifications and hypotheses, we will give a short description of this experiment and the LAST MINUTE corpus, which is the result of previous research.

3.1 Wizard of Oz Experiment LAST MINUTE

The WOz experiment and the resulting LAST MINUTE corpus were developed as a research tool to investigate subjects during an interaction with a speech-based interactive dialog system, including a problem-solving task with planning, re-planning and strategy change [15]. All tasks had to be solved by users with the help of a solely speech-controlled computer system. In accordance with the central design feature of WOz experiments, this system was controlled by hidden human operators. The subjects believed they communicate with an autonomous computer-system. A male sounding, clearly computerized voice (MARY TTS, mary.dfki.de) was chosen to reinforce the feeling of interacting with a computer system [5].

According to Frommer et al. [13] as well as Rösner et al. [5], the experiment was executed as described in the following: At first, the system introduced itself and asked some personal questions, the so called personalization module. The system explained users that this information is needed for individual adaptation. After that, the actual last minute module [5] began with the explanation of the task. Subjects had to pack a suitcase for a suggested summer vacation for fourteen days in a predefined time. They were informed that detailed weather information will be gathered and provided later. Participants could choose items out of twelve categories (e.g. tops, shoes, accessories), which were presented in a predefined order on a screen in front of them. This stage is called "baseline" (BSL). Within the interaction course, particular restrictions, namely challenges, occur. The first of these challenges is called "weight limit barrier" (WLB). Here, users were informed that their suitcase is confined by the airlines' weight limit. New items could be added only when others were unpacked before. As a result, participants had to adapt to this unexpected condition and to cope with their possibly emerging stress. After they passed more than half of all categories the final information regarding the destination was revealed. The vacation resort was located in the southern hemisphere where the seasons are switched. Now, subjects had to pack for cold climate, which means they had to change their strategy. This challenge is called "weather information barrier" (WIB). Apart from time and weight restrictions, this rendered the packing process even more complicated. In this situation, about half of participants got an empathic intervention inviting them to express their actual feelings. The remaining time could be used for correction, and is called "revision stage" (RES). In the end, participants had the chance to explicate how satisfied they were with the content of their suitcase [5, 13].

3.2   Modification of the Wizard of Oz Experiment LAST MINUTE

For the purpose of our prospective research we modified the established WOz experiment to focus on users' perceptions of the system voice. Particular attention is paid to users' individual ratings of the system and its voice as well as possible changes in users' affective states during the course of interaction.

With respect to prior results, we modified the personalization module to avoid primary uncertainty regarding the system and the interaction [16] and to strengthen the sympathy of users towards the system in the beginning. The intervention was removed because of its indistinct effects [19].

There will be two experimental groups: One half of the participants will interact with the artificial voice which was already used in the prior experiments; the other half will interact with an anthropomorphic voice (IVONA TTS, www.ivona.com). We paid attention to use male voices to avoid the aforementioned gender effects. The setting stays equal for both groups. We expanded the experiment with two rating phases to gather information of actual user conditions and to detect significant changes during the interaction. Altogether, we survey users' conditions and perceptions in three particular experimental phases as described below (also Fig. 1).

The first rating occurs before the start of the experiment. Here, we survey general information about the user, like socio-biographic variables and experience with technical devices. Furthermore, we measure users' task-related motivation (Achievement Motives Scale, AMS) [20] and their actual affective state (Positive and Negative Affect Schedule, PANAS) [21]. This rating phase represents the *Baseline* (see Fig. 1) for further points of measurement. The actual experiment begins after this phase.

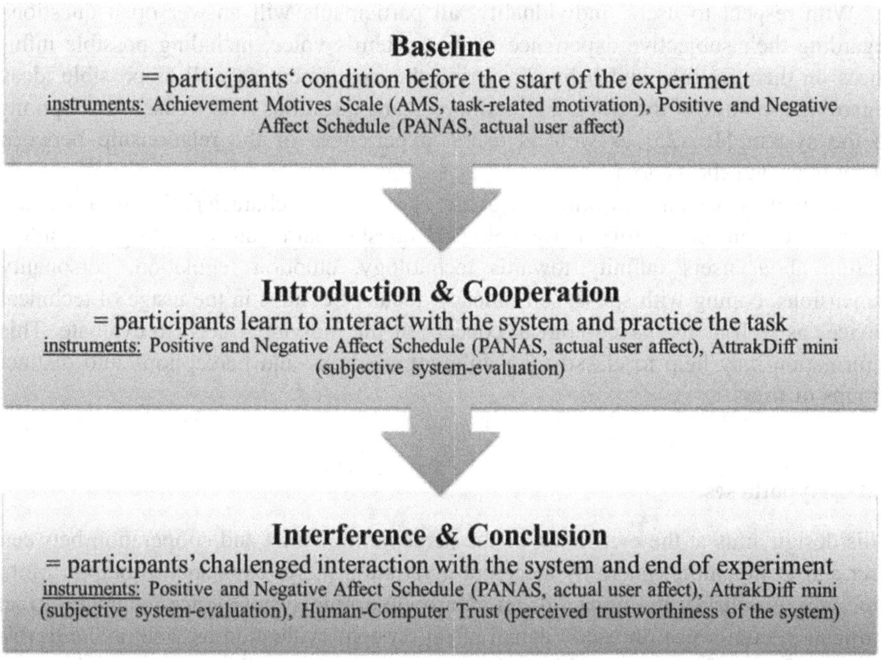

Baseline

= participants' condition before the start of the experiment

instruments: Achievement Motives Scale (AMS, task-related motivation), Positive and Negative Affect Schedule (PANAS, actual user affect)

Introduction & Cooperation

= participants learn to interact with the system and practice the task

instruments: Positive and Negative Affect Schedule (PANAS, actual user affect), AttrakDiff mini (subjective system-evaluation)

Interference & Conclusion

= participants' challenged interaction with the system and end of experiment

instruments: Positive and Negative Affect Schedule (PANAS, actual user affect), AttrakDiff mini (subjective system-evaluation), Human-Computer Trust (perceived trustworthiness of the system)

Fig. 1. The three rating phases during the modified WOz experiment

Participants pass through the personalization module to get to know the system (*Introduction*), and immediately start with the last minute module. Here, users are enabled to practice the task while packing the first three categories (tops, jackets & coats, trousers & skirts) (*Cooperation*). After finishing the third category, the second system rating occurs. Here, we measure the actual affective state (PANAS) again and also the subjective system-evaluation by using a shortened version of the AttrakDiff (AttrakDiff mini) [22], which quantifies hedonic and pragmatic product quality. This rating happens aside the experimental screen, which ensures objective appraisal by participants without the effect of politeness towards the system [23]. After that, the last minute module continues. During this last phase, participants have to face all challenges (WLB, WIB and RES, see Sect. 3.1) (*Interference*) and to finish the task (*Conclusion*). The third and last rating occurs after the system-initiated goodbye. The applied questionnaires gather information about users' present affective state (PANAS), final subjective system-evaluation (AttrakDiff mini) and the perceived trustworthiness of the system (Human-Computer Trust) [24].

Therefore, we have three particular rating phases during the experiment: the Baseline, the Introduction & Cooperation as well as the Interference & Conclusion (as shown in Fig. 1). By doing so, we want to evaluate possible changes in users' emotional states during these phases. Furthermore, we want to survey differences in the subjective system-rating and perceived trustworthiness of both groups. A comparison of all ratings between the experimental groups may offer a profound basis for reaching the intended research goals.

With respect to users' individuality, all participants will answer open questions regarding their subjective experience of the system's voice, including possible influences on their feelings and behavior during the experiment as well as possible ideas regarding a change of the voice. Furthermore, some questions refer to users' ascriptions to the system [16, 25] as well as users' experiences of the relationship between themselves and the system.

We will also gather information about specific user characteristics in a second, separate session. Standardized psychological questionnaires are used to gather information about users' affinity towards technology, emotion regulation, personality dimensions, coping with stress, self-efficacy, locus of control in the usage of technical devices as well as the psychological concept of the individual need to evaluate. This information may help to classify the different reactions and perceptions into distinct groups of users.

3.3   Hypotheses

This design aims at the evaluation of the perception of trust and cooperation between user and Companion-system by means of a variation in system's speech-output. More precisely, we survey the impact of an anthropomorphic system-voice compared to an artificial system-voice on users' actual affect, system evaluation as well as the development of trust. Furthermore, this design serves to detect possible correlations between the perception of the system voice and specific user characteristics, e.g. gender, personality dimensions or affinity towards technology.

With regard to the previous explanations, we suppose that the anthropomorphic voice has a more positive influence during the interaction with the simulated Companion-system, compared to the artificial voice. The anthropomorphic voice may increase users' perceived trustworthiness. Furthermore, the possibly cooperative relationship between user and simulated Companion-system will be influenced during the phase of Interference & Conclusion to an unacquainted extent.

Hence, several hypotheses were formulated:

1. Regarding the phase of Introduction & Cooperation, we expect more positive affect (PANAS) and a higher system rating (AttrakDiff mini) of those users who interact with the anthropomorphic voice in comparison to the other group.
2. Both experimental groups have to face the barriers during the phase of Interference & Conclusion and will show lower system-rating (AttrakDiff mini), compared to the phase of Introduction & Cooperation.

Especially the change between cooperative interaction (second rating phase) to possibly interfered (or even failed) interaction (third rating phase) seems interesting. But here, we can just formulate explorative questions:

3. Will significant differences occur between the two groups regarding their perceived trustworthiness and subjective system-evaluation for the third rating phase?
4. Will significant differences occur between the two groups regarding users' affective state for the second and third rating phase?

5. Are there significant influences of user characteristics on the following goal criteria: perceived trustworthiness, subjective system-evaluation and users' emotional state?

The human-like voice may rather evoke the assumption of competence in users which possibly can or cannot be satisfied during the interaction. Trust issues and higher levels of negative affect may be the result. As mentioned before, the perception of system-voices is strongly influenced by user characteristics. Even if we suppose that the anthropomorphic voice may evoke more positive affect in general, individual preferences and perceptions have to be taken into account, too. Therefore, it seems possible for some users that they perceive the artificial voice as less competent, and thus may more likely forgive mistakes.

Besides these assumptions, the design of the study shall help to get a profound understanding of the effects of several user characteristics (e.g. personality dimensions, coping with stress, motivation, self-efficacy) on the preference of a specific system voice.

4 Outlook

The experiment takes place in a research lab of the Otto von Guericke University Magdeburg. A small sample of six participants already passed a test phase. The first (not systematically analyzed) results show that they indeed experience different, albeit marginal affective states during the interaction. Of course, we will need a greater sample size to support our hypotheses. We plan experimental group sizes of about 30 participants for statistical evaluation of all measurements. In order to reduce influences based on participants' age or gender, both experimental groups will be homogeneous regarding these characteristics (only students aged 18 to 28, gender balanced).

The inclusion of actual affective user states and a profound understanding of users' subjective perceptions of UCI are required for the development of Companion-systems, which shall be experienced as supportive, empathic and trustworthy partners by their individual users.

Acknowledgements. The presented study is performed in the framework of the Transregional Collaborative Research Centre SFB/TRR 62 "A Companion-Technology for Cognitive Technical Systems" funded by the German Research Foundation (DFG). The responsibility for the content of this paper lies with the authors. We are grateful for cooperation in this study regarding technical implementation, modification and computer science aspects to the research group of Dietmar Rösner, including Rico Andrich and Rafael Friesen. Furthermore, we want to thank Ralph Heinemann and Michael Tornow for the additional assistance regarding technical implementation of the experimental setting.

References

1. Wendemuth, A., Biundo, S.: A companion technology for cognitive technical systems. In: Esposito, A., Esposito, A.M., Vinciarelli, A., Hoffmann, R., Müller, V.C. (eds.) COST 2102. LNCS, vol. 7403, pp. 89–103. Springer, Heidelberg (2012)

2. Karitnig, A.: Analyse von künstlichen und natürlichen Sprachausgabesystemen im Smart-Home-Bereich. In: Hitz, M. Leitner, G., Kruschitz, C. (eds.) HASE 2010 – HCI Aspects of Smart Environments, pp. 29–38. Klagenfurt (2010). http://www.uni-klu.ac.at/tewi/downloads/HASE10_Conference_Proceedings.pdf

3. Suzuki, N., Katagiri, Y.: Prosodic alignment in human-computer-interaction. Connect. Sci. 19(2), 131–141 (2003)

4. Waytz, A., Heafner, J., Epley, N.: The mind in the machine: anthropomorphism increases trust in an autonomous vehicle. J. Exp. Soc. Psychol. 52, 113–117 (2014)

5. Rösner, D., Frommer, J., Friesen, R., Haase, M., Lange, J., Otto, M.: LAST MINUTE: a multimodal corpus of speech-based user-companion interactions. In: Calzolari, N. (Chair), Choukri, K., Declerck, T., Doğan, M.U., Maegaard, B., Mariani, J., Moreno, A., Odijk, J., Piperidis, S. (eds.) Proceedings of the Eight International Conference on Language Resources and Evaluation (LREC 2012), p. 96. European Language Resources Association (ELRA), Istanbul, Turkey (2012)

6. Picard, R.W.: Affective Computing. MIT Press, Cambridge (1997)

7. Wolff, S., Kohrs, C., Scheich, H., Brechmann, A.: Temporal contingency and prosodic modulation of feedback in human-computer interaction: effects on brain activation and performance in cognitive tasks. In: Heiß, H.-U., Pepper, P., Schlingloff, H., Schneider, J. (eds.) Informatik 2011, Berlin, GI-Edition. LNI, vol. 192, p. 238. Koellen, Bonn (2011)

8. Hudlicka, E.: To feel or not to feel: the role of affect in human-computer interaction. Int. J. Hum Comput Stud. 59, 1–32 (2003)

9. Nass, C., Moon, Y.: Machine and mindlessness: social responses to computers. J. Soc. Issues 56(1), 81–103 (2000)

10. Wolff, S., Brechmann, A.: Carrot and stick 2.0: the benefits of natural and motivational prosody in computer-assisted learning. Comput. Hum. Behav. 43, 76–84 (2015)

11. Partala, T., Surakka, V.: The effects of affective interventions in human-computer interaction. Interact. Comput. 16, 295–309 (2004)

12. Nass, C., Lee, K.M.: Does computer-synthesized speech manifest personality? Experimental tests of recognition, similarity-attraction, and consistency-attraction. J. Exp. Psychol. 7(3), 171–181 (2001)

13. Frommer, J., Rösner, D., Haase, M., Lange, J., Friesen, R., Otto, M.: Project A3 prevention of negative courses of dialogues: wizard of Oz experiment operator's manual. Working Paper of the Collaborative Research Project/Transregio 62 "A Companion Technology for Cognitive Technical Systems". Pabst Science Publication, Lengerich (2012)

14. Haase, M., Lange, J., Frommer, J.: Eigenschaften von Nutzern in der Mensch-Computer-Interaktion. In: Peters, S. (ed.) Die Technisierung des Menschlichen und die Humanisierung der Maschine: Interdisziplinäre Beiträge zur Interdependenz von Mensch und Technik. Mitteldeutscher Verlag, Halle (Saale) (2015)

15. Rösner, D., Haase, M., Bauer, T., Günther, S., Krüger, J., Frommer, J.: Desiderata for the design of companion systems. KI - Künstliche Intelligenz 30(1), 53–61 (2016)

16. Krüger, J., Wahl, M., Frommer, J.: making the system a relational partner: users' ascriptions in individualization-focused interactions with companion-systems. In: Berntzen, L., Böhm, S. (eds.) Proceedings of the Eighth International Conference on Advances in Human Oriented and Personalized Mechanisms, Technologies, and Services (CENTRIC 2015), pp. 47–53. IARIA (2015). http://www.iaria.org/conferences2015/CfPCENTRIC15.pdf

17. Frommer, J., Rösner, D., Andrich, R., Friesen, R., Günther, S., Haase, M., Krüger, J.: LAST MINUTE: an empirical experiment in user companion interaction and its evaluation. In: Companion-Technology: A Paradigm Shift in Human-Technology Interaction. Springer, Heidelberg (in press)

18. Lexow, A., Andrich, R., Rösner, D.: LAST MINUTE: User perception of the computer voice. In: Biundo-Stephan, S., Rukzio, E., Wendemuth, A. (eds.) Proceedings of the 1st International Symposium on Companion-Technology (ISCT 2015), Ulm, pp. 137–142 (2015). http://vts.uni-ulm.de/doc.asp?id=9771

19. Wahl, M., Krüger, J., Frommer, J.: From anger to relief: five ideal types of users experiencing an affective intervention in HCI. In: Berntzen, L., Böhm, S. (eds.) Proceedings of the Eighth International Conference on Advances in Human Oriented and Personalized Mechanisms, Technologies, and Services (CENTRIC 2015), pp. 55–61. IARIA (2015). http://www.iaria.org/conferences2015/CfPCENTRIC15.pdf

20. Lang, J.W.B., Fries, S.: A revised 10-item version of the achievement motives scale: psychometric properties in German-speaking samples. Eur. J. Psychol. Assess. **22**(3), 216–224 (2006)

21. Krohne, H.W., Egloff, B., Kohlmann, C.-W., Tausch, A.: Untersuchungen mit einer deutschen Version der "Positive and Negative Affect Schedule" (PANAS). Diagnostica **42**, 139–156 (1996)

22. Hassenzahl, M., Burmester, M., Koller, F.: AttrakDiff: Ein Fragebogen zur Messung wahrgenommener hedonischer und pragmatischer Qualität. In: Szwillus, G., Ziegler, J. (Hgg.) Mensch & Computer 2003 (Berichte des German Chapter of the ACM), Bd. 57, S. 187–196. Vieweg + Teubner Verlag, Wiesbaden (2003)

23. Reeves, B., Nass, C.: The Media Equation: How People Treat Computers, Television, and New Media Like Real People and Places. Cambridge University Press/CSLI, New York (1996)

24. Madsen, M., Gregor, S.: Measuring human-computer trust. In: Gable, G., Vitale, M. (eds.) 11th Australasian Conference on Information Systems, vol. 53, pp. 6–8 (2000)

25. Krüger, J., Wahl, M., Frommer, J.: Users' relational ascriptions in user-companion interaction. In: 18th International Conference on Human-Computer Interaction, 17–22 July, Toronto, Canada. LNCS. Springer, Heidelberg (accepted)

Expression of Emotions by a Service Robot: A Pilot Study

Angela Giambattista[1], Luís Teixeira[2], Hande Ayanoğlu[2(✉)],
Magda Saraiva[2], and Emília Duarte[2]

[1] DICDEA Department, Second University of Naples, via Roma 29,
81031 Aversa, Italy
angela.giambattista@unina2.it
[2] UNIDCOM, IADE – Creative University, Av. D. Carlos I, 4,
1200-649 Lisbon, Portugal
lmteixeira@fmh.ulisboa.pt, {hande.ayanoglu,
emilia.duarte}@iade.pt, magda.saraiva@gmail.com

Abstract. A successful Human-Robot Interaction (HRI) depends on the empathy that the robot has the capability of instantiating on the user, namely through the expression of emotions. In this pilot study, we examined the recognition of emotions being expressed by a service robot in a virtual environment (VE), by university students. The VE was a corridor, neutral in terms of context of use. The robot's facial expressions, body movements, and displacement were manipulated to express eight basic emotions. Results showed that participants had difficulties in recognizing the emotions (33% of success). Also, results suggested that the participants established empathy with the robot. Further work is needed to improve the emotional expression of this robot, which aims to interact with hospitalized children.

Keywords: Human robot interaction · Emotional design · User experience · Healthcare · Service robot

1 Introduction

The robotics field, initially, had as main objective the production of industrial robots that are able to replace humans in the most routine and dangerous tasks [1]. However, recently, it is possible to witness a paradigm shift with the appearance of service robots [2–5]. Service robots are intelligent artificial partners that interact with humans to promote social and intellectual benefits. In this sense, today, the disciplines such as robotics, computer science, and design, among others are focusing on Human-Robot Interaction (HRI) [6]. This type of robots is mainly intended to interact, accompany and help humans while they perform their work and daily tasks [1]. In order to interact with humans, robots should have characteristics that make for an effective and fluent interaction. However, to interact with a robot is significantly different than interacting with another human, even when sharing the same capacities and communication skills, either verbal (e.g., speech) or nonverbal (e.g., facial expressions). It is known, through studies in Psychology and Sociology, that emotions play a fundamental role in the

A. Marcus (Ed.): DUXU 2016, Part III, LNCS 9748, pp. 328–336, 2016.
DOI: 10.1007/978-3-319-40406-6_31

individual's behavior regulation in social contexts [7]. Emotions are what allow the human initiate, maintain, and/or terminate, a relationship or interaction with the environment and with other humans [8].

In the design field, the importance of emotions in the idealization of objects and products, in addition to the components of usability, are also recognized. In this context Emotional Design [9] emerges, based on the premise that products and objects that are able to elicit emotions in the user (positive emotions, preferably), allow a greater and better human-product interaction.

Taking into account the fundamental role that emotions play in human interaction processes, it is believed that a service robot must involve artificial intelligence with emotions [10]. HRI is only effective if the robot is able to express emotions [11]. Robots must be able to recognize emotions expressed by humans and respond accordingly, including those that are empathic responses. In other words, this inter-action should be as similar as possible to the interaction between humans, but it must be taken into account that, despite it being possible for robots to recognize the emo-tional states of humans and respond in accordance with them, this does not occur in the same way as the interaction between humans. This is because robots are unable to attribute cognitive meaning to an experience or situation as humans can do [12].

However, humans do not interact only based on emotions. Humans also interact through facial expressions, speech, body movements, among others [13]. It is in this context that humanoid robots appear. Human-like bodies of humanoid robots enable humans to intuitively understand their gestures and cause people to unconsciously behave as if they were communicating with humans, that is, if a humanoid robot effectively uses its body, people will communicate naturally with it [14].

In this context, it is important to understand the essential features that are inherent to a successful HRI and, therefore, provide fundamental guidelines for the design of robots (i.e., service robots).

This paper presents a pilot study on the emotional design of a service robot being used in healthcare contexts for children [15]. The main purpose was to define how the robot would express eight emotions (i.e., joy, trust, fear, surprise, sadness, disgust, anger, and anticipation) by using components such as facial expressions (e.g., eyes, mouth), body movements (e.g., head, arms) and displacement (e.g., back and forward, turns, sideways). Recommendations regarding the design of this type of robot are practically non-existent; consequently, this study seeks to complete/enhance this important gap and contributes to this expanding area of research. The use and the creation of a functional robot involve various costs, including time and economic ones. However, these costs may be reduced through the use of Virtual Environments (VEs). Virtual Reality has important advantages, as a research tool, such as the opportunity to conduct a myriad of evaluations without a physical fully functional prototype, the high replicability of the experiments, and the easy manipulation of the robot's design variables (e.g., facial expressions), with good internal, external and ecological validi-ties. Moreover, the use of VEs for the evaluation of user experience is still largely unexplored.

2 Method

The method is divided into three stages: Definition; Design; and Test, as described next.

2.1 Stage 1 - Definition

At the outset of the study, this stage was conducted aiming to define a specific combination of components (i.e., facial expressions, body movements and displacement) that would represent a given emotion for which the robot's expressions could be created.

Participants. Ten undergraduate Design students participated, aged between 19 and 21 ($M = 19.40$; $SD = 0.66$) years old, equally distributed by gender.

Stimuli and apparatus. Eight target emotions; i.e., joy, trust, fear, surprise, sadness, disgust, anger, and anticipation were selected, gathered from Plutchik's theory [16]. The procedure took place in a photography studio of IADE's Media Lab in which a video camera was used for the data collection. A squared area of 2 by 2 meters was marked in the studio's floor, inside which the participants should perform. To better simulate the robot's behavior, two arms made of cardboard were attached to the arms of the participants.

Procedure. Upon arrival, participants received a brief explanation about the purpose of the study and an informed consent was obtained. After dressed with the cardboard arms, they were given instructions to follow and were requested to perform each one of the emotions. It was stressed that they should mimic a robot, as such, their movements should be, to some extent, constrained; e.g., they could move their arms only up and down, walk forward backward and move sideways, rotate their head and body to the left and right, but they could not bend their body. All participants were requested to perform a training session. After they declared that they were able to perform the procedure as requested, the experimental session began. Following the training, participants were requested to perform the emotions that were printed in a sheet of paper. The order of presentation of the emotions was randomized. After the participant had finished the performance of each emotion, the researcher asked him/her about dubious facial expressions or movements. The experimental session ended after the 8 emotions were performed.

Results. Two independent researchers analyzed all the recorded videos in an attempt to identify the characteristics that, according to the participants, would express better each emotion. Special attention was given to the facial expression (eyes and mouth), arms and body movement (up and down; forward or backward). The researchers, working individually, filled a table identifying the features for each emotion. At the end of this process, the two observations were compared and all discrepancies were resolved with the help of the research team. The results were implemented to the robot as shown in the Fig. 1.

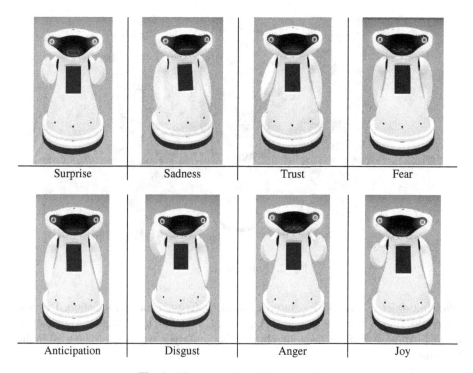

Surprise	Sadness	Trust	Fear

Anticipation	Disgust	Anger	Joy

Fig. 1. The expression of the 8 emotions

2.2 Stage 2 - Design

This stage aimed to program the virtual robot prototype to express the 8 emotions, based on the features defined in the previous step. For that, a Virtual Environment (VE) was created which was contextual neutral, approximately 5 m long. The robot was placed inside the VE (see Fig. 2). Both the robot and the VE were created using Rhinoceros and then exported to Unity 3D.

For the Testing stage, the scene was envisioned as follows: The robot started approaching through the end of the corridor. In the beginning, the robot would move to be closer to the participants while remaining completely on the screen (i.e., approximately 2.3 m away from the participants). During this movement, the robot was exhibiting a Neutral emotion (i.e., arms rested, mouth was a single line and the eyes were lit but without any level of glow), so that the participants become accustomed to the VE. Afterwards, the robot would perform the first emotion (each emotion was displayed for 10 s), and at the end of each the participants had to match the emotion displayed with one in a list of 16 possibilities. The emotions displayed by the robot were changed by a keypress, by the researcher. Between each presented emotion, the robot would return to its position in front of the participants and remained turned off (i.e., arms rested, eyes and mouth turned off) until the researcher would activate the next emotion. So as not to create an order effect of the emotions presentation, two randomized sequences were created, where the emotions were presented in the

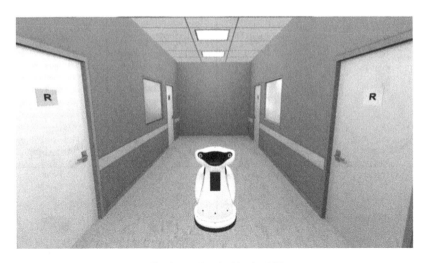

Fig. 2. Robot inside the VE

following order: Sequence 1 - Surprise, Sadness, Trust, Fear, Anticipation, Disgust, Anger, Joy; Sequence 2 - Sadness, Fear, Trust, Joy, Surprise, Anger, Anticipation, Disgust. At the end of this task, the virtual robot prototype was ready to be used in the Test stage.

2.3 Stage 3 - Test

This stage aimed to test the extent to which the robot was able to display the intended emotion in a way that was correctly identified by the participants. To do so, participants were requested to watch the robot performing and identify the emotion being acted.

Participants. 13 participants volunteered in this experiment. 7 were female (53.8%) and 6 males (46.2%) aged between 19 and 37 ($M = 24.6$; $SD = 5.02$) years old.

Materials and design. The experiment was conducted using a 3D projection-based virtual reality system, with a 1280×720 pixels resolution at 120 Hz. Participants sat 100 cm away from the wall screen and wore 3D shutter glasses. The experiment took place in a darkened room to prevent outside distractions. The stimuli were the 8 emotions expressed by the robot in the VE, as described before.

A questionnaire based on Lakatos et al. [17] was administered divided in three parts: (1) Before the interaction with the robot; (2) During the interaction; and (3) After the interaction. **Part 1** begins with demographic questions (e.g., age, degree). Afterwards, a brief definition about service robots was given and it was asked if the participant had previous contact with a service robot (if yes, the participant must indicate the context) and if the participant had a service robot. A *Technological Attitude Scale,* consisting of 9 affirmations followed, aiming to understand the participant's relationship with technology. A five-point Likert scale (1 - I Strongly Disagree; 2 - I Disagree; 3 - Undecided; 4 - I Agree, 5 - I Strongly Agree) was employed. Then, to assess the participants' opinion about robots the *Perception Scale about Robots* was applied, which is based on the Negative Attitudes Toward Robots Scale [18]. This questionnaire had 12 items and the same scale used as previous. **Part 2** was presented during the interaction with the robot and aimed to assess the participants' ability to identify the emotion being expressed by the robot. The participants should select either one emotion from a list of sixteen emotions (8 emotions under study plus 8 distracting emotions - Anxiety, Irritation, Shame, Contempt, Guilt, Pleasure, Despair, Proud), or the option "none of the above emotions is correct". The participants did this matching for every emotion expressed. After the interaction with the robot, **Part 3** of the questionnaire was presented. This part aimed to understand the participants' perception of the virtual prototype of the robot. In this sense, three questions were asked to the participants, using the same Likert scale mentioned above: 1. I would feel comfortable if I had to interact with this robot; 2. I did not like having this robot in my house; 3. I would not feel sorry if I had to destroy this robot. Finally, participants were also asked about the perceived robot's gender and about what function they think that the robot can perform.

Procedure. Participants performed the experiment at IADE-UX.Lab. Upon arrival, participants read the informed consent form containing brief information about the objectives of the study, and were warned for the possibility of slight negative effects due to the use of 3D glasses (e.g., nausea). Once informed consent was acquired, participants answered the Part 1 of the questionnaire. Then they were asked to watch the robot's performance, while wearing the 3D glasses, and reply to the Part 2 of the questionnaire. After they did so for the 8 emotions, they responded to the Part 3 of the questionnaire. The total duration of the procedure was of about 15 min. At the end of the experiment participants were thanked, debriefed and dismissed.

3 Results and Discussion

The small number of participants did not allow to conduct quantitative analyzes of the data, by which a qualitative analysis is presented.

With regard to Part 1 of the questionnaire, it was found that only 3 participants had been in contact with a service robot in past. Regarding the Technological Attitude Scale, it is of note that, on average, participants considered their technological knowledge as good, enjoying exploring new technological devices. Moreover, participants revealed that they are afraid that robots are used for bad purposes, and they are afraid that in the future the robots might dominate society. It notes also that the participants would like to have a service robot in their homes, and they think that the service robots are useful. These results suggest that participants have a positive attitude towards technology and service robots.

The most important data from this pilot study is related with the ability to correctly recognize the emotion being expressed by the robot (Part 2 of the questionnaire). Table 1 shows the associations between the displayed emotions and the listed emotions.

Table 1. Associations between the displayed emotions and the listed emotions

	1	2	3	4	5	6	7	8	9	10	11	12	13	14	15	16	17
1	7			4											2		
2		6		2							4						1
3			2		2			6	1				1				1
4				3		3			3	1				1			2
5				6				1					1	1		1	3
6				2		1			2	2			1		1		4
7			1	1					5	3					3		
8								9						3		1	

Note. Basic emotions (1 – Surprise; 2 – Sadness; 3 – Trust; 4 – Fear; 5 – Anticipation; 6 – Disgust; 7 – Anger; 8 – Joy); Distractive emotions (9 – Anxiety; 10 – Irritation; 11 – Shame; 12 – Contempt; 13 – Guilt; 14 – Pleasure; 15 – Despair; 16 – Proud); 17 – None.

Results revealed that participants had some difficulty in recognizing the emotions expressed by the robot, since the emotions are only correctly recognized in 33% of cases. However, while looking at the recognition for each of emotions separately, it is possible to understand that two of the emotions are correctly recognized by more than 50% of the participants: joy (56%) and surprise (54%). Also anticipation and sadness were recognized correctly in 46% of the cases. On the other hand, the other emotions attain a low percentage of correct recognition: fear (23%), trust (15%), disgust (8%) and anger (0%). It should be noted that the participants could choose an emotion from 16 possible (8 target emotions, and 8 distracting emotions).

The trust emotion was wrongly identified by 46% as joy. One possible explanation for the poorly identified emotions can be the limitation of the robot's mouth design, e.g., displaying a smile can be easily confused with a state of contentment/happiness. Furthermore, it is also highlighted the fact that trust is not an emotion that is considered by many authors as a basic emotion e.g., [19], and this may explain the difficulty of recognizing it. Disgust was identified as anxiety, shame or fear in 46% of the cases, or selected as not corresponding to any emotion of the list (31%). This may be due to the fact that for this emotion, the robot raises one arm at the face level and this movement can be interpreted as hiding the face as a sign of shame or fear. Moreover, a large number of the participants were not able to identify disgust emotion. This demonstrates the need to reprogram this emotion. With regard to anger, it was 61% of the time confused with anxiety or irritation. This is because, and according to the participants' feedback, the arms movements of the robot (up and down relatively quickly), gives the idea of anxiety and impatience. Furthermore, participants showed some difficulty in distinguishing anger and irritation, this could be due to the fact that in Portuguese language they are very similar concepts. However, despite the low level of correct recognition, there is a tendency that negative emotions are recognized as negative (e.g., anger-irritation), and positive emotions as positive (e.g., joy-pleasure); i.e., there is congruence in the recognition of the emotions valence.

In Part 3 of the questionnaire, participants answered a few questions about the robot. Participants revealed that they would feel comfortable if they had to interact with this robot, also they said they would like having this robot in their homes and they felt sorry if they had to destroy it. These results suggested that the robot creates some degree of empathy with the participants. With regard to the robot gender, 10 participants said that the robot does not have a defined gender, and the remaining 3 participants said that it is male. Regarding the function of the robot, the participants answered that it would be a robot to help with housework and a companion robot for people with disabilities, elderly and children.

4   Conclusion

The main objective of this study was to examine the recognition of emotions being expressed by a service robot in a Virtual Environment (VE). Thus, in the stage Definition, a set of components was defined that the robot should perform to express the emotions. The Design stage's aim was to program the virtual robot prototype, based on the components defined in the Definition stage, using a VE. Finally, in the Test stage, the goal was to test the virtual prototype robot, in order to understand if the emotions were correctly identified and recognized by the participants.

The results showed that the participants had some troubles to recognize correctly some of the emotions defined (i.e. fear, disgust, trust, and anger). However, through the feedback given by the participants, with respect to the difficulties experienced during the test, it was possible to identify some problems in the presentation of some of those emotions. For future work it is intended to implement some changes in the expressions of these emotions, making them easier to recognize by manipulating/changing (i.e., eyes, mouth) and/or adding different components (i.e., eye brows).

Acknowledgements. The authors would like to thank Isabel Ferreira and João Sequeira, from the MOnarCH Project for the encouragement and the opportunity to use the virtual prototype of the robot.

References

1. Siegel, M., Breazeal, C., Norton, M.: Persuasive robotics: the influence of robot gender on human behavior. In: IEEE/RSJ International Conference on Intelligent Robots and Systems, pp. 2563–2568. IEEE Press, New York (2009)
2. Goris, K., Saldien, J., Lefeber, D.: Probo: a testbed for human robot interaction. In: ACM/IEEE International Conference on Human Robot Interaction, pp. 253–254. IEEE Press, New York (2009)
3. Graaf, M., Allouch, S.: Exploring influencing variables for the acceptance of social robots. Robot. Auton. Syst. **61**, 1476–1486 (2013)

4. Hollinger, G.A., Georgiey, Y., Manfredi, A., Maxwell, B.A., Pezzementi, Z.A., Mitchell, B.: Design of a social mobile robot using emotion-based decision mechanisms. In: IEEE/RSJ International Conference on Intelligent Robots and Systems (IROS), pp 3093–3098. IEEE Press, New York (2006)

5. Oh, K., Kim, M.: Social attributes of robotic products: observations of child-robot interactions in a school environment. Int. J. Des. **4**, 45–55 (2010)

6. Breazeal, C.: Designing Sociable Robots. MIT Press, Cambridge (2002)

7. Plutchik, R.: The Emotions. University Press of America, Lanham (1991)

8. Frijda, N.: The Emotions. Cambridge University Press, Cambridge (1986)

9. Norman, D.: Emotional Design: Why we Love (or Hate) Everyday Things. Basic Books, New York (2004)

10. Picard, R.: Affective computing. Technical report, MIT Media Laboratory - Perceptual Computing Section, vol. 321, pp. 1–16 (1997)

11. Picard, R.: Towards computers that recognize and respond to user emotion. ibm systems J. **39**, 705–719 (2000)

12. Blow, M., Dautenhahn, K., Appleby, A., Nehaniv, C., Lee, D.: Perception of robot smiles and dimensions for human-robot interaction design. In: 15th IEEE International Symposium on Robot and Human Interactive Communication, pp. 469–474. IEEE Press, New York (2006)

13. Bartneck, C.: How convincing is Mr Data's Smile: affective expressions of machines. User Model. User Adap. Interact. **11**, 279–295 (2001)

14. Kanda, T., Iwase, K., Shiomi, M., Ishiguro, H.: Moderating user's tension to enable them to exhibit other emotions. In: Kanda, T., Ishiguro, H. (eds.) Human-Robot Interaction in Social Robots, pp. 299–311. CRC Press Taylor & Francis, Florida (2005)

15. MonarCH Project. http://monarch-fp7.eu/

16. Plutchik, R.: Emotion: A Psychoevolutionary Synthesis. Harkes & Row, New York (1980)

17. Lakatos, G., Gácsi, M., Konok, V., Brúder, I., Bereczky, B., Korondi, P., Miklosi, A.: Emotion attribution to a non-humanoid robot in different social situations. PLoS ONE **9**(12), e114207 (2014)

18. Nomura, T., Suzuki, T., Kanda, T., Kato, K.: Altered attitudes of people toward robots: investigation through the Negative Attitudes toward Robots Scale. In: AAAI-06 Workshop on Human Implications of Human-Robot Interaction, pp. 29–35. AAAI Press, California (2006)

19. Ekman, P., Friesen, W., Ellsworth, P.: Emotion in the human face. Cambridge University Press, Cambridge (1982)

An Exploratory Study on Consumer's Needs on Smart Home in Korea

Sunwoo Kim[1(✉)] and Jeonghyuk Yoon[2]

[1] SK telecom, Seoul, Republic of Korea
sunwoo7.kim@gmail.com
[2] LG Electronics, Seoul, Republic of Korea
jeonghyuk@hotmail.com

Abstract. In the middle of transformation to IoT society, interests on smart home services are increasing. While the needs on smart home can be different by culture and lifestyle, there are only a few studies on smart home user experiences in Korean situation.

Six focus group discussions (FGD) were conducted and the main findings were as follows; first of all, whereas smart home is still new concept for general consumers and IoT is felt rather far from their everyday lives, smart home services with tangible benefits were acceptable. In addition, the adoption of smart home is related with user's lifestyle. However, concerns on customer care and privacy are critical barriers for its adoption.

In the new era of IoT, it is important to understand consumer's attitudes and experiences towards smart home services. The service providers are encouraged to plan and develop the user oriented services and marketing communications.

Keywords: Smart home · Home IoT · Korean case study · Consumer needs

1 Introduction

In the middle of transformation to IoT society, interests on smart home services are increasing from both consumer and industry sides. Smart home is defined as "a residence equipped with technology that facilitates monitoring of residents and/or promotes independence and increases residents' quality of life [1]". Recently, the concept of smart home services is being expanded to various smart devices which is located at home and can be self-automated, remote-controlled through mobile phone or PC outside home.

Among various industries utilizing IoT, smart home services are expected to have a great growth potential in near future. Gartner even forecasted that "a typical family home could contain more than 500 smart devices by 2022 [2]". Telecommunication industries are also very interested in smart home market. Verizon Wireless and AT&T in the United States and NTT docomo in Japan are already providing smart home service in each region. In the United States, for example, where the detached houses are popular, smart home services are being evolved focusing on the home security related services.

© Springer International Publishing Switzerland 2016
A. Marcus (Ed.): DUXU 2016, Part III, LNCS 9748, pp. 337–345, 2016.
DOI: 10.1007/978-3-319-40406-6_32

In Korea, domestic telecommunication service providers such as SK telecom, KT and LG U+ started to launch smart home services in 2015 spring such as home monitoring camera, gas locking service, door locking service, remote-controlled boiler and dehumidifier, etc. LG U+ was reported that the number of Home IoT service monthly subscriptions were more than 100 thousand households [3].

Though it is important to understand consumers' attitudes and lifestyle related with smart home for user oriented technology development, most of researches have been focused on smart home in the perspective of elderly care in the aging and aged society ([4–7]). Only a few studies started to explore young and middle-aged consumers' perceptions towards smart home and the use cases ([8]). Moreover, while the needs on smart home can be different by culture and lifestyle, studies on smart home user experiences in Korean situation were rarely visited.

This paper aims to explore consumer's general perception on smart home and to discover triggers and barriers for smart home adoption by households. The article begins with background of this study including the definition of smart home and a brief literature review on smart home. Subsequently, findings from focus group discussion conducted in Korea were reported. Finally, implications and suggestions for further research are provided.

2 Background

2.1 The Definition of Smart Home

In accordance with the traditional concept of automated and/or ubiquitous home, a smart home has been defined as "a residence equipped with a communications network, linking sensors and domestic devices and appliances which can be remotely monitored, accessed or controlled and which provides services that respond to the needs of its inhabitants ([5, 6, 8])".

Smart home services, which pursue comfortable, safe, economic and pleasant life, are classified into six sub categories by its value such as smart home appliances, home automation, security, healthcare, green home, and smart TV & home entertainment service [9]. Smart home services related with home security and automation have been dominant because safety is the most important basic function of human value especially at home or personal/families' shelter.

2.2 Research Review

Except studies on elderly people's needs on smart home, most of prior researches on smart home were focused on housewives' needs. This is because smart home services are being established at home, which is traditionally perceived as female's territory. However, a recent research [10] showed that smart home can be adopted by various user segments, such as female housewives, male, elderly people and young generation in 20's. Another study in Korea [11] also showed that single female household had high interests on smart home CCTV in the perspective of security.

In addition, a Qualitative study [8], which was conducted in three European countries, UK, Germany and Italy, reported that tangible benefits and increases of quality of live will be the drivers for smart home development. But the potential barriers of smart home service adoptions existed such as lack of understanding of smart home technology, concerns on technology failure or difficulties in use, privacy and/or security concern, and loss of consumer freedom.

3 Methods

This study adopted focus group discussion to explore consumers' perceptions in a qualitative way. Six focus groups were conducted with 37 participants from Seoul metropolitan area in Korea (see Table 1). Each session of FGD consisted of 4 to 7 consumers. Two focus groups were consisted of smart home users who are currently using one or more smart home services and other four focus groups were targeting potential customers. Three intender group of smart home and one low interest group discussion were conducted and intender groups were consisted of three household types; single household, newly wedded couple and household with children. All six focus group sessions were conducted in October 2015.

The participants were recruited through a marketing research agency and paid incentive money in order to compensate their time. Prior to discussion, every consumer was well informed of research background, main discussion agendas, gratitude provision and signed a nondisclosure agreement and a declaration of consent agreeing to be recorded to allow the voice to be scripted only for research purposes. The participants were also informed that all comments were recorded but would be anonymized prior to analysis.

Each group session consisted of two parts; the first part was focused on consumer perceptions and expectations towards smart home and the second part focused on the real use cases, triggers and barriers of smart home adoption. Whereas intender group discussions were more focused on their perceptions and expectations towards smart home, user group discussions were more focused on their real use cases, and perceived values and pain points. All the six discussion sessions were transcribed and an iterative analysis between the transcripts was conducted to discover the common themes of consumer perceptions and attitudes to smart home.

4 Results

4.1 Perceptions on Smart Home

The participants identified a wide range of issues which fits into three themes as s Table 1 summarizes. The three themes included general concept of smart home services, perceived values of smart home, and concerns on smart home technology. Firstly, most of participants mentioned "automatic", "remote control", "controllable outside", "always connected", and "ubiquitous."

Table 1. Group participant profile

No.	Group characteristics	Number of people
1	User group 1 : Telco smart home	5
2	User group 2 : Non-Telco smart home	4
3	Intention group 1 : Single family	7
4	Intention group 2 : Newly wed	7
5	Intention group 3 : Family w/children	7
6	Low interest group	7

Intender groups felt more positive towards smart home services with describing it as "advanced", "sophisticated", "up to date", and "cutting edge", technology". Among intender group, there were differences between households in a family with children and households in a single family or newly wedded couple without a child. Whereas housewives in a family with children valued smart home as a device which is helpful, comfortable, caring for everything in the household, and is able to provide spare time with lessening the burdens of household choirs, single family and newly wedded couples were mostly focused on the value of safety, and relief from anxiety on security (Table 2).

In the other hands, low interest group mentioned rather negative expressions towards smart home services such as "unfamiliar", "not yet", "unbelievable", "untrustworthy", "vague", and "frustrated". In addition to malfunction and privacy concerns which were mentioned by every group, low interest group showed ethical concerns on smart home services such as human alienation.

Table 2. Perceptions on smart home

		Intender			Low interest group
		Single household	Newly wedded couple	Family with children	
Concept & basic attributes	Automatic	√	√	√	√
	Remote control	√	√	√	√
	Always connected		√		
	Ubiquitous		√		
	Fast/speed	√	√		√
	Convenient	√	√	√	√
	Efficient	√			√
	Time saving			√	√
	Cost saving	√			
	Customized	√			

(*Continued*)

Table 2. (*Continued*)

		Intender			Low interest group
		Single household	Newly wedded couple	Family with children	
Positive values	Advanced	√	√	√	
	Up to date	√	√	√	
	Sophisticated			√	
	Cutting edge		√		
	Relief, security	√	√		
	Helpful			√	
	Showing off			√	
	Spare time			√	
	Care for everything			√	
General concerns on smart home	Malfunction	√	√	√	√
	Not necessary		√	√	√
	Planned obsolescence		√	√	
	Untrustworthy			√	√
	Unfamiliar				√
	Vague				√
	Unbelievable				√
	Frustrated				√
	Hard to use				√

(*Concerns on smart home by low interest group*)

"*It should be useful but what shall I do if machines do all the things? What do I live for? Machines do too many things and would overwhelm us.*"

"*It is really efficient but people may lose their memory, as we can't remember the phone number after using a smart phone. My movement will also decrease if every activity is substituted by artificial intelligence.*"

"*It would be scaring if everything is controlled by technology. I just want to get a help when I asked to do it. I need the right of choice as a master of my home. I am not a puppet.*"

4.2   Triggers and Barriers of Smart Home Adoption

Whereas smart home is still new concept for general consumers and IoT is felt rather far from their everyday lives, smart home services with tangible benefits were acceptable. The main triggers for smart home adoption was as follows; first of all, Users felt satisfaction more on frequently used smart home services such as automatic gas locking services, because consumers felt it useful when it is related with their daily concern or anxiety such as gas leak. The core benefit of the smart home service is relief from the concern and anxiety, which were traditionally thought as uncontrollable.

(Gas locking service use cases)

"I use the gas locking service several times even in a day. When I am not sure if I closed the gas valve right after getting out of the kitchen, I just check it through my smart phone. I can solve my issues even without walking a few steps, which is very useful and satisfying."

"My mother always forgets to close the gas valve and I am really relieved from the anxiety with the gas locking service."

In addition, the adoption of smart home is related with user's lifestyle. For example, pet owners felt home monitoring cameras and automatic adjustable lighting useful when they were on vacation or out of home leaving their pet at home where their pet is very used to. They were able to watch and give a talk to pet and even turn on and off the lights in the evening and in the morning when they are travelling abroad. While self-adjusting thermostat and boiler were welcomed by families with a baby or little kids to adjust temperature and make home cozy right before they arrived home from outside, remote controlled gas locking service were a cool factor for working house-wives and elderly families.

(CCTV use cases)

"It is really innovative to use CCTV for home security, which is never imaginable 10 year ago. I live alone in a detached house and always had concern on robbery/theft of parcel delivery before installing CCTV. I feel secure now."

"CCTV is very useful because there is a baby and a pet as well in my family, because I can take care of them partially even when I am out of home."

(Automatic adjustable lightening use cases)

"My dog is too shy to leave it at the dog hotel while I am out of home. She feels rather comfortable at home but is afraid of darkness. Automatic adjustable lighting is very useful in this situation. If my trip is not longer than 2 days, she rather wants to stay at home. I leave enough food and turn on the light at night and off in the morning."

Whereas smart home provides convenient life for consumers, there also exist some barriers for its adoption. It was hard to figure out the exact reason when malfunctions happened. Secure internet broadband services and electricity is prerequisite of smart home service. In addition, responsive customer feedback & repair is required to avoid embarrassing experiences, if smart home is aiming to be a life platform. For instance, one pet owner confessed they had to come back home to take their pet in the middle of their journey when the smart home app didn't work well outside.

(Embarrassing experiences with system malfunction)

"It happened in the new year's day last year. We were in the middle of journey to my parents' home for a short visiting trip without taking my pet. But when I tried to access the smart home

system provided by our apartment, it didn't work well. Though I made several calls to the office, there was no way to solve it because it happened during the big national holidays. We had to come back to home to take my dog. I was really embarrassed."

(Concern on after sales service)

"When the smart home application doesn't work, it may be hard to know what the real issue is. Various problems can be considered such as WiFi disconnection, application error, or malfunction of sensors embedded in the smart home appliances. If we need to contact each service provider separately, it would be very painful. All the communication channels should be integrated into single source for a quicker resolution."

Privacy and user information protection is another concern. Whereas the home monitoring camera is very useful for pet care and security, there is a trade-off between the usefulness and the privacy safety. There should be a possibility of 3rd person access to recorded images, which has to be saved somewhere in the cloud storage for the mobile phone access.

(Privacy concerns on CCTV)

"Convenience always goes with dangerousness, never safe. Every moment in my house is recorded and can be accessed through my smart phone and laptop, which means that anyone can access it."

4.3   Expectations Towards Smart Home

When consumers were asked about their expectations towards smart home in near future, most of their imaginations were related with smart home appliances and home automation. Smart home appliances which can be controlled from outside were said to be useful for families with children.

(An expectation on a smart microwave oven)

"When I am late, my child sometimes uses microwave oven for herself. I am always afraid of her being injured. Hope that I can cook from outside and let her have it after checking the temperature."

(An expectation on a smart air purifier)

"For families with children or little babies, automotive air purifier will be very useful, which is enable to measure the amount of indoor fine dust and purify air. The automatic control of temperature and humidity would be also beneficial for families with little babies."

Smart home appliances were also attractive even to single families and newly wedded couples without children. They had interests in doing household choirs such as laundry washing, vacuum cleaning or grocery shopping outside home to save their time.

(An expectation on a smart washer)

"I am almost outside during day time and have trouble to find time for laundry washing, because washing laundries at night time is not recommended in apartments. I hope that I can

do laundries when I am out of home or one hour before I come home through smart home services."

(An expectation on a smart refrigerator)

"I always do grocery shopping in the mobile shopping mall while I am commuting and sometimes have no ideas what I have in my refrigerator. I expect a smart refrigerator which informs me of grocery shopping items or allows smart home services to do grocery shopping based upon information gathered by scanning the quantities and/or status of food items in the refrigerators."

Whereas families with children, single families and newly wedded couples liked the remote control function of smart home, FGD participants recommended smart home to elderly families or households with disabled because of home automation function of smart home.

(Smart home recommendations to elderly or disabled people)

"It is likely to be more useful for elderly families or households with disabled persons but they may feel uncomfortable with it. For elderly or disabled people, automated control would be rather useful than remote control."

5   Discussions

In the new era of IoT, it is critical to understand consumer's attitudes and experiences towards the newly introduced smart home services. This research aimed to provide exploratory views of smart home service user's experiences in the Korean context for a user-oriented smart home service design. Families with children showed the biggest interests on smart home services but busy single families and newly wedded couples were also interested in smart home if they are well informed based upon their lifestyle needs. It is time to call further researches on smart home to discover user's basic needs on the smart home by various consumer segments and to encourage the service providers to plan and develop the user oriented services and marketing communications.

Moreover, it is important to provide universal service design for the smart home market formation, which is compatible with all peripheral devices and products regardless of the OS and manufacturers. In Korea, for example, the market share of android phone is much higher than that of IOS and the smart home services are mostly customized for android OS. It would be also painful if users need to download several smart home apps for each product or service. Users are not able to purchase all their home appliances from the same manufacturers to make them connected, either. The most compatible and integrated service design will be the key success factor of smart home.

In the future researches, influencing factors on smart home adoption need to be discovered in the perspective of consumer psychology such as technology acceptance or technology readiness, etc. In addition, it is important to explore smart home user's experience in their daily life contexts to design the most easy to use smart home platform.

References

1. Augusto, J.C., Nugent, C.D.: Smart homes can be smarter. In: Augusto, J.C., Nugent, C.D. (eds.) Designing Smart Homes. LNCS (LNAI), vol. 4008, pp. 1–15. Springer, Heidelberg (2006)
2. Middleton, P., Koslowski, T., Angela, M.: Forecast analysis: Internet of Things, endpoints and associated services, worldwide, 2014 update. Gartner (2014)
3. The number of Home IoT service subscription in LG U Plus over 0.1 million. ET news, January 2016. Accessed on 29th Feb 2016)
4. Demiris, G., Hensel, B.K.: Technologies for an aging society: a systematic review of smart home applications. IMIA Yearbook Med. Inform. 3, 33–40 (2008)
5. Chan, M., Esteve, D., Escriba, C., Campo, E.: A review of smart homes-present state and future challenges. Comput. Methods Prog. Biomed. 91, 55–81 (2008)
6. Chan, M., Campo, E., Esteve, D., Fourniols, J.: Smart homes-current features and future perspectives. Maturitas 64, 90–97 (2009)
7. Le, Q., Nguyen, H.B., Barnett, T.: Smart homes for older people: positive aging in a digital world. Future Internet 4, 607–617 (2012)
8. Balta-Ozkan, N., Amerighi, O., Boteler, B.: A comparison of consumer perceptions towards smart homes in the UK, Germany and Italy: reflections for policy and future research. Technol. Anal. Strat. Manag. 26(10), 1176–1195 (2014)
9. Smart home industries and policy status. Korea Association of Smart Home (2014)
10. Kim, H.J., Yeo, J.S.: A study on consumers' levels of smart home service usage by service type and their willingness to pay for smart home services. Consum. Policy Educ. Rev. 11(4), 25–53 (2015)
11. Weekly focus: 2015 Korean smart home market, focusing on the needs towards small things. In: LG Business Insight, pp. 18–24, 29 July 2015

MUVA: A MUltimodal Visceral Design Ambient Device

Robert Kivac, Sune Øllgaard Klem, Sophus Béneé Olsen,
Amalie Bækgaard Solander, Simon Dyrberg von Spreckelsen,
Evangelia Triantafyllou$^{(\boxtimes)}$, and Georgios A. Triantafyllidis

Department of Architecture Design and Media Technology,
Aalborg University Copenhagen, Copenhagen, Denmark
{rkivac14,sklem15,sboll3,asolan15,
svonspl5}@student.aau.dk,
{evt,gt}@create.aau.dk

Abstract. This paper presents MUVA (MUltimodal Visceral design Ambient device), a prototype for a storytelling light- and sound-based ambient device. The aim of this device is to encourage social interaction and expand the emotional closeness in families with children where at least one parent has an irregular work schedule. MUVA differs from the other ambient devices, because it is targeted to children, and it adopts a visceral design approach in order to be appealing to its users. It is a raindrop-shaped lamp, which features audio playing, while its light color is affected by the audio playing. MUVA can be used by parents to store pre-recorded audio of themselves telling stories, which their children can listen to when they are away. In order to investigate if MUVA is appealing to its users and if it creates feelings of closeness between parents and children when the first are absent, we conducted interviews and observations of children and an online survey study with parents. Our preliminary evaluation failed to provide solid evidence on the development of feelings of closeness. However, the majority of children participating in our test found the record function of the product enjoyable, while the majority of parents thought MUVA would be a fun communication method. Finally, our evaluation indicated that both parents and children would prefer another shape and design.

Keywords: Ambient device · Storytelling · Children · Visceral design · Ambient light

1 Introduction

The family structure has changed drastically over the last 60 years. In post-modern families, it is common that both parents join the workforce, which has resulted in a decline in social interaction between the members in a family [5]. According to a study published in 2001, only 1 % of mothers were stay-at-home mothers in Denmark [5]. In another study, Deding et al. [11] found that 25 % of men and women in Denmark believe that they have trouble in finding a balance between their work and family life. Among the factors affecting this balance, Deding et al. focused on "working non-working hours".

© Springer International Publishing Switzerland 2016
A. Marcus (Ed.): DUXU 2016, Part III, LNCS 9748, pp. 346–356, 2016.
DOI: 10.1007/978-3-319-40406-6_33

The technological revolution has made work away from the workplace and during non-working hours more common, because it made possible 24-hour contact with the workplace. This availability is known as borderless work [15]. This constant availability has resulted in an increased working load for employees and hence for parents, because it made the boundaries between work and leisure time fluid [8]. Deding et al. [11] found in 42 % of Danish families at least one parent has an irregular work schedule, i.e. work during weekends, evenings or nights, while in 14 % of them both parents have such a work schedule.

Such changes in post-modern families have an influence on the parenting time devoted to children [12]. When both parents work, time spent by parents with their children often decreases. However, parenting time plays an important role on a child's life, since interaction with the caregivers is paramount for the child's mental and social development [4]. On the short-term parental absence may affect the wellbeing, the social behavior and the mood of children [9]. Leibowitz [18] has also found that first-grade children exhibited significant differences in verbal and mathematical competence that reflected variations in inherent ability but also on the amounts of time and other resources offered by among others parents. In the long-term, parental absence during childhood may have great consequences during children's adult life. Parental absence has been related to development of depression in later life, as well as a negative effect on children's education and academic qualifications [2, 9].

Storytelling is a great tool for bonding between adults and children and it can also be used as a tool to create a relaxed and intimate atmosphere [1]. Wright has also stressed the importance of storytelling in childhood: "*We all need stories for our minds as much as we need food for our bodies*" [25]. Research has also shown that parents' reading contributes to better language development among children [23]. During the last decade storytelling has also received increasing attention because of its potential to promote engagement, enjoyment and fun in interactive digital environments [13].

This paper presents MUVA (MUltimodal Visceral design Ambient device), a prototype for a storytelling light- and sound-based ambient device. The aim of this device is to encourage social interaction and expand the emotional closeness in families with children where at least one parent has an irregular work schedule.

The rest of the paper is organized as follows. Section 2 presents similar approaches in the field of ambient devices and interactive storytelling, and Sect. 3 discusses the design of MUVA. Section 4 describes the technical implementation, while Sect. 5 presents data on the evaluation of our prototype. Section 6 discusses the evaluation results, while Sect. 7 concludes this paper with directions for future work.

2   Background

In the field of interactive storytelling, Zhou et al. [26] developed the "Magic Story Cube", a prototype of an interactive cube for storytelling, which featured augmented reality and tangible interaction. The Magic Story Cube employed multiple modalities including speech, 3D audio and 3D graphics to provide the user (especially children) with multi-sensory experiences in the process of storytelling. Zhou et al. found that this prototype can make storytelling more appealing and understandable to children compared to traditional children's books.

In the last years, there have been developed ambient devices that use light and/or sound and provide different kind of information [24]. An ambient device presents information within a space through subtle changes in light or sound, which can be processed in the background of awareness. Therefore, it uses the physical environment as an interface to provide information without distraction [19]. An example of an ambient device is the Ambient Orb, which is a wireless frosted-glass ball glowing in different colors to display changes in e.g. stock market, traffic, pollen, and weather forecast (www.ambientdevices.com/about/consumer-devices).

Nabaztag is another ambient device shaped as an interactive bunny featuring an adjustable light in the belly, recording/playing of audio messages, as well as Wi-Fi communication with other paired bunnies (http://www.nabaztag.com/). It can also provide information about stocks, traffic, and weather and can create notifications for incoming e-mails, SMS etc.

Angelini et al. [3] presented the anthropomorphic lamp called ADA (Anthropomorphic Display of Affection), which allows displaying and collecting user's emotional states. ADA displays the emotional information changing colors and facial expressions and it allows interaction through tangible gestures typically used in social interactions by humans.

Kowalski et al. [17] developed the Cubble, an ambient device, which uses light for enabling partners in long-distance relationships to share their emotions, simple messages and remote presence. Kowalski et al. found that people, who used the Cubble, reported that it encourages a more frequent message exchange, resulting in a stronger emotional closeness.

The Cubble indicates that an ambient device can be used to enhance communication and maintain emotional closeness between people being apart. In this paper, we present MUVA, a prototype for an ambient device. MUVA differs from the aforementioned devices, because it is targeted to children, and it adopts a visceral design approach in order to be appealing to and entertaining for its users [21]. Our goal was to produce a storytelling ambient device, which would create the emotional state of closeness between absent parents and their children by featuring specific appearance and functionality. Since bedtime storytelling is a well-established tradition in many Danish families [6], we decided to elaborate on storytelling and provide an alternative communication method between absent parents and their children. The following section presents the design of this novel ambient device based on the principles of the visceral design theory.

3   Design of the Prototype

MUVA is a prototype for an interactive, light- and sound-based ambient device, which is created as a storytelling night lamp for children. The light of this night lamp can be adjusted to a bedtime story that has been pre-recorded by an adult.

In order to come up with a satisfying design for the night lamp, we took several aspects into consideration such as its shape, light, color, sound and personalization.

MUVA is meant to please two individuals – the child and the parent. Hence we tried to produce a lamp that is visually pleasing for the child having it in her bedroom, while incorporating functions that make it easy to use and appealing to parents. We utilized therefore the principles of visceral design.

Visceral design is an emotional design theory wherein the physical features (e.g. size, shape, color and appearance) are dominant, since these factors create an immediate emotional impact on the user [21]. By following a visceral design approach, the aim is to produce an artifact that is attractive and creates enjoyment. In order to create an appealing product for children, we first researched what kind of shapes and appearances appeal to children by exploring popular characters from children's movies. Through this research, we found that in order to construct a likeable and appealing character or product for children, it should include rounded edges and curved figures. This is based on the assumption that rounded edges and curves are associated with something positive, good and likable.

Based on these findings, we created different sketches to come up with the exterior design for MUVA (Fig. 1). However, we decided to go with a simple design instead of a character, because we wanted the ambient light in the night lamp to be the main visual focus. Finally, we chose for MUVA to have the shape of a water drop (Fig. 2). Furthermore, we chose to make MUVA small enough in order to be portable. We decided on portability in order to be possible for children to get attached to the lamp, since they will be able to move around with it or bring it along when outside of home.

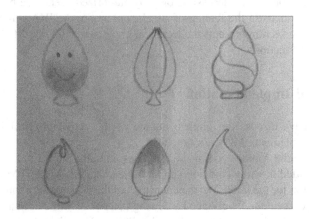

Fig. 1. Different design sketches for MUVA

As far as the color of MUVA is concerned, we chose to provide children with the opportunity to select their preferred color. As Cherry [9] mentions: *"...feelings about colour are often deeply personal and rooted in your own experience or culture."*, so we decided that it was important for MUVA to be adjustable in order to cater for different preferences. The light of MUVA reacts also to the audio being played while in the storytelling mode. The light brightness changes according to the frequency of the sound signal being played.

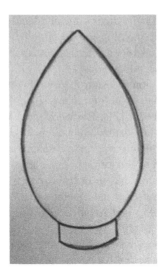

Fig. 2. The chosen shape of a water drop

MUVA's main function is the ability to playback a recorded sound. Parents can use MUVA to store pre-recorded audio files of them reading a story, which their children can listen to when they are away. We chose also to implement a password function for MUVA, in order for it to be accessible only by authorized users. We believe that this feature may also increase the feeling of attachment among MUVA's users.

The following section presents the technical implementation of a MUVA prototype and its featured functions.

4   Technical Implementation

In this section we discuss the implementation of the actual physical lamp and the software that implements MUVA's functions.

In order to build a prototype of the lamp, we initially built a model in Autodesk Maya. We exported the Maya model as an STL file to Autodesk 123D Make, where we created a skeleton for the lamp. We then constructed the skeleton in 3 mm. wood with a laser cutter. We made the lampshade by sewing patches of white cotton cloth together to fit the skeleton. MUVA gets its light by Philips Hue light bulb [16]. We also constructed a pedestal in wood, which acts as a compartment for storing the electronic elements of the lamp. Furthermore, the pedestal acts as a foothold for the socket for the Philips Hue light bulb and hides the wireless speaker.

MUVA contains four different functions, the main function being light reacting to a sound input and three supporting functions, namely a color changing function, a timer function and a password function. These functions were all created in the open source programming language Processing [22], with the use of its Minim and Voce libraries and the Philips Hue software.

While in playback mode, changes in the frequency of the sound being played result in changes in the brightness of a Philips Hue light bulb. Therefore, we implemented a function for converting the audio signal from the time domain to the frequency domain by using a Fast Fourier Transformation. Once in the frequency domain, the brightness is mapped to the amplitude of a specific frequency range, resulting to low amplitudes representing low brightness fluctuation, and high amplitudes representing high brightness fluctuation. As far as the light color is concerned, we developed a color changing function in order for the child to be able to choose the color of MUVA's light bulb. For the two aforementioned functions, we used the Philips Hue Bridge API's, which are the primary tools for controlling the Philips Hue light bulbs. The API is a RESTful interface over HTTP. This means that controlling the light bulbs can be achieved wirelessly.

The audio recording function makes it possible for parents/adults to record a story through a computer before going away, or while being away. This feature gives the parents the opportunity to interact with their children through storytelling even when the parents are not physically present. MUVA features also a timer function that makes it possible for parents to set MUVA to start at a desired time. When the timer goes off, the lamp will start to glow and change color, as well as play a melody. This function will give an indirect notification that the child has to get ready to go to bed.

We developed also a password function in order to give MUVA a more special and personal attachment for the child. By using the speech synthesis and recognition library Voce, the user (e.g. children) is able to choose a password, which MUVA will be able to recognize and accept when spoken into the lamp. Moreover, the pre-recorded story will only be played when the password is accepted.

All these functions were implemented and installed to the aforementioned physical prototype. The final prototype is shown in Fig. 3.

Fig. 3. The implemented MUVA prototype

5 Evaluation

For the evaluation of the MUVA prototype, we employed a convergent parallel mixed research method [10]. The purpose of this explorative evaluation was to investigate user experience and user feelings on the exterior design of MUVA and to explore parents' intention to use such an ambient device. In order to gather data, we conducted two different tests: group interviews and ethnographic observations of children when exposed for the first time to MUVA [7], and an online questionnaire for parents [14].

For recruiting participants for the tests, two non-probability sampling methods were used, namely quota sampling for the children and snowball sampling for the parents. The sample consisted of 6 to 8 year old Danish children, and Danish parents with children in the age of 6 to 12 years.

The first test was conducted at a primary school in the region of Copenhagen, Denmark. During this test, three group interviews were conducted. We interviewed groups of two to three children during each interview. Children of each group reported to be friends with each other. Group A consisted of three boys, Group B consisted of three girls and Group C consisted of two boys. The test took place in an artificial environment, and around a semi-structured interview. Each session lasted approximately 30 min and consisted of three parts:

1. An interview, with questions on preferences and habits regarding bedtime story-telling, night lamps, and first impression on MUVA.
2. A demonstration of MUVA and observations of children's reaction to it.
3. Collection of children's opinions regarding the functionality as well as the design of MUVA, by using our own version of the Smiley-based Affective Instrument (SBAI) as a projective technique [20].

The SBAI method was employed instead of a Likert scale, because not all children at the age of our participants master numbers and reading. Normally, the SBAI method consists of nine options but for simplicity reasons we chose to use only five options (Fig. 4). The different smileys from the SBAI method were given the following interpretations (Smiley numbers from Fig. 4):

Smiley	Fun	Design	Color	Size	Total
1.	2	0	4	5	11
2.	0	0	0	0	0
3.	3	2	1	1	7
4.	1	2	0	0	3
5.	2	4	3	2	11
Total:	8	8	8	8	32

Fig. 4. Children's responses collected by the Smiley-based Affective Instrument

- Smiley 1: A very negative response to the question.
- Smiley 2: A negative response to the question.
- Smiley 3: An indifferent response to the question.
- Smiley 4: A positive response to the question.
- Smiley 5: A very positive response to the question

During the initial part of the interview, we found that not all children are used to listen to bedtime stories. Furthermore, only four of them reported that they parents often were absent in the evenings. Finally, seven out of eight children had a night lamp in their room.

Through ethnographic observations during the first test, it was found that eight out of eight children showed interest when they were introduced to MUVA, while five of them found the record function amusing. Children expressed preferences on the light color of MUVA and they liked the idea that they could customize the color of the light bulb. Furthermore, five of them proposed that the lamp should be shaped as a character. None of the children could guess that MUVA had the shape of a water drop.

The data collected through the SBAI method was clustered in four overall categories regarding the MUVA characteristics: fun, design, color, and size (Fig. 4). Summing up the responses to all characteristics, we conclude that 44 % of the opinions towards MUVA were positive, while 34 % were negative. Subsequently, focusing on aspects regarding MUVA's physical appearance (design, color, and size), we observe again more positive responses than negative (45.8 and 37.5 % respectively).

The second test involved an online survey, which consisted of two parts:

1. Demographic data collection.
2. Information on MUVA and collection of opinions on the use of MUVA.

We gathered 27 responses from parents of children aged 6 to 12. 81.5 % of them reported reading bedtime stories to their children, while the vast majority of them (89 %) contact their children by phone when they are away. 59.3 % of the respondents reported that MUVA would be a fun way of communicating with their children

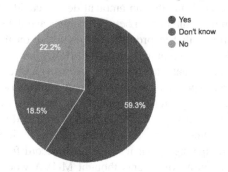

Do you think MUVA would be a fun way of communicating with your child/children?

- Yes
- Don't know
- No

22.2%
18.5%
59.3%

Fig. 5. Parents' responses to the question "Do you think MUVA would be a fun way of communicating with your child/children?" (N = 27)

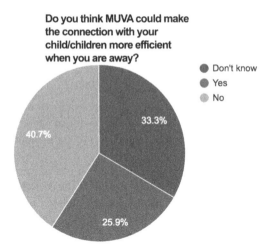

Fig. 6. Parents' responses to the question "Do you think MUVA could make the connection with your child/children more efficient when you are away?" (N = 27)

(Fig. 5), but only 25.9 % reported that MUVA could facilitate the communication with their children when they are away (Fig. 6). Finally, 33.7 % could see themselves using MUVA in general.

6   Discussion

A mutual decline in social interaction between members of the family is happening in the modern society. This means that parents do not always have enough time to spend with their children. However, it is of great importance for parents to interact with their children throughout different stages of their lives, to ensure a healthy social and mental development. Research conducted by Kowalski et al. [17] indicated that ambient devices could assist in establishing an emotional closeness between people being away. Therefore, there is some evidence that an ambient device could serve as an approach towards improving the mutual interaction between parents and their children. However, our preliminary evaluation failed to provide solid evidence on this direction. Nevertheless, answers provided by parents indicated that MUVA has some fun elements that could attract children's and parents' attention. By following a visceral design approach, we sought to create a prototype, in which physical appearance would create feelings of attachment and closeness to children. Our data from interviews and observations of children and from an online survey study with parents indicated that both parents and children would prefer another shape and design. However, it was noted that the majority of children participating in our test found the record function of the product enjoyable and that the majority of parents thought MUVA would be a fun communication method. Lastly, one third of the parents could see themselves using MUVA. This implicates that further development could be continued with focus on a redesign of MUVA's appearance.

7 Conclusion

The purpose of this study was to investigate if a light- and sound-based ambient device could improve communication and create feelings of closeness between children and their absent parents. With this aim, a prototype of an interactive ambient night lamp called MUVA was developed that provided parents with the opportunity to read bedtime stories to their children even when they are away from home. With MUVA, parents can record and store themselves reading bedtime stories for their children. MUVA is able to display light changing according to the frequency of the audio played, and change color depending on user's preference. In the future, we would like to develop a new version of a MUVA prototype, taking into account the evaluation results presented in this paper. Moreover, we would like to test MUVA in a natural environment over a longer period of time, in order to be able to gather valid data on the development of feelings, since this process requires time to evolve.

References

1. Aiex, N.: Storytelling By children (1988). http://www.vtaide.com/png/ERIC/Storytelling.htm. Accessed on 20 Oct 2015
2. Amato, P.R., Booth, A.: Consequences of parental divorce for adult well-being. Soc. Forces **69**, 895–914 (1991)
3. Angelini, L., Caon, M., Lalanne, D., Abou khaled, O., Mugellini, E.: Towards an anthropomorphic lamp for affective interaction. In: Proceedings of the Ninth International Conference on Tangible, Embedded, and Embodied Interaction, Stanford, California, USA, pp. 661–666 (2015)
4. Astingston, J., Edward, M.: The development of theory of mind in early childhood, pp. 1–7 (2010)
5. Christoffersen, M.N., Mørck, Y., Sørensen, K.M.: Ungdomssociologi. Forlaget Columbus, Copenhagen (2001). ISBN: 87-7970-023-3
6. Bak, L., Epinion, Leadership, P.: Danskernes kulturvaner 2012. Kulturministeriet (2012)
7. Bjørner, T.: Qualitative Methods for Consumer Research. Hans Reitzel, København (2015). ISBN: 978-87-412-5853-9
8. Bjørnstrup, V., Matthiesen, T., Skov, O.: Identitet og senmodernitet – Med stress som case (2013). ISBN: 978–87-616-6190-6
9. Cherry, K.: Color Psychology (2015). http://psychology.about.com/od/sensation andperception/a/colorpsych.htm. Accessed on 16 Dec 2015
10. Creswell, J.W.: Research Design: Qualitative, Quantitative and Mixed Methods Approaches, 4th edn. Sage Publications, Thousand Oaks (2014)
11. Deding, M., Lausten, M., Andersen, A.: Børnefamiliernes Balance Mellem Familie- og Arbejdsliv, pp. 1–140 (2006). ISBN: 87-7487-837-9
12. Dencik, L.: Growing up in the post-modern age: on the child's situation in the modern family, and on the position of the family in the modern welfare state. Acta Sociol. **32**(2), 155–180 (1989). doi:10.1177/000169938903200203
13. Garzotto, F., Paolini, P., Sabiescu, A.: Interactive storytelling for children. In: Proceedings of the 9th International Conference on Interaction Design and Children, pp. 356–359 (2010)
14. Gillham, B.: Developing a Questionnaire, 2nd edn. Continuum International Publishing Group, London (2000)

15. Gonas, L.: Balancing family and work to create a new social order. Econ. Ind. Democracy **23**(1), 59–66 (2002)
16. Koninklijke Philips Electronics N.V.: Philips Hue. United States of America (2012)
17. Kowalski, R., Loehmann, S., Hausen, D.: Cubble: A multi-device hybrid approach supporting communication in long-distance relationships, pp. 201–204 (2013)
18. Leibowitz, A.: Home investments in children. Marriage, family, human capital, and fertility. J. Polit. Econ. **82**(2), 111–135 (1974)
19. Markopoulos, P., Ruyter, B., Mackay, W.: Awareness systems advances in theory. Methodol. Des. **1**, 27–29 (2009)
20. Moore, A., Steiner, C., Conlan, O.: Design and development of an empirical smiley-based affective instrument, pp. 1–12 (2013)
21. Norman, D. (ed.): Emotional Design: Why we Love (or Hate) Everyday things, 1st edn., pp. 20–70. Basic Books, New York (2004)
22. Reas, C., Fry, B.: Processing (Version 3.0.1) Fathom Information Design, UCLA Arts Software Studio, NYU's ITP, Boston, Los Angeles, New York (2001)
23. Sénéchal, M., LeFevre, J.A., Hudson, E., Lawson, E.P.: Knowledge of storybooks as a predictor of young children's vocabulary. J. Educ. Psychol. **88**(3), 520 (1996)
24. Wisneski, C., Ishii, H., Dahley, A., Gorbet, M., Brave, S., Ullmer, B., Yarin, P.: Ambient displays: turning architectural space into an interface between people and digital information. In: Yuan, F., Konomi, S., Burkhardt, H.-J. (eds.) CoBuild 1998. LNCS, vol. 1370, pp. 22–32. Springer, Heidelberg (1998)
25. Wright, A.: Storytelling with Children. Oxford University Press, Oxford (1995)
26. Zhou, Z., Cheok, A., Pan, J., Li, Y.: Magic story cube. In: Proceedings of the 2004 ACM SIGCHI International Conference on Advances in Computer Entertainment Technology, ACE 2004, pp. 364–365 (2004)

IoT Connectivity Interface in Tizen: Smart TV Scenarios

Gaeun Lee[1,2(⊠)] and Minjin Rho[1,2]

[1] Seoul R&D Campus, Seongchon-Gil, Seocho-Gu, Seoul, Korea
[2] Samsung Electronics Co. Ltd., Seoul, Korea
{gganni.lee,mj.rho}@samsung.com

Abstract. As we are moving towards the Internet of Things (IoT), the number of devices and sensors deployed around the world is growing at a rapid pace. A new approach, control interface for the next era of IoT is necessary. IoT will fundamentally affect all of us. As digital devices become increasingly complicated, TV includes many smart functions as connecting diverse devices. Therefore, complicated interaction and unnecessary functions caused many other problems. The aim of this study is to highlight the Everything's Guide (ETG) feature of Samsung's new Tizen Operating System (OS), with respect to the most talked about IoT scenarios. ETG also converts Smart TV into an IoT hub, leaving users with an altogether new experience of TV watching. It talks about the new created interface, considering user interactions as primarily. With increase of devices controlled by users and things based on the sensor, it's essential to define such an interface, which is user centric, simplified in nature and easy to use.

Keywords: Iot (Internet of Things) · Smart homes · Connectivity · Controller · User interface · Smart TV

1 Introduction

In the recent years, the internet has drastically changed the way we live. The use of smart devices having RFID's and sensors has increased exponentially [1]. According to the Gartner, the number of connected devices in the IoT(Internet of Things) will increase 30 times approximately 26 billion devise by 2020 [2]. The IoT vision expects to empower the perception of the real world and seamless interactions. Numerous smart objects are directly related to the physical world and have the communication and computation capabilities to connect and interact with their surroundings. The data or services offered by such objects can give information about the physical world and allow interaction with it [3]. The main thought of the IoT is an extension of the Internet into the physical world, to involve interaction with a physical objects in the environment. The idea is to connect every object via Internet and make them communicate. IoT is expected to offer advanced connectivity for devices, systems, and services that goes beyond machine-to-machine communications (M2 M), and covers a variety of protocols, domains, and applications [4]. Connectivity is one of the most critical factors that may affect as a great benefit to various domains for the next era of the IoT.

© Springer International Publishing Switzerland 2016
A. Marcus (Ed.): DUXU 2016, Part III, LNCS 9748, pp. 357–364, 2016.
DOI: 10.1007/978-3-319-40406-6_34

Everything is connected around us and leads to various connectivity issues [5]. With technologies evolving everyday the connectivity issues are resolved to give better performance and end results [6]. The IoT does not revolutionize our lives or the field of computing. It is another step in the evolution of the Internet we already have [7]. It is important to make any devices to connect all the time with the most efficient connection methods. When it comes to control these multiple IoT devices, complex interfaces are getting generated [8]. It is hard to find having concrete rules for user interface on the existing smart TV. Samsung's Tizen OS aim's at redefining the User Experience of controlling multiple IoT devices, by introducing Everything's Guide (ETG) for Smart TV.

2   IoT Connectivity Interface

2.1   Exploring IoT Opportunities in Smart TV

Smart TV's potential as IoT device has not been fully utilized. A Smart TV can be utilized for the information storage, data visualization, interaction point, data processor and data source [9]. The smart phone is preferred as controllers because of their connectivity and evolving technology. However, the screen size of the smart phone becomes a bottleneck when it comes to displaying of huge data. Any size of device, from small screens (Smart phone, Tablet) to the large screen (TV), should be considered concrete rules for designing user interfaces. In the connected environment, it is very important to make any devices to connect with the most efficient connection and displaying methods. If the designer do not consider how to make user-centric interface on IoT, complex and unnatural interaction methods cause many other issues [5]. In this scenario, the convenience of technology is considered important over human comfort. In this aspect, we prototype ETG as part of the Tizen OS project and talk about the ETG design which is an integral part of the Tizen OS. The new interface for TV that helps you control connected things, parallel while watching your favorite TV channel. If we look around to see the emerging trends among all big companies in today's date, we realize that they are moving towards visualizing IoT into reality. The most challenging aspect is to make all the things (sensors and RFID's etc.) to communicate with each other [1]. Few of the trending projects like; Google's Project Brillo and Weave, Apple's Home Kit, they have visualized the need and initiated bold steps towards making seamless connectivity as a dream for the common man. There are many good implementation cases about seamless connectivity between devices in the smart home development [5]. However, surrounding Things and the interface of Device are too focused on the Protocol standard; there is less improvement in effectiveness of user interfaces and consideration of mental model of the users [3]. The most of current researchers focuses on the communication and networking aspects between the devices that are used for sensing and measurement of the real world objects [5]. Therefore, we must introduce design concepts like Everything's Guide with design features, mainly focusing on User Interactions. Below is the outcome of the prototype, implementation of the ETG interface into TV and Smartphone. The design process for the ETG guide in Tizen OS can be explained as below (Fig. 1).

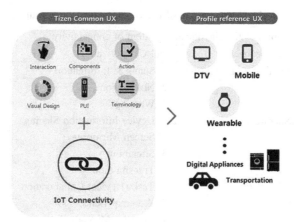

Fig. 1. Key role of IoT Connectivity in Tizen platform

2.2 Designing ETG for Tizen OS

The common guideline for Tizen provides common styles for diverse devices such as smart phones, wearables, TV and IVI (in-vehicle infotainment), keeping connectivity as the main focus. Every device has specialization of functions [6]. The Tizen OS aims to offer a unified experience across multiple devices, and TV is one of the device that can expect to see it. IoT should be encouraged by a hybrid architecture which comprises a wide range of devices and architectures. It becomes difficult for each device to expand easily due to its OS. Therefore, consistency in the interface, along with easy connectivity with surrounding devices such as TV or smartphone is the best solution. The purpose of this study is to explore challenges in implementing cases about seamless connectivity experience. Prototyping ETG as part of the Tizen OS project is meaningful in the view of user centric design approach and application of IoT. In this scenario, TV provides a wide screen for displaying lots of connected devices better. Trial on TV interface as ETG is suitable for visualizing various graphical information [4]. While designing for the structure of ETG, we needed to consider how we would absorb many legacies and low power sensor devices and their interfaces. For optimization, we assume an environment as the smart home environment and designed an interface for this situation.

Table 1 indicates the connectivity of use cases that can be generated in the smart home environment. This table is based on user's needs of connectivity. Even with multiple connected devices, designing simpler user interface can be possible. To deal with different devices and access their information is very essential. The structure of ETG should be accessible and flexible enough to deal with many connecting devices. All the connected things can be viewed on the Smart TV. They can be edited and modified based on the user needs. The remote control of the TV is the main input and core-control devices [5]. Considering limitations of remote controls and usability issues, an optimized design was evolved to control all things. Based on Table 1, Fig. 2 defines the structural understanding of ETG guide. It has been proposed Suggestion as Recommend in ETG.

Table 1. Categorization of use cases in smart home situation

Examples of the classification system of connectivity	
Big Categorization	Small Categorization
1. Monitoring & Sensing	1-1. Status & Information
	1-2. Notification
	1-3. Warning
2. Sharing	2-1. Device Information Sharing
	2-2. Screen Mirroring
	2-3. Streaming
	2-4. Transmission
	2-4. Task (Device) Collaboration
	2-5. Web experience
3. Control	3-1. Remote (Manual) Control
	3-2. Rule based automation (IFTTT)
	3-3. Contextual Trigger (Intelligence)
	3-4. Task (Device) Collaboration
4. Suggestion	4-1. Information
	4-2. Contents
	4-3. Devices
	4-4. Control
	4-5. Task (Mode)
	4-6. Services

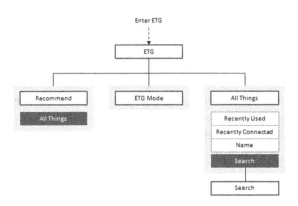

Fig. 2. Structure of ETG Guide in Tizen TV

An ETG guide at a broad level can be categorized into 3 sections: Recommend Area, Mode Area, All Things. The Recommend Area can be considered as the first step to adaptive behaviors within an smart home environment. For the specific functions of different section refer Table 2 below, along with Fig. 3a, b and c.

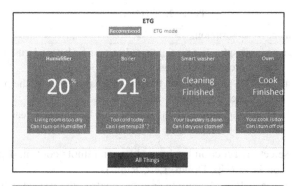

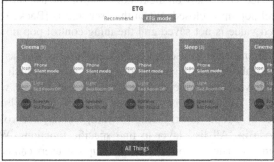

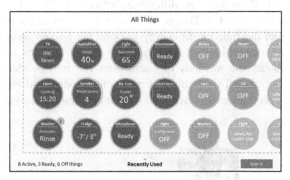

Fig. 3. (a) Recommend area of ETG, (b) Mode List area of ETG, (c) All things of ETG

As mentioned earlier, TV's remote control plays an important role in the user experience while operating the ETG guide. Figure 4 shows 4-way keys on the remote control. Figure 5(a) and (b) shows user interface that is designed and how to controls interface. For the user's convenience and consideration of mental model of the users, all the controls are mapped to the four (up/down/right/left) keys of the remote. In general, the most natural way of controlling TV is using the remote control.

The flow of the activities after the user selects the desired connected thing to edit is as below:

- Thing Control is displayed when the user selects the particular thing on All things screen.

Table 2. ETG sections

Fig	OSD Element	Description
3(a)	Recommend Area	Display notification-based recommendations in the list, which are relevant to things.
3(b)	Mode List Area	Display the mode that the user has created for the particular status. User can edit and add the mode.
3(c)	All things	Display recently used things on All Things Screen.

- The user can select the function by 4-way keys on remote control. 4-way keys mean 4-way navigation keys (Up, Down, Left, Right).
- When the user selects [OK] key on the remote control, the last set value is saved and the thing control pop up is closed. When the user selects [Back] key on the remote control, changed value is not saved and the thing control pop up is closed.

IoT implementation needs to use existing framework as well as existing interactions. As mentioned above, we have provided three layers, which contain different connected device. However, with the increase of things and devices, we have to reduce the depth to enter the 'All lists' layer and cover all users' needs while they are using 'Recommend' layer or 'Mode' layer. Going forward, we may use voice interaction or provide search mode in 'All list' layer to find specific functions. With the growing number of things in IoT, The 'Recommend Area' support users can easily access what they want to control. There are some differences between traditional interaction design and designing for the Internet of Things. When it comes to interaction on TV, the user is available to select the function by 4-way keys on the remote control. User is now available to operate many things at home by 4-way navigation keys and screen cursors of ETG. In the future, the methods of interactions can be extended in many ways (Voice, Gesture control on TV). Dialogue between the product and the user can have a profound impact on the experience and, when implemented well, can provide

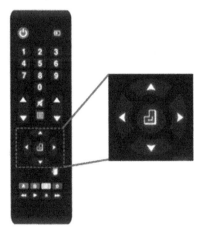

Fig. 4. Way keys on remote control

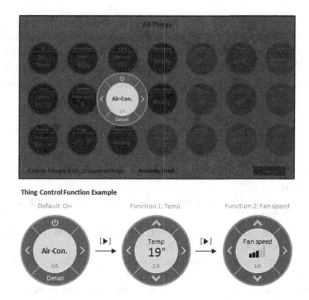

Fig. 5. (a) Things control in All Things of ETG, (b) Example of Things control function

emotional rewards to the user. If we branch these new interfaces such as above in smart phone or TV, the value of user experience will be increased in Tizen platform-based devices.

3 Conclusion

This study presents ETG as a new approach of control interface for the next era of the IoT. Samsung's ETG for Tizen OS has proven the potential to add a new dimension to the IoT world by enabling seamless connectivity and ease of use between smart objects. As we move from small screens (Smart phone, Tablet) to large screens(TV), more information can be provided in meaningful ways for users. More users are trying to control and manage expanding numbers of devices and content in a less demanding, but in more convenient way. In the near future, the tizen platform automatically recognizes IoT devices, which offers users easier, more convenient TV experiences to the users. The ETG shows a user centric design approach, making it the most differentiating OS available among the other existing platforms. The ETG reduces the burden of using many remote controllers to manage various devices connected to users' smart TVs. User centric interaction (4-way mapping) and visualized thing on TV are meaningful trials. As the case of IoT application, this allows user to interact with their environment. Going forward, it can be claimed that Tizen has opened new possibilities for connecting objects. A direction has been set where in the capabilities of Smart TV are being explored. Its emphasis on the use of remote control, which is today's era is the simplest, most devices comprising a mental model which a small child as well as a senior person can use, is creditable. Furthermore, its open source design makes its application extendable to any imagined smart objects. The goal of this study is not only to offer a unified IoT experience on Tizen platform but also to appreciate the findings and discuss their applicability towards the IoT. Expectations are that the new approach of Tizen will add more values of users' TV experience, not only enjoying traditional broadcasting programs but also IoT services generated by connecting things.

References

1. Atzori, L., Iera, A., Morabito, G.: The internet of things: a survey. Comput. Netw. **54**(15), 2787–2805 (2010)
2. Da Xu, L., He, W., Li, S.: Internet of things in industries: a survey. IEEE Trans. Ind. Inform. **10**(4), 2233–2243 (2014)
3. De, S., et al.: An internet of things platform for real-world and digital objects. Scalable Comput. Pract. Exper. **13**(1), 45–58 (2012)
4. Holler, J., et al.: From Machine-to-machine to the Internet of Things: Introduction to a New Age of Intelligence. Academic Press, Oxford (2014)
5. Choi, B., Lee, Y., Park, S.S.: A research of user interface design elements on smart TV. In: ADADA, pp. 219–222 (2014)
6. Cho, J.Y., Lee, H.S., Lee, B.G.: Connectivity issues on IoT business-the Korean case of smart home network. In: Second International Conference on Electrical, Electronics, Computer Engineering and their Applications, EECEA 2015, p. 120 (2015)
7. Perera, C., Zaslavsky, A., Christen, P., Georgakopoulos, D.: Context aware computing for the internet of things: a survey. IEEE Commun. Surv. Tutor. **16**(1), 414–454 (2014)
8. Chorianopoulos, K.: User interface design principles for interactive television applications. Int. J. Hum. Comput. Interact. **24**(6), 556–573 (2008)
9. Sawh, M.: Samsung Tizen OS: 6 Things You Need To Know (2014). http://www.trustedreviews.com/opinions/samsung-tizen-os-features#plQ6wCXG6bYU6zGJ.99

A Framework for Designing UX of Sharing 'Internet of Things (IoT)' System and Service: Case Study of UX Development of Community Laundry Machines

Minjoo Lee[(⊠)], Dasom Jeong, Hayoung Jeong, Enoch Lee, and Moonkyu Song

Handong Global University, Pohang-si, Gyeongsangbuk-do, Korea
minjoooolee@gmail.com, jeongglory@gmail.com, enoch2110@gmail.com, {kate9902,pacify30}@naver.com

Abstract. The objective of present case study is to design user experience (UX) of an IoT system and service for sharing devices, community laundry machine. Due to distinctive usage situations of the system such as community machines, multiple users, and use of IoT technology, it was identified that a distinctive usage model and design framework are required rather than conventional UX design frameworks. Based on the unique usage model, a series of UX design process was performed including an interactive prototype as conceptual design. We expect the framework and process of the study would provide UX designers with insights to design such novel system/service environments.

Keywords: UX design · Community system and service · Multiple users · IoT

1 Introduction

The life style using products and services is being transformed to a new aspect using more emerging technologies including mobile devices and 'internet of things' (IoT). In addition to this, a concept of 'community products' in terms of 'sharing economy' has been expected to be an important trend of the new life style in near future, such as 'Uber' and 'AirBnB.' Even though many companies and researchers have developed various products and services that use the concept of IoT, most of them seem to focus on implementation of technologies such as sensors and network, rather than active efforts to consider and reflect the users' needs in terms of the principles of user-centered design and UX design.

Historically, a model of computer-supported cooperative work (CSCW) was used to identify such interactive systems used by multiple users, since various users access the system and communicate information regardless of time and space [1, 2]. However, we initially expected that the UX development for the 'community product' would require a different design framework beyond traditional interactions for single user or, even, multi-user situations (CSCW), due to a different usage model.

© Springer International Publishing Switzerland 2016
A. Marcus (Ed.): DUXU 2016, Part III, LNCS 9748, pp. 365–372, 2016.
DOI: 10.1007/978-3-319-40406-6_35

With this in mind, the objectives of this study were to conduct a UX design development for a community product integrated with IoT as well as to identify different design and development framework for the system and service. A series of user requirements analyses and conceptual design including development of usage model, framework, and task flow were conducted to achieve the objectives. A facility of community laundry machines in a University dormitory was used for the UX development including user requirement analysis, system and service design, and prototyping and user interface (UI) design in a mobile device.

2 User Requirement Analysis

A facility of community laundry machines in student dormitory of Handong Global University in South Korea was selected for the target system. The dormitory consists of seven buildings with 3-5 stories in each building. Approximately 90 students reside in a floor and they share one or two laundry machines in each floor. Thus there are about 5 machines in each building.

In order to collect and analyze users' implicit/explicit requirements for the system and service in the situation, various methods were employed. Since the service and system using IoT for the community machine has not introduced in the market, the user requirement analysis was focused on understanding current users' usage model and explicit concerns as well as on developing new system/service framework to resolve their concerns on the system. Conventional methods to capture user requirements in terms of user studies were used including focus group interview, contextual inquires, in-depth interview, video ethnography, and survey using actual target users [3].

In this section, interesting results of the user requirement analysis in the study is provided along with unique usage model for the community IoT system.

2.1 Current Users' Explicit Concerns and Behaviors

The analyses of user studies revealed several general issues on current system. In general, the primary concerns were inefficient waiting time due to messed order of the machine use among multiple users and a lack of confidence to other unknown users in a same community such as invasion of privacy.

As examples of inefficient waiting time, a current active user (a user in use) who was waiting the completion of his/her laundry showed frequent movements between his/her room to the laundry machine to check the completion or spent meaningless time near the machine because there is not a substantial way to monitor current status of washing or drying from the machine in own room. Other users who are waiting his/her turn for use of the machine also had to frequently check the completion of current use by physical movements between rooms. Even other waiting users for second or later had to spend substantial efforts to check the completion of current and previous uses of the machine. Many actual users complained the problems during the user studies.

If a current user missed picking up his/her laundry right after the completion, a next user who had waited his/her turn had to wait another time until the current user's pick up. If the current user did not appear to pick up on time, the next user moved the current user's completed laundry to other places (e.g., shelves) to start his/her laundry. In this case, the current (or previous) user would feel unpleasant experience such that other unknown person touched his cloth, sometimes, including underwear. The students in the study also expressed a concern of a lack of communication between users in the community for the use of machine. Therefore, we initially thought that the issues could be resolved using new service and system design in terms of UX, especially using network between laundry machine and personal device (e.g., smartphone), which is a basic concept of IoT. That is, the laundry machine has own function to detect the current status and expected completion (or waiting) time for multiple users as well as notify them to multiple users. Each user in current use and a line also can check the status and receive messages from the machine, using individual device such as smartphone.

2.2 Development of a Usage Model

Based on the analysis, a usage model was developed for the system and service. Since the use situation between system and users are different to the conventional single user system, a use model for multiple users was attempted to generate. Initially, a conceptual use model of CSCW was considered to apply, which represents the use of system for multiple user. Figure 1 shows the historical categories of CSCW system and instance applications of each category, identified by Shneiderman and Plaisant [2]. As shown in the Fig. 1, the CSCW systems are categorized by time of use (synchronous vs. asynchronous) across space of use (remote vs. co-located) among users.

However, we realized that the framework for CSCW was not applicable to develop a usage model for the present study. We could identify the primary reasons of this mismatch. First, while the users in CSCW are cooperating for achieving a common goal (e.g., completion of discussion for decision making or document preparation),

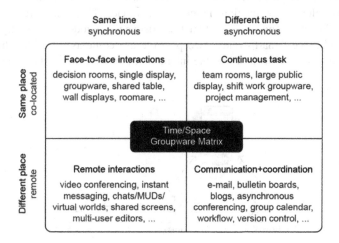

Fig. 1. Time/space four-quadrant matrix model of group-supported work [2]

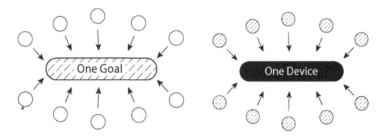

Fig. 2. The traditional CSCW usage model(left) and the Community IoT Product Usage Model (right) (Note: blank item represents personal devices, slash textured item represents goals to achieve, and solid filled item represents a IoT device)

the users in the present study have own goal (e.g., "completion of laundry of my clothes," "reservation for next use") regardless of other users. Second, while the CSCW users use their own device to complete the common goal, the users in the present study use own personal device (e.g., smartphone) to access the main device (e.g., laundry machine). Figure 2 shows the conceptual differences in usage models between traditional CSCW system and the present study, community IoT service and system. Consequently, the multiple users in CSCW works together with distributed cognition [4] while the multiple users in the present community system/service share specific system across time and space.

In addition to this, as a result of usage model development for the present study, four main agents were observed and identified, including: a present user who is currently using a laundry machine, the laundry machine with IoT equipment, a first waiting person of the machine, and other waiting persons. However, it was assumed that every human user has own mobile device to communicate between agents such as human users or the machine. Figure 3 shows general relations among the four agents in the service.

Based on the usage model, a list of general user tasks was identified, which are expected to implement as functions in the system/service. The tasks were identified two dimensions, the space and time of interactions between main device (laundry machine) and personal device (smartphone). Two possible use contexts were identified for the space category (see Table 1). First, the interaction could be done where the main and

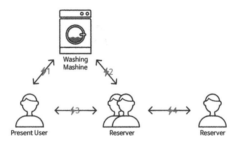

Fig. 3. Four agents (users and device) consisting the service

Table 1. Time/space matrix model of community laundry system

		Time		
		Before Reserved time	**On Reserved time**	**After Reserved time**
Space (main and personal devices)	**Same Place**	(no interaction but physical interaction between user & machine)	Authentication	(no interaction but physical interaction between user & machine)
	Remote Place	Check availability, waiting line, etc. Make reservation	Evaluation of previous users	Pick-up message

the personal device are in the same place such as in the laundry room. In this case, along with a long-distance network such as internet protocol through Wi-Fi or data service for smart phone, a simple short-distance network such as Bluetooth or Near Field Communication (NFC) could be used for the authorization. Second, the user can access the main device using his/her personal device in a remote place (e.g., own room or outside of building) to check the status of the main device like a typical IoT system. In this case, a long-distance network would be needed to connect the devices.

Three possible use contexts were identified for the time dimension in perspective of user to complete own purpose, including: (1) Before reserved time: because the laundry machine is being used for previous user's purpose, he/she would check the expected completion time for previous user and the number of previous users in the waiting line, and reserve his/her order on the specific machine; (2) On reserved time: when the user starts using the machine. The user needs to authorize him/herself in front of the main machine as well as evaluates previous user's manner for the community system; and (3) After reserved time: when the laundry machine is finishing the washing. The user would receive a push message to pick up the laundry few minutes earlier its completion.

3 Development

3.1 Task Flow Chart

Based on the usage model and the general tasks list, detailed problems and requirements for each agent as well as what kinds of information need to be delivered between agents to resolve the problems were identified, along with considerations of personal privacy. Then a conceptual service model was developed in forms of UX service flow chart. Figure 4 shows a sample of the service flow chart. The service chart was used to identify groups of features and functions of the service. The three main features were: (1) 'washing reservation' to determine the order of the laundry machine use among

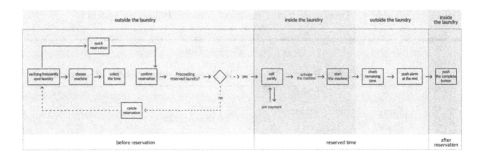

Fig. 4. A sample of service flow chart

users; (2) 'self authentication' to check the present user at his/her reserved time, and (3) 'laundry monitoring' to provide users with current status of the washing in real time. Some distinctive functions for the service also were identified including, for example, 'poke' to send an anonymous push notification for the previous user to pick up his/her completed laundry and 'manner evaluation' to evaluate other users' manner to the community machine.

3.2   Concept UI Design

In order to validate the suggested UX design along with features and functions, a prototype of user interface in a mobile phone was developed. Figure 5 shows 3 sample screenshots of the smartphone application UI. (It should be noted here that the UI was designed in Korean.) Figure 5 (a) is a 'Reservation' screen which shows current status of laundry machines in each building with multiple floors. A user can check which machine is being currently available, otherwise, when the current use for previous user

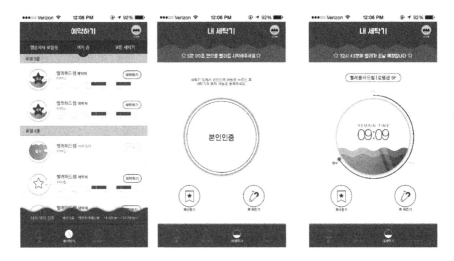

Fig. 5. Sample screen shots of UI prototype: (a) Reservation; (b) Authentication; and (c) Status Monitoring

would be finished, and how many users are waiting the machine in the line for each machine. Finally, the user can select and reserve a specific laundry machine which seems to be most feasible. When a user received a message from system notifying that his/her order becomes to ready, the user needs to authorize himself/herself in front of the reserved machine using own smartphone application depicted in Fig. 5 (b) ('Authentication'). After the user starts his laundry, the user may check the status of the machine washing his/her laundry in a remote place, using the UI screen shot in Fig. 5 (c). As shown in Fig. 5 (c), the UI provides the user with remained time to complete the laundry using various ways such as clock and progress bar.

3.3 Concept System Development

A hardware prototype of laundry machine integrated with IoT device (Raspberry Pi) also has been developed to build and aggregate the comprehensive system including the laundry machine and smartphone application. However, due to the limited time and resource, a series of evaluations by experts (e.g., walkthrough and heuristic evaluation) has been conducted for usability evaluation to revise the UI. More elaborative usability test using actual users for evaluating aggregated UX service will be conducted in near future in more realistic situations.

4 Discussion and Conclusion

The present research shows a case study to design a comprehensive UX for community system with IoT, which is a laundry system in a dormitory. Through the study, it was able to confirm that:

First, UX development of communal environment revealed respectively unusual usage models as it must consider multiple user UX simultaneously. During developing the usage model and its framework, it was identified that the model of CSCW was not applicable to the current study due to differences in purposes among users toward the sharing system, even though multiple users need to access the system regardless of space and time. Second, some unique features, such as push alarm or manner evaluation, were needed to enhance the inter-user credibility to serve as differentiated using models. Third, the development of higher fidelity prototype including hardware, software, network, and service seems to be necessary to reflect users' potential and tangible needs.

The primary limitation of this study is that the comprehensive system was not evaluated in terms of usability test and acceptability. As mentioned, even though several expert evaluations were conducted for the UI of the smartphone application, it would not represent actual acceptability for overall UX of the system to be perceived by actual target users. Therefore, it would be desirable to assess overall system/service through appropriate evaluation methods, rather than traditional heuristic methods or usability tests for simple UI with a single user.

Finally, the present study itself is expected to provide a better UX environment to the dormitories and community laundries, the typical environment of communal washing. Also, we expect that the study could be a precedence case of UX development and framework research for the new communal usage environment. The study would serve as a preliminary case of an application of the IoT technology to the sharing economy as well.

Acknowledgement. This study was supported by a 'University for Creative Korea' Grant to Handong Global University through the Ministry of Education, South Korea. We would like to thank professors InWook Choi and Sang-Hwan Kim for advising the study and manuscript preparation.

References

1. Dewan, P., Choudhary, R.: A high-level and flexible framework for implementing multiuser user interfaces. ACM Trans. Inf. Syst. (TOIS) Spec. Issue User Interface Softw. Technol. **10** (4), 345–380 (1992)
2. Shneiderman, B., Plaisant, C.: Designing the User Interface: Strategies for Effective Human-Computer Interaction, 5th edn. pp. 360–402. Pearson, London (2009)
3. Vermeeren, A.P.O.X., Law, E.L.-C., Roto, V., Obrist, M., Hoonhout, J., Mattaila, K.V.: User experience evaluation methods: current state and development needs. In: NordiCHI 2010 Proceedings of the 6th Nordic Conference on Human-Computer Interaction, pp. 521–530 (2010)
4. Dix, A., Finlay, J., Abowd, G.D., Beale, R.: Human-Computer Interaction, 3rd edn. pp. 504–508. Pearson, Harlow (2004)

Evaluation of an Inverse-Kinematics Depth-Sensing Controller for Operation of a Simulated Robotic Arm

Akhilesh Kumar Mishra[1], Lourdes Peña-Castillo[1,2], and Oscar Meruvia-Pastor[1(✉)]

[1] Department of Computer Science, Memorial University of Newfoundland, St John's, Canada
{Akm565,Lourdes,Oscar}@mun.ca
[2] Department of Biology, Memorial University of Newfoundland, St John's, Canada

Abstract. Interaction using depth-sensing cameras has many applications in computer vision and spatial manipulation tasks. We present a user study that compares a short-range depth-sensing camera-based controller with an inverse-kinematics keyboard controller and a forward-kinematics joystick controller for two placement tasks. The study investigated ease of use, user performance and user preferences. Task completion times were recorded and insights on the measured and perceived advantages and disadvantages of these three alternative controllers from the perspective of user efficiency and satisfaction were obtained. The results indicate that users performed equally well using the depth-sensing camera and the keyboard controllers. User performance was significantly better with these two approaches than with the joystick controller, the reference method used in comparable commercial simulators. Most participants found that the depth-sensing camera controller was easy to use and intuitive, but some expressed discomfort stemming from the pose required for interaction with the controller.

Keywords: Gesture-based controllers for robot arm manipulation · Depth-sensing cameras and short-range RGBD sensors · Inverse and forward kinematics · User studies

1 Introduction

Human-Computer Interaction using depth-sensing cameras has captured the imagination of enthusiasts and researchers alike. Depth-sensing cameras are especially suited for spatial manipulation tasks, and are nowadays used in many areas, including mobile computing, gaming and robotics [1–4]. After the introduction of the first Kinect, a new group of depth-sensing cameras with a much closer range of interaction appeared in the market, allowing for the technology to be used in a wider variety of applications in desktops, laptops, wearable and mobile devices [5–9].

In this article, we investigate a depth-sensing camera controller based on inverse-kinematics for placement tasks using a robot arm simulator, and describe a user

A. Marcus (Ed.): DUXU 2016, Part III, LNCS 9748, pp. 373–381, 2016.
DOI: 10.1007/978-3-319-40406-6_36

study to evaluate participants' performance using short-range depth-sensing camera controllers against comparable off-the-shelf controllers.

2 Related Work

In recent years there has been a significant increase in the usage of robotic arms that require human manipulation in industrial, medical and offshore applications.

One of the earliest manipulation problems studied in the field of robotics was the insertion of a peg into a hole using a robotic arm while preventing the wedging or jamming of the peg [10]. Since then, there have been significant advances in manipulation techniques and robot control. There are many techniques for manipulating a robot arm, such as the Titan IV robot arm, involving position-controlled manipulators [11–13], joystick based controllers [11, 14], speech [15, 16], gesture based controllers [2, 3, 17], computer simulations [18, 19], and even smartphones [20]. To help training operators to control a robotic arm, there are virtual simulators like GRI Simulations Inc.'s VROV manipulator trainer [19], which help a user train on a particular robotic arm type using either a master controller or a joystick. Compared to joysticks, master controllers are more sophisticated and expensive devices. On the other hand, joysticks are more affordable, but not as convenient as master controllers, since they are generic use products designed for gaming which do not exactly map to the functionalities of master controllers.

In this research, we evaluated alternatives to control robots arms using off-the-shelf input devices, such as cameras and keyboards. Previous methods which use either stereo cameras or depth-sensing cameras to control a robot are described in [2–4]. To manipulate the simulated robotic arm used in this study, we implemented the method presented by Mishra et al. [21]. In that approach, the user specifies the target position of the robot actuator by moving his/her hands in front of a depth-sensing camera. The depth camera returns the coordinates of the users' hand and the coordinates are passed as target position to an inverse kinematics module, where the joint angles for the arm simulator are calculated using CCD [22]. After the joint angles have been calculated, the robot arm simulator module applies the rotations and the end-effector reaches the target.

3 Methods

We compared user performance using the inverse-kinematics control method proposed by Mishra et al. [21] to control a robot-arm of type Titan IV (Fig. 1a) against user performance using two other common control devices: keyboards and joysticks. Keyboards were selected for comparison because most users are familiar with the use of keyboards, while the joystick controller is the reference interface used in some commercial simulators. Master controllers, such as the one shown in Fig. 1b, were not included in this study because they are costly (in the range of tens of thousands of dollars) and highly specialized devices not usually available to most users.

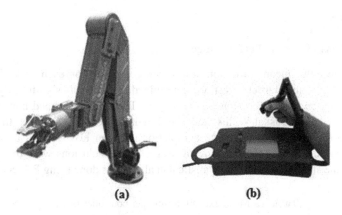

(a)   (b)

Fig. 1. (a) Titan 4 robotic arm (b) Master controller for Titan 4 robotic arm. Image credit: Copyright 2005FMC Technologies, Inc.

The goal of the study was to find answers to three main questions: (1) How will users' performance with a depth-sensing camera control system compare to their performance using the other alternatives? (2) How long do users needed to get used to each method? (3) Which controller will users prefer the most?. To answer the above mentioned questions and to evaluate in more detail the user's impressions on the different type of controllers, a robot arm simulator shown in Fig. 2 was developed to carry out the study.

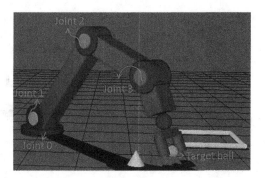

Fig. 2. Robot arm simulated with OpenGL.

3.1   User Study

Our user study had a balanced design with 18 participants recruited, 2 tasks, 3 controllers and 6 orderings of controller usage. An ordering of controller usage, for example, was to use first the keyboard controller, second the depth camera controller, and third the joystick controller. Each user performed each task 10 times with each controller in the assigned order of usage. Their task completion times were recorded and their feedback with regard to the different controllers was collected with an exit questionnaire.

4 Results

4.1 Analysis of Users' Performance

Table 1 shows the mean execution times per controller for each task. Using the Shapiro-Wilk test and Bartlett's test, we determined that our data significantly deviated from normality and had heterogeneous variances. Thus, we performed non-parametric tests, such as the Kruskal-Wallis and the Friedman test, in addition to two-way ANOVA to test whether the average completion time per task differed between controllers when considering the ordering of usage. The conclusions were the same irrespective of the statistical test used. Statistical analysis was done using R (version 3.1.1).

Table 1. Mean execution time per controller (secs.)

Controller	Keyboard	Camera	Joystick
Task 1	17.3 ± 14.5	18.1 ± 11.9	28.7 ± 12.9
Task 2	29.6 ± 17.5	30.8 ± 13.4	38.0 ± 17.6

Figure 3 shows the completion times per controlling device per task. The average completion time for both tasks varied significantly depending on the controller used (p-value < 2e-16 and p-value = 6.78e07 for Task 1 and Task 2 respectively).

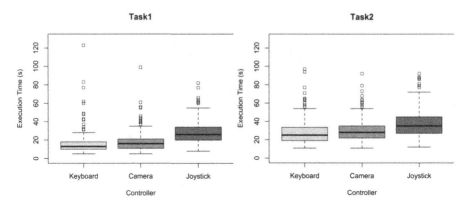

Fig. 3. Execution times per controller for Task 1 and Task 2. The black lines inside the boxes indicate the median completion time, the bottoms of the boxes are at the 25 percentile and the tops are at the 75 percentile.

The results indicate that the depth-sensing camera controller and the keyboard controller allowed for similar levels of user performance. User performance with these two approaches was significantly better than their performance using the joystick controller, which is the reference method used in comparable commercial simulators. Our results also show that there is a significant learning effect in the case of the depth-camera controller, which was also perceived by the participants (see Fig. 4).

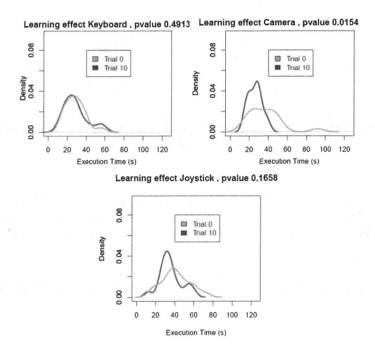

Fig. 4. Learning effect for each input device for Task 1 and Task 2 (Color figure online)

4.2 User Perception and Preference

This section discusses the data gathered from the exit questionnaire.

Participants' perception on ease of use, ease of learning, usefulness, ergonomics, performance and overall preference for each controller was collected. Participants found that the depth-sensing camera controller was both easy to use and intuitive, but expressed some discomfort during interaction. This discomfort is a known usability problem of vision-based gesture interactions [23].

Perception of Ease of Learning. The majority of participants found the three controllers easy to learn, with 15 participants (83.33 %) strongly agreeing that the depth-camera method was easy to learn, 14 participants (77.78 %) strongly agreeing that the keyboard method was easy to learn, and 12 participants (66.66 %) strongly agreeing that the joystick method was easy to learn. The complete results about the perception of ease of learning are shown in Fig. 5.

Perception of Performance. No participant found the performance of the controllers inappropriate (Fig. 6). More than 88 % of the participants agree that the performance of the depth-camera and keyboard controllers was appropriate.

Perception of Ease of Use. Figure 7 shows the user responses about whether each input device was easy to use. Users rated the depth-camera and keyboard as easy to use. The joystick was rated slightly lower as compared to other input devices. In general, users found all the devices easy to use.

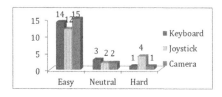

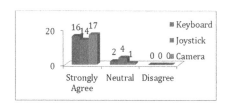

Fig. 5. Perception of ease of learning (Color figure online)

Fig. 6. Perception of performance (Color figure online)

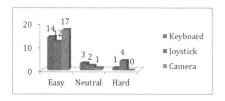

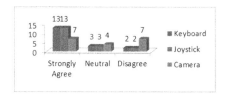

Fig. 7. Perception of ease of use (Color figure online)

Fig. 8. Ergonomics rating of each controller (Color figure online)

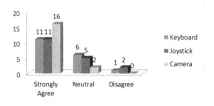

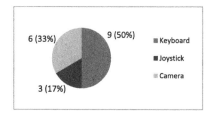

Fig. 9. Usefulness rating of each controller (Color figure online)

Fig. 10. User responses for least amount of training time (Color figure online)

Perception of Ergonomics. The depth-camera interface was rated lower in ergonomics ratings when compared to both the keyboard and the joystick interface. Figure 8 shows the user responses about ergonomics of each input device. Only 7 out of 18 participants reported that the depth-camera was an ergonomic interface and some of the unstructured user feedback (discussed below) provided some further insight into this result.

Perception of Usefulness. The depth-camera interface was rated highest in usefulness when compared to both the keyboard and the joystick interface (Fig. 9), with 16 out of 18 participants strongly agreeing that the depth-camera was a useful interface with the rest being neutral about it, whereas the keyboard and joystick controllers were found useful by 11 participants.

Perception of Training Time. Figure 10 illustrates that 9 participants (50 %) believed that the keyboard took the least amount of training time. The depth-camera was rated second in training time, with 6 participants (33 %) saying that the depth-camera

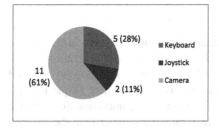

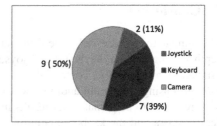

Fig. 11. Users' perception of performance after training (Color figure online)

Fig. 12. Overall input controller preference (Color figure online)

requires the least amount of training. The joystick was rated lowest as only 3 participants (17 %) said that joystick requires the least amount of training. We believe this impression was caused because the joystick was controlled using forward kinematics, making it harder to use than the other alternatives.

Perception of Performance after training. Figure 11 shows that 11 (61 %) participants reported that the depth-camera performs best after training, 5 (28 %) participants reported that keyboard performs best and only 2 (11 %) participants chose the joystick as best performer after training and practice. It is interesting to note that users favored the depth-camera controller after training, even though they performed equally well with the keyboard.

Overall Preference. Figure 12 shows user's overall controller preference. 9 participants (50 %) responded that they preferred the most the depth-camera controller. The second most preferred controller by 7 participants (39 %) was the keyboard. The least preferred option is the joystick controller which is the controller preferred by 2 participants (11 %).

Written User Feedback. The questionnaire also asked participants to write comments about the experiment and the interface. With respect to the depth camera position, some users reported that the camera position played an important role in overall performance of the depth-camera controller. The depth-camera was mounted on top of the desktop monitor like a webcam and, for some users, that was not a convenient position. One participant suggested that, instead of mounting the depth-camera on top of the monitor, the depth-camera should be kept beside the keyboard on the same plane as the keyboard, facing upwards so that the user does not have to lift their hand too high to interact with the camera. Also, another user suggested that there should be a support for the elbow if the camera was to be mounted on top of the desktop monitor. Causing discomfort is a known usability problem of vision-based gesture interaction systems and there are steps that can be taken to reduce fatigue, as proposed by [23]. Another alternative to reduce fatigue is to implement a hand gesture control system providing tactile feedback to the user's hand, such as the one proposed by Kim et al. [24].

5 Conclusion

We comparatively assessed three different devices to control a robotic arm, namely, depth-sensing camera, keyboard and joystick. To do this, we developed a robot arm simulator which could be controlled using a standard keyboard, a gaming joystick and a depth-sensing camera. In addition, we conducted a user study where 18 participants were recruited to participate. Our results indicate that the task completion times for the depth-camera and the keyboard controllers were significantly lower than the joystick controller, without any significant statistical difference observed between the depth-camera and the keyboard. Our results also show that there is a significant learning effect in the case of the depth-camera controller which was also perceived by the participants. While participants had a positive perception of all three controllers, 50 % of the users reported that they would prefer the depth-camera interface over the joystick and the keyboard interface. The reason why the joystick was least preferred could be related to the fact that the joystick was using forward kinematics and its execution times are significantly longer, compared to the depth-camera and the keyboard.

References

1. Lun, R., Zhao, W.: A Survey of Applications and Human Motion Recognition with Microsoft Kinect. Int. J. Pattern Recogn. Artif. Intell. (2015)
2. Corradini, A., Gross, H.: Camera-based gesture recognition for robot control. In: 2000 Proceedings of the IEEE-INNS-ENNS International Joint Conference on Neural Networks. IJCNN 2000 (2000). doi:10.1109/IJCNN.2000.860762
3. A. Anonymous: Real-time 3D pointing gesture with kinect for object-based navigation by the visually impaired. Presented at Biosignals and Biorobotics Conference (BRC), 2013 ISSNIP (2013). doi:10.1109/BRC.2013.6487535
4. Suay, H.B., Chernova, S.: Humanoid robot control using depth camera. In: 2011 6th ACM/IEEE International Conference on Human-Robot Interaction (HRI) (2011)
5. 31 October 2014. http://www.roadtovr.com/nimble-sense-kickstarter-virtual-reality-oculus-rift-time-of-flight-input/
6. Leap Motion Controller, 10 June 2015. https://www.leapmotion.com/
7. Microsoft Kinect for Windows V2, 25 June 2015. https://www.microsoft.com/en-us/kinectforwindows/
8. Intel Real Sense SDK, 16 June 2015. https://software.intel.com/en-us/intel-realsense-sdk
9. Project Tango, ATAP, 25 June 2015. https://www.google.com/atap/project-tango/
10. Whitney, D.E.: Quasi-static assembly of compliantly supported rigid parts. J. Dyn. Syst. Measur. Control **104**(1), 65–77 (1982)
11. Sian, N.E., Yokoi, K., Kajita, S., Kanehiro, F., Tanie, K.: Whole body teleoperation of a humanoid robot - development of a simple master device using joysticks. In: 2002 IEEE/RSJ International Conference on Intelligent Robots and Systems (2002). doi:10.1109/IRDS. 2002.1041657
12. Manikandan, R., Arulmozhiyal, R.: Position control of DC servo drive using fuzzy logic controller. In: 2014 International Conference on Advances in Electrical Engineering (ICAEE) (2014). doi:10.1109/ICAEE.2014.6838474

13. Jan, V., Marek, S., Pavol, M., Vladimir, V., Stephen, D.J., Roy, P.: Near-time-optimal position control of an actuator with PMSM. In: 2005 European Conference on Power Electronics and Applications (2005). doi:10.1109/EPE.2005.219516

14. Lu, Y., Huang, Q., Li, M., Jiang, X., Keerio, M.: A friendly and human-based teleoperation system for humanoid robot using joystick. In: 2008 7th World Congress on Intelligent Control and Automation, WCICA 2008 (2008). doi:10.1109/WCICA.2008.4593278

15. Ng-Thow-Hing, V., Luo, P., Okita, S.: Synchronized gesture and speech production for humanoid robots. In: 2010 IEEE/RSJ International Conference on Intelligent Robots and Systems (IROS) (2010)

16. House, B., Malkin, J., Bilmes, J.: The VoiceBot: a voice controlled robot arm. In: Proceedings of the SIGCHI Conference on Human Factors in Computing Systems (2009). http://doi.acm.org/10.1145/1518701.1518731. doi:10.1145/1518701.1518731

17. Oniga, S., Tisan, A., Mic, D., Buchman, A., Vida-Ratiu, A.: Hand postures recognition system using artificial neural networks implemented in FPGA. In: 30th International Spring Seminar on Electronics Technology (2007). doi:10.1109/ISSE.2007.4432909

18. Chen, C.X., Trivedi, M.M., Bidlack, C.R.: Simulation and animation of sensor-driven robots. IEEE Trans. Robot. Autom. 10(5), 684–704 (1994). doi:10.1109/70.326572

19. (18/06/2015). VROV Manipulator Trainer [VROV Manipulator Trainer]. http://www.grisim.com/products/vrov-virtual-remotely-operated-vehicle/

20. Parga, C., Li, X., Yu, W.: Tele-manipulation of robot arm with smartphone. In: 2013 6th International Symposium on Resilient Control Systems (ISRCS) (2013). doi:10.1109/ISRCS.2013.6623751

21. Mishra, A.K., Meruvia-Pastor, O.: Robot arm manipulation using depth-sensing cameras and inverse kinematics. Oceans - St. John's (2014). doi:10.1109/OCEANS.2014.7003029

22. Kenwright, B.: Inverse kinematics - cyclic coordinate descent (CCD). J. Graphics, GPU & Game Tools, 177–217 (2012)

23. Hincapié-Ramos, J.D., Guo, X., Moghadasian, P., Irani, P.: Consumed endurance: a metric to quantify arm fatigue of mid-air interactions. Presented at Proceedings of the SIGCHI Conference on Human Factors in Computing Systems. 2014, Available: http://doi.acm.org/10.1145/2556288.2557130. doi:10.1145/2556288.2557130

24. Kim, K., Kim, J., Choi, J., Kim, J., Lee, S.: Depth camera-based 3D hand gesture controls with immersive tactile feedback for natural mid-air gesture interactions. Sensors (Basel) 15(1), 1022–1046 (2015). doi:10.3390/s150101022

The Simpler the Better: How the User-Inspired Innovation Process (UIIP) Improved the Development of RelaxedCare – the Entirely New Way of Communicating and Caring

Martin Morandell[1(✉)], Sandra Dittenberger[2], Andrea Koscher[2],
Emanuel Sandner[1], and Mirsolav Sili[1]

[1] Health & Environment Department, AIT Austrian Institute of Technology,
Biomedical Systems, Wr. Neustadt, Austria
{martin.morandell,emanuel.sandner,
mirsolav.sili}@ait.ac.at
[2] NDU New Design University, Sankt Pölten, Austria
{sandra.dittenberger,andrea.koscher}@ndu.at

Abstract. "Is my mom doing okay right now?" Answering this question at a glance and in an unobtrusive way could relieve stress for informal caregivers. This was the primary goal of the RelaxedCare project. Involving end-users in the development process of research projects in this domain is perceived as a "must", but the extent to which this is actually done varies greatly. This paper describes how applying the "User Inspired Innovation Process" which involved more than 200 end-users throughout the development process has influenced the functions, design and context of use of the final prototype.

Keywords: User inspired innovation process · User centered design · Ambient assisted living

1 Background

Informal caregivers are a major pillar of the social care system in most of the countries. Taking care of a family member or another close person can be on one hand an enriching, positive experience; but very often, especially when the caregiving task lasts over a long period of time and the person in need of care has, for example, a neurodegenerative disease, informal caregivers (IC) have a high risk of feeling continuously stressed and overburdened. A representative study [1] conducted in Austria in 2005 showed that 80 % of the people in need of care (referred as "assisted persons") receive their care by informal caregivers (IC) at home. More than 66 % of these IC's feel overburdened by that task sooner or later, resulting in a decreased quality of the interaction between the two parties.

One of the major problems ICs face is how to assure the well-being of the AP when the IC is alone at home. Hence personal visits and frequent phone calls are the logical consequence and the most common approach to deal with this situation.

© Springer International Publishing Switzerland 2016
A. Marcus (Ed.): DUXU 2016, Part III, LNCS 9748, pp. 382–391, 2016.
DOI: 10.1007/978-3-319-40406-6_37

1.1 Aim of the Project

RelaxedCare wants to increase the quality of communication by reducing the number and necessity of these short, but time-consuming status checks. RelaxedCare aims to provide a system to keep the IC updated on the overall well-being of the AP in a passive and pervasive way, so as to reduce the burden of caregiving and thereby enhance the quality of life of people in care situations and the bond between IC and AP.

1.2 State of the Art

A major aim of Active and Assisted Living (AAL) is to enable people to live longer more independently at home [2, 3].

User Involvement. There is no doubt that users must be involved in the development of Assistive Technology, but the extent to which this is actually done varies greatly by project.

Many apply various user-involvement methods, but most of them do not follow a concrete process. Standards like ISO 9241-210 (Ergonomics of human-system interaction) [4] help by supplying a more standardized development cycle which involves users at selected development phases. The FURTUNE Guidelines [5] give advice on how to involve primary end users into the research process– but still, end-users could influence the development of technical-solutions much more if they are involved in further ways.

The Ambient Assisted Living Joint Programme provides a catalogue [6] that suggests different user involvement methods for different phases of an AAL project, but this is not necessarily combined with a concrete process of how to use them.

Technology. At the moment there are just a few existing solutions on the market that inform one about the state of an assisted person. Some of these solutions (available only in the US) offer information about the current state of the assisted person via a user interface such as a webpage [7–10]. They have been described in more detail in [11].

2 Methodology

As user involvement is a continuous and active part of the development, the technical approach is also briefly described in this section.

2.1 Technical Approach

For RelaxedCare, two major technology fields are of primary interest – Behavior Pattern Recognition and Ubiquitous Computing.

Mark Weiser, describes ubiquitous computing in [10] as "the method of enhancing computer use by making many computers available throughout the physical environment, but making them effectively invisible to the user." This is a major challenge for RelaxedCare – both, the user interfaces and the smart home sensor network have to integrate into the living environments of the end-users.

In the field of Ambient Assisted Living, behavior pattern recognition (BPR) is a common research topic for the last 10 years. In particular, efforts were put on the detection of "activities of daily living". Based on smart home sensor networks, these activities of daily living are processed and changes recognized. On the other side, ubiquitous and pervasive computing methods aim to create systems that integrate into the environment. RelaxedCare tries to combine those two approaches to develop an information and communication system that connects people in care situation.

The concept of RelaxedCare. To gain user acceptance and a high degree of usability, we aim to provide the IC a pervasive, ubiquitous, low-barrier object as user interface that becomes part of the living environment. The basic idea behind the RelaxedCare system is illustrated in Fig. 1 and described below.

Fig. 1. The RelaxedCare concept – the Assisted Person on the upper part, the Informal Caregiver on the lower part.

At the AP's home, illustrated in the upper part of the picture, a smart home system is installed. Various sensors detect when the user is active, e.g. motion sensors in the living room, pressure sensors in the bed or door sensors on the refrigerator or entrance door. This information is collected within an AAL middleware platform and behaviour pattern methods are then applied on these data, yielding a wellbeing status. This status is then relayed to the IC side, as represented in the lower part of the picture. Whether the IC is at home or at work, the well-being state will be presented in an unobtrusive way such as a colour-coded lamp or a digital picture specific to the well-being state. When the IC is mobile, the same information is available via a smart-phone app. When the well-being state changes, the information can be tracked by the IC, thus keeping the IC always informed about the current well-being of the AP.

To gain user acceptance and a high degree of usability, we aim to provide the IC a pervasive, ubiquitous, low-barrier object as user interface that becomes part of the living environment."

2.2   User Involvement Methodology

The ISO 9241-210 standard offers information about the involvement of end-users in different phases of a product development process. Lessons learned in applying this process methodology in other projects show that the steps of the ISO 9241-210 standard are often executed by different expert groups (e.g. technology development, design and user research) within the project. This can create stumbling blocks to a smooth and efficient workflow and inter-group communication because this process model doesn't address individuals directly.

To overcome this identified gap a process methodology was chosen which addresses not only the involvement of end-user in the product development process but also offers a guideline for the involvement of each team member to actively involve him - or herself in every step of the process.

The User Inspired Innovation Process. The User Inspired Innovation Process UIIP [13] offers a process methodology designed from an individual's point of view. The key question for this process methodology is: "where and how can I actively contribute to the different steps of the product development process?" The UIIP combines the guideline for involving end-users (ISO 9241-210 standard) with a guideline for the involvement of each team member in a holistic product development process.

The UIIP consists of 7 steps: (a) ignite, (b) perceive, (c) collect, (d) decode, (e) assemble, (f) experiment and (g) merge. The step 'ignite' aims to create an understanding and inclusion of each team member's creative potential; to exchange experiences and information with other team members; and to build bridges to other knowledge areas. On an anthropological level, the step 'perceive' is used as an awareness-building phase for the target groups of the project and their life contexts. Especially human values, needs, emotions, behaviour, and used technology items are addressed. The step 'collect' brings a mix of design and ethnographic research methods to bear, like audio-/visual documents and materials, camera surveys with contextual interviews, perspective-sorting studies, user workshops, cultural probes and studies, etc.

Subsequently, the step 'decode' involves the sorting, grouping and interpreting of the collected data. Findings from these qualitative inquiries are used to inspire the team to create new project approaches. An example is shown in Fig. 2. During the 'assemble' step the team creates ideas, prototypes them and develops use cases and scenarios. Proofs of concept with users and the incorporation of given feedback to the created concept characterizes the 'experiment' step of the process. Finally, the 'merging' of the concept with developed technology and created business cases takes place.

Fig. 2. The cube of Requirements: It consists of small cubes. Each cube represents key findings from one method of the first end-user requirements study.

3   Execution

The research process for the first end-user requirements engineering study was designed as an unstandardized, qualitative research study (Flick, 2009). This was a comparative study broken down into five phases, employing eight methods in total deriving a) from the field of design research (Assumption Personas and Personas, Show and Tell Method, Cultural Probes and Design Workshop) and b) from the field of qualitative social research (Questionnaire, Focus Group Discussion and Contextual Inquiry Interview). The applied research methods focused on uncovering relevant factors for assessing user needs and wishes at an early stage of the project. The study design, with its mix of methods deriving from the aforementioned research areas, was chosen to ensure rich output as a basis for the subsequent project development process. This first research period lasted from June to September 2013. A total of 207 test persons participated, split between the two user groups – informal caregivers (average age 77 years) and assisted persons (average age 66 years) – and comprising 155 females and 52 males.

3.1   Lessons from the First Phase

We learned that caregiving in families is not unidirectional. Even though the younger generation is more seen as the "informal caregiver", they are still the children of their parents, and hence the "assisted persons" still care about their child and their family members. A major lesson from this was that most of people in need of care do not want to put extra burden on their family members and thus avoid asking for help. Hence, a new way of communication is needed that enables them to ask for help, a phone call or a visit with a very low barrier. Furthermore we learned a lot about the attitude of people towards technology, their favorite places in their homes and which aspects of technology usage in their everyday life are preferred. After the execution of all research methods from the first user requirements study, the initial Assumption Personas which had been defined in a common team creation process were compared with the findings for each user group, and several major changes had to be made. One of the major findings revealed that the average age for caregivers and their assisted persons, originally defined to be 30 + and 75 + respectively, had to be changed to 50 + and 80 +. Concerning activities of daily living and preferred objects of everyday life, various similarities among the group of the caregivers and the group of the assisted persons could be identified (Fig. 3).

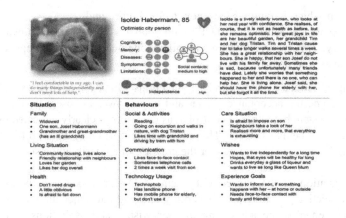

Fig. 3. Detailed Persona at the end of the analysis phase 1

Based on the findings of the first user requirements engineering study and the defined use cases and scenarios, five different design concepts were elaborated. In a common team election process, three out of the five design concepts which had been developed by the design team, were chosen. In order to prepare the next step of the development process in which the developed design concepts would be tested in an informal usability test with end-users of both target groups, the three design concepts were prototyped and visualized with appropriate everyday use scenarios. The informal usability test was then conducted to gather first user impressions of the proposed concepts, in order to be able to refine the concepts in an early stage of the product development for integrating the most promising aspects into prototype I.

3.2   Lessons from the Second Phase

The second end-user research study was created as a qualitative research study applying the method of design workshops, which included several sessions deriving from the field of design research. The design workshops consisted of three different sessions: round-table discussions, model building sessions and voting sessions, within the framework of the different types of messages and the cubes appearance in terms of color, material, surface structure and size.

The second research study focuses on two end-user groups: informal caregivers and young people with an average age of 17. Those groups were chosen bearing in mind the findings of the first end-user study, which revealed that the product and the services developed within this project have to address first of all informal caregivers followed by the assisted persons – but might also beyond that affect the whole family, from younger to older people. The design workshops took place in January 2015. All in all, 9 informal caregiver and 10 youths participated, with a respective average age of 17 and 72 years.

The conclusions drawn from the second user requirements study comprised recommendations for the embodiment of prototype II.

Addressing the user-group of the informal caregiver, we had to realize that the project has to face two kinds of users within this one target group:

- One group which is familiar with new technologies, and
- one group which is not at all facile with – and is even skeptical towards – new technology. This group may own a mobile phone but prefer not to depend on it and often leaves it at home.

Creating a modular system with basic functions which can later be extended might help to overcome the acceptance barrier and to empower the users to not to be controlled by the system but rather to control it, as the findings clearly indicated that people hate the feeling of being surveyed. This empowerment will play an important role when going to market and enables moreover the creation of an easily understandable market message.

The translation of the chosen User-Centred Design process methodology from theory into practice generally went smoothly and without major difficulties. The iterative process enabled the addressing of user wishes and aspirations in our design proposals. The concrete feedback sessions on the developed concepts and design proposals led to continuous refinement of the overall system design. Lessons learned from other projects show that the steps of the User-Centred Design process are often executed by different expert groups, e.g. technology development, design and user research, of the project. At project's start we defined our goal as the involvement of all experts from different fields in each step of the product development process. Since we are currently running the field trials of our developed system and the research project is near its end, some conclusions can be drawn concerning our own lessons learned from the implementation of this approach to the applied process.

During this translation process we identified some areas for improvements. As mentioned before, we were well aware that the User-Centred Design Process offers information about the involvement of end-users in different phases of a product development process and that we had to keep an eye on the involvement of team members of our different expert fields in each process phase. During the work on the project we realized that we still hadn't managed to overcome the identified gap between the expert groups of technical development, design and user research sufficiently. One conclusion from this could be that the User-Centred Design process model doesn't address individuals – meaning the team members of the different expert groups – directly. Following this thought, we conclude that one possibility for filling the identified gap could be raising the personal motivation for each team member to actively involve oneself in every phase of the process.

4   Results

RelaxedCare is the entirely new way of communicating and caring: allowing more communication from the assisted person's side while unobtrusively keeping informal caregivers worry-free and informed about the assisted person's wellbeing state. The second prototype is depicted in Fig. 4. It consists of a elegantly-designed RelaxedCare cube and a smartphone app.

At the assisted person's home, the cube is connected to a smart home system. Innovative behaviour pattern recognition methods detect the wellbeing state of the user, including activity level, social interaction and daily life routines.

On the informal caregiver's side, the wellbeing status is displayed in a pervasive way via the wellbeing indicator on the in the front of the RelaxedCare cube and the app.

The cube also enables both sides to send simple messages using an innovative interaction design: placing tiles with specific icons on top of the cube. Asking for help, requesting a call or saying "I am thinking of you" has never been simpler than with RelaxedCare.

Fig. 4. The RelaxedCare second prototype consisting of the RelaxedCare Cube with tiles and the RelaxedCare App.

Concerning the chosen methods for the user research studies of the project, the arrangement to divide the whole study into five phases where design research and qualitative social research methods were applied alternately has proven to be a fruitful approach. Each method gave clues which led to the refinement of the successive method – in other words, the generated findings from each step enabled the team to broaden the view on the target groups and to define the successive methods in an even more target-oriented way. The research methods deriving from two research realms had been chosen for specific questions whose answers were required to inform the product development process. The findings indicate that the combination of methods of qualitative social science in combination with methods of design research in generative sessions have the potential to offer insights in the area of knowledge what people know, feel and dream of. This can ultimately lead to the possibility of extracting tacit and latent knowledge of the target groups we design for and of course will be of great importance for a holistic project development in general.

The active user involvement of more than 200 end-users shifted the primary focus of the technology development from "informing the ICs" to a new form of communication between IC and AP. The original focus would have put even a certain stigma on the assisted person. Shifting the focus towards bilateral communication and providing both parties with the same tool – the RelaxedCare cube – enables them to meet more on the same level. "Caring about each other" and increasing the bond between IC and AP makes RelaxedCare more a "lifestyle object" and moves it away from the telecare field.

Lessons learned from previous projects indicate that closing the gap between the technical, design and user research experts is a success parameter for a technology development project. In RelaxedCare we aimed at applying a holistic product development process, defining a way for a close collaboration of team members from various fields with a broad variety of knowledge areas and experiences, like technology development, system design, interaction and product design, user requirements research and usability. Therefore we applied the ISO 9241-210 standard for the User-Centred Design (UCD) process methodology in the project and decided to combine it with the systematic involvement of project team members from different expert fields to every step of the applied process.

After almost three years of working on the project's design and technical development, we are currently evaluating our final system definition and its concrete results (prototype II) in field trials in Austria and Switzerland with the end-users of the project.

Acknowledgements. The project RelaxedCare (www.relaxedcare.eu) is co-funded by the AAL Joint Programme and the following National Authorities and R&D programs in Austria (bmvit, FFG, Programm benefit), Switzerland (OPET), Slovenia (MIZS) and Spain (National Institute of Health Carlos III, and Ministerio de Industria, Energía y Turismo (MINETUR)).

References

1. Pochobradsky, E., Bergmann, F., Brix-Samoylenko, H., Erfkamp, H., Laub, R.: Situation pflegender Angehöriger. BM für soziale Sicherheit, Generationen und Konsumentenschutz, Wien, Austria (2005)
2. Catalogue of Projects. The Central Management UNIT (CMU), AAL JP, Belgium (2014)
3. Engel, S.: Angehörigenberatung — Verbesserung. der Situation pflegender Angehöriger als ein zentrales Arbeitsfeld der Gerontopsychologie. In: Gerontopsychologie, pp. 195–212. Springer Vienna (2008)
4. International Organization for Standardization. ISO 9241-210:2010 Ergonomics of human-system interaction – Part 210: Human-centred design for interactive systems (2012), 10 February 2016. http://www.iso.org/iso/catalogue_detail.htm?csnumber=52075
5. Fortune: The 7 principles, 10 February 2016. http://www.fortune-net.de/principl.htm
6. Active and Assisted Living Programme: Toolbox Methods of User Integration for AAL Innovation. AALA_ToolboxA5_online.pdf, 10 February 2016. http://www.aal-europe.eu/wp-content/uploads/2015/02/
7. BeClose, 10 February 2016. http://beclose.com/
8. Live!y, 10 February 2016. http://www.mylively.com/
9. Healthsense, 10 February 2016. http://healthsense.com/
10. POM Peace of Mind, Project leaflet Andreas Kreiner, 10 February 2016. www.modernfamilies.net/peace-of-mind/
11. Morandell, M., Steinhart, J., Sander, E., Dittenberger, S., Koscher, A., Biallas, M.: RelaxedCare: A Quiet Assistant for Informal Caregivers, CCCIC CSCW 2014, Baltimore (USA), 15.-19.02.2014. In: Proceedings of the ACM CSCW Workshop on Collaboration and Coordination in the Context of Informal Care, pp. 11–21 (2014)
12. Weiser, M.: Some CS issues in ubiquitous computing. Commun. ACM Spec. Issue Comput. Augmented Environ. Back Real World 36(7), 75–84 (1993)
13. Dittenberger, S.: User-inspired Innovation Process. NDU, Sankt Pölten (2012)

Design Factors for the Location
and Arrangement of Control Actuators

Weiyu Sun[1], Junmin Du[2,3], Huimin Hu[4(✉)], and Xuehuan Hu[1]

[1] School of Energy and Power Engineering, Beihang University, Beijing, China
[2] School of Transportation Science and Engineering, Beihang University,
Beijing, China
[3] Airworthiness Technologies Research Center, Beihang University,
Beijing, China
[4] Ergonomics Laboratory, China National Institute of Standardization,
Beijing, China
huhm@cnis.gov.cn

Abstract. Location and arrangement of control actuators have a significant impact on operation safety and efficiency. In order to benefit from the proper location and arrangement of control actuators, a large amount of factors need to be considered in the design process. In this paper, three types of main design factors were summarized through literature research, including operators physical characteristics, task operation properties and control actuators features. Meanwhile, the priority of these factors (detailed in indexes) were determined by questionnaire investigation. The results showed that the top priority indexes were anthropometric dimensions, limbs reachable area, comfortable area, operation accuracy, visual checking, avoiding interference, friction, the control actuators type of hand and foot manipulate, the control actuators functions of on/off or start/stop, safety or emergency device, importance of control actuators, and operator habits.

Keywords: Control actuators · Location and arrangement · Design factors

1 Introduction

Location and arrangement are concerned significantly during the design process of control actuators. They have strong impact on operation safety and efficiency. If the location and arrangement of control actuators are unsuitable, misoperations and low efficiency may be caused. Even more, operators fatigue and joint diseases may occur. Proper location and arrangement of control actuators are essential for improving operation safety, efficiency, comfort, and reducing operators' fatigue and potential healthy risk in the field of automobile and aircraft industry, machinery etc.

In the design process, a large amount of factors should be considered for obtaining proper location and arrangement of control actuators. Many guidances and standards have been published to instruct the design of control actuators location and arrangements by different organizations and departments all over the world, such as ISO 9355-3: 2006, BS EN 894-4: 2010, GB/T 14775-93 etc. Although those guidances and

A. Marcus (Ed.): DUXU 2016, Part III, LNCS 9748, pp. 392–400, 2016.
DOI: 10.1007/978-3-319-40406-6_38

standards mentioned many design factors for the location and arrangement of control actuators, the key point of each document is quite different with each other, and the design factors are relatively scattered. Moreover, there is no guide to represent the priority of these factors, which sometimes make the designer feel difficult to balance them during the design period for control interface.

This paper aims to summarize the design factors for the location and arrangement of control actuators, and determine the priority of these factors (detailed in indexes). Literature research and questionnaire investigation were carried out focusing on the control actuators' location and arrangement. Three types of main influence factors were summed up, including the operators physical characteristics, task operation properties and control actuators features. Total 47 indexes of these factors were conducted and investigated. The priority indexes in the design of control actuators location and arrangement were obtained. The results are helpful for understanding the design factors of control actuators location and arrangement, as well as providing references for human machine interface design.

2 Main Design Factors of Control Actuators Location and Arrangements

2.1 Literature Research

Multiple standards were reviewed, including international, European and Chinese standards. The key words for literature searching were control actuators, location, arrangement, control region, control area and control actuators design. Literature analysis focused on the design requirements of control actuators location and arrangements. The analysed standards primarily included ISO 9355-3: 2006 (International standard), BS EN 894-4: 2010 (European standard), GB/T 14775-93 (Chinese national standard), etc.

Based on the analysis of these standards, three types of main design factors for location and arrangement of control actuators were summarized. They were operators physical characteristics, task operation properties and control actuators features. The details are described as following.

2.2 Three Types of Main Design Factors

2.2.1 Operators Physical Characteristics

The operators physical characteristics include anthropometric dimension and operation postures.

(1) Anthropometric dimensions

Anthropometric dimensions contribute to the reachable area of limbs. It is the first considered factor for the control actuators location and arrangement design. The operation areas are various for people with different height and limbs length. Therefore, in the design process of control actuators location and arrangement, users' body dimensions should be considered seriously, so as to satisfy the reachable requirements of most people, avoid unreachable problems, and locate control actuators with proper locations.

Anthropometric dimensions are classified to static and functional dimensions. Static dimensions refer to dimensions which are measured when human body are static. The measurement of static dimensions are carried by different postures, including standing, sitting, kneeling and prone postures [1]. Height, eye height, shoulder height, elbow height, sitting height, sitting eye height, sitting cervical height, sitting shoulder height are all belong to static dimensions.

Functional dimensions refer to reachable area when people participate in some functional activities. Functional dimensions are measured in dynamic mode of human body. They are the motion range dimensions produced by joint movement angle and limbs length.

Most countries or states have their own standard on local population anthropometric dimensions. In China, the national standard GB/T 5703—1999 (*Human body measurement infrastructure for technical design*) regulates 32 static dimensions and 13 functional dimensions in standing and sitting postures. These dimensions are given at 1, 5, 50, 95, 99 percentile respectively [2]. The proper position of control actuators, related to human reachability domains, should be determined by anthropometric data of appropriate percentile. For example, automobile driver seat is usually designed based on the anthropometric dimensions from 5 percentile of female to 95 percentile of male, thus to satisfy most people with seating comfortably.

(2) Operation postures

Operation postures have significant effect on operation energy consumption, reachable area and operation stability, thus influence on the selection of control actuators location and arrangement [3].

First of all, the maximum force of certain limb changes dramatically with different postures. Therefore, the postures influence body energy consumption a lot, and then influence operation duration time, fatigue and health. In order to improve the operation endurance and mitigate the negative effects on human health, operators' postures must be considered when designers determine the control actuators location and arrangement.

Second, operation postures influence limbs reachable area. For instance, the reachable areas are quite different between the standing and sitting posture. Obviously, the reachable height of upper limbs in standing posture are much more taller than that in sitting posture. The location and arrangement of control actuators is definitely different in these two postures, no matter operating by hand or by foot.

Finally, operation postures affect operation stability. For example, human body stability is not high in standing posture, although the flexibility is high because people can turn around and move the body to operate. On the contrary, the operation stability is relatively higher in sitting posture, which could reduce operation error rate.

In the design process, when operation postures are not determined, designers can choose appropriate location and arrangement of control actuators to help operators operating with comfortable postures. On the other hand, when the operation postures have been determined, location and arrangement of control actuators can be optimized to reduce fatigue and improve comfort of operators.

2.2.2 Task Operation Properties

Task operation properties include operating accuracy, speed and force, efficiency, visual checking, tactile detect, sensibility to errors, wearing gloves and easy cleaning. Task operation properties have dramatic impact on the location and arrangement of control actuators.

(1) Operation efficiency

High efficiency requirement of task operation means that the control actuators should be easily detected and reached, so that the control actuators should be arranged in places close to human body or to the most frequently used controls. Meanwhile, the efficiency also requires that the control actuators should be arranged in a regular and orderly way. The number of control actuators around the certain control actuator should be limited. The distance that need to be completed by hand or foot should be reduced via putting the control actuators on suitable locations. For instance, in cars, the position of handbrake is close to the operation lever. It is convenient for driver to move hand from operation lever to control handbrake, which is very important in emergency condition. This arrangement can not only reduce the recognizing and judging time, but also can reduce the possibility of operating error, so as to improve the operation efficiency [4].

(2) Speed

To satisfy the high requirements of speed, the control actuators are generally required to be placed in a convenient location, as well as a comfortable position. Continuous operation would decrease the operation speed gradually if the position of control actuators causes discomfort to operators. The comfortable position keeps a suitable distance with human body, neither too far nor too close. Too far from human body costs longer time to contact control actuator. Too close to human body may not allow limbs to extent completely and may cause uncomfortable postures. In addition, appropriate distance between control actuators is needed under the condition of high speed requirement. Large distance is helpful for avoiding misoperations, but would increase operation duration time.

(3) Force

Considering force requirement, the determination of control actuators location should be combined with human limbs movement characteristics. When large operation force is needed, control actuators should be located in positions centered with human torso, so that the relative large force can be exerted by operators. These positions should not only satisfy the requirements of force, but also should not cause excessive consumption of human body energy.

(4) Visual checking

When the visual detect is needed in operation, operators must observe and operate the control actuators simultaneously, otherwise mistakes may occur. Control actuators should be arranged in the field of vision and close to human body, so as to reduce the time to observe and recognize. Feedback device (if any) should keep appropriate distance with control actuators. For example, if the feedback device is a display, the distance between the display and the control actuators should allow operators to catch the feedback information quickly and clearly. At the same time, the direction of information display should be consistent with the movement direction of the control actuators, that is display-motion consistency.

(5) Tactile detect

When there is a requirement of tactile detect in operation, operators' attention is usually occupied fully by other things, or the control actuators locate far from the operators. If the task operation need tactile check, the control actuator should be arranged in positions easy to be operated and keep a suitable distance with surrounding control actuators in order to reduce the possibility of misoperation. In other words, the control actuators should locate within the reachable area of human limbs. There should be as few as possible control actuators around the target control actuator so as to avoid misoperation. It is noteworthy that the operators' hand or foot movement from the initial position to the target control actuator should not be hampered by other control actuators. An example is the location of the accelerator and brake pedal in cars. The two pedals are in a short distance with each other, and there is no other control actuator between them. Drivers get benefits from this design because their attention are mainly painted on road, then moving the foot from the accelerator pedal to the brake pedal primary relies on tactile detection.

(6) Sensibility to errors

The more sensitive to errors, the more important the task operation is. This kind of task operation is the key factor affecting operational safety. In order to make the operators to reach and operate control actuators accurately and quickly in emergency, the control actuators should be located in positions that can be easily observed and reached by the operator.

(7) Wearing gloves

Hand sensibility decreases and finger becomes thicker when operator wears gloves. The most concerned problem is misoperation. Enlarging the distance between control actuators is an effective way to avoid misoperation.

(8) Easy cleaning

Some machines has the requirement of easy cleaning. The control actuators on these machines should be enlarged, so as to provide enough space for cleaning.

2.2.3 Control Actuators Features

Control actuators features refer to physical features, functions and using environment of control actuators.

(1) Physical features

Physical properties of the control actuator include the type, color, shape, dimensions and size. In order to lower the visual errors, as well as decrease the recognition time, the control actuators could be grouped by the principle of similarity according to type, color, shape or size. If the type of control actuators is different, the proper distance between them should be determined by combination with motion way of control actuators [5]. For example, the distance between knobs and buttons should guarantee fingers to operate freely without obstacle if these two types of control actuators are used together.

(2) Functions of control actuators

Functions of control actuators include emergency, switch operation and general operation. Various functions usually contribute to various locations. It is well known that control actuators used in emergency should be located in striking and maneuverable places so that operators can react quickly and correctly. But for the control actuators for general operation, because of its less impact on safety and low error sensitivity, they are just required to be located in human limbs reachable area.

(3) Using environment

Using environment refers to spaces or surfaces for locating and arranging control actuators. The limitation of space or surface size make the range for locating control actuators reduced, and the distances between control actuators limited. Locations of control actuators may be differed when the size of space or surface is different, In this situation, the location and arrangement of control actuators should be designed with the consideration of using context, combining with other factors, such as human limbs motion characteristics and control actuators function.

3 Priority Indexes of the Design Factors

3.1 Method

Many detailed indexes were involved in the three types of factors described above related with the design of control actuators location and arrangement. In order to find out the priority indexes, a questionnaire survey was carried out. Total 47 indexes, which may have influence on control actuators location and arrangement design, were included in the questionnaire, shown as following.

- Type of control actuators (hand and foot manipulate, voice and eye control)
- Dimensions of control actuators
- Function of control actuators (on/off or start/stop, general control actuators, safety or emergency device)
- Anthropometric dimensions (anthropometric static dimensions, functional dimensions, limbs reachable area and comfortable area)
- Task operation properties (operation accuracy, speed, force, visual checking, tactile detect, avoiding interference, friction, wearing gloves and easy cleaning)
- Operation movement characteristics (movement type, movement axis, movement direction, movement continuity, angle of rotation for continuous rotary, repetitive movement, duration time, order, static posture holding time, supporting)
- Hand grip characteristics (grip type, hand part of applying force, applying force method)

- Grouping (whether to group, frequency of transforming operation between different groups, distance in group, distance between groups, number of control actuators in a single group)
- Importance of control actuators
- Using frequency of control actuators
- Correspondence with visual display
- Coding
- Operator habits

The participants were asked to evaluate the importance of each index according to their experience. A five-point Likert scale was used in the evaluation, ranging from "not important at all" to "very important".

3.2   Participants

Total 26 participants coming from machinery company and automobile company attended the investigation. Their ages were from 26 to 45 years old. Their career experiences were 3 to 24 years. For their job title, 17 of them were designers of control actuators, 9 of them were testers of control actuators. The investigation scene is shown in Fig. 1.

(a) Designers of control actuators   (b) Testers of control actuators

Fig. 1. Investigation scene

3.3   Results

By the analysis on the investigation data, the top priority indexes for control actuators location and arrangement were found out. The top priority indexes were regarded as having larger impact on the location and arrangement, and should be considered firstly in design period. Besides, the secondary priority indexes were also obtained.

(1) Operators physical characteristics

All of the indexes in anthropometric dimensions were evaluated as the top priority indexes, including anthropometric static dimensions, functional dimensions, limbs reachable area and comfortable area. Besides the anthropometric, operator habits was also evaluated as the top priority indexes.

For the secondary priority indexes, most of the indexes in hand grip characteristics were regarded as in this level, including hand part of applying force (finger/palm), applying force method(normal/tangential direction). In addition, movement type (linear/rotary), movement axis, and movement continuity (continuous/discrete) of operation movement characteristics were also considered as secondary priority indexes.

(2) Task operation properties

The top priority indexes were operation accuracy, visual checking, avoiding interference, and friction. Operation force were considered as secondary priority index. Other indexes of the task operation properties were evaluated as less important, such as operation speed, tactile detect, wearing gloves and easy cleaning.

(3) Control actuators features

The top priority indexes were the control actuators type of hand and foot manipulate, the control actuators functions of on/off or start/stop, safety or emergency device, importance of control actuators. The distance between control actuators with similar functions or different functions, whether grouped or not, were regarded as the secondary priority indexes.

All other indexes that not belonged to the top or secondary priority indexes were evaluated as not priority. Those indexes can be considered later in the design period.

4 Conclusion

Through the literature research related with the design of control actuators location and arrangement, the three type of main design factors were summarized, including operators physical characteristics, task operation properties and control actuators features. According to the investigation of detailed indexes of these design factors, the top priority indexes were found out, which should be considered firstly in the design period. These top priority indexes were anthropometric static dimensions, functional dimensions, limbs reachable area, comfortable area, operation accuracy, visual checking, avoiding interference, friction, the control actuators type of hand and foot manipulate, the control actuators functions of on/off or start/stop, safety or emergency device, importance of control actuators, and operator habits. In addition to the top priority indexes, the secondary priority indexes were also presented.

The research results are useful for human machine interface designers to comprehend the design factors and priority indexes in the design process of control actuators location and arrangement. What's more, the design indexes concluded in this paper can be used to evaluate existing location and arrangement of control actuators with problems of uncomfortable operation, high rate of misoperation or heavy load of operation.

It is helpful for checking out the problems in the existing interface and amending the unreasonability related with location and arrangement of control actuators.

References

1. Ju, F.: Research on aircraft cockpit ergonomic design, pp. 6–7. Northwestern Polytechnical University of China, Xi'an (2007)
2. GB/T 5703—1999, Human body measurement infrastructure for technical design. Standards Press of China, Beijing (1999)
3. BS-EN 894-4:2010, Safety of machinery—Ergonomics requirements for design of displays and control actuators Part 4: Location and arrangement of displays and control actuators, pp. 8–12. BSI Standards Publication (2010)
4. ISO 9355-3:2006(E): Ergonomic requirements for the design of displays and control actuators, Part 3: Control actuators, pp. 4–13. The International Organization for Standardization (2006)
5. GB/T 14775-93: General ergonomics requirements for controller, pp. 1–2. Standards Press of China, Beijing (1993)

Building a Soft Machine: New Modes of Expressive Surfaces

Amy Winters[⊠]

Royal College of Art, Textiles, Kensington Gore, SW7 2EU London, UK
amy.winters@network.rca.ac.uk
http://www.rainbowwinters.com

Abstract. This paper will investigate how the distinct role of the textile designer can enrich the design process in HCI. It will advocate embodiment as a design methodology by focusing on a subjective, visceral engagement with material and physical computing using tacit textiles expertise. This theoretical premise is explored drawing on the fields of soft robotics, organic user interfaces and transitive materials for the fabrication of a responsive textile composite. The research uses a range of theoretical references to support its concepts of design thinking and computational materiality and deploys the methodological process of autoethnography as a qualitative system for collecting and evaluating data on the significance of textile thinking. This research concludes that there are insights gained from the creative practice experimental methods of textile thinking in HCI that can contribute to the commercial research and development field in wearable technology.

Keywords: Material · Expressive surfaces · Aesthetics · Soft composite · Soft robotics · Wearables

1 Introduction

1.1 Background

The human body and its component parts are, within a consumer electronics cultural setting, frequently referred to as 'body real estate' [1]. It is commodified, objectified and compartmentalized by companies and research laboratories eager to commercialize and exploit the 'hot trend' of 'Wearables' [2] - smart watches, bands and headgear embedded with sensing capabilities, which quantify, measure and calculate. As an exhibitor at the International Consumer Electronics Show (CES 14, 15) and Consumer Electronics Week (CE 13), the author witnessed an emerging commercial interest from fashion and entertainment organizations seeking convergences. The majority of 'wearables' on display face issues of market unacceptability and statistical data designed in the context of industrial engineering design practices. The consequences, as exposed by the wearable technology trend of wristwear, are systems that fail to acknowledge the complexity of being in this world [3].

Technologies acting at the interface of the body in HCI, offer an opportunity to extend, explore and re-define user-experience. Yet the objectified standardization

© Springer International Publishing Switzerland 2016
A. Marcus (Ed.): DUXU 2016, Part III, LNCS 9748, pp. 401–413, 2016.
DOI: 10.1007/978-3-319-40406-6_39

commonly found in a Cartesian-inspired design of human-machine integration can isolate us within a fixed chain of procedures and overlook opportunities to develop embodied, sensitive and nuanced methods of expression.

The embodiment theories of Maurice Merleau-Ponty [4] provide an alternative to René Descartes' dualism of a radical separation of mind and body – thus offering a holistic lens to view and design a 'soft machine' through the active participation of the lived body in different stages of the design process. Moreover, digital critic Jaron Lanier argues in favor of re-designing machines by developing and articulating self-expression [5].

Since 2010, there have been key developments in the arena of turning wearable computing into forms that are more expressive. Increasingly, textile designers with an affinity towards technology and its multi-sensory capabilities are re-branding as 'Materials-experience designers', 'Trans-disciplinary designers' and 'Materiologists' as ways and means to describe their emerging position. It is within the commercial wearable technology field itself that we can now interrogate developments. Gaps identified include a lack of sensory 'material' awareness and experimentation. 'Cute Circuit', one of the leading players in expressive wearable technology has found success as a platform to popular culture through celebrity endorsement and soft electronics [6]. However, a focus on advancing purely the technology (miniaturization of LED components embedded into garments) can result in a limited visual and sensory language. 'The Unseen', in contrast, employ a materials-led approach of 'Material Alchemy' experimenting with a range of responsive printed inks, such as heat-sensitive (thermo chromic), and wind-sensitive (piezochromic) on such natural materials as feathers and leather [7]. Despite this, the brand defines its practice in opposition to the computational due to hard, clunky components and mainstream associations with consumer-led wearable technology.

This paper will position a relationship between both material and computational practices. Thinking through physical prototyping and reflexive practice is at the core of the textile designer's work. Therefore, an engagement with the textile practice allows the exploration and experimentation of computational design through material, allowing the maker to express their tacit knowledge. Conversely, the computational, rather than being just a collection of clunky components used to measure and quantify, can be applied to 'textiles thinking' as a tool for experiential, interactive and aesthetic capabilities.

Subsequently, novel ways of designing the soft machine are now considered by contesting user-led design in favor of design through exploration. Firstly, through a contextual case study of the author's work on wearable technology and secondly through a series of small-scale composite experiments in 'visceral softness.'

1.2   Case Study of the Author's Work

In its autoethnographic approach, the author's personal experience as a wearable technology designer is used as a contextual starting point to position experiential as opposed to user-led design in HCI (Fig. 1).

Fig. 1. Left: Thunderstorm Dress, Right: Garden Dress

In 2010, the author founded 'Rainbow Winters', a brand seeking to express the emotive and aesthetic expression of technology [8]. The sound-reactive 'Thunderstorm Dress' (2010), as an example, turned the wearer into a living Thunderstorm with an aim to create 'visual music'.

John McCarthy et al. introduced the experiential as a type of user experience within HCI [9]. The 'visceral' visual connection to experience, rather than usability, meant that the prototype reached a wider audience (fashion industry [10] and mainstream news [11]) than was usually prevalent amongst traditional function-led wearable technology. The 'color-sensitive' Garden dress developed at the Royal College of Art (2014); Craft-based techniques such as hand printing and embroidery were appropriated alongside a soft circuit, micro-controller and sensor as a method to blend the physical and the digital.

The physical experience of making each component of the prototype led to new awareness on the limitations of expression in current technology such as the LEDs and Electroluminescence, with their one dimensional, emissive and binary expressional capabilities. Yet, this binary method is alien for textile designers who work in a distinctive way using explorative, unplanned, non-linear, experimental, unknown and unforeseen outcomes. The relationship between the senses and arts practice can be defined by Sarah Pink's sensory ways of knowing [12].

Could therefore, an inherently subjective and reflective qualitative design methodology, such as autoethnography, which explicitly seeks to evoke the experience of the maker, be placed within HCI?

2 Related Work

2.1 Material Lens HCI

Framed within a material lens, this paper intends to translate embodiment as a design methodology by engaging the human body beyond the conventional screen-pointer interface. The application of computational components to flexible, soft substrates blurs the boundaries between the physical and the digital, thus transforming our notion of materiality.

Several researchers have discovered the potential of Soft Materials within HCI [13] to perform as a convergence tool between the physical and digital. Anna Vallgårda et al. [14], and Robles and Wiberg [15] articulate a new vocabulary in computational material design by advocating a material strategy and position aesthetics as a driver for novel computational materiality [16]. Whilst Frankjaer and Gilgen define the Soft User Interface [SUI] as technology ingrained within flexible materials [17].

We can, therefore, infer that there is a requirement for design to appropriate its own material language and methodologies in the research and development process of advanced materials – especially, if designers may concentrate on attributes such as form, expression and aesthetic. The Design-Science, Technology, Engineering, Maths model [D-STEM] proposed by Toomey et al. [18] calls on designers to apply intuitive and non-intuitive methods in the development of smart materials as part of their materials toolbox. An experiential understanding of these novel materials gives the designer new knowledge to understand innate characteristics and affordances [18]. Ylva Fernaeus et al. for example, introduces 'soft hard-ware' as 'electronic components, coating, and shells built from soft, malleable materials' [19].

Under the wider term of 'Programmable Materials', the emerging fields of Transitive Materials [20], Organic User Interfaces [20], and Soft Robotics [21] can redefine our understanding of both computation and interaction [22].

'Transitive Materials' unite physical materials, and their unique and diverse properties, with the computational [20]. These novel substrates fused with computational properties offer an opportunity to explore interaction through adaptive surface properties [23] stimulating both visual and tactile senses, which may not be apparent in flat interfaces with emissive light changes.

Organic User Interfaces (OUI) can be defined as a user interface with a non-flat display. Holman et al. use the textiles analogy of knitwear to ask what computers would look like if designed with a delicate sensibility [24] and explore the physical materiality of paper as being malleable and possessing haptic, visual cues.

Traditionally robots are comprised of inflexible, hard material and joints. The emerging field of Soft Robotics uses flexible materials such as soft elastomers embedded with sensing and actuating properties [25].

Rolf Pfeiffer et al. advocate embodiment as a methodology in bio-robotics; embodiment becomes an 'enabler for cognition' [26], especially as soft robotics use flexible and soft materials which require manipulation [26]. Further, composite structures are used as a technique in soft robotics to combine the mechanical properties of different materials [27]. Pneumatic networks, for example (networks of small channels in elastomeric materials) [27] can open design opportunities within wearables due to their flexible and conformable nature.

Until now, soft robotic applications have been limited to function-led products such as a pneumatic glove for hand rehabilitation [28]. Within the textile domain soft robotics remains under-explored even though both subjects focus on the innate characteristics of 'soft'- stretchy, malleable, fluid, tender, manipulated, adaptable, sensorial, sensation and highly tactile.

2.2   Textiles Thinking

What assumptions can we challenge for textile design? Its ubiquity and lack of critical design discourse hide an effective methodology, which is ripe for development, to re-define user experience within HCI. By moving the machine into the realm of 'soft' - adaptable, shape-shifting and ubiquitous textiles, this paper will pose the question: 'why does 'soft' matter?'

This study is based on the premise that the textile designer can appreciate and respond to complex emotional and aesthetic influences. Claire Pajaczkowska argues that an embodied relationship with material stimulates a distinctive type of thinking [29]. As illustrated by Textile designer, Rachel Phillpott, whose practice is character-ized as a playful manipulation of materials driven by embodied knowledge with the potential to expand from an anticipated guideline in creating new inventions [30].

Sensibility within the context of re-defining user-experience has been represented by McCarthy et al. as sensory fluency [31]. This particular sensitivity to material experience detailed as delicacy, subtlety, intuition, feeling, responsiveness and per-ceptiveness, is embedded within the tacit knowledge of the textile designer who makes use of a range of sensory clues.

Textile theorist Elaine Igoe contests Nigel Cross's non-acknowledgement of methods used by designers who have a close understanding and unique relationship with materials (textiles, fashion, jewellery, ceramics, glass). The designers reviewed by Cross in developing 'Designerly ways of thinking' [32] all share a similar background (industrial, product, engineering design) and apply user-led design methodologies which focus on functionality and practical applications. Igoe asserts that the textiles design process needs to be articulated to validate a critical awareness of its distinctive type of design thinking with its own 'specific methodologies' [33]. This utilization of tacit textiles knowledge is transformed to create surfaces, which are aesthetic, haptic and engage directly with the subjectivity of the maker [33].

Textiles sensibility needs to enter a dialogue with HCI to enrich the discourse in wearable technology and as a method and process of innovation within a growing commercial arena, which needs further validation. In this light, McCarthy et al. align with Igoe in placing equal importance on sensation and cognition [31]. Materials can play an essential part in brand positioning therefore, qualitative perceptual qualities such as tactility, visual impact and user experience play a role [34]. Donald A Norman's framework for analyzing design on an emotional level constitutes the fol-lowing: Design evokes an emotional response at three different levels: the visceral, the behavioral and the reflective [35]. Behavioral design relates to functionality and usability favored by traditional HCI user-experience. The 'visceral' relates directly to our experiential and sensorial experience where the material rules supreme - physical features (look, feel, sound) prevail (shape, form, physical feel and texture).

Industrial design can find design processes used in the more affective disciplines such as textiles, fashion and theatrical design challenging. Norman characterizes emotions as fundamental to fashion [35] yet translating a mood, expression or feeling is inherently subjective and not quantifiable; film-makers for example do not start out their process with earnest user studies and insights. Therefore, the nature of industrial design and the design methods with a pre-disposition towards use and usability mean expressive and emotional methods are often overlooked. This user-led approach to design, which Cross advocates tends to reduce people to grouped commonalities, which this research argues, would by default, reduce expressional capabilities. Norman aligns with this approach claiming that user-centered design is not always appropriate for either visceral or reflective design [35].

2.3   Affect and Visceral Engagement with Material

This research frames the design of the soft machine within the 'Visceral' layer of emotional design as charted by Norman [35]. Visceral is a theme often found in the context of theater and film for the creation of 'affect'. Youn-Kyung Lim et al., for their part, explore emotional experience in interaction design - using Norman's definition of 'Visceral' as 'perceptually-induced reactions' which relate directly to our physical senses [36].

Positioning textiles as an interface for the experiential, can we imagine a 'visceral soft system' that engages our body and its sensory experience: optical, acoustic, olfactory, tactile, thermal, kinaesthetic, proprioceptive, visceral and cross-modal? An experiential textiles interface could be described as translating one subjective experience into another, a human transitional experience. However, in traditional computation the computer engineers build the tools that are invariably technically driven [37] and designers/artists are thus limited to using these tools.

Framing the design of the soft machine within the 'visceral' layer of emotional design offers an opportunity for expressive surfaces to be fabricated through programmable matter. Norman speaks of future machines as layered systems of affect [35]. The textiles designed through 'visceral softness' are designed for purpose, to translate a 'visceral experience'. They cannot be replicated through standard off-the-shelf materials but go through a range of textile processes by the designer.

Textiles have the potential, within the field of HCI, to offer magical, functional, ubiquitous, accessible, intimate, curious and multi-dimensional behaviors. McCarthy et al. for example, re-examine user-experience as felt experience through the concept of 'enchantment'. They question how designers can use this tool in the design of interactive systems within HCI to build affective attachments through the sensuality of the artefact, a playful regard of material and the potential of its transformational qualities [31]. Ling Yao et al. have developed a technical framework for pneumatically actuated composites illustrating for example dynamic texture change and composite sensing layering [38]. A function-led approach of developing potential application such as a shape changing mobile is employed. However, the point of departure in this paper is located within 'sensory making' as described by Pink with particular attention to sensory perception and experience [12]. We build on Yao's framework by fabricating interactive pneumatic and fluidic surface design within specific 'textiles thinking' methods. Developing the 'sensory engagement' layers of the composite through experimentation with surface design, color, texture and pattern.

3 Soft Responsive Composite Textile

3.1 Methodology

Through a textile design composite, we can now introduce the term 'visceral softness' and advocate an approach that builds the 'machine' on the principles of embodied interaction.

The ground-work for the 'textile thinking' experimental process within HCI is laid out as a detailed set of instructions in the context of Autoethnography, a distinctly subjective iteration of traditional design thinking models that includes human experience [39] as well as the embodied experience of materials. We draw on Pink's notion that sensory participation is a reflexive and experiential process [12]. By seeking out directly subjective, tacit knowledge, the author is thus positioned as a researcher and participant in a method that encompasses human experience, experience of materials, as well as problem solving.

The instructional method serves to translate tacit textile knowledge into an explicit and reproducible process. Further, we wish to build on an emerging methodology within HCI to translate the experiential; Kristina Hook for example uses autoethnography as a tool to convert embodied experiences into new knowledge [40].

3.2 Composite Experiments: Visceral Softness

This initial stretchable composite prototype uses off-the-shelf materials as a 'technology blue-print' using a 3 V air motor, 12 V peristaltic pump, sound sensor and proximity sensor. The composite layers comprise of (1) Active texture and (2) Fluidic Actuation. To move the composite into an autonomous soft prototype, we propose in the next iteration to include the layers of (3) soft circuit and (4) battery. The 'sensory engagement' layers (active texture and fluid actuation) combine traditional textile craft techniques used in print and mixed media (surface disruption, layering and interruption).

This materials-engaged and explorative method of working builds upon emerging approaches, which consider the embodied and experiential value within HCI as opposed to a function-orientated, user-centred approach. Examples include Heekyoung Jung's 'materiality understood through exploration rather than use' [41, 42], Felicia Davis's, 'research through material' [42], and Coelho et al. fusion of new technologies with craft as a basis for manifesting unexpected design opportunities [23].

3.3 Instructional Method for Building a Soft Machine

These instructions have been adapted from the 'Soft Robotics' Toolkit, an open-source resource to contribute to the advancement of soft robotics from the Whitesides Research Group, Harvard University [43]. In our process, we use a metaphor of cooking, with a range of options to be adapted for each layer.

Ingredients

- Required materials: silicon (Eco-flex 00-30), 3 V pneumatic mini pump, 12 V peristaltic pump, 1 mm I.D x 2 mm O.D clear translucent silicone tubing (for fluidic layer but size is interchangeable), 1.5 mm I.D x 3 mm O.D polyethylene tubing (active texture layer), non-woven fabrics Vilene (Lutradur 30 gm).

- Optional materials: silicone pigments, colored powders, fibers (in different colors, we used fibers also found in applications such as prosthetic make-up, model-making garden fiber), 3D printed molds for elastomer channels.
- Tools: scissors, pins, cutting knife, metal baking tray, disposable gloves, wooden stir sticks, soldering iron, latex gloves, mixing/measuring cups.
- Optional: sublimation printer, heat-press, 3D printer for molds.

Step One: Inspiration Devise a mood board (a collection of textures, colors and images) to capture thoughts, glimpses, nuances and impressions. This experiment used for example macro-photography to explore surface through organic forms, texture, and the secret enchantments of the natural world. Textile designers often use found materials or pictorial experiences to convey a tone or atmosphere and will embed physical tactile references and unconventional materials into their experimental processes to create brand new forms. This mood board will be the blueprint for feeding into the 'sensory-engagement' layers of the composite. Images and thoughts expressed in a quick, instinctive, visceral manner.

The composition of the mood-board invited a story of interaction to investigate experiential textiles creating novel interactive expressive surfaces. Suggestive ideas started to emerge such as skin and water gasping, breathing acoustics, swarm, bass, beat.

Step Two: Electronic System. Assemble the circuit. Inputs: gesture sensor APDS-9960, electret microphone BOB-09964. Outputs: 3 V pneumatic motor, 12 V peristaltic pump. Control: Arduino Pro Mini 3.3 V data processor. Power: 9 V batteries (X 2), step-down voltage regulator D15V35F5S3. We use a sound and proximity sensor but the sensors can be interchanged depending on the interaction required (Fig. 6).

Fig. 2. Left: Silicon Mixture and ingredients [colored powder, gold-flakes, grass fibers, beads, yarns]. Middle: Multilayer making process. Right: Multi-layer composite with active texture and fluid actuation. (Color figure online)

Step Three: Composite Fabrication

- Sublimation print to a non-woven polyester (Lutradur 30). Heat from a soldering iron can be used to distress the material and re-imagine surface qualities, structures and textural qualities.

- Mix part A and part B Ecoflex into a measuring cup equally. Spread a very fine layer over the printed fabric samples. Cure for four hours.
- Pour a layer of EcoFlex on a baking tray (layer 1), pigments and fibers can be mixed to create a variety of tensile strengths. Mixed-media layering involves freely combining any and all kinds of materials that you want to use in creating the composite. Painterly methods of layering, dripping, pouring, and glazing enable expressivity and the multi-layer structures evoke a tactile quality where human-made imprecision is a desired part of the result (Fig. 3).
- Active texture layer: Coat the edges of (layer 1) with a small amount of Ecoflex to bond and place on the cured printed fabric sample (this forms as an adhesive) (Fig. 5). Cure for four hours. Use a pin to insert a hole for tubing into layer 1.
- Fluidic layer: fix silicon tubing onto the printed fabric sample with EcoFlex. Here we use fluids as a display surface as an alternative to compressed air (Fig. 4).

Fig. 3. Left: Pouring silicon over grass fibers. Right: Form adapted from Pneu-Net elastomer channel molds.

Fig. 4. Tests on sound-activated fluid-actuation layer. Composite embedded with grass fibres and silicon tubing.

Step Four: Testing. Together with the aforementioned Design-STEM model proposed by Toomey et al., this method calls for designers to assert both a sensory and a technical fluency in the development of smart materials. In a commercial context this would mean that the designer, rather than accepting a submissive role in STEM developments, would instead move 'to one of active influence and effect from within this arena' [18]. 'Textiles thinking' is discovered through a direct visceral engagement with physical materials and experimental technology to uncover subjective capabilities such as imagination, touch and material manipulation.

It was interesting to note the difference between the objective methods (assembly of the circuit) and the subjective methods (mood-board, material experimentation) (Figs. 2 and 6).

3.4   Future Development

This paper demonstrates an embryonic prototype of a responsive composite textile interface with active texture and fluidic actuation. Technical limitations include a reliance on conventional, rigid electronics to connect the sensors and actuators. In addressing limitations, further development will comprise the integration of soft printed conductive circuits, assembly of multiple micro-pumps (Mp6 Bartels) [44] and flexible battery to devise a soft autonomous system suitable for wearable applications (Fig. 6).

Soft, stretchable electronics have been defined by Rus et al. as the next stage in the growth of soft robotics and material machines [26], which our next development would hope to exploit.

Further, McCarthy et al. place the concept of 'enchantment' within a commercial context suggesting application such as 'wearable technology' [31]. The instructional

Fig. 5. Tests on proximity-sensitive active texture layer. Composite embedded with prosthetic makeup 'flesh' fibers and textile yarns.

Fig. 6. Left: Current prototyping circuit. Right: Next iteration of portable micro-pumps for wearable applications.

method on textiles thinking within HCI will be tested on a range of participants with the aim of informing research and development strategies in wearable technology with qualitative research data.

4 Conclusion

The results obtained from the literature survey and autoethnographic approach to designing a soft responsive composite, indicate that this may only be the beginning of a discourse into how 'visceral material exploration' contributes to the design discourse of Wearables. An evaluation strategy will be constructed to survey key stakeholders including textile designers, R&D departments and commercial tradeshow platforms such as CES. Alongside autoethnographic data, this will provide further evidence that design usability can be expanded to include experience, advocating a material based approach to constructing the soft machine.

Acknowledgements. The author would like to thank Clive Hudson at Programify for support with electronic circuit fabrication and coding.

References

1. Dvorak, J.: Moving Wearables into the Mainstream, p. 107. Springer, Heidelberg (2008)
2. Marketsandmarkets.com,: Wearable Technology Market by Product - 2020| Marketsand Markets. http://www.marketsandmarkets.com/Market-Reports/wearable-electronics-market-983.html
3. Damasio, A.: Descartes' error, p. 249. Vintage, New York (2006)
4. Merleau-Ponty, M.: Phenomenology of Perception. Humanities Press, New York (1962)
5. Lanier, J.: You Are Not a Gadget, p. 191. Alfred A. Knopf, New York (2010)
6. CUTECIRCUIT: tshirtOS. http://cutecircuit.com/tshirtos/
7. Seetheunseen.co.u: T H E U N S E E N. http://seetheunseen.co.uk
8. Rainbowwinters.com: Rainbow Winters – homepage. http://www.rainbowwinters.com
9. McCarthy, J., Wright, P.: Technology as Experience. MIT Press, Cambridge (2004)
10. Steele, C.: PCMag's Coco Rocha Explores CE Week's Wearable Tech. http://uk.pcmag.com/consumer-electronics-reviews-ratings/14462/news/pcmags-coco-rocha-explores-ce-weeks-wearable-tech
11. Walker, R.: Fashion's big brands follow the money to join the wearable tech revolution. http://www.theguardian.com/technology/2015/feb/14/fashion-phones-wearable-technology
12. Pink, S.: Situating Sensory Ethnography: From Academia to Intervention. In: Doing Sensory Ethnography. pp. 7–22 (2009)
13. Buechley, L., Coelho, M.: Special issue on material computing. Pers. Ubiquit. Comput. **15** (2), 113–114 (2010)
14. Vallgårda, A.: A material strategy: exploring material properties of computers. Int. J. Des. **4**, 3 (2010)
15. Robles, E., Wiberg, M.: Texturing the "material turn" in interaction design. In: Proceedings of the Fourth International Conference on Tangible, Embedded, and Embodied Interaction - TEI 2010 (2010)

16. Vallgårda, A., Redstorm, J.: Computational composites. In: Proceedings of the SIGCHI Conference on Human Factors in Computing Systems - CHI 2007 (2007)

17. Frankjaer, T., Gilgen, D.: Wearable Networks, Creating Hybrid Spaces with Soft Circuits. In: Marcus, A. (ed.) DUXU 2014, Part II. LNCS, vol. 8518, pp. 435–445. Springer, Heidelberg (2014)

18. Toomey, A., Kapsali, V.: D-STEM: a design led approach to STEM innovation. In: A Matter of Design: Making Society through Science and Technology (2014)

19. Fernaeus, Y., et al.: Touch and feel soft hardware. In: Proceedings of the Sixth International Conference on Tangible, Embedded and Embodied Interaction - TEI 2012 (2012)

20. Coelho, M., et al.: Programming reality. In: Proceedings of the 27th International Conference Extended Abstracts on Human Factors in Computing Systems - CHI EA 2009 (2009)

21. Verl, A., et al.: Soft Robotics. Springer, Heidelberg (2015)

22. Jacob, R., et al.: Reality-based interaction. In: Proceeding of the Twenty-Sixth Annual CHI Conference on Human Factors In Computing Systems - CHI 2008 (2008)

23. Coelho, M., Zigelbaum, J.: Shape-changing interfaces. Pers. Ubiquit. Comput. 15(2), 161–173 (2010)

24. Holman, D., Vertegaal, R.: Organic user interfaces. Commun. ACM 51(6), 48 (2008)

25. Rus, D., Tolley, M.: Design, fabrication and control of soft robots. Nature 521(7553), 467–475 (2015)

26. Pfeifer, R., et al.: How the body shapes the way we think, pp.19, 30. MIT Press, Cambridge (2007)

27. Marchese, A., et al.: A recipe for soft fluidic elastomer robots. Soft Robot. 2(1), 7–25 (2015)

28. Polygerinos, P., et al.: Towards a soft pneumatic glove for hand rehabilitation. In: 2013 IEEE/RSJ International Conference on Intelligent Robots and Systems (2013)

29. Pajaczkowska, C., Jefferies, J., et al.: The handbook of textile culture, making known, The Textiles Toolbox- Psychoanalysis of Nine types of Textile Thinking, p. 79. Bloomsbury Academic (2015)

30. Philpott, R.: Engineering opportunities for originality and invention: the importance of playful making as developmental method in practice-led design research. Studies in Material Thinking (2013)

31. McCarthy, J., et al.: The experience of enchantment in human–computer interaction. Pers. Ubiquit. Comput. 10(6), 369–378 (2005)

32. Cross, N.: Design Thinking, p. 67. Berg, Oxford (2011)

33. Igoe, E.: The tacit-turn: textile design in design research. J. Text. Des. Res. Pract. 1(1), 5–8 (2013)

34. Schifferstein, H., Wastiels, L.: Sensing Materials. Materials Experience, pp. 15–26 (2014)

35. Norman, D.: Emotional design, p. 63, 93, 97. Basic Books, New York (2004)

36. Lim, Y., et al.: Emotional experience and interaction design. In: Peter, C., Beale, R. (eds.) Affect and Emotion in Human-Computer Interaction. LNCS, vol. 4868, pp. 116–129. Springer, Heidelberg (2008)

37. Berzowska, J., Bender, W.: Computational expressionism, or how the role of random () is changing in computer art. In: Proceedings of SPIE 3644. Human Vision and Electronic Imaging, vol. 3644 (1999)

38. Yao, L., et al.: PneUI. In: Proceedings of the 26th Annual ACM Symposium on User Interface Software and Technology - UIST 2013 (2013)

39. Ellis, C., et al.: Autoethnography: an overview. Forum Qual. Sozialforschung / Forum: Qual. Soc. Res. 12, 1 (2010)

40. Höök, K.: Transferring qualities from horseback riding to design. In: Proceedings of the 6th Nordic Conference on Human-Computer Interaction Extending Boundaries - NordiCHI 2010 (2010)
41. Jung, H., Stolterman, E.: Digital form and materiality. In: Proceedings of the 7th Nordic Conference on Human-Computer Interaction Making Sense Through Design - NordiCHI 2012 (2012)
42. Davis, F.: The textility of emotion. In: Proceedings of the 2015 ACM SIGCHI Conference on Creativity and Cognition - C&C 2015 (2015)
43. Softroboticstoolkit.com: Design. http://softroboticstoolkit.com/book/pneunets-design
44. Bartels-mikrotechnik.de: Bartels Mikrotechnik GmbH – Home. http://www.bartels-mikrotechnik.de

Study of Usability Evaluation on Display Interface for Intelligent Electric Cooker

Yanlong Yao[1(✉)], Yinxia Li[1], Hui-min Hu[2],
Yunhong Zhang[2], and Siyuan Liu[1]

[1] School of Mechanical Engineering,
Zhengzhou University, Zhengzhou 450001, China
582901493@qq.com
[2] Ergonomics Laboratory, China National Institute of Standardization,
Beijing 100000, China

Abstract. With the development of technology, the electric cookers have become more and more powerful, more and more complex, then bring new usability problems, such as difficult operation, unclear of function meaning. Aiming at these ergonomics problems, this study first proposes to use a combined means of usability testing and EEG to evaluate display interface of electric cookers. The index system of intelligent electric cooker display interface ergonomic evaluation is built on questionnaire survey and research on the related documents. The three chosen intelligent electric cookers are evaluated on this basis. Consequently, ergonomics problems of electric cooker display interface are discovered and related proposals for improvement are proposed. These ergonomic problems, which are found to avoid problems in the design and redesign process of intelligent electric cooker, provides direction of designing the electric cooker display interface.

Keywords: Intelligent · Electric cooker · Display interface · Ergonomics · Evaluation

1 Introduction

With the rapid development of technology, the functions of electric cooker become more and more, and the operation is more and more complex, then many ergonomics problems, such as the operation becomes hard, function definition is not clear and so on, come along. This violates the user's pursuit of convenient, simple and efficient, it is a great strike to the user's interest, also hinders the development of intelligent electric cooker.

In view of the above problems, it is necessary to make a scientific and reasonable evaluation on display interface for intelligent electric cooker, thus can provide a reference for the design and redesign of intelligent electric cooker, and improve human-computer interaction.

A. Marcus (Ed.): DUXU 2016, Part III, LNCS 9748, pp. 414–424, 2016.
DOI: 10.1007/978-3-319-40406-6_40

2 Determination of the Evaluation Method

The usability evaluation is one of the main methods of evaluation for display interface. There are many traditional usability evaluation methods, such as heuristic evaluation, usability testing, cognitive walk-through, action analysis, structured and unstructured interview, and questionnaire survey model. These methods have been widely applied in many evaluation processes, suitable for variety of interface design and development, and each has its benefits and drawbacks1.

With the development of cognitive science, physiology and psychology, and so on, some scholars begin to use the method of cognitive psychophysiology such as eye movement and electroencephalograph (EEG) technology, to research the usability2.

This study first proposes to use a combined means of usability testing and EEG technology to evaluate display interface of electric cookers.

This method mainly includes three steps:

1. Determine test plan: It mainly includes establishing the index system, designing the experiment tasks and settings the experimental process.
2. Evaluation process: Evaluate the evaluation objects according to the test plan.
3. Analyze the results and write reports: Analyze and arrange the results of test, and write related reports.

3 Establishing the Evaluation Index System

The index of the usability is the evaluation index that reflect the degree of products available for related users, in the usability research and practice [3]. According to the view of International Standardization Organization (ISO) and experts in the field that usability includes three main aspects, which is efficiency, learnability and satisfaction [4, 5, 6, 7, 8], The index system of intelligent electric cooker display interface, are constructed, through a questionnaire survey and combining with the existing research results [9], besides, the characteristics of the three chosen sample electric cooker to be tested are also taken into account. The index system is shown in Table 1, which O stands for overall goals, $O_i (i = 1, 2, \cdots, 7)$ stands for sub-goals, U_k stands for Index layer.

4 Determination of the Weight for Each Evaluation Index

4.1 G1 Method

This study use the G1 method to determine the weight for each evaluation index of intelligent electric cooker. G1 method is an improved method which roots in AHP method and overcomes the defect of the AHP method, put forward by Northeastern University professor Guo Yajun. The basic principle of this method is sorting all the index of the same index layer first, according to certain evaluation criteria. Then assign the importance of adjacent index quantitatively according to the identified method.

Table 1. The index system of intelligent electric cooker display interface usability evaluation

Overall goal layer	Sub-goal layer	Sub-sub-goal layer	Index layer	Index
O The Usability evaluation Index for display & control system of intelligent electric cooker	O_1 : Display Device	O_{11} : Display interface layout	U_1 : Display interface layout	U_{11} : Is the location of display interface suitable?
				U_{12} : Is the slope of the operation interface easy to operate and view?
				U_{13} : Is the size of the operation panel easy to view?
		O_{12} : Information readability	U_2 : Information readability	U_{21} : Is the grouping for the interface of the electric cooker suitable and clear?
				U_{22} : Can the function keys and display be distinguished clearly?
				U_{23} : Is each part of the cooker easy to be found?
				U_{24} : Is the options clearly visible?
				U_{25}: Are the characters on the panel clear?
				U_{26} : Is the contrast between the characters and the background suitable?
				U_{27} : Are the procedure, function names and the graphic symbol easy to understand?
		O_{13} : Information clarity	U_3 : Information clarity	U_{31} : After choose a function, can user clearly know if it is selected?
				U_{32} : Is the current operating status clear?
		O_{14} : Error Proofing Design	U_4 : Error Proofing Design	U_{41} : Are the operation mistakes easy to correct?
				U_{42} : Are the prompts indicates easy to detect?
	O_2 : Control device	O_{21} : Design of control device	U_5 : Design of control device	U_{51} : Is the size (lengths, widths or diameter) of the button (physical/touch buttons) suitable?
				U_{52} : Are characters on the button clear?

(Continued)

Table 1. (*Continued*)

Overall goal layer	Sub-goal layer	Sub-sub-goal layer	Index layer	Index
				U_{53} : Is the depth of the button pressed level suitable?
				U_{54} : Do people know how to operate each control unit?
				U_{55} : Is the function adjustment easy to operate?
				U_{56} : Does the direction of the movement displayed accord with common motion?
		O_{22} : Control device layout	U_6 : Control device layout	U_{61} : Is the space (crosswise/lengthways) between two buttons suitable?
				U_{62} : Is the layout (location/inclination) of the button suitable?
		O_{23} : Usability of control program	U_7 : Usability of control program	U_{71} : Is the cook program convenient to adjust?
				U_{72} : Are the parameters (cooking time/rice varieties/rice's taste) easy to adjust?
				U_{73} : Is the function (order/cancel) easy to adjust?
	O_3 : Consistency between display and control device	$O31$: Space consistency	U_8 : Space consistency	U_{81} : Does the key and its corresponding display interface have a clear space position contact?
		O_{32} : Motion consistency	U_9 : Motion consistency	U_{91} : Is operation and the corresponding display information is consistent on the movement direction?
		O_{33} : Habits consistency	U_{10} : Habits consistency	U_{101} : Are operation and the corresponding display information in accordance with conventional habits?

The Weight Factors of each index in the same index layer can be got through calculating the results of sorting and assignment [10, 11]. For example, if the evaluation index set of one index layer is $\{u_1, u_2, \ldots u_n\}$, then the steps of the method are:

Sorting the importance of the index. If the importance of index $\{u_i\}$ is greater (or not less) than index $\{u_j\}$, according to some evaluation criteria, marked as $\{u_i \succ u_j\}$.

Experts in the related field are asked to choose the most important index (only one) in the evaluation index set according to some evaluation criteria. Then choose the most important index (only one) in the rest index according to the same evaluation criteria. After n times of choosing, a sole relationship of importance is determined as formula (1):

$$\{u_1 \succ u_2 \succ \cdots \succ u_n\} \tag{1}$$

Assigning u_{k-1} and u_k through comparing and judging the importance of them. If the ratio of the importance of u_{k-1} and u_k, namely w_{k-1}/w_k, is as formula (2) shown, according to the judgement of experts.

$$w_{k-1}/w_k = r_k, k = n, n-1, \cdots, 3, 2 \tag{2}$$

The assignment of r_k can refer to Table 2.

Table 2. Reference values of r_k

r_k	Note
1.0	Index u_{k-1} has the same importance with index u_k
1.2	Index u_{k-1} is slightly more important than index u_k
1.4	Index u_{k-1} is obviously more important than index u_k
1.6	Index u_{k-1} is strongly more important than index u_k
1.8	Index u_{k-1} is extremely more important than index u_k

Calculating the weight coefficient w_k. The weight coefficient w_i for index u_i can be calculated through formulas (3) and (4), according to r_k, then the weight coefficients of all index in the index set $\{u_1, u_2, \cdots, u_n\}$ can be got.

$$w_n = \left(1 + \sum_{k=2}^{n} \prod_{i=k}^{n} r_i\right)^{-1} \tag{3}$$

$$w_{k-1} = r_k w_k, k = n, n-1, \cdots, 3, 2 \tag{4}$$

When the number of experts is more than 16, the weight coefficient of the evaluation objects changes to be stabilized, that is to say the current weight coefficient is reliable [12]. So this study hired 20 experts, considering the actual situation. The 20 experts gave their own judgment on the same issue at the same time.

4.2 The Results and Analysis of Weight Coefficient

According to the result of the research and formulas 3 and 4, it is easy to obtain the weight of each index, as follows:

$$\{W_{o_1}, W_{o_2}, W_{o_3}\} = \{0.32, 0.33, 0.35\},$$

$$\{W_{o_{11}}, W_{o_{12}}...W_{o_{14}}\} = \{0.24, 0.27, 0.26, 0.23\},$$

$$\{W_{o_{21}}, W_{o_{22}}, W_{o_{23}}\} = \{0.34, 0.31, 0.35\},$$

$$\{W_{o_{31}}, W_{o_{32}}, W_{o_{33}}\} = \{0.32, 0.33, 0.35\},$$

$$\{W_{u_{11}}, W_{u_{12}}, W_{u_{13}}\} = \{0.36, 0.33, 0.31\},$$

$$\{W_{o_{21}}, W_{o_{22}}...W_{o_{27}}\} = \{0.14, 0.15, 0.16, 0.14, 0.11, 0.11, 0.16\},$$

$$\{W_{u_{31}}, W_{u_{32}}\} = \{0.52, 0.48\},$$

$$\{W_{u_{41}}, W_{u_{42}}\} = \{0.46, 0.54\},$$

$$\{W_{u_{51}}, W_{u_{52}}...W_{u_{56}}\} = \{0.15, 0.17, 0.14, 0.21, 0.20, 0.13\},$$

$$\{W_{u_{61}}, W_{u_{62}}\} = \{0.49, 0.51\},$$

$$\{W_{u_{71}}, W_{u_{72}}, W_{u_{73}}\} = \{0.36, 0.34, 0.30\}.$$

5 Evaluation Case

5.1 Experiment Device

The experiment proceeded in the usability lab, and the UX office system provided a whole-process monitor. The EEG data is provided by NeuroEdu device. NeuroEdu adopts portable brain wave device as the front-end EEG measuring equipment which can capture the EEG data and other psychological state parameters of subjects. The equipment is very easy to wear, to use, safe and comfortable, stable and reliable at the same time. The main indicators to be measured is sentiment index and caution index. "Caution index" indicates the current "caution indicator" or "concentration level" of users, and reflects the level of users' concentration. The mental status, such as upset, trance, inattention or anxiety will reduce the value of "caution index". "Sentiment index" parameter indicates the current "tensity" of users. "Caution index" and "sentiment index" indicate the users' caution index level and sentiment index level with a definite value among 1-100. If the value is higher than 60, then it indicates that the subject is in a high level of concentration and tension.

5.2   Experiment Evaluation Team

The evaluation team is composed of conductor and several reviewers. The conductor leads the reviewers to perform the pre-set task and evaluate the parameters that need to be evaluated. Beside this, the conductor needs to record the process of the experiment also.

The reviewers most are consumers. They can be common consumers or specialists with professional experience. The common consumers can put forward their subjective feelings or estimate. And the specialists can give some professional advises.

Nielsen and Landauer find a functional relationship between the number of usability problems and the number of participants. When there are more than 12 participants, almost all problems could be found13. So in this experiment, the number of reviewer is 12.

5.3   Evaluation Objects

Considering the characteristics of intelligent electric cooker, this study selects 3 typical electric cookers, marked as sample 1, sample 2, and sample 3. The buttons on sample 1 and sample 2 are physical buttons, and the buttons on sample 3 are touch buttons. Sample 1 has 21 adjustable programs. Sample 2 has 20 adjustable programs, and sample 3 has 12 adjustable programs. Since the versatility and complexity of display interface for intelligent electric cooker, it isn't scientific to evaluate on the whole. Thus, according to the analysis of display interface for intelligent electric cooker, this study will evaluate from 10 aspects, such as the display interface layout, information readability, etc. As shown in Table 1.

5.4   Evaluation Process

This study uses a method that combined usability test and EEG to evaluate display interface of electric cookers. The evaluation process can divide into 4 stages.

1. Preparatory stage. In the preparatory stage, the tester need to prepare 3 intelligent electric cookers and set experiment tasks. According to people`s habits and the consideration of the characteristics of each selected electric cooker, this study chooses three typical tasks and one open task for each reviewer. Typical tasks are stewing, cooking congee, and reservation timing.
2. Reviewers recruit stage. The result of experiment has a great relationship with reviewers, so the reviewers recruit is very important. The reviewer must have a certain discernment and experience of using intelligent electronic device.
3. Evaluation stage. This stage is the core of the whole evaluation. It is divided into three parts. The first part is a preparation for the next parts. After the subjects wear the NeuroEdu hair band, the conductor open the video monitoring equipment. In the second part, the conductor introduces the display interface of the three intelligent electric cookers, and explains the evaluation index system to the reviewers. If the reviewers have any questions, the conductor has a responsibility to explain and

demonstrate. In the third part, the reviewers perform the evaluation under the conductor's guidance. The reviewers operate the tasks on the usability testing record chart one by one, then grade the three-class index on the user experience score chart. The scale of marks is a five-grade marking system. At the same time, the conductor records the problems during the evaluation and the number that error appears, etc.

4. Result output and analysis stage. After the evaluation, the tester process the evaluation data collected. The data is classified into two kinds, usability data and EEG data. Usability data contains quantitative data and qualitative data. The quantitative data includes the reviewers' grade of three-class index, the time needed to complete the tasks and the number error appears, etc. The qualitative data includes the usability problems that reviewers find during the evaluation. The basis of quantitative data is qualitative data. The conclusion made from quantitative data could be proved by qualitative data; EEG data contains caution index and sentiment index.

6 Analysis of the Results

6.1 Analysis of Usability Results

Analysis of Qualitative Results. By summarizing the usability problems put forward by reviewers, the three electric cookers can meet the basic needs of people, but still have some usability problems. For sample 1: the space consistency between display device and control device doesn't conform people's usage habits; and the reservation timing function is very complex to use. For sample 2: the motion consistency and habit consistency between display device and control device doesn't conform to people's habits. It causes people don't know how to operate it. Besides, the color contrast of background and fonts is not very obvious. The button isn't sensitive and people can't conform the current operation status. For sample 3: the display interface is too small, and the fonts is not very clear; the variation of screen colors is unreasonable; the information display doesn't conform to people's habits and the functional adjustment is complex.

Analysis of Quantitative Results. Summarize the time needed to complete the former 3 tasks and the percentage of error, the results shown as the Tables 3, 4, and 5. It can be seen from the table that sample 1 is superior to sample 2 and sample 3.

According to the score of every index given by reviewers and the relevant index weight product, the usability score of sample 1, 2, 3 are 4.23, 3.83, and 3.82,

Table 3. The statistical result of the cooking task

Sample number	Average time needed to complete the task (s)	Percentage of error	Mean value of users' satisfaction score
Sample 1	37.0	0 %	4.2
Sample 2	50.0	17 %	2.9
Sample 3	45.8	8 %	3.0

Table 4. The statistical result of the porridge task

Sample number	Average time needed to complete the task(s)	Percentage of error	Mean value of users' satisfaction score
Sample 1	36.0	8 %	3.8
Sample 2	36.2	8 %	3.6
Sample 3	38.3	8 %	3.4

Table 5. The statistical result of the making an appointment time task

Sample number	Average time needed to complete the task(s)	Percentage of error	Mean value of users' satisfaction score
Sample 1	26.9	0 %	3.9
Sample 2	32.4	0 %	3.8
Sample 3	27.8	8 %	3.6

respectively. Both users' satisfaction and usability score can declare the usability design of sample 1 is better.

Global Analysis. As far as the qualitative results can indicate that sample 1 has less of usability problems. As far as the quantitative results can indicate that sample 1 has a higher score and users' satisfaction score. Sample 2 and sample 3 have a little distinction. We can draw a conclusion that the number of functions is out of proportion as usability. More functions don't mean good usability.

6.2   Statistical Analysis of EEG Results

The EEG results are arranged as Table 6 shown. It is indicated that the usability design of these 3 electric cookers is good, because the percentage of average value over 60 for caution index and sentiment index are very low. But, on the other hand, it is indicated that when subjects operate these three electric cookers, they would feel tense. Because the percentage of maximum value over 60 for caution index and sentiment index are very high. Furthermore, the percentage of sample 3's each index are lower than the other two sample. It has a relationship with the simple operation program, which could reduce the mental burden of users.

6.3   Analysis of Global Results

From the usability test result and EEG test result, it can be seen the usability design of these three electric cookers is relatively good. But there are still some error ratio, and the users' satisfaction score is not that high. The user would feel tense during operating the electric cooker. Therefore, these three electric cookers should do something to improve their effectiveness, efficiency and users' satisfaction combining their characters to make human-machine interaction more friendly.

Table 6. The statistical result of EEG experiment

Sample number	Sample 1	Sample 2	Sample 3
Percentage of max. value over 60 for caution index	92 %	92 %	81 %
Percentage of avg. value over 60 for caution index	25 %	22 %	14 %
Percentage of max. value over 60 for sentiment index	83 %	81 %	81 %
Percentage of avg. value over 60 for sentiment index	0	6 %	6 %

7 Conclusion

The aim of evaluation is finding the problem and solving the problem. This paper used a method that combined usability test and EEG to find problems existed in the display interface of electric cookers. This article is of great significance:

- Using NeuroEdu equipment to evaluate the usability of electric cookers, we can monitor the changing emotion of subjects during the experiment, and we can understand the users' needs, so that we can improve the display interface.
- By using an innovative method that combined traditional usability test and modern electroencephalograph (EEG), we can find usability problems from both subjective and objective aspect, and solve these problems to improve the usability of intelligent electric cookers.
- This study provides a direction for the display interface design of intelligent electric cookers. It makes the target consumers experience the product innovation as early as possible. This study can shorten the product innovation process, in order to reduce the defect after the product come into the market, improve the product quality.

References

1. Wang, J.: A literature review of progress in foreign usability research. New Technol. Libr. Inf. Serv. **2009**(09), 7–16
2. Wang, B., Sheng, J., Li, Y.: Summary of human-machine interface usability testing and evaluation research. Mod. Comput. **16**, 26–28 (2012)
3. Zheng, Y., Liu, Y., Wang, Q.: A survey on evaluation index system of product usability. Chin. J. Ergon. **20**(3), 83–86 (2014)
4. ISO (International Standards Organization). ISO 9241-11. Ergonomics of human system interaction (Part 11: Human-centered design for interactive systems). ISO, Geneva, Switzerland (2008)
5. Nielsen, J.: Usability Engineering, pp. 188–225. Morgan Kaufmann, San Francisco (1994)
6. Hou, W.: The Research of University Portal Interface Usability Design. Harbin Engineering University, Harbin (2013)

7. Nie, D., Wang, X.-W., Duan, R.-N., Lv, B.-L.: A survey on EEG based emotion recognition. Chin. J. Biomed. Eng. **31**(4), 595–604 (2012)
8. Yuan, H.: Study on Classification of Emotion Based on EEG. Nanjing Normal University, Nanjing (2014)
9. China Standard Certification Co., Ltd. Ergonomic evaluation of six electric cooker. Chin. Appliance **2014**(11), 70–72
10. Guo, Y.: Comprehensive Evaluation Theory and Method. Science Press, Beijing (2002)
11. Junjie, G.: Research on Ergonomics Comprehensive Evaluation of Wheel House to Vehicle. Zhengzhou University, Zhengzhou (2014)
12. Li, Y., Yuan, X., Yang, C.: Weight factors determination of the evaluation indexes of cockpit ergonomics. Acta Aeronaut. Astronaut. Sin. **27**(3), 370–373 (2006)
13. Dong, J., Fu, L., Rao, P.: Human-Machine Interaction– User-Centered Design and Evaluation, 3rd edn. Tsinghua University Press, Beijing (2010)

Research on User Experience Driven Product Architecture of Smart Device

Jiaming Zhong, Di Wang, Nan Liang, and Liqun Zhang$^{(\boxtimes)}$

Design Management Institute, Shanghai Jiao Tong University, Shanghai, China
zhanglliqun@gmail.com

Abstract. With the development of information technology in recent years, smart device becomes the most popular topic of product design. Our research attempted to use smart device product as breakthrough point, choosing myopic treatment instrument as object to make further exploration. We first made a prototype design for the myopic treatment instrument. After collecting the corresponding users data of the prototype, the data was resolved, filtered and analyzed by the statistical methods. Through the research, we found that smart device had already made a big influence on product architecture design. The finding of smart device product oriented to user experience innovation can provide help and reference for the future design of smart device product.

Keywords: User experience · Smart device · Product design · Data analysis

1 Introduction

Recently, the rapid development of electronic technology leads the product to be intelligence. Now smart device has become the focus of each product area. In CES ASIA 2015, smart home and wearable device become the most popular product of electronics show. After Apple launched the new product "Apple Watch", other companies joined in the same area one after another, while the concept of "smart home" also swept the global world. Meanwhile, the World Internet Conference has been held twice. None of the internet enterprise can avoid the topic of smart device in discussing the future of the Internet. The major enterprises like Alibaba and Tencent pointed out that smart device would be the next innovative direction of the Internet. Now smart device quickly build its own ecosphere by "hardware" plus "service". And the customer which smart device faces to has changed from the young or geek to normal people. A series of excellent smart devices including smart band, smart watch is approaching the public life through the good product design. In return, the popularity of smart device also affects the product architecture.

Figure 1 shows that the number of global internet device increase at a high speed from 2010. The Internet magnates evaluate the smart devices as the next market of billions level. With numerous smart devices released, we found that the feature of combining software and hardware and connectivity made the smart device different from the traditional industrial product in product design. The traditional product innovation was driven by technical innovation, but the smart device focused on mining potential user demand to achieve innovation of user experience.

© Springer International Publishing Switzerland 2016
A. Marcus (Ed.): DUXU 2016, Part III, LNCS 9748, pp. 425–434, 2016.
DOI: 10.1007/978-3-319-40406-6_41

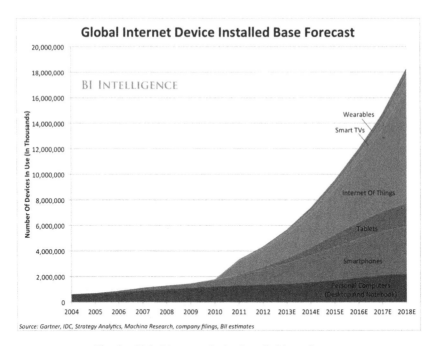

Fig. 1. Global internet device installed base forecast

2 Related Work

We chose myopic treatment instrument as experiment object as it was different from the smart glasses. It lacked of typical product and could not be classified as smart glasses. Unlike the Google Glass or some virtual reality devices, it aimed at the medical cure, which contains different requirement of appearance and function. According to the investigation, the myopia rate is about 22 % and in China, almost 4 hundred million people are myopia and the rate reach up to 33 %, which may even rise. The myopia has already become a big problem in China. Concerned as a way to prevent or remit myopia, the myopic treatment instrument is created to focus on the people who are myopia or may become myopia, especially children in 7 to 18 years old.

Through the market research, we found the most effective method of the treatment whose theory is to make the visible things away in order to adjust the eye muscles to release the eyeball. Currently, the treatment instrument based on the theory is quite simple. It is realized by some mechanical structure and is not smart at all. So we made some changes on the instrument to intelligentize it. During the transformation, we conduct some user investigation and depth interview to collect the key point of user experience, which contains:

- The perspective of existing myopic treatment instrument is negative
- The feature which users most care is medical effect, comfort and appearance.
- Safe, technical, comfortable and portable are the key words that users describe the ideal instrument.

- Users are willing to accept the suggestion sent by the smart device and they believe it is more correctly than their own experience.

Based on the user research, we made a prototype design (Fig. 2). We set a series of colors, which user can select their favourite one, to fit the users personalization. Undertint was used to construct the atmosphere of safety and modernization. The materials of the prototype include plastic, glass, and rubber. Metal was abandoned because of its weight can not fit the glasses. Real product may use carbon fiber instead. The inside part of frame is made of rubber so as to transform to fit different size of head. The sensors and data acquisition units are packaged on the side and behind so user would not feel uncomfortable or weird about the structure of the product.

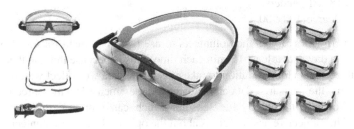

Fig. 2. Product prototype

Meanwhile we conceive the interface of application (Fig. 3). It contains the data collected under different circumstances. According to the commerciality and enjoyment, we engaged the social sharing. The interface can show about the usage and the result measured by the instrument. It would also estimate the degree of fatigue in order to give the correct suggestion. The application interface aimed to show the user how high the degree of myopia and what he should do to relax his eyes.

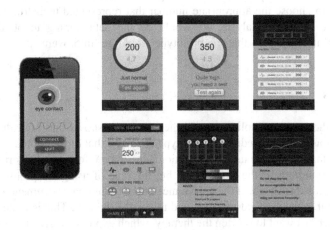

Fig. 3. Application interface

3   Experiment

After we created a model of smart myopic treatment instrument by prototype design, we need to test its function module and explore the link between smart device and product architecture. We take an experiment by comparing the prototype and traditional treatment instrument. Volunteers would take part in two similar test to help us find out the difference of two instruments. We would observe the usage of two products, obtain the responsive data collect by sensors. The data mining can help us to acquire the preference and habit of users, also would contribute the algorithm of suggestion. As the traditional treatment instrument does not have any sensor, so we would do the statistic record manually. The research needs several volunteers and the basic requirements are:

- Age 10-18, all genders.
- Myopia degree 100-500.

The experiment requires the volunteers to use two instrument for about one week, at least once a day and at least 15 min each time. This is because that the therapy of the instrument requires a long duration to take effect. The data we collect would be divided into two parts: the measured data and subjective assessment. The measured data means the data directly collected by the sensors, which can represent the usage of each volunteer. The subjective assessment is about the opinion from the volunteer of the user experience that would help us to improve the product.

To analyze the measured data, a SPSS file has been created including all of the collected data. In the file, we used descriptive statistics and cross-comparison of each volunteer, including these:

1. According to the statistics, analyze the time and rate of usage of two treatment instruments.
2. Analyze the change in visual acuity of the single volunteer and judge whether the suggestion given about using eye is correct and timely.
3. Compare the usage of each volunteer by correlation analysis.
4. Four groups of antonym adjective are digitized before given to each volunteer and they had to choose the appropriate number that represented their true feelings.
5. According to those analysis, we would do the data mining to obtain the real requirement of users so that the prototype would get improvement.

4   Results

Figure 4 is the usage of volunteers. In the picture, it shows that both durations are normal distribution. The median of prototype is 35 and that of traditional instrument is 22. It means that volunteers used the traditional instrument for a much shorter time, just satisfied the standards of the experiment, but the time of using the prototype is more than 30 min. It is because that the appearance of the traditional instrument always hints the user that it is the medical machine and this is the therapy. This is quite oppressive and make user just want to shorten the therapy, which express clearly on the using time. On the other hand, the prototype is much more like a normal glasses as it just has two

Frequency Table

prototype(min)

Valid		Frequency	Percent	Valid Percent	Cumulative Percent
Valid	30	1	1.3	1.3	1.3
	31	1	1.3	1.3	2.5
	32	5	6.3	6.3	8.8
	33	12	15.0	15.0	23.8
	34	10	12.5	12.5	36.3
	35	15	18.8	18.8	55.0
	36	15	18.8	18.8	73.8
	37	7	8.8	8.8	82.5
	38	6	7.5	7.5	90.0
	39	5	6.3	6.3	96.3
	40	3	3.8	3.8	100.0
	Total	80	100.0	100.0	

tradition(min)

Valid		Frequency	Percent	Valid Percent	Cumulative Percent
Valid	19	3	3.8	3.8	3.8
	20	13	16.3	16.3	20.0
	21	14	17.5	17.5	37.5
	22	15	18.8	18.8	56.3
	23	12	15.0	15.0	71.3
	24	8	10.0	10.0	81.3
	25	8	10.0	10.0	91.3
	26	4	5.0	5.0	96.3
	27	1	1.3	1.3	97.5
	28	2	2.5	2.5	100.0
	Total	80	100.0	100.0	

Descriptive Statistics

	N	Minimum	Maximum	Mean	Std. Deviation
prototype(min)	80	30	40	35.30	2.218
tradition(min)	80	19	28	22.45	2.116
Valid N (listwise)	80				

Fig. 4. Usage of the single volunteer

more lenses. It is easy for the volunteer to be used to the product. If someone who has already wear glasses, it would be much easier and cost less time to get started. As we all known, the time of using has been defined and has a minimum. If the users can not reach the standard, the effect of the instrument will be greatly reduced. Thus, from this standpoint, the prototype does much better than the traditional one.

For reasons of timing, we do not get a much detail report of the visual acuity change. The picture (Fig. 5) shows that the visual acuity change within a narrow range, although the volunteer is at the age that their visual acuity can change rapidly. We can not say that the instrument actually prevents or relieve the myopia. As the nuance of the sight, we also sent the different message including warning and congratulations. According to the feedback of volunteers, we calculate that more than 80 % of the suggestions are correct and in time.

We found no significant correlation between the utilization rate and the visual acuity of each user as they do not have the same usage scenarios (Fig. 6). Someone is eager to cure the myopia while others do not think it is a big problem. The mentality is the determining factor that affect the usage of the product. And most people preferred to take treatment at night. There is less time for them in the morning or afternoon as they have their jobs to finish. Night is the best time for relax and taking the therapy.

In the antonym section, we use four groups of adjective antonym which includes "comfortable-uncomfortable", "portable-ponderous", "safe-dangerous", "modern-vintage". The volunteers should mark two instruments from 0 to 5 point after they take the therapy. The higher score the instrument gets, the better performance it shows. As we can see (Fig. 7), the prototype gets the higher point of comfortable and portable. Its appearance and materials convince the volunteer that it is the better choice. Both instruments are believed to be safe because they are recognized to a medical treatment instrument. We found that the prototype only get a little bit higher score in "modern-vintage". The reason might be that the appearance of the prototype is just like

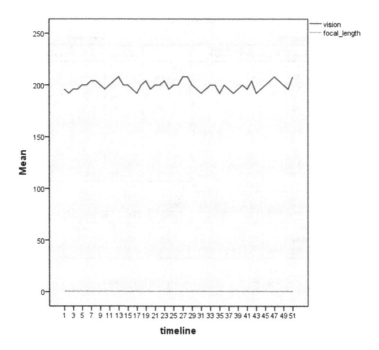

Fig. 5. Visual acuity change

ANOVA

		Sum of Squares	df	Mean Square	F	Sig.
morning	Between Groups	16.100	8	2.013	.	.
	Within Groups	.000	1	.000		
	Total	16.100	9			
afternoon	Between Groups	25.600	8	3.200	1.600	.548
	Within Groups	2.000	1	2.000		
	Total	27.600	9			
night	Between Groups	11.600	8	1.450	.	.
	Within Groups	.000	1	.000		
	Total	11.600	9			

Fig. 6. OneWay ANOVA analysis

the normal glasses which could not convince users to be a tech device and they even did not realize it as a smart device. To sum up, the prototype performs better than the traditional instrument. Because of the statistics is based on the current volunteers, so it only represents these volunteers' opinion and we would consider to expand the number of participants.

During the analysis, we found that our prototype has a competitive advantage in traditional treatment instrument. There are several features which make it a well-designed product:

prototype

Descriptive Statistics

	N	Minimum	Maximum	Mean	Std. Deviation
comfortable_ uncomfortable	10	3	5	4.10	.738
portable_ponderous	10	3	5	4.00	.818
safe_dangerous	10	4	5	4.60	.516
modern_vintage	10	3	5	4.10	.568
Valid N (listwise)	10				

tradition

Descriptive Statistics

	N	Minimum	Maximum	Mean	Std. Deviation
comfortable_ uncomfortable	10	2	4	3.00	.667
portable_ponderous	10	1	4	2.70	.949
safe_dangerous	10	3	5	4.00	.667
modern_vintage	10	2	5	3.90	.876
Valid N (listwise)	10				

Fig. 7. Antonym analysis

- The style of the prototype is quite like the normal glasses which can reduce the learning cost.
- Time of using meets the standard of therapy while the traditional one can not reach, which means the treatment is much better and more effective.
- The accuracy of the suggestions which the prototype provides failed to achieve our expectation. The usage scenario sometimes interferes the judgement generated by existing algorithm. And this is going to be improved.

5   Conclusion and Future Work

In the research, we invited several volunteers to take part in the experiment. We obtained the data of them by observation and collection. To explore the link between smart device and product architecture, we conducted the data mining and acquire many information about our prototype. The whole process led to an conclusion: we thought that the smart device provided a better user experience to conduct the product design and we believed that this could lead the revolution of product architecture and user experience.

First is the diversity of user experience. The model of smart device is the combination of software and hardware. User can experience the product through the application on the mobile phone as well as focusing on the appearance. Designer should pay more attention on the digital screen as interaction design now does not only means the operation we do in reality, but also on the website and mobile devices. Taking our prototype as example, we provide a series of application user interface including test data, suggestion, social sharing and so on. The well-designed interface can attract the attention of users, which can maintain user's dependence on product.

Secondly, timeliness is a potential key-point of interaction that many designers do not realize. People always want the initial reactions or feedbacks return from the product. Just like a conversation, the quick response makes the talk heated and no response just ends the talk. In the usage of product, some volunteers complain about that they do not know whether the product is active or what step they have reach. One way to solve the problem is add guiding lights, but it is quite strange for some wearable devices because it makes people seem odd or embarrassed, which prompt users stop using the product any more. The smart device has a smart solution that it sends the information on the mobile devices which is timely and natural.

Another point is about the accuracy. User experience is measured or estimated by user interview. One thing has already caused attention that people are not willing to show their real face to the interviewer. This leads the question that the interviewees give the answer they really choose or just to fulfill the investigation. Only the experienced UX designer or interviewer can lead the interview to tell the truth in a relax environment. However, the smart device avoid this defect because it certainly collect the data which shows the real usage of one user. Numbers don't lie, what we need is an accurate algorithm and enough data. The accuracy will increase as the size of data grows larger. And then the big data can simulate users' behavior and habit.

The last one is the persistence. After the product gathers the first batch of users, customers and company can communicate on the platform created by the smart device. Based on the data mining, fast iteration is applied to the product. The part which users are dissatisfied with can be find out and improve quickly while the core competencies are preserved.

To summarize, we conducted an experiment of smart device focusing on the myopia treatment instrument. The experiment collected data from volunteers and conducted the data mining. We not only do the data analysis but also discuss the link between smart device and user experience. We believed that the smart device could challenge the traditional user experience and product architecture. Smart device could provide better user experience than traditional industrial product as it based on the platform built by the Internet.

During the research, we did not take an experiment with larger scale for the reason of time and fund. We hope to carry out a larger and longer experiment if possible. The number of volunteers can enrich the database and make the statistics more accurate. And the long-term track on the volunteers can not only update the database but also modify and improve the product prototype.

In the future, we will focus more than the myopia treatment instrument but also other smart devices. When new smart devices created by the technology companies, we will choose the typical and general ones to make more test and research. We will pay attention to the new technology which can be applied to just like augmented reality.

References

1. Hassenzahl, M., Tractinsky, N.: User experience-a research agenda. Behav. Inf. Technol. 25(2), 91–97 (2006). Taylor & Francis
2. Mandryk, R.L., Inkpen, K.M., Calvert, T.W.: Using psychophysiological techniques to measure user experience with entertainment technologies. Behav. Inf. Technol. 25(2), 141–158 (2006). Taylor & Francis
3. Mack, Z., Sharples, S.: The importance of usability in product choice: a mobile phone case study. Ergonomics 52(12), 1514–1528 (2009)
4. Karapanos, E.: User Experience over Time. In: Karapanos, E. (ed.) Modeling Users' Experiences with Interactive Systems. SCI, vol. 436, pp. 61–88. Springer, Heidelberg (2013)
5. Bargas-Avila, J.A., Hornbæk, K.: Old wine in new bottles or novel challenges: a critical analysis of empirical studies of user experience. In: CHI 2011 Proceedings of the SIGCHI Conference on Human Factors in Computing Systems, pp. 2689–2698. ACM, New York (2011)
6. Rusu, C., Rusu, V., Roncagliolo, S., González, C.: Usability and user experience: what should we care about? Int. J. Inf. Technol. Syst. Approach 8(2), 1–12 (2015)
7. Wei, L., Hu, R., Qian, Y., Wu, G.: Enable device-to-device communications underlaying cellular networks: challenges and research aspects. IEEE Commun. Mag. 52(6), 90–96 (2014)
8. Page, T.: Application-based mobile devices in design education. Int. J. Mob. Learn. Organ. 8(2). inderscienceonline.com (2014)
9. Jaramillo, D., Katz, N., Bodin, B., Tworek, W., Smart, R., Cook, T.: Cooperative solutions for Bring Your Own Device (BYOD). IBM J. Res. Dev. 57(6), 5:1–5:11 (2013). IEEE Xplore Digital Library
10. Want, R., Schilit, B.N., Jenson, S.: Enabling the internet of things. Computer 48(1), 28–35 (2015)
11. Canfora, G., Mercaldo, F., Visaggio, C.A., D'Angelo, M., Furno, A., Manganelli, C.: A case study of automating user experience-oriented performance testing on smartphones. In: 2013 IEEE Sixth International Conference on Software Testing, Verification and Validation (ICST), pp. 66–69 (2013)
12. Mayer, S., Tschofen, A., Dey, A.K., Mattern, F.: User interfaces for smart things - a generative approach with semantic interaction descriptions. ACM Trans. Comput.-Hum. Interact. 21(2), 1–24 (2014). ACM, New York
13. Rallapalli, S., Ganesan, A., Chintalapudi, K., Padmanabhan, V.N., Qiu, L.: Enabling physical analytics in retail stores using smart glasses. In: MobiCom 2014 Proceedings of the 20th Annual International Conference on Mobile Computing and Networking, pp. 115–126. ACM, New York (2014)
14. Stefana, M., et al.: Clinical and surgical applications of smart glasses. Technol. Health Care 23(4), 381–401 (2015)
15. Wiederhold, B.K.: Time to port augmented reality health apps to smart glasses? Behav. Soc. Netw. Cyberpsychology 16(3), 157–158 (2013)
16. Ok, A.E., Basoglu, N.A., Daim, T.: Exploring the design factors of smart glasses. In: 2015 Portland International Conference Management of Engineering and Technology (PICMET), pp. 1657–1664 (2015)
17. Le, H., Dang, T., Liu, F.: Towards long-term large-scale visual health monitoring using cyber glasses. In: PervasiveHealth 2013 Proceedings of the 7th International Conference on Pervasive Computing Technologies for Healthcare, ICST, pp. 200–207 (2013)

18. Gudlavalleti, V.S.M., Allagh, K.P., Gudlavalleti, A.S.V.: Self-adjustable glasses in the developing world. Clin. Ophthalmol. **8**, 405–413 (2014)
19. Lucero, A., Lyons, K., Vetek, A., Järvenpää, T., White, S., Salmimaa, M.: Exploring the interaction design space for interactive glasses. In: CHI EA 2013 CHI 2013 Extended Abstracts on Human Factors in Computing Systems, pp. 1341–1346. ACM, New York (2013)

Author Index

Printed in the United States
By Bookmasters